Life SCIENCE DAYBOOK

In Collaboration with NSTA

TEACHER'S EDITION

Great Source
EDUCATION GROUP
A Houghton Mifflin Company

Acknowledgments

Reviewers

Charles M. Harmon
Los Angeles Unified School District
Los Angeles, California

Maxine Rosenberg
Curriculum Consultant
Newton, Massachusetts

Dwight Sieggreen
Hillside Middle School
Northville, Michigan

Thomas Vaughn
Arlington Public Schools
Arlington, Massachusetts

Credits

Writing: Bill Smith Studio
Editorial: Great Source: Fran Needham, Marianne Knowles, Susan Rogalski; Bill Smith Studio
Design: Great Source: Richard Spencer; Bill Smith Studio
Production Management: Great Source: Evelyn Curley; Bill Smith Studio
Cover Design: Bill Smith Studio

National Science Teachers Association: Tyson Brown, Carol Duval, Juliana Texley, Patricia Warren, Stephen J. Farenga

Photos

Page iii: PhotoDisc; **iv:** PhotoDisc; **1:** PhotoDisc; **2:** PhotoDisc; **3:** © Hutchings Photography/Corel; **4:** © Galen Rowell CORBIS; **8:** PhotoDisc; **9:** CORBIS/Royalty Free; **12–13:** PhotoDisc; **15:** Painet, Inc.; **16–17:** Painet, Inc.; **17:** ©J. Bavosi/Photo Researchers, Inc.; **18–19:** PhotoDisc; **21:** © K. Porter/Photo Researchers, Inc.; **22–23:** PhotoDisc; **24:** PhotoDisc; **26–27:** PhotoDisc; **28–29:** PhotoDisc; **30:** © G. Murti/Photo Researchers, Inc.; **33:** PhotoDisc; **35:** © Claude Edelmann/Photo Researchers, Inc.; **36–37:** PhotoDisc; **39:** © Keith Porter/Photo Researchers, Inc.; **40:** © Dr. Neal Scolding/Photo Researchers, Inc. ; **42–43:** ArtToday; **44:** NASA; **48:** PhotoDisc; **50:** Digital Vision; **51:** PhotoDisc; **53:** PhotoDisc; **54:** PhotoDisc; **56–57:** Corel; **58:** PhotoSpin; **58–59:** PhotoDisc; **60–61:** PhotoDisc; **62:** Hutchings Photography; **64–65:** PhotoDisc; **65:** © Kevin Fugate; **68–69:** PhotoDisc; **70–71:** © Biophoto Associates/Photo Researchers, Inc.; **72:** Corel; **74a:** PhotoDisc; **74b:** © Joe McDonald/CORBIS; **76:** Corel; **77:** © AFP/CORBIS; **80:** PhotoDisc; **81a:** PhotoDisc; **81b:** © D Suzio/Photo Researchers, Inc.; **82:** PhotoSpin; **83:** © STR/Reuters/TimePix; **84–85:** PhotoDisc; **84a:** © STR/Reuters/TimePix; **84b:** PhotoDisc; **84c:** PhotoDisc; **84d:** Corel; **86–87:** CORBIS; **87a:** Corel; **87b:** ArtToday; **87c:** Corel; **87d:** ArtToday; **90:** Corel; **92:** PhotoDisc; **93:** Corel; **94a:** PhotoDisc ; **94b:** PhotoDisc; **95:** PhotoDisc ; **96–97:** PhotoDisc; **98:** © Oliver Meckes/Nicole Ottawa/Photo Researchers, Inc.; **99:** Painet, Inc.; **100:** PhotoDisc; **101:** © Bettmann/CORBIS; **102:** ©Scimat/Photo Researchers, Inc.; **104:** © L. West/Photo Researchers, Inc.; **105:** Corel; **107a:** Corel; **107b:** © N. Poritz/Photo Researchers, Inc.; **107c:** Corel; **108a:** © S. Dalton/Photo Researchers, Inc.; **108b:** © S. Dalton/Photo Researchers, Inc.; **109:** Corel; **110:** Corel; **111:** Rick and Nora Bowers/Visuals Unlimited; **114:** © Tom Brakefield/CORBIS; **116–117:** Painet, Inc.; **119:** Corel; **120–121:** Corel; **122:** © Stuart Westmorland/CORBIS; **123a:** Corel; **123b:** © Kennan Ward/CORBIS; **123c:** corel; **124:** Ron Leighton; **125:** ©Peter Slater/Photo Researchers Inc.; **128:** PhotoDisc; **130a:** PhotoDisc; **130b:** © Sally A. Morgan;Ecoscene/CORBIS; **131:** © Nuridsany et Perennou/Photo Researchers, Inc. ; **132:** Corel; **134:** © Nathan Blow/AllSport; **135:** Zigy Kaluzny/Stone; **136:** PhotoDisc; **137:** Hutchings Photography; **138–139:** PhotoDisc; **140:** Hutchings Photography; **141:** Corel; **142:** Corel; **143:** Hutchings Photography; **144:** PhotoDisc; **146:** Corel; **147:** © Susan Leavines/Photo Researchers; **148–149:** ArtToday; **150:** PhotoDisc; **151:** © Doug Martin/Photo Researchers, Inc.; **154:** Corel; **155:** Corel; **156:** PhotoDisc; **157:** Courtesy of Marcus E. Raichle, M.D.; Washington University School of : Medicine; **159:** PhotoDisc; **160–161:** © A Hobson/Photo Resarchers, Inc.; **163:** PhotoDisc; **164–165:** PhotoDisc; **166:** © Biophoto Associates/Photo Researchers, Inc.; **167:** © Bettmann/CORBIS ; **168–169:** © Bettmann/CORBIS; **169:** Bettmann/CORBIS; **169:** © Bettmann/CORBIS; **171:** © S. Stammers/Photo Researchers, Inc.; **172:** © Getty Images; **173:** PhotoDisc; **174:** PhotoDisc; **178:** © Galen Rowell/CORBIS; **182:** © Frank Lane Picture Agency/CORBIS; **184:** PhotoDisc ; **188:** Corel ; **189:** Corel; **191:** Corel; **193:** Corel; **195:** Corel; **196–197:** Corel; **198:** PhotoDisc; **199:** Corel; **200–201:** Corel; **204–205:** PhotoDisc; **209:** Corel; **210–211:** Corel; **213:** PhotoDisc; **214:** PhotoDisc; **216–217:** PhotoDisc

Cover: All images PhotoDisc

Illustration: Thomas Gagliano

Printed in the United States of America.
ISBN-13: 978-0-669-49250-7 ISBN-10: 0-669-49250-7
6 7 8 9 10 — DBH — 10 09 08 07

Why NSTA Worked On These Books

Scientists write letters, argue incessantly, make mistakes, suffer from jealousy, exhibit both vanity and generosity—all while striving in diverse ways to enlarge human understanding. Among the most important skills they possess is the ability to communicate ideas, defend them against critics, and modify their own positions in the face of contravening evidence. Every literate person—every scientifically literate person—must do this.

The National Science Teachers Association (NSTA) is pleased to participate in the publication of these Science Daybooks because they bring together science, reading, and writing. Most important: The primary sources in the Daybooks—first-hand accounts that scientists and researchers use to communicate their ideas—firmly place science in the context of human endeavor.

What NSTA Did

From the outset, NSTA staff and members collaborated with Great Source editors and developers to ensure that the Daybooks were created from a teacher's perspective and were based on the National Science Education Standards. We helped link important topic areas with primary sources. We suggested activity ideas at the pilot stage and reviewed those submitted by authors during development. We reviewed the teaching plans that accompany student lessons and supported these plans with tips, warnings about misconceptions, and brief activities taken from articles in *Science Scope*—NSTA's middle school peer-reviewed journal. NSTA also provides the *sci*LINKS® extensions that appear throughout the book, directing readers to Web sites that offer further information, additional lessons, and activities.

What Is NSTA

NSTA is the largest organization in the world committed to promoting excellence and innovation in science teaching and learning for all. To address subjects of critical interest to science educators, the NSTA Press publishes projects of significant relevance and value to teachers of science—books on best teaching practices, books that explain and tie in with the National Science Education Standards, books that apply the latest science education research, and classroom activity books. NSTA also considers novel treatments of core science content and is especially eager to publish works that link science to other key curriculum areas such as mathematics and language arts. Hence this project.

Let Us Hear From You

We hope teachers and students benefit from this innovative approach to learning science. Tell us what you think of this joint effort by e-mailing daybooks@nsta.org. For more information about NSTA, please visit our Web site at www.nsta.org.

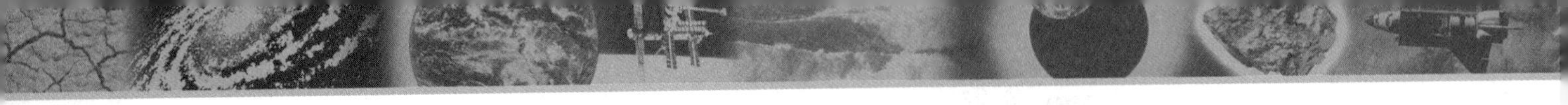

How to Use This Book 5

Scope and Sequence 6

UNIT 1 Cells 8

Chapter 1
STRUCTURE OF A CELL

Opener 10A

1 **Sentries at the Gate** *The cell membrane controls what goes into and out of the cell.* 10

2 **All Kinds of Parts** *The cell is made up of many organelles.* 14

3 **The Nucleus and DNA** *The nucleus controls the functioning of the cell's other organelles.* 18

Chapter 2
CELLS AT WORK

Opener 20A

4 **Energy for Life** *During cellular respiration, mitochondria release energy by breaking down glucose.* 20

5 **Photosynthesis** *During photosynthesis, plant cells change carbon dioxide and water into glucose.* 24

6 **All Together Now** *Cellular respiration and photosynthesis are complementary processes.* 28

Chapter 3
CELL DIVISION

Opener 30A

7 **One Becomes Two** *During mitosis, a cell divides to produce two daughter cells, each with the same number of chromosomes as the parent cell.* 30

8 **The Sorcerer's Apprentice** *Cell growth is exponential.* 34

9 **Cells Out of Control** *Cancer is cell division out of control.* 38

Chapter 4
WHEN CELLS GET TOGETHER

Opener 40A

10 **All Charged Up** *Cells use electricity to communicate.* 40

11 **Growing Tissue** *Scientists have found a way to grow tissue from an adult's stem cells.* 44

12 **Organ Misfire** *When an organ is not functioning normally, other organs are affected.* 48

UNIT 2 Heredity, Diversity, and Change

UNIT 2 Heredity, Diversity, and Change 50

Chapter 5 HOW GENES WORK

Opener 52A

13 **Your Genes and Chromosomes** *DNA contains the instructions for all of an organism's physical traits.* 52

14 **In-gene-ius!** *Gregor Mendel investigated inherited traits in pea plants.* 54

15 **Custom Corn** *Selective breeding produces organisms with desirable traits.* 58

Chapter 6 GENES AND PEOPLE

Opener 62A

16 **Single-Gene Human Traits** *Some human physical traits are controlled by a single gene.* 62

17 **The Blue People of Kentucky** *Blue-tinged skin is caused by the recessive form of a gene.* 64

18 **More Than Just Genes** *Genes alone do not determine all of a person's characteristics.* 68

Chapter 7 MOST LIKELY TO SURVIVE

Opener 72A

19 **The Right Stuff** *Adaptations enable a species to survive in its environment.* 72

20 **Tall, Gray, and Tuskless** *In some populations of Asian elephants, the gene for growing tusks is being lost due to illegal hunting.* 76

21 **New and Improved** *Adaptive radiation and convergent evolution are two results of natural selection.* 80

Chapter 8 ONE HUNDRED MILLION KINDS OF THINGS

Opener 82A

22 **What's in a Name?** *When scientists discover a new organism, they must determine how it fits into the scientific classification system.* 82

23 **We Are Family** *Organisms are sometimes reclassified based on new evidence.* 86

24 **It's Classified!** *A dichotomous key helps identify organisms by presenting a series of choices.* 90

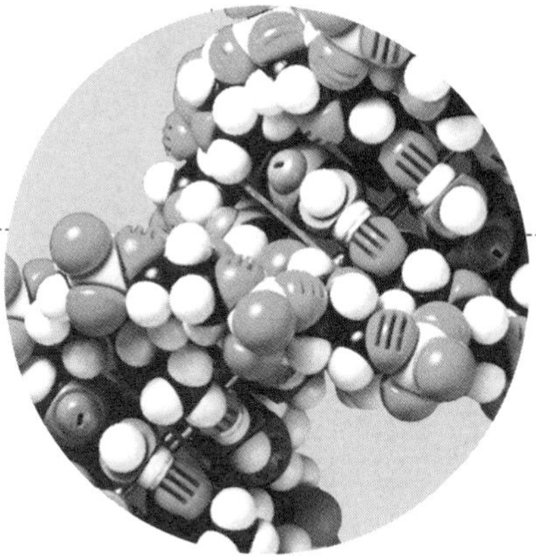

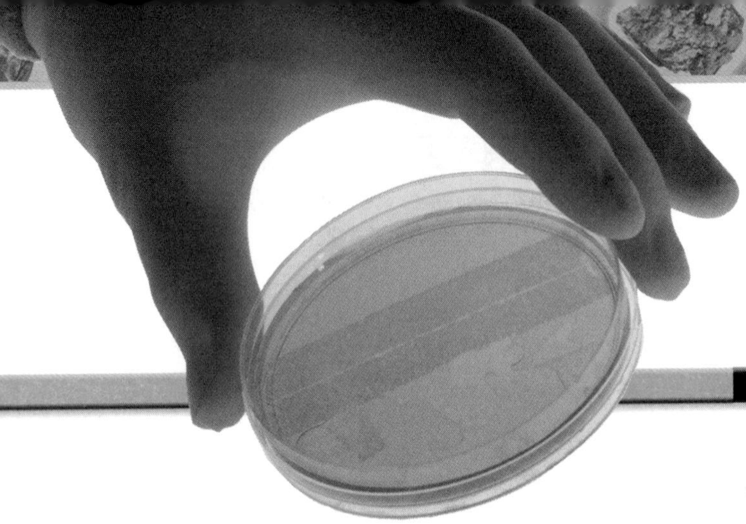

UNIT 3 Living Things 92

Chapter 9 **BACTERIA**

Opener 94A

25 **More Bacteria for Your Buck** *Bacteria thrive on paper money.* 94

26 **The Bad Guys** *Some bacteria are deadly.* 98

27 **Bacteria at Work** *Some bacteria help keep us healthy.* 102

Chapter 10 **HOW INSECTS GET AROUND**

Opener 104A

28 **Walk Like an Insect** *An insect's body structure makes it stable as it walks.* 104

29 **Jump!** *Structures for jumping help insects survive.* 108

30 **Flights of Fancy** *Flying and migration are structural and behavioral adaptations of some insects.* 110

Chapter 11 **KILLER WHALES: WOLVES OF THE SEA**

Opener 114A

31 **Sounds of the Sea** *Killer whales use sound to navigate and to communicate under water.* 114

32 **The Hunters** *Killer whales show cooperative behavior when hunting.* 118

33 **Name That Whale** *Marine biologists use a system to identify individual killer whales.* 122

Chapter 12 **PLANT ADAPTIONS**

Opener 124A

34 **Mistletoe, Birds, and Trees** *Mistletoe plants depend on symbiotic relationships with other organisms to survive.* 124

35 **Not Your Usual Carnivores** *Some plants have adaptions that enable them to capture and consume insects.* 128

36 **What Attracts Insects to Flowers?** *Flowers have features that attract insects.* 132

UNIT 4 Human Body Systems 134

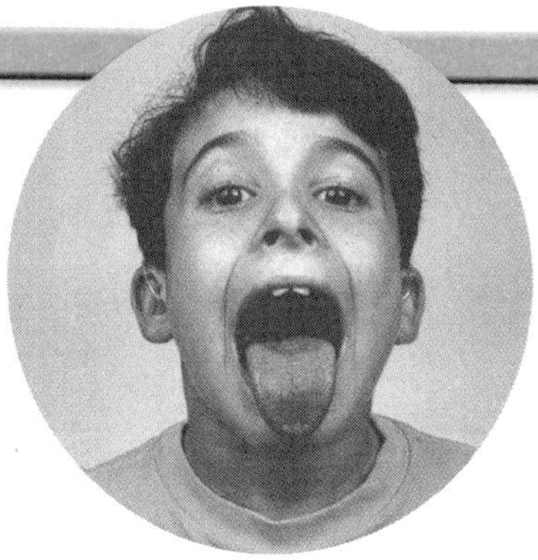

Chapter 13 — COMING TO OUR SENSES

Opener 136A

37 **Testing Taste Buds** *Scientists are investigating whether humans can taste fat.* 136

38 **Balancing Act** *Our inner ears help us maintain balance.* 140

39 **How Does It Feel?** *Our sense of touch provides important information about our environment.* 142

Chapter 14 — BODY WORK

Opener 146A

40 **In One End...** *The digestive system breaks down food and absorbs nutrients.* 146

41 **The Beat Goes On** *The health of the circulatory system is affected by diet and behavior.* 150

42 **On the Move** *The human body has three types of muscle tissue: skeletal muscle, cardiac muscle, and smooth muscle.* 154

Chapter 15 — A MIND OF ITS OWN

Opener 156A

43 **Brain Scan** *Different parts of the brain do different things.* 156

44 **Sleep On It** *Sleep may play an important role in learning.* 158

45 **Seeing Things** *The brain interprets what the eye sees.* 162

Chapter 16 — DISEASES THROUGH TIME

Opener 166A

46 **Conquering Polio** *Vaccines help the body's immune system fight the viruses that cause polio.* 166

47 **The Buzz on Malaria** *Malaria is an infectious disease that continues to plague the world today.* 170

48 **Help Yourself Stay Healthy** *Infectious diseases can be prevented.* 172

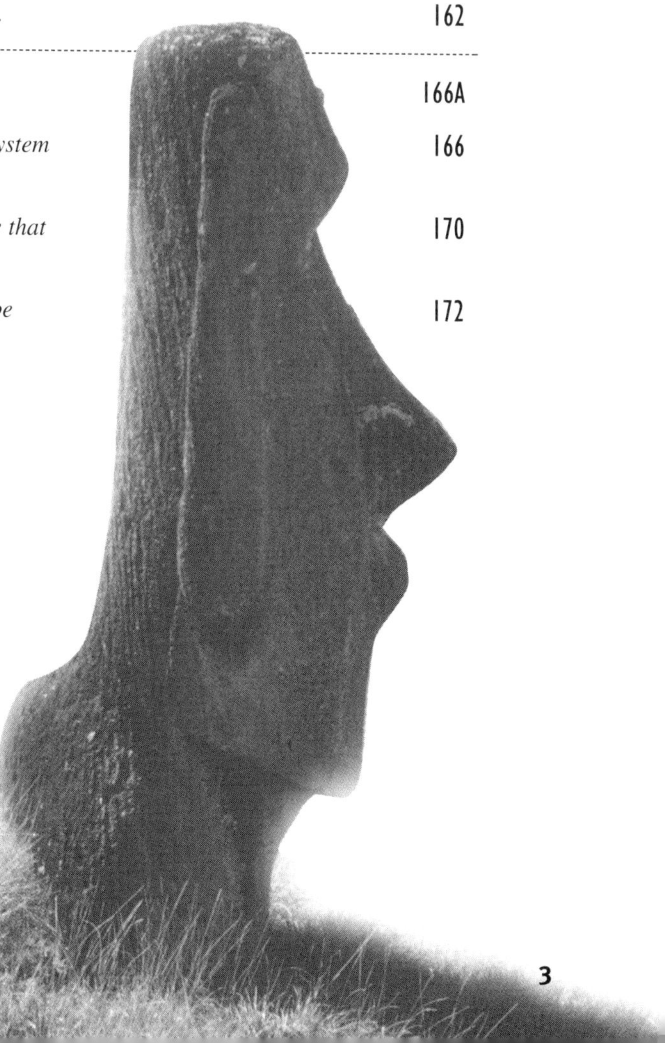

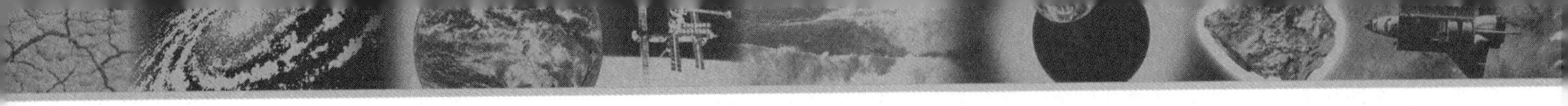

UNIT 5 Ecology

UNIT 5 Ecology 176

Chapter 17 — POPULATIONS, COMMUNITIES, AND ECOSYSTEMS

Opener 178A

49 **The Cane Toad Invasion** *Cane toad populations in Australia have grown at an alarming rate.* 178

50 **Poison Toads** *A cane toad population interacts with other populations in its community.* 182

51 **Bad Neighbors** *Cane toad populations affect their entire ecosystem.* 186

Chapter 18 — UNDER THE GRASSLAND SKY

Opener 188A

52 **Eat or Be Eaten** *Coyotes and rodents illustrate predator-prey feeding relationships in a desert ecosystem.* 188

53 **A Place of Their Own** *Different species can survive in the same ecosystem by occupying different habitats.* 192

54 **The Fragile Land** *Humans often make changes that affect ecosystems.* 196

Chapter 19 — RAIN FOREST

Opener 198A

55 **Let It Rain** *The tapir's structural adaptations enable it to survive in its tropical rain forest ecosystem.* 198

56 **The Seeds of Biodiversity** *Tapirs serve an important role in maintaining the biodiversity of the tropical rain forest.* 202

57 **Going, Going... Gone?** *If the deforestation of tropical rain forests is not slowed, one of Earth's most valuable ecosystems will be destroyed.* 206

Chapter 20 — PROTECTING EARTH

Opener 208A

58 **The Lesson of Easter Island** *The earliest civilization on Easter Island destroyed the island's natural resources.* 208

59 **People Make a Difference** *Human population growth has a direct impact on aquatic ecosystems.* 212

60 **Be an Eco-Hero** *Biodiversity can be found in even a small plot of land.* 214

Glossary 218

Rubric 225

Copymasters 226

Index 232

Credits 236

How to Use This Book

The Great Source *Life Science, Earth Science, and Physical Science Daybooks* are designed to be flexible resources for you to use with your students. Here are a few suggestions for incorporating them into your science curriculum.

Use the *Science Daybooks* as the core of your science program. Throughout the *Science Daybooks,* the lessons reference *ScienceSaurus®*, a middle school science handbook, and *sci*LINKS®, to provide a complete foundation for a middle school science curriculum. *ScienceSaurus* is a comprehensive reference aligned with the *National Science Education Standards* (grades 5–8), and models scientific investigation and inquiry. The *sci*LINKS Web site provides students with a logical next step to the process of finding out more. With the *Science Daybooks*, we initiate this process by providing students with snippets of readings from "real" science materials. These engage them in the discovery process, and help them apply what they've learned in extended activities. These readings were carefully selected to provide meaningful investigations into every area described by the *National Science Education Standards.* However, unlike a textbook approach that requires students to read about an array of science topics, the *Science Daybooks* allow the students to "get specific" and do the science.

For example, when we study ecosystems, students gain a basic understanding of factors that affect populations and relationships between populations by referencing topics 130 through 135 in *ScienceSaurus.* Then in one of 12 *Life Science Daybook* lessons from the Ecology Unit, students focus on predator-prey relationships as they read actual field notes of a coyote study in southeastern Arizona. They analyze data and draw conclusions. They challenge the researchers' conclusions, suggesting questions for further study. They make predictions. And, they apply what they've learned by researching state and local wildlife management plans. Students go to the *sci*LINKS® Web site and enter keywords "Ecosystem" and "Food Webs" and connect to a vast number of appropriate Web sources providing additional research information, case studies, and activities. And, they can do additional research and design their own investigations using the models and guidelines found in the *ScienceSaurus* (topics 001–019 and 410–426) and experience the process of "full inquiry," as outlined in the *National Science Education Standards.*

Supplement your existing science program. The units and topics in the *Science Daybooks* match up with those in most current textbooks. Pick and choose units or chapters as you teach those topics during the year.

Extend science after school or during the summer. It can be difficult to do everything you would like in science class. You may want to extend students' science time to after school. The wealth of extended activities in the *Science Daybooks* allows students (as individuals and/or small groups) to pursue different investigations throughout the year and report their findings to the class. Many of the activities were culled from the best of NSTA's *ScienceScope*, a professional journal for middle school science teachers.

Prepare students for high-stakes assessments with opportunities to write and communicate about science. Most often, state assessments require students to read, comprehend, and write about both fiction and nonfiction passages. The *Science Daybooks* promote critical reading, writing, and thinking about science.

Weave into an integrated science curriculum. Since the *Science Daybooks* are small, inexpensive, and portable, a set of three books can be purchased for the students in the first year of a three-year integrated science curriculum. Determine the units to teach in each of the three years, and pass the books along to the next-level teacher at the end of the year.

There are many ways to make good use of the *Science Daybooks* in your classroom. In whatever way you choose to use them, be assured that these materials provide a foundation for a complete and effective curriculum for the middle school grades.

Scope and Sequence

Correlation with National Science Education Standards, Grades 5–8

UNIT ▶	UNIT 1												UNIT 2								
CHAPTER ▶	Ch. 1			Ch. 2			Ch. 3			Ch. 4			Ch. 5			Ch. 6			Ch. 7		
LESSON ▶	1	2	3	4	5	6	7	8	9	10	11	12	13	14	15	16	17	18	19	20	21
Unifying Concepts and Processes																					
Systems, order, and organization	•	•	•		•	•	•			•	•	•	•	•	•	•	•				
Evidence, models, and explanation	•	•		•	•	•	•	•		•	•			•		•	•	•		•	
Change, constancy, and measurement				•	•	•	•	•	•										•	•	•
Evolution and equilibrium															•				•	•	•
Form and function	•	•	•	•	•	•	•	•	•	•	•	•	•	•	•				•		•
Science as Inquiry																					
Abilities necessary to do scientific inquiry	•				•													•			
Understanding about scientific inquiry			•								•			•							
Physical Science																					
Transfer of energy	•			•	•	•				•											
Life Science																					
Structure and function in living systems	•	•	•	•	•	•	•	•	•	•	•	•	•	•	•				•		•
Reproduction and heredity			•				•	•					•	•	•	•	•	•	•	•	•
Regulation and behavior	•	•	•	•		•	•	•	•	•		•									
Populations and ecosystems																					•
Diversity and adaptations of organisms														•	•				•	•	•
Science and Technology																					
Abilities of technological design											•										
Understanding about science and technology			•								•										
Science in Personal and Social Perspectives																					
Personal health												•					•	•			
Populations, resources, and environments															•			•		•	
Natural hazards									•										•		
Risks and benefits																					
Science and technology in society			•								•				•					•	
History and Nature of Science																					
Science as a human endeavor			•								•			•							
Nature of science					•	•					•			•							
History of science			•											•							

			UNIT 3												UNIT 4												UNIT 5											
Ch. 8			Ch. 9			Ch. 10			Ch. 11			Ch. 12			Ch. 13			Ch. 14			Ch. 15			Ch. 16			Ch. 17			Ch. 18			Ch. 19			Ch. 20		
22	23	24	25	26	27	28	29	30	31	32	33	34	35	36	37	38	39	40	41	42	43	44	45	46	47	48	49	50	51	52	53	54	55	56	57	58	59	60
Unifying Concepts and Processes																																						
●	●	●		●	●	●	●	●	●	●	●	●	●	●				●	●	●	●	●	●	●	●	●	●	●	●	●	●	●	●	●	●	●	●	●
	●	●	●	●		●	●	●	●	●	●	●	●	●	●	●	●	●		●	●	●	●	●	●		●	●	●	●	●	●		●				
			●												●		●		●			●			●		●	●	●	●		●	●	●	●	●	●	●
	●				●																				●				●				●					
●	●	●			●	●	●	●				●	●	●	●	●	●	●	●	●	●	●	●	●				●					●	●				
Science as Inquiry																																						
●		●												●	●	●	●	●				●								●	●							●
●	●	●	●		●				●	●	●	●			●							●		●				●		●	●			●				●
Physical Science																																						
							●		●																													
Life Science																																						
●	●	●			●	●	●	●				●	●	●	●	●	●	●	●	●	●	●	●	●				●					●	●				
●	●											●													●		●	●					●					
					●	●	●	●	●	●	●	●							●		●	●				●		●	●		●			●				
									●	●	●	●	●														●	●	●	●	●	●	●	●	●	●	●	●
●	●	●	●	●	●	●	●	●	●	●	●	●	●	●											●		●	●			●		●	●				●
Science and Technology																																						
																								●														
Science in Personal and Social Perspectives																																						
			●	●	●												●	●	●	●	●	●		●	●	●												
			●	●																					●		●	●	●	●	●	●	●	●	●	●	●	●
			●	●	●												●							●	●	●		●			●	●		●	●	●	●	
																			●					●		●	●	●			●	●			●			
																								●		●	●	●		●					●		●	
History and Nature of Science																																						
●	●		●							●	●	●										●		●						●	●			●	●			
●	●	●	●						●	●	●	●		●	●	●	●	●				●		●						●	●			●				●
	●			●							●													●														

About the Photo

In this photo, fibrin threads trap human red blood cells as a blood clot forms. Unlike other human cells, red blood cells do not have a nucleus.

About the Reading Selections

The reading selections included in the student book include square brackets and points of ellipses—a series of three or four points (periods). Such substitutions were made to simplify or shorten the text. If students are not familiar with these forms of punctuation, offer the following explanations:

- Square brackets show that other words were substituted for words in the original text.
- Points of ellipsis show that words were left out of the original text. Within a sentence, three points are used. At the end of a sentence, four points are used—three points of ellipsis plus the period that ends the sentence.

About the Charts

A major goal of the *Science Daybooks* is to promote reading, writing, and critical thinking skills in the context of science. The charts below describe the types of reading selections included in this unit and identify the skills and strategies used in each lesson.

UNIT 1 Cells

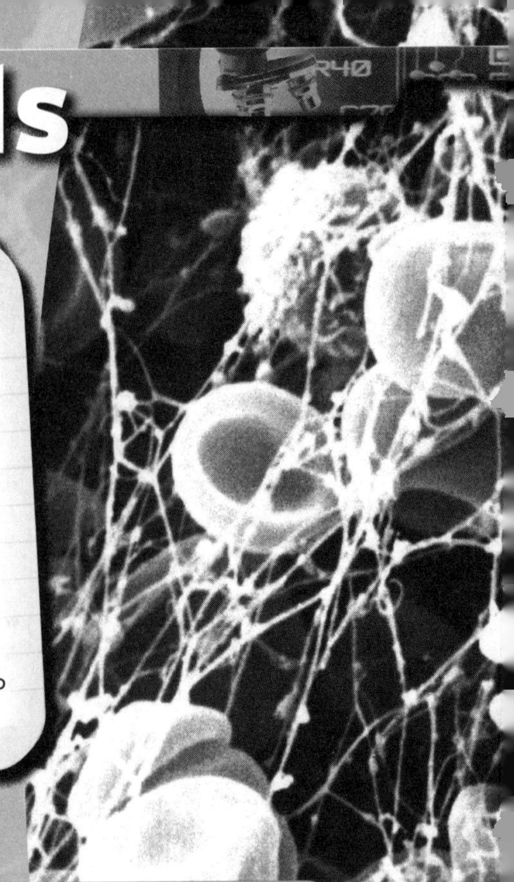

Do you know why cells are called "cells"?

The first person to observe cells was an English scientist named Robert Hooke. In 1665, Hooke looked at a piece of cork using a microscope and drew a comparison between what he saw and something he was already familiar with. He thought that the sections making up the cork looked like the rooms that monks lived in, which are called "cells." Hooke decided to call the cork sections "cells," too.

In this unit, you will learn all about cells, the small but complex building blocks of all living things. Cells carry out all the activities that keep a living thing alive. For example, they take in nutrients, water, and air. They get rid of wastes, use energy, grow, and reproduce themselves. You'll also learn how cells join together to form tissues, organs, and organ systems. Finally, you'll learn what can happen when cells stop functioning normally.

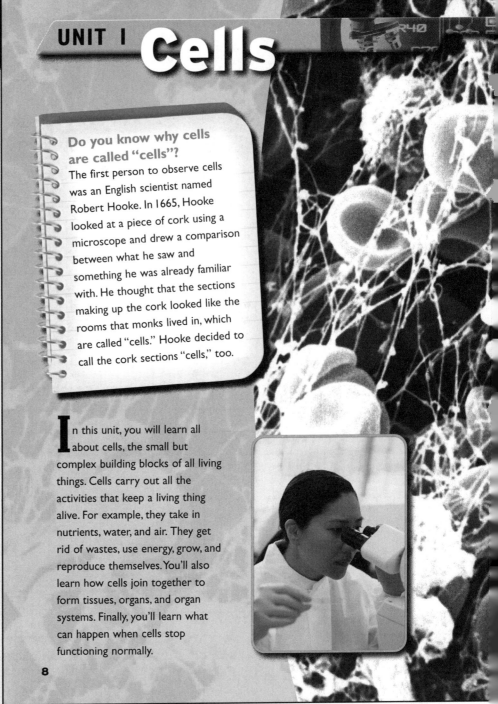

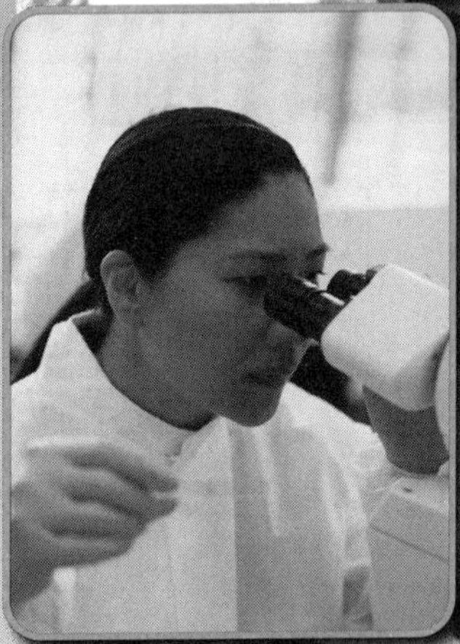

8

SELECTION	READING	WRITING	APPLICATION
CHAPTER 1 • STRUCTURE OF A CELL			
1. "Heads Out—Tails In" (nonfiction science book)	• Make a list • Directed reading	• Conduct an experiment • Record observations • Opinion statement	• Draw a diagram
2. "The Cell as a City" (nonfiction science book)	• Brainstorming • Critical thinking	• Graphic organizer	• Write a dialogue
3. "Clones: Double Trouble?" (children's magazine article)	• Main idea	• Main idea • Supporting details	• Write a poem
CHAPTER 2 • CELLS AT WORK			
4. "Charles Wallace's Mitochondria" (science fiction book)	• Concept map • Directed reading	• Brainstorming • Draw conclusions	• Write a dialogue
5. "Dancing Chloroplasts" (science news magazine)	• Record observations • Critical thinking • Support an opinion	• Make comparisons • Draw conclusions	• Conduct an experiment
6. "From Sugar-Making to Sugar-Burning" (medical school Web site)	• Directed reading • Compare and contrast	• Reexamine • Write a persuasive paragraph	• Make a poster

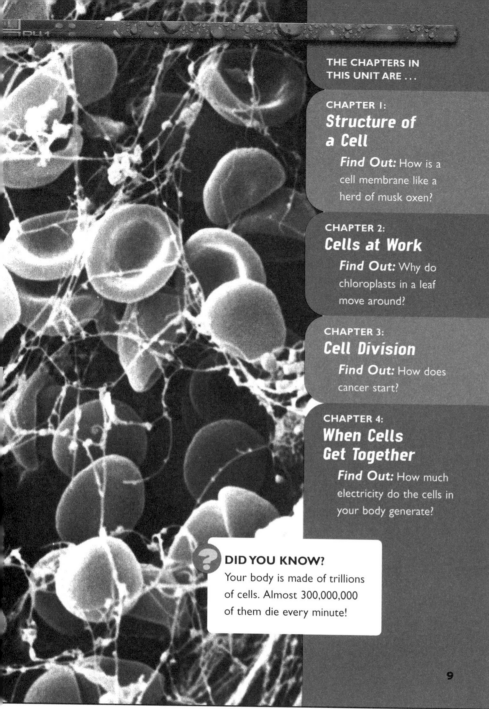

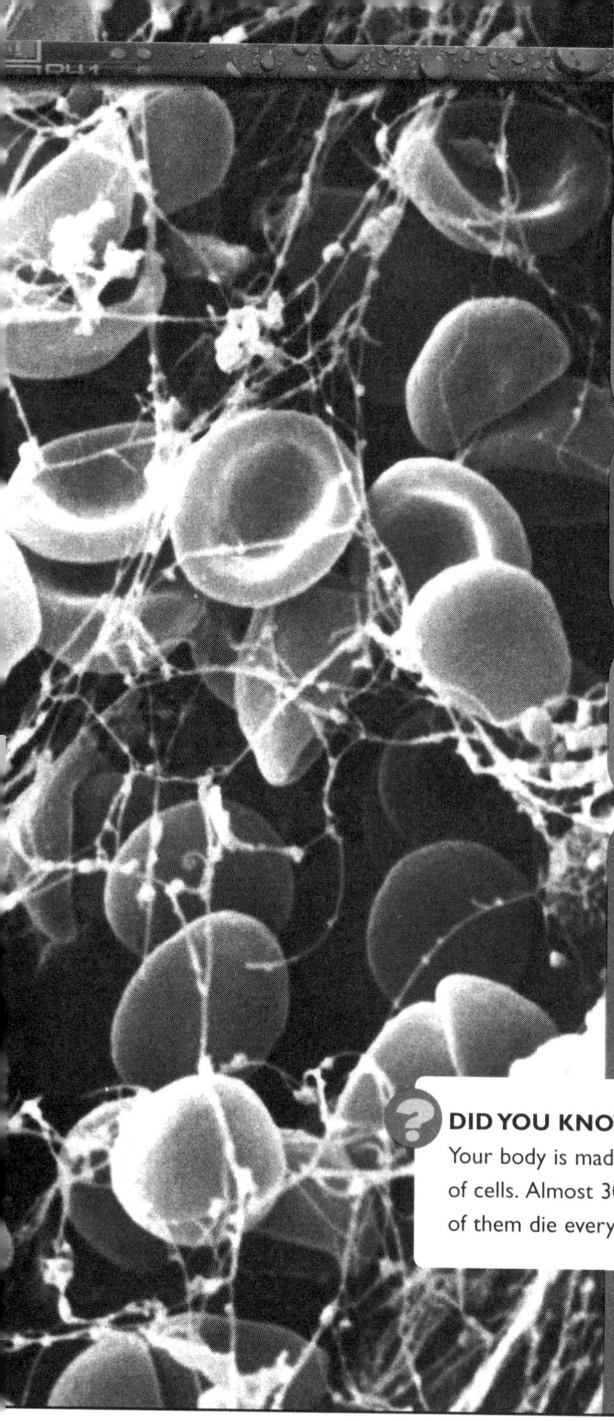

THE CHAPTERS IN THIS UNIT ARE . . .

CHAPTER 1:
Structure of a Cell

Find Out: How is a cell membrane like a herd of musk oxen?

CHAPTER 2:
Cells at Work

Find Out: Why do chloroplasts in a leaf move around?

CHAPTER 3:
Cell Division

Find Out: How does cancer start?

CHAPTER 4:
When Cells Get Together

Find Out: How much electricity do the cells in your body generate?

DID YOU KNOW?
Your body is made of trillions of cells. Almost 300,000,000 of them die every minute!

Answers to *Find Out* Questions

CHAPTER 1
A cell membrane surrounds the cell and protects its contents just like musk oxen protect their calves by forming a circle around them. (p. 11)

CHAPTER 2
Chloroplasts move into lighted areas of the leaf to absorb sunlight for photosynthesis and into shaded areas when the light is too intense. (p. 24)

CHAPTER 3
Cancer starts when the controls that tell cells when to stop dividing do not work normally and the cells keep dividing uncontrollably. (pp. 38–39)

CHAPTER 4
enough to power a 40-watt light bulb (p. 41)

SCILINKS
THE WORLD'S A CLICK AWAY
www.scilinks.org
Keyword: Current Research
Code: GSSD04

SELECTION	READING	WRITING	APPLICATION
CHAPTER 3 • CELL DIVISION			
7. "Where Do Cells Come From?" (nonfiction science book)	• Make a list • Critical thinking	• Draw and label model • Explain model • Conduct research	• Record research findings in table • Defend conclusion
8. "Exponential Growth" (nonfiction science book)	• Make a prediction • Critical thinking	• Make comparisons • Analyze and explain	• Hands-on activity • Write comparisons • Write analysis and explanation
9. "Cell Activity Gone Wrong" (medical school Web site)	• Critical thinking	• Make comparisons • Conduct research	• Compare research findings • Write investigation question
CHAPTER 4 • WHEN CELLS GET TOGETHER			
10. "The Body Electric" (university science Web site)	• Brainstorming • Critical thinking • Draw a diagram	• Interpret scientific diagram • Make inferences • Conduct research	• Write research review
11. "Tissue Engineering" (NASA Web site)	• Write opinion • Critical thinking • Generate questions	• Interpret scientific diagram • Make inferences • Draw conclusion	• Write a haiku poem
12. "Hyperthyroid Blues" (health Web site)	• Preview • Critical thinking	• List reference results in table	• Write analysis from table

Structure of a Cell

LESSON 1

Sentries at the Gate

Point of Lesson: ***The cell membrane controls what goes into and out of the cell.***

Students first consider the role of boundaries (such as fences) in everyday life, then relate the concept of boundaries to the functions of the cell membrane. An activity in which students observe changes in a hen's egg demonstrates that cell membranes allow some materials to pass through them but not others.

Materials

Science Scope Activity (p. 10B, p. 11, and p. 13), for the class:

- research sources that include colorful diagrams of animal cells and organelles
- wide variety of construction materials (cardboard, paper, wood, paint, nails, yarn, fabric, glue, tape, and the like)

Activity (p. 12), for each group:

- 1 raw egg
- 3 large clear plastic cups
- vinegar
- corn syrup
- water
- 25-cm piece of string
- metric ruler

Connections (p. 12), for the class:

- research sources about structures used as boundaries

Laboratory Safety

Review the following safety guidelines with students before they do the Activity in this lesson.

- Do not taste anything in the laboratory.
- If you have an allergy to eggs, let your lab partner handle the egg.
- Handle the egg gently to avoid breaking it, especially after its shell is removed.
- Clean up spills immediately.
- Wash your hands thoroughly after the activity.

LESSON 2

All Kinds of Parts

Point of Lesson: ***The cell is made up of many organelles.***

A book excerpt introduces organelles by drawing an analogy between a cell and a city. Students work with the analogy to correlate the role of each major organelle to the function of a person, service, or organization within a city. They then apply their knowledge by writing an imaginary dialogue between two different organelles in which each argues that it is most important to the cell as a whole.

Materials

none

LESSON 3

The Nucleus and DNA

Point of Lesson: ***The nucleus controls the functioning of the cell's other organelles.***

A magazine article describing the creation of Dolly the cloned sheep reinforces for students the role of a cell's nucleus. Students explain why replacing the nucleus of a sheep egg cell with the nucleus from an adult sheep's cell would cause the egg to develop into a copy of that adult. Students summarize this newsworthy event in a limerick about Dolly, focusing on the role of the cell nucleus.

Materials

none

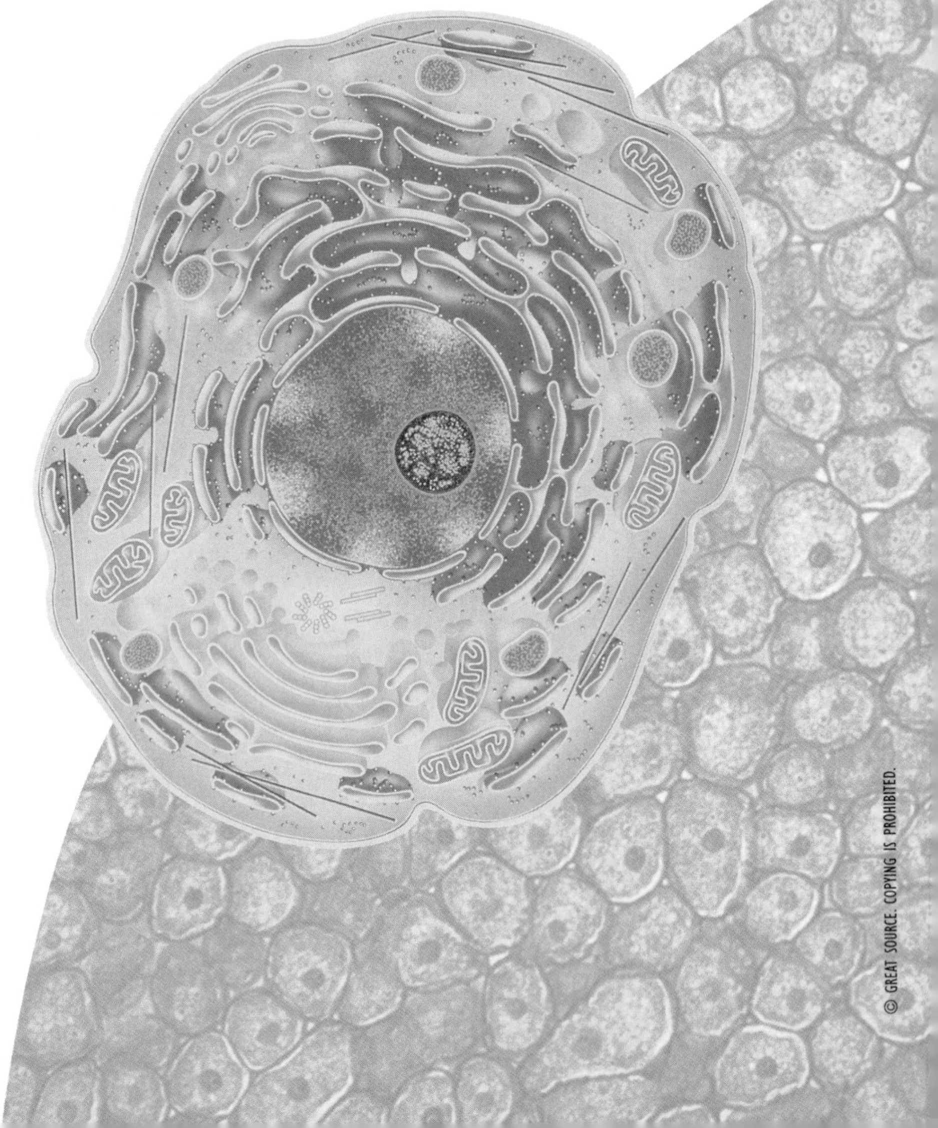

Science Scope Activity

Walk-in Cell

NSTA has chosen a Science Scope *activity related to the content in this chapter. The activity begins here and continues in Lesson 1, pages 11 and 13.*

Time: ongoing (partial use of class time)
Materials: see page 10A

As an ongoing project throughout this chapter, students can create a walk-in model of a cell. The size of the model and the materials of which it is made can be varied to suit your classroom. Provide biology textbooks and other references with colorful diagrams that students can use as the basis for designing and constructing the model. The "walk-in cell" will provide a dramatic educational exhibit for other classes or for visitors on Parents Night.

(continued on page 11)

Background Information

There about 200 different types of cells in the human body, varying in size from a few micrometers in diameter to over a meter in length (a nerve cell). The number and type of organelles and other structures vary among cells, depending on the cell's function. For example, muscle cells contain structures called myofilaments, which allow the cells to contract and produce movement. Some cells within the eye have special organelles that enable them to detect light.

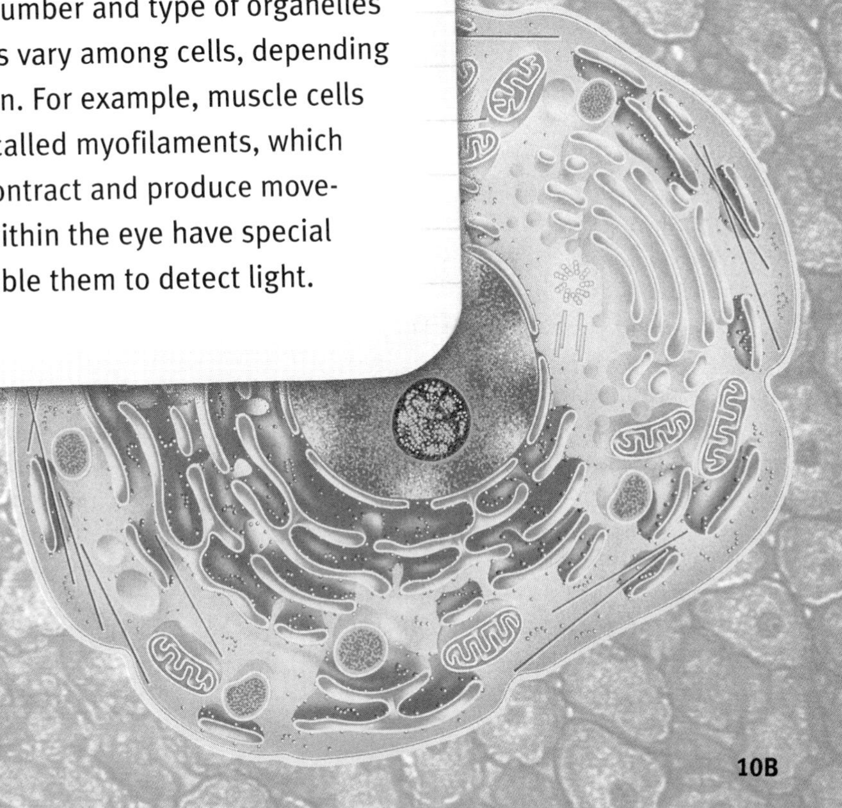

Point of Lesson
The cell membrane controls what goes into and out of the cell.

Focus
- Systems, order, and organization
- Evidence, models, and explanation
- Structure and function in living organisms
- Regulation and behavior

Skills and Strategies
- Comparing and contrasting
- Collecting and recording data
- Interpreting data
- Observing
- Recognizing cause and effect
- Making inferences
- Making and using models
- Abilities necessary to do scientific inquiry

Advance Preparation

Vocabulary
Make sure students understand these terms. Definitions can be found in the glossary at the end of the student book.

- bacteria
- cell
- fat
- molecule
- nutrient
- organism

(continued on page 11)

Structure of a Cell

Sentries at the Gate

There are many structures inside a cell. What keeps the structures inside the cell and keeps out things that can damage those important structures? The cell membrane.

Your body contains billions of cells! Cells are the building blocks of life. Some organisms are made up of only one cell, while others are made up of millions of cells. Imagine that your fingertip is the size of a room and the room is filled with rice grains. Each grain would represent one cell. Can you imagine the number of cells in your fingertip?

Cells are filled with a fluid called cytoplasm. A thin membrane surrounds every cell. This membrane forms a boundary between the inside of the cell and its surroundings.

Before You Read

THINK ABOUT IT Boundaries keep things in and out. For example, a fence marks the boundary of a yard. The fence also keeps the pet dog and the young children in. It keeps strange dogs and bicyclists out.

- ***Think about the boundaries in your environment. Name five boundaries that you can see around you. For each one, tell what marks the boundary. List what is kept in and what is kept out by the boundary.***

Accept all reasonable answers. Example: A refrigerator's door and walls keep the cold air in and the warm air out.

TEACHING PLAN pp. 10–11

INTRODUCING THE LESSON
This lesson introduces the structure and function of the cell membrane.

Ask students how big they think an average-size human cell is. Then point out the rice-grain analogy in the first paragraph on this page. Ask students to think of other analogies to describe the size of cells.

Some students may think that cells are as small as molecules or atoms; others may think they are large enough to see with the unaided eye. Emphasize that most cells can be seen only with a microscope. Only large egg cells, such as a chicken egg, can be seen without a microscope. Also explain that cells are made of molecules that in turn are made of atoms; the cells themselves are not as small as a molecule or atom.

Before You Read

THINK ABOUT IT Focus on the function of the cell membrane by noting that it surrounds and protects the cell's contents much like a fence or wall protects a field. Point out that although the cell membrane forms a boundary, it allows materials to pass through it.

Encourage students to think of boundaries that separate, such as the walls of a swimming pool or the latex of a balloon. Discuss the title of this lesson in relationship to the function of the cell membrane. Emphasize that both "keeping in" and "keeping out" make up the "sentry" role of the membrane "gate."

Read

It can be easier to understand something new by comparing it with something else.

Heads Out—Tails In

When danger threatens, musk oxen gather in a circle—heads and horns to the outside, tails to the inside—sheltering their calves in the center. This circle of protection illustrates one of life's organizing **principles**—a difference between in and out. Life's chemicals need to be kept close together so that they can meet and react readily. The inner environment needs a saltiness, acidity, temperature, etc., different from the outside. These differences are **maintained** by some form of protective barrier, such as a baby's skin, a clam's shell, or a cell's membrane.

The membrane surrounding each of our cells behaves something like the threatened musk oxen. The fat molecules that make up the membrane have a water-liking head and a fat-liking tail. Heads face outside toward the watery environment beyond the cell; tails face inward. Since the inside of a cell also has a watery environment, a second row of fat molecules lines up tail-to-tail with the outer layer, heads facing inward. With this structure creating an inside and an outside, life can do its work.

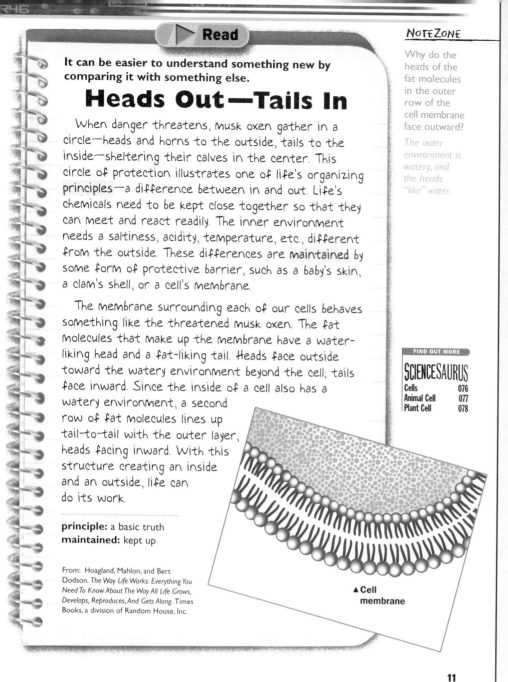

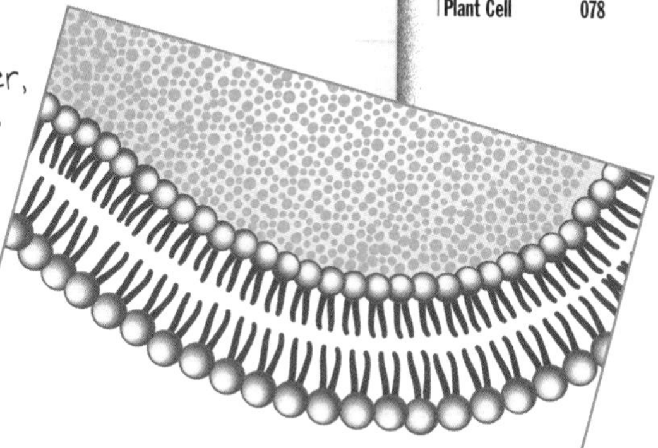

▲Cell membrane

principle: a basic truth
maintained: kept up

From: Hoagland, Mahlon, and Bert Dodson. *The Way Life Works: Everything You Need To Know About The Way All Life Grows, Develops, Reproduces, And Gets Along.* Times Books, a division of Random House, Inc.

NOTEZONE

Why do the heads of the fat molecules in the outer row of the cell membrane face outward?

The outer environment is watery, and the heads "like" water.

FIND OUT MORE

SCIENCESAURUS

Cells	076
Animal Cell	077
Plant Cell	078

11

(continued from page 10)

Materials

Gather the materials needed for ***Science Scope Activity*** (p. 10B, p. 11, and p. 13), ***Activity*** (p. 12), and ***Connections*** (p. 12).

Science Scope Activity

(continued from page 10B)

1. Divide the class into six groups, and explain the role of each group:
   Group 1 will build the cell body and set up the display.
   Group 2 will research cell structure and the function and size of cell parts.
   Group 3 will design and construct the cell organelles.
   Group 4 will create a pamphlet that describes the model and the actual cell structures it represents. These pamphlets will be given out to visitors who tour the walk-in cell.
   Group 5 will create labels for the cell organelles that explain their functions.
   Group 6 will be the Test Your Knowledge Committee. These students will create a game to test visitors' knowledge.

(continued on page 13)

Read

This reading compares the cell membrane to a herd of musk oxen protecting their young. Tell students that this analogy may help them understand how a cell membrane functions, but it does not mean that molecules in the membrane "choose" to arrange themselves as a protective barrier, as the musk oxen do. The oxen are aware of what they are doing; molecules in the membrane are not. Have students identify the sentence in the reading that compares the outer row of fat molecules in the cell membrane to the outward-facing musk oxen (second paragraph, third sentence).

Some students may think that the area between the two rows of molecules is the "inner environment" mentioned in the reading's first paragraph. Point out that the two rows of fat molecules *together* form the cell membrane; the "inner environment" is the speckled area of the diagram.

CHECK UNDERSTANDING

Skill: Making and using models

Ask groups of students to demonstrate the structure and function of the cell membrane by arranging themselves to model the membrane and materials entering and leaving the cell. (Students should form one outward-facing ring and a second, inward-facing ring inside it, resembling the diagram on this page.)

More Resources

The following resources are also available from Great Source.

SCIENCESAURUS

Cells 076
Animal Cell 077
Plant Cell 078

READER'S HANDBOOK

Focus on Science Concepts 132
Comparison and Contrast 278
Elements of Graphics: Diagram 552

MATH ON CALL

Gathering Data: Recording Data 268
Displaying Data in Tables and Graphs: Data in Tables 285

Connections

Time: will vary
Materials: research sources about structures used as boundaries

SOCIAL STUDIES Have students research different types of protective boundaries used in the past, such as medieval perimeter walls and moats, Hadrian's Wall, the Great Wall of China, the Berlin Wall, and circles of wagon trains. Encourage students to find out about the functions of such boundaries—keeping out intruders, keeping in inhabitants, or isolating inhabitants from disease.

Activity

MAKE COMPARISONS The cell membrane controls the movement of nutrients, water, salts, and other substances into the cell and the movement of wastes out of the cell. The membrane also keeps out harmful bacteria, viruses, and other things that could damage the cell.

Water and other materials pass through the membrane and into or out of the cell by a process called *osmosis*. Using an egg to represent a cell, you can see osmosis in action.

WHAT YOU'LL NEED:
- **1 raw egg**
- **3 large clear plastic cups**
- **vinegar**
- **corn syrup**
- **water**
- **25-cm piece of string**
- **metric ruler**

1. Measure the circumference of the egg by wrapping the string around the egg's middle. Then measure that distance with the ruler. Record that measurement in the chart below.
2. Put the egg in one of the cups, and cover it with vinegar. Leave the cup in the refrigerator for three nights. Examine and measure the egg each day, and record your observations.
3. Carefully take the egg out of the cup. (The shell should be dissolved.) Rinse the egg with water and carefully measure its circumference again.
4. Put the egg in the second cup and cover it with corn syrup. Leave the cup in the refrigerator overnight.
5. Rinse the egg with water, measure its circumference, and put it in the third cup. This time, cover the egg with water. Leave the cup in the refrigerator overnight. Measure the egg's circumference again.

Day	Circumference	Observations of Egg	Observations of Liquid
Start	*Measurements will vary.*	*has white/brown shell*	*Vinegar is clear; bubbles and fizzing around egg.*
After first night in vinegar	*Circumference remains constant.*	*Shell is thinner.*	*fizzing and small bubbles around egg*
After second night in vinegar	*Circumference remains constant or decreases.*	*Egg shell is nearly dissolved.*	*fizzing and small bubbles around egg*
After third night in vinegar	*Circumference increases.*	*shell fully dissolved; egg rises; can see yolk*	*Level of liquid decreases.*
After one night in corn syrup	*Circumference decreases.*	*Egg has shriveled and become firmer.*	*Level of liquid increases.*
After one night in water	*Circumference increases.*	*Egg is larger again.*	*Level of liquid decreases.*

12

TEACHING PLAN pp. 12–13

Activity

Time: 5–10 minutes each day for 6 days
Materials: (per group) 1 raw egg, 3 large clear plastic cups, vinegar, corn syrup, water, 25-cm piece of string, metric ruler

MAKE COMPARISONS Review the process of osmosis. Stress that substances always move from the area of higher concentration to the area of lower concentration. In this activity, water, vinegar, and corn syrup pass through the membrane enclosing an egg.

- Have students work in groups of three, taking turns measuring the egg.
- Caution students to handle the egg gently to avoid breaking it. This is particularly important once the shell is removed.
- If necessary, demonstrate the measuring technique described in step 1.
- Make sure students understand that the egg's shell is not the membrane. Point out that the shell protects the inner membrane, which looks like a thin film in a raw egg.
- The vinegar used in step 2 will somewhat solidify the inner egg so it can be handled more easily.
- Students could use a slotted spoon to hold the egg when they measure it in step 3.
- Arrange for space in a refrigerator easily accessible by students.

Propose Explanations

▸ ***Why did you need to remove the shell from the egg?***

to expose the membrane

▸ ***What did you observe after you left the egg in syrup? Why do you think this happened?***

The syrup got watery and the egg got much smaller. Water must have passed out of the egg through the membrane.

▸ ***Why didn't the syrup pass into the egg?***

The syrup molecules must have been too big to go through the membrane.

▸ ***What did you observe after you left the egg in water? Why do you think this happened?***

The water level in the cup became lower, and the egg became bigger. Water must have moved through the membrane and into the egg.

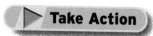

Take Action

DRAW DIAGRAMS A pack of wolves approaches a herd of musk oxen and tries to attack and kill a calf. Draw a diagram to show how the herd protects its young. Then draw another diagram to show how the cell membrane protects the cell's contents from attacking bacteria.

Science Scope Activity

(continued from page 11)

2. Clear an area in the classroom where the walk-in model can be conveniently built and left up for awhile. Depending on the complexity of the model, it should be wide enough so that two people can walk around inside it comfortably.
3. Different organelles should have their own "stations" inside the cell where materials and information are displayed. When visitors tour the model, student volunteers can serve as tour guides to explain the cell structures and answer questions.

Assessment

Skill: Drawing conclusions

Use the following question to assess each student's progress:

What are the functions of the cell membrane? (It forms the outer boundary of the cell, protects and isolates the interior of the cell from the outside environment, and maintains differences in saltiness, acidity, and temperature between the cell's interior and the outside environment.)

Propose Explanations

If students have difficulty answering the questions in this section, have them reread the Activity's introductory paragraphs on page 12. Then review the process of osmosis using a simple diagram on the board: a large circle to represent the cell, 10–12 small circles inside the cell to represent water molecules, 8–10 medium-size circles outside the cell to represent corn syrup molecules, and arrows to show that water molecules move from inside the cell (the area of higher concentration) through the membrane and into the corn syrup (the area of lower concentration).

If students need help answering the second and fourth questions, use the analogy of a sponge getting smaller as water evaporates from it and getting larger as it absorbs water.

Take Action

DRAW DIAGRAMS Students' diagrams should include the following:

- heads and horns of oxen facing the outside
- two rows of molecules forming the cell membrane
- oxen and molecules tightly grouped to avoid gaps
- wolves outside the circle of oxen; at least one bacterium outside the cell membrane
- young oxen inside the circle

UNIT 1 Cells

CHAPTER I / LESSON 2

Point of Lesson
The cell is made up of many organelles.

Focus
- Systems, order, and organization
- Form and function
- Structure and function in living systems

Skills and Strategies
- Making inferences
- Communicating
- Classifying
- Comparing and contrasting
- Interpreting scientific illustrations

Advance Preparation

Vocabulary
Make sure students understand these terms. Definitions can be found in the glossary at the end of the student book.

- carbohydrate
- cell
- cell membrane
- cytoplasm
- DNA
- molecule
- nutrient
- protein

Structure of a Cell

All Kinds of Parts

If you think a cell is small, imagine how small the structures inside it must be!

A cell is complex. It contains many smaller structures, called *organelles.* Each organelle has a particular job to do to keep the cell working properly. The organelles are found in the cytoplasm that fills the cell. Organelles in an animal cell include lysosomes, the golgi apparatus, ribosomes, the nucleus, the endoplasmic reticulum, and mitochondria. The diagram on page 17 shows what these organelles look like.

Before You Read

STAYING ALIVE All living things need nutrients, water, and air. They need a suitable place to live. They grow and change. In addition, all living things sense and respond to changes inside them and in their surroundings, and they reproduce.

- ***You just read about what living things need to stay alive. What do you think a single cell needs to do in order to stay alive?***

Possible answers: take in food, water, and air; get rid of wastes; use the energy from food; reproduce; change; respond to changes inside and around them; grow

TEACHING PLAN pp. 14–15

INTRODUCING THE LESSON
This lesson presents the organelles found in all eukaryotic cells and the organelles' functions. Ask students if they can name any of the parts inside a cell. Students may recall at least the nucleus from their previous science classes.

Some students may not realize that a cell contains many different parts and may think that a cell is more like a chicken egg—a large nucleus (the egg's yolk) surrounded by fluid. Direct students' attention to the illustration of an animal cell on page 17 and ask them to note the various parts that are shown and labeled.

Before You Read

THINK ABOUT IT Students should understand that an individual cell must do the same things that an entire organism must do in order to survive. Ask: *Why do cells need to perform these functions?* (A cell is a living thing.)

Read

The parts of a cell can be compared to things we know well.

The Cell as a City

The cell itself is...comparable to a small city, with functions assigned to tiny workers within its walls....

Inside the cell membrane, the city of the cell is populated by...little workers, called organelles, that perform the services that keep the cell alive. They can be compared to the workers, factories, and transportation and communication systems that are vital to a working community.

For example...the mitochondria burn the carbohydrate fuel that is taken into the cell.... [M]itochondria are rather like power plants burning coal to make the electricity that keeps the city running....

vital: necessary
burn: combine with oxygen to release energy

From: Shroyer, Jo Ann. *Quarks, Critters, and Chaos: What Science Terms Really Mean.* Prentice Hall General Reference.

NOTEZONE

Jot down a question about cells to ask your teacher.

FIND OUT MORE

SCIENCESAURUS

Animal Cell	077
Plant Cell	078
Cell Processes	079

SCILINKS. THE WORLD'S A CLICK AWAY

www.scilinks.org
Keyword: Cell Structure
Code: GSLD01
Keyword: Eukaryotic Cells
Code: GSLD02

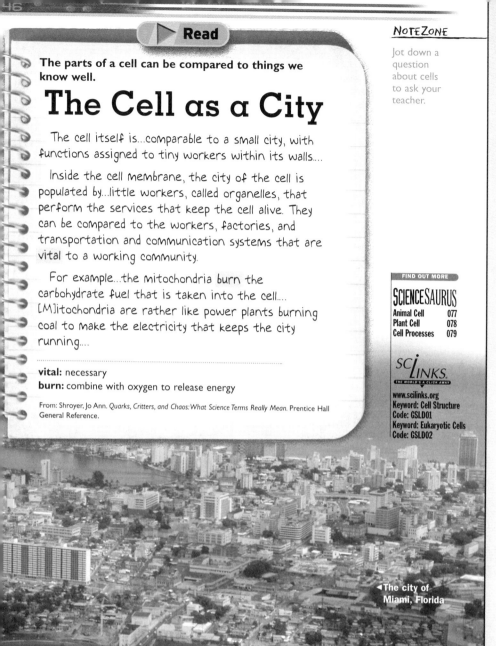

◄The city of Miami, Florida

Enrichment

Ask students if they can think of other complex systems besides a city that are made up of many individually functioning parts that work together. (Examples: a sports team, a construction crew, a hotel or other building) Discuss how these large systems satisfy their basic needs, and ask students to brainstorm similarities and differences between them. Focus on how individual parts of each system work together for the good of the whole.

Read

Some students may not be familiar with the transportation or communication systems that are part of a working community. Discuss students' own community as an example.

Point out that the reading's author calls organelles "little workers." Ask students to explain how this term helps the reader understand what organelles are. (It compares something new to something that the reader already knows.)

CHECK UNDERSTANDING

Skill: Comparing and contrasting

Ask: *What are some of a cell's basic needs that are the same as the entire organism's needs?* (taking in nutrients, water, and air; growing; reproducing; eliminating wastes; generating energy from food)

More Resources

The following resources are also available from Great Source and NSTA.

ScienceSaurus

Animal Cell	077
Plant Cell	078
Cell Processes	079

Reader's Handbook

Comparing and Contrasting	42
Focus on Dialogue	360

SCILINKS. THE WORLD'S A CLICK AWAY

www.scilinks.org
Keyword: Cell Structure
Code: GSLD01
Keyword: Eukaryotic Cells
Code: GSLD02

Connections

MUSIC Have students compare an orchestra or band to a cell. Ask them to identify the various instruments and their unique sounds. Ask: *What organizes and coordinates the musicians?* (the conductor or band leader) *Which part of a cell is like a conductor or band leader?* (the nucleus) *How are the instruments like the organelles in a cell?* (Each type of instrument has a

(continued on page 17)

Explore

The first person to see a cell was Robert Hooke, a British scientist. In 1665 Hooke used a simple microscope to observe dead cork cells. After his discovery, many centuries passed before scientists learned that cells contain organelles such as mitochondria. Each organelle plays a specific role in helping the cell function.

CELL CITY The reading compared mitochondria to a city's power plants. See if you can match each of the other organelles with a city structure that performs a similar function.

CELL PART	CITY STRUCTURE
Mitochondria: provide energy for the cell by breaking down sugar	city government offices; library
Golgi apparatus: packages materials and proteins to move them out of the cell	fuel refinery; waste processing plant
Nucleus: contains the cell's DNA; gives instructions to produce proteins; is the control center of the cell	power plants
Lysosomes: break down nutrients into more usable molecules; digest the cell's waste products	packaging and shipping center
Ribosomes: produce proteins	bus and subway systems inside the city
Endoplasmic reticulum: packages proteins and releases them out of the cell; carries materials around the cell	factories

16

Teaching Plan pp. 16–17

Explore

CELL CITY Help students find key words that link the cell parts to the city structures. For example, "energy" would indicate "power," and "control center" would suggest "government." In some cases, the same words are used. "Waste," mentioned in the description of lysosomes, relates directly to "waste processing plant." Help students differentiate between moving proteins and materials out of the cell and moving them around inside the cell.

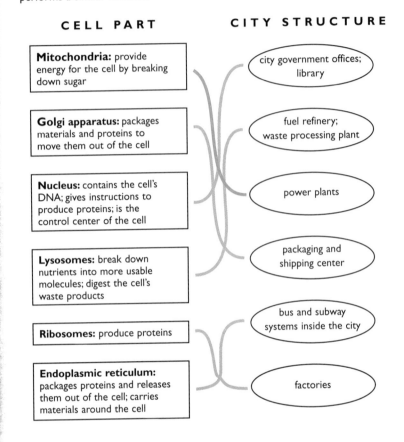

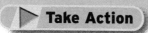

Take Action

WRITE A DIALOGUE A dialogue is a conversation between at least two people. Choose two of the organelles listed on page 16. Then write a dialogue between them in which they argue about which of them is more important to the cell's survival.

Answers will vary. Dialogues should include some structural and functional facts about each organelle discussed in this lesson.

ANIMAL CELL

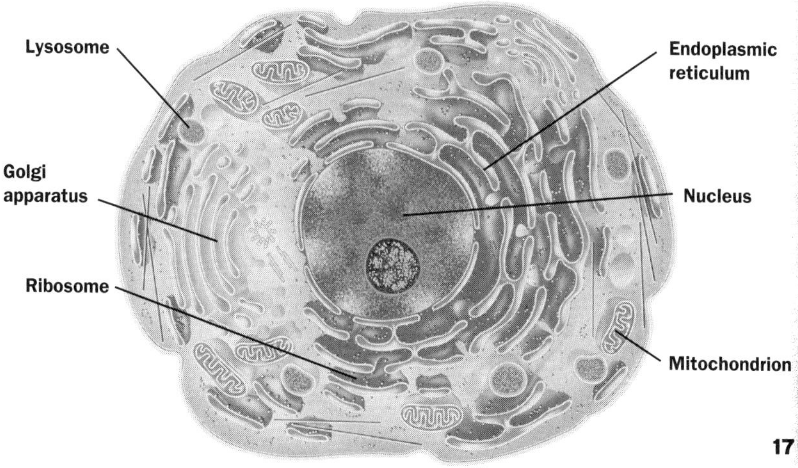

17

(continued from page 16)

different part to play in the music, as organelles do in a cell. Both the musicians and organelles must work together.)

Assessment

Skill: Drawing conclusions

Use the following question to assess each student's progress:

What are some of the functions that organelles perform? (provide energy by breaking down nutrients; produce proteins; move proteins out of the cell; move materials around inside the cell; get rid of waste products; nucleus controls other organelles)

Take Action

WRITE A DIALOGUE To prompt students' ideas, have them review examples of dialogue found in plays or books of nonfiction or fiction. Tell students to liven up their dialogues by giving human personality traits to each organelle, such as the nucleus being a bossy know-it-all and the mitochondria being constant complainers because they have to do all the work.

Review students' dialogues, and choose three or four that are particularly good in terms of both the science content and interest level. Ask pairs of volunteers to act out the dialogues. Give each pair its dialogue beforehand so the students can read it through and prepare their presentations.

Point of Lesson

The nucleus controls the functioning of the cell's other organelles.

Focus

- Systems, order, and organization
- Structure and function in living systems
- Reproduction and heredity
- Understanding about science and technology
- Science as a human endeavor
- History of science
- Understanding about scientific inquiry

Skills and Strategies

- Communicating
- Making inferences
- Recognizing cause and effect

Advance Preparation

Vocabulary

Make sure students understand these terms. Definitions can be found in the glossary at the end of the student book.

- chromosome
- DNA
- egg
- gene
- nucleus
- organelles
- organism
- sperm

The Nucleus and DNA

Every cell contains organelles. But where is the information that tells the organelles what to do? In the nucleus.

All plant and animal cells have a nucleus. The nucleus contains the cell's chromosomes, which are made of DNA. It is the DNA in the nucleus that determines what kind of organism the cell is part of—a frog, an oak tree, a fruit fly, a human, or whatever. Except for egg and sperm cells, the nucleus of every cell in an organism's body has a complete copy of that DNA. Knowing this, scientists searched for a way to produce an entire organism using just a cell's nucleus. In 1997 they finally succeeded.

Read

NOTEZONE

Circle the two things the scientists joined together to create Dolly.

Clones: Double Trouble?

Scientists called [Dolly the sheep] "a mind blower," "an awesome work" and "science fiction come true."... Dolly seemed to take her stardom in stride, nibbling straw and blinking softly. But news of her existence caused global excitement.

Dolly is a clone. From the length of her eyelashes to the swirling pattern of her wool, she's an exact copy of another sheep, an adult female, or ewe (pronounced *yew*).

Her life began in a laboratory. Scientists took one cell from a ewe and placed its nucleus, the command center containing the cell's genes, inside a sheep egg cell. The egg's own nucleus had been removed. After a zap of electricity, the cell began behaving like a newly fertilized sheep egg. It divided into more cells. The scientists placed the cluster of cells into the womb of another ewe, where it continued to develop into a lamb. The ewe gave birth to Dolly [in July 1997]. Tests show that she's identical to the ewe whose single cell created her.

From: "Clones: Double Trouble?" *Time for Kids*. Time Inc. (www.timeforkids.com/TFK/magazines/story/0,6277,93229,00.html

FIND OUT MORE

SCIENCESAURUS

DNA	115
Genes	116
Cloning	120

TEACHING PLAN pp. 18–19

INTRODUCING THE LESSON

This lesson explains the role of the cell's nucleus using the example of cloning.

Ask students if they know what cloning is. Some students may not know that cloning is done at the genetic level. Explain that the cloning process involves taking the nucleus of one cell with its complete set of DNA and placing it into an egg cell whose nucleus has been removed. The egg cell then begins dividing to grow into a new organism. Emphasize that only one "parent" is involved in cloning—the organism that had the original nucleus in one of its cells.

Read

The reading uses some terms that may be unfamiliar to students. Explain the terms "mind blower," "take her stardom in stride," and "science fiction come true" as needed.

In the NoteZone task, make sure students distinguish between the nucleus that was removed from the sheep egg cell and the nucleus that was introduced into it. Also clarify that the "cluster of cells" was placed into the womb of another ewe, not the womb of the ewe that contributed the nucleus.

Explore

To increase understanding of the cloning process, have students explain in their own words the difference between the nucleus removed from one ewe's egg cell and the nucleus taken from the second ewe's body cell. Help students realize that the nucleus removed from the ewe's egg cell lacked a complete set of DNA. In order to have a complete set, the egg would have to be fertilized by a ram's sperm, and only then would it be able to begin dividing. Explain that the zap of electricity activated the cell division process.

Explore

▸ ***Why would placing a cell nucleus inside a nucleus-free egg cell enable the egg to begin dividing?***

The DNA inside the nucleus has all the instructions to tell the cell when to divide.

▸ ***Why was the new ewe identical to the ewe that the scientists took the cell nucleus from?***

By taking the ewe's cell nucleus, they were taking all the instructions to create the exact cells that made up the ewe.

Take Action

WRITE A POEM A limerick is a poem with five lines. Lines 1, 2, and 5 rhyme, and each line has 8 to 10 syllables. Lines 3 and 4 rhyme, and each line has 5 or 6 syllables. Write a limerick about Dolly using what you know about the cell nucleus.

Students' poems should have the correct limerick structure and include facts from the lesson.

19

More Resources

The following resources are also available from Great Source.

ScienceSaurus

DNA	115
Genes	116
Cloning	120

Reader's Handbook

Making Inferences	40
Drawing Conclusions	41
Reading Science	100
Rhyme Scheme	462

Assessment

Skill: Drawing conclusions

Use the following question to assess each student's progress:

Suppose two lambs look identical. One lamb was produced through cloning a cell from a ewe, and the other was the natural offspring of a ram and the same ewe. How could a scientist tell the difference between the two lambs? (Examine the DNA of the two lambs, the ram, and the ewe. The cloned lamb's DNA would be identical to the ewe's DNA. The natural offspring's DNA would be a combination of the ram's and the ewe's DNA.)

Take Action

WRITE A POEM Write the following limerick on the board to help guide students in creating one about Dolly. Ask a volunteer to come up to the board and break the lines into syllables with slash marks. Then have students count the syllables in each line.

There was an old person of Fife
Who was greatly disgusted with life;
They sang him a ballad
And fed him on salad,
Which cured that old person of Fife.

Point out that limericks usually have a sing-songy quality and are humorous, with the last line being like the punch line of a joke. Encourage students to create imaginative rhymes such as "nucleus" and "new to us."

CHECK UNDERSTANDING

Skill: Recognizing cause and effect

Ask: *Why did scientists have to insert a nucleus from another ewe into the nucleus-free egg cell in order to produce a clone?* (Without a nucleus and a complete set of DNA, the egg cell would not begin dividing, even with a zap of electricity.)

Cells at Work

LESSON 4

Energy for Life

Point of Lesson: ***During cellular respiration, mitochondria release energy by breaking down glucose.***

In her novel *A Wind in the Door*, Madeline L'Engle describes a character in danger of dying from lack of energy because of a problem with his mitochondria. In this lesson, students first consider what energy sources their bodies have and how their bodies use that energy. They then read an excerpt from the novel and use the chemical equation for cellular respiration to analyze the science in this piece of science fiction.

Materials

none

LESSON 5

Photosynthesis

Point of Lesson: ***During photosynthesis, plant cells change carbon dioxide and water into glucose.***

A report on a science team's investigation into chloroplasts introduces students to the concept of photosynthesis and an analysis of the equation describing this chemical reaction. Students then conduct their own investigation to determine the location of stomata on plant leaves. They analyze their experiment to see if the results support their hypotheses, then suggest other possible explanations for their outcomes.

Materials

Before You Read (p. 24), for each pair or group:
- one or more green plants

Science Scope Activity (p. 20B and p. 25), for each student or pair:
- Grasshead Data Collection Sheet (copymaster page 226)
- grass seed
- nylon stocking
- sawdust (about 2 cupfuls)
- 2-liter plastic bottle
- scissors
- glue gun (share with class)
- 2 plastic eyes or buttons
- plastic-coated wire
- rubber bands
- cup
- water

Experiment (p. 26), for each group:
- 1 healthy plant
- petroleum jelly

Laboratory Safety

Review the following safety guidelines with students before they do the Science Scope Activity and the Experiment in this lesson.
- Handle sawdust and grass seed carefully so you do not inhale them.
- Use the hot glue gun under supervision. Avoid skin contact with hot glue. It will cause burns.
- Do not taste any substance in the laboratory.
- Be careful using sharp objects. Always cut in a direction away from yourself and away from others.
- Handle plants and living things with care.
- Wash your hands thoroughly after the activity.

LESSON 6

All Together Now

Point of Lesson: ***Cellular respiration and photosynthesis are complementary processes.***

A scientist's response to a student's question about respiration in plants leads students into a comparison of the net equations for photosynthesis and cellular respiration. Students observe that the products of photosynthesis are needed for cellular respiration, and vice versa. They then create a poster summarizing the relationship between the two processes.

Materials

Explore (p. 29), for each student:
- posterboard
- markers

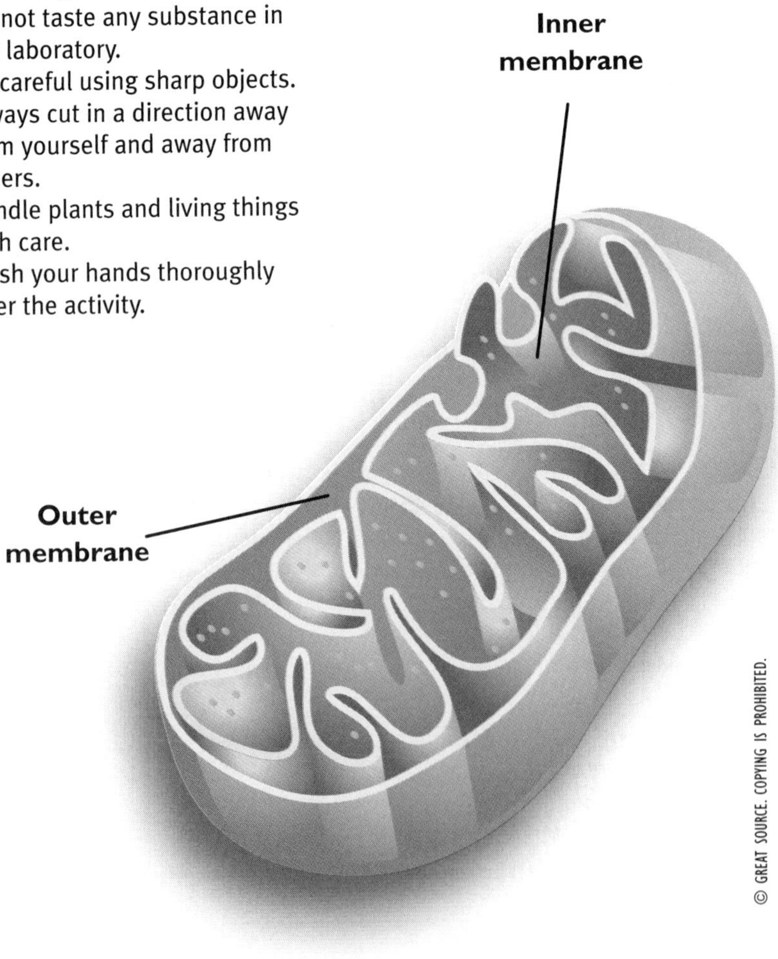

Science Scope Activity

Make a Grasshead

NSTA has chosen a Science Scope *activity related to the content in this chapter. The activity begins here and continues in Lesson 5, page 25.*

Time: 35 minutes

Materials: see page 20A

This activity demonstrates that plants need sunlight in order to produce their own food through photosynthesis and that varying levels of light intensity affect plant growth.

Procedure

Give each student a copy of the Grasshead Data Collection Sheet and the following instructions:

1. Cut off the top part of the stocking and discard it. Keep just the bottom part up to the ankle.
2. Place a small handful of grass seed into the toe of the stocking.
3. Mix some water with 2 cupfuls of sawdust. Fill the stocking with sawdust, and tie a knot to close it.

(continued on page 25)

Background Information

Lesson 4

An actual disease caused by mitochondrial dysfunction was reported in 1960 by two Swedish researchers, whose patient remained thin despite eating large amounts of food and sweated even in the coldest weather. The researchers concluded that the patient's muscle mitochondria could not make as much energy as they should, and the unused fuel was converted into heat production.

Lesson 6

The lesson presents the summary, or net, chemical equations for both cellular respiration and photosynthesis in order to emphasize that the end results of the two processes are complementary. In fact, both processes are quite complex; each involves a series of several chemical reactions involving other molecules. Details of both processes are commonly included in high-school level biology curricula.

Point of Lesson

During cellular respiration, mitochondria release energy by breaking down glucose.

Focus

- Form and function
- Structure and function in living systems
- Regulation and behavior

Skills and Strategies

- Concept mapping
- Evaluating source material
- Making inferences
- Drawing conclusions
- Generating ideas
- Communicating

Advance Preparation

Vocabulary

Make sure students understand these terms. Definitions can be found in the glossary at the end of the student book.

- cell
- chemical equation
- chemical reaction
- energy
- mitochondria
- nutrient
- organelles
- organism

ENERGY FOR LIFE

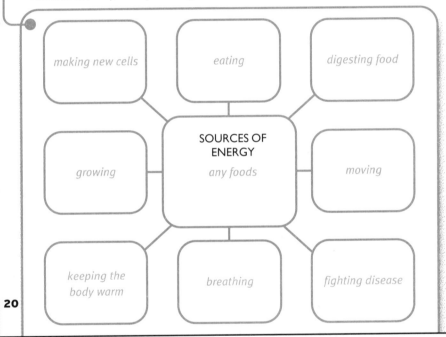

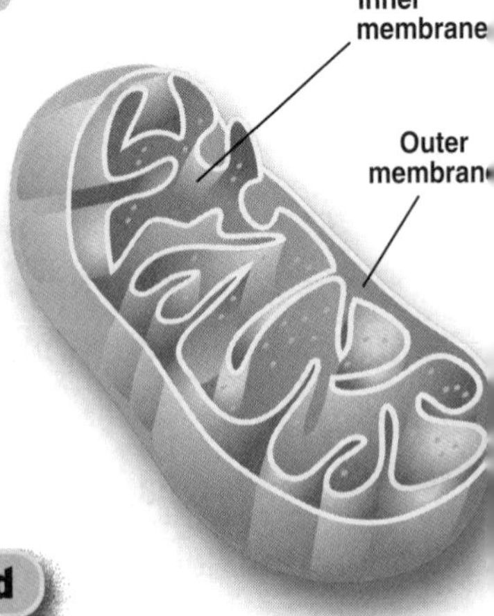

▼ Structure of a mitochondrion

Believe it or not, we humans cannot live without mitochondria!

Mitochondria are one type of organelle found in cells. In the mitochondria, the energy that is stored in nutrients is released so the cell can use it.

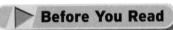

Before You Read

THINK ABOUT IT No organism can survive without energy. How do *you* get and use energy? In the concept map below, list some things in the center box that are sources of energy for your body. In the other boxes, list ways your body uses energy.

Answers will vary. Examples are given below.

SOURCES OF ENERGY: *any foods*

- *making new cells*
- *eating*
- *digesting food*
- *growing*
- *moving*
- *keeping the body warm*
- *breathing*
- *fighting disease*

TEACHING PLAN pp. 20–21

INTRODUCING THE LESSON

This lesson introduces one cell organelle, the mitochondrion, and its role in cellular respiration. Explain that mitochondria can be found in most cells. Eukaryotic cells—cells that contain a nucleus with a membrane—also contain organelles with membranes, including mitochondria. These cells are found not just in humans but in all animals, flowering plants, algae, fungi, and protists.

Ask students what people need to do to take care of their bodies. (Answers should include maintaining a healthy weight, exercising regularly, getting enough sleep, and eating healthy foods.) Ask students whether they think sugar is good or bad for the body. Discuss the difference between refined sugar—the type of sugar found in cookies, candy bars, soft drinks, and the like—and the sugars that are found naturally in fruits and vegetables (fructose and glucose), milk (lactose), and honey (fructose and glucose). Explain that these "simple sugars" are not harmful but are necessary for good health.

Before You Read

THINK ABOUT IT Before students complete the concept map, briefly discuss how the body uses energy. Be sure students take into account involuntary muscle activity and bodily processes that continue even while we sleep.

Read

In the science fiction novel *A Wind in the Door*, Charles Wallace, an unusual six-year-old, has something wrong with his mitochondria. Mr. Jenkins and Margaret, Charles's sister, are trying to find out how to help him.

Charles Wallace's Mitochondria

"Charles Wallace will die if his mitochondria die. Do you understand that?"

Mr. Jenkins shook his head. "I thought he was making things up with his big words. I thought he was trying to show off. I didn't know there really were mitochondria."

Blajeny turned to Meg. "Explain."

"I'll try. But I'm not sure I really understand either, Mr. Jenkins. But I do know that we need energy to live. Okay?"

"Thus far."

She felt Blajeny kything information to her, and involuntarily her mind sorted it, simplified, put it into words which she hoped Mr. Jenkins would understand. "Well, each of our mitochondria has its own built-in system to limit the rate at which it burns fuel, okay, Mr. Jenkins?"

"Pray continue, Margaret."

"If the number of farandolae in any mitochondrion drops below a critical point, then hydrogen transport can't occur; there isn't enough fuel, and the result is death through energy lack."

Blajeny: a character in the book, a teacher from the universe
kything: in the book, an imaginary way of communicating mind-to-mind, without words
involuntarily: not by choice
farandolae: imaginary microscopic beings that—only in the story—live inside mitochondria

From: L'Engle, Madeline. *A Wind in the Door.* Farrar, Straus, & Giroux.

NOTEZONE

Underline the plural of mitochondrion.

Circle what happens if a mitochondrion can't function.

Draw a box around the name of the fictitious parts of a mitochondrion.

FIND OUT MORE
SCIENCESAURUS
Animal Cell 077
Cell Processes 079
Animal Physiology 105

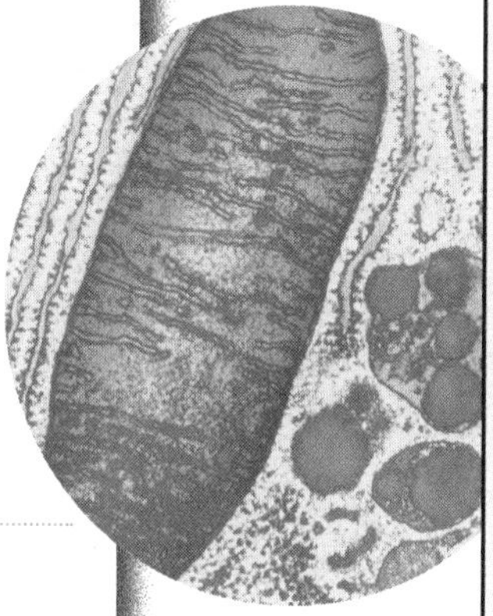

▲ **Mitochondrion viewed with a microscope**

21

Enrichment

Ask students to write short science fiction stories using information about mitochondria and cellular respiration. Invite groups of three to five to work together. Have students begin by brainstorming ways to use the information they have learned. Then have them choose a dramatic fictional problem involving mitochondria and a simple plot that shows its solution. Remind students that they can stretch the facts but should use some basic science concepts. Post the groups' stories on the bulletin board so the class can read them.

Read

Begin by discussing the genre of the story excerpt. Point out that although science-fiction writers research science facts to make their stories more interesting and believable, they also often stretch these facts. Advise students to look at the definitions below the reading to learn which elements are fictional before they complete the NoteZone activity.

After students complete the NoteZone activity, ask them which word they drew a box around. Then ask: *What do you think "hydrogen transport" means?* (Record students' questions and comments so they can check them later with new information that they learn.) *What does the word "fuel" refer to?* (energy from food)

CHECK UNDERSTANDING

Skill: Making and using models

Ask students to draw cartoons that show the series of steps needed to obtain and use energy. Tell students to create four to six frames (as in a comic strip). Then have them make a drawing in each frame to depict how a person takes in food and how the mitochondria release the energy in nutrients and disperse it throughout the cell. Students can write captions to explain the process.

More Resources

The following resources are also available from Great Source.

SCIENCESAURUS

Animal Cell 077
Cell Processes 079
Animal Physiology 105

READER'S HANDBOOK

Drawing Conclusions 41
Concept Map 137
Focus on Dialogue 360
Becoming a Context Clue Expert 615

WRITE SOURCE 2000

Writing Dialogue 190

Explore

EXAMINE AN EQUATION Mitochondria burn fuel to provide our cells with energy. An important chemical reaction called *cellular respiration* takes place in the mitochondria. The chemical equation for cellular respiration looks like this.

$$C_6H_{12}O_6 + 6O_2 \rightarrow 6CO_2 + 6H_2O + \text{energy}$$

glucose + oxygen → carbon dioxide + water + energy

WHAT THE EQUATION MEANS During cellular respiration, a type of sugar called glucose is broken down. This happens only with the help of oxygen. Carbon dioxide, water, and energy are given off. Some of the energy is in the form of heat that keeps our bodies warm, and some of the energy is used to keep our cells alive.

FIGURE IT OUT

- ***Why do we need to breathe in oxygen?***

We need oxygen for cellular respiration in the mitochondria of our cells.

- ***Where would you expect to find more mitochondria—in very active cells such as those in your heart and liver, or in less active cells such as those in your earlobes? Explain your answer.***

In cells that are very active; active cells require more energy, and it's the mitochondria that release the energy in glucose.

Propose Explanations

DRAW CONCLUSIONS Margaret says that Charles will die if his mitochondria die.

- ***Knowing what you do about mitochondria, would you agree? Explain your answer.***

Yes; we depend on our mitochondria to release the energy in glucose to keep our cells alive.

22

TEACHING PLAN pp. 22–23

Explore

EXAMINE AN EQUATION Begin by defining *elements* as simple substances that cannot be broken down any farther. Explain that scientists have assigned letter symbols to elements—for example, C for carbon, H for hydrogen, and O for oxygen. Molecules are formed when elements link together. In the equation on this page, letter groups show formulas for molecules. A subscript number after a symbol shows the number of atoms present. A number before a symbol indicates the number of molecules.

Discuss the fact that chemical equations can express complicated information using just a few symbols and numbers. Learning to read chemical equations is a valuable scientific tool.

WHAT THE EQUATION MEANS Read aloud the formula for glucose: 6 atoms of carbon, 12 atoms of hydrogen, and 6 atoms of oxygen. Ask volunteers to read the formulas for oxygen, carbon dioxide, and water. Ask what happens during cellular respiration. (Glucose and oxygen are changed into carbon dioxide and water, and energy is released.)

FIGURE IT OUT Discuss how the equation answers the first question. (On the left side, the equation states that oxygen is needed.) For the second question, encourage students to use logic to draw conclusions. (More mitochondria are needed where more energy is needed.)

► *What would happen to our cells without the mitochondria?*

Our cells could not function and would die.

Take Action

WRITE A DIALOGUE Imagine that you are Margaret. Any problems your brother had in the past with his mitochondria have been cured. But you're still interested in mitochondria. Write a dialogue, like the one between Margaret and Mr. Jenkins, in which you explain to a friend why mitochondria are important. Include facts that you have learned about what occurs in the mitochondria.

Students' dialogues will vary but should include the following information: Mitochondria release the energy stored in nutrients so the cell can use it. Cellular respiration, a chemical reaction essential for life, occurs in the mitochondria. Students may also describe the process of cellular respiration, which is explained in "What the Equation Means" on the previous page.

23

Assessment

Skill: Drawing conclusions

Use the following questions to assess each student's progress:

Do you think cellular respiration is an efficient way for your body to get energy? Why or why not? (Students should understand that the process is very efficient because each cell performs a very small task. In this way, every part of the body gets energy.)

Propose Explanations

DRAW CONCLUSIONS Explain to students that their conclusions must be based on facts they have read in this lesson. If students have difficulty, prompt them by asking: *What parts of Charles Wallace's body need energy, and how would he obtain this energy if he had no mitochondria?* (Every part of his body needs energy. He would not be able to obtain energy if he had no mitochondria.)

Take Action

WRITE A DIALOGUE Explain that a dialogue is a written conversation. Encourage students to look again at the dialogue in the reading to see how it is constructed. You may need to review the use of quotation marks and paragraph indentations as they are used in the reading. Also remind students that in a dialogue, people speak in an easy, conversational style. Encourage students to explain what they have learned as if they were actually talking with a friend. Allow class time for students to read their dialogues aloud with a partner. You may also want to encourage students to research mitochondria and cellular respiration on the Internet before writing their dialogues.

Point of Lesson

During photosynthesis, plant cells change carbon dioxide and water into glucose.

Focus

- Evidence, models, and explanation
- Structure and function in living systems
- Abilities necessary to do scientific inquiry

Skills and Strategies

- Interpreting data
- Comparing and contrasting
- Developing hypotheses
- Collecting and recording data
- Identifying and controlling variables
- Drawing conclusions

Advance Preparation

Vocabulary

Make sure students understand these terms. Definitions can be found in the glossary at the end of the student book.

- cell
- chemical equation
- chemical reaction
- control
- energy
- experiment
- gene
- glucose
- hypothesis
- mitochondria
- nutrient
- organelles

(continued on page 25)

Photosynthesis

You're lucky! You get to eat great-tasting food to get energy. Plants have to make their own food!

Plant cells are different from animal cells. Like animal cells, plant cells have mitochondria, but they also have another kind of energy-converting organelle called a *chloroplast*. Chloroplasts are not found in animal cells.

Before You Read

POWER PLANTS Take a look at a green plant. What are some ways that it obtains the energy and nutrients it needs to stay alive?

It has roots to take in water and minerals. It has leaves to take in sunlight and gases.

Read

A team of Japanese scientists, led by Masamitsu Wada, is studying how chloroplasts move in green plants.

Dancing Chloroplasts

Inside each plant cell, light-gathering chloroplasts dance out of a cell's shaded edges to soak up the sun or back into that shade when the light is too intense....

Chloroplasts...capture light energy from the sun and use it to convert carbon dioxide and water into oxygen and food. The tiny spherical or disk-shaped chloroplasts contain the pigment chlorophyll, which gives green plants their color.

When light is weak, like on a cloudy day, the chloroplasts spread across the upper faces of the cells on a leaf, giving it a deeper green color. In intense sunlight, chloroplasts retreat to the cells' edges, making leaves look pale. Both reactions depend on the amount of...light reaching the cells.

TEACHING PLAN pp. 24–25

INTRODUCING THE LESSON

In this lesson, students learn about photosynthesis and perform an experiment to determine the location of stomata on leaves.

Ask students how plants are different from animals. Encourage students to talk about the way plants look as well as the ways they grow and the conditions they need to grow.

Students may think that only plants carry out photosynthesis and release oxygen into Earth's atmosphere. Explain that algae and some protists, such as euglena, also conduct photosynthesis. In fact, most of the oxygen on Earth is produced by microscopic marine organisms called *phytoplankton*.

Before You Read

Time: 15 minutes
Materials: one or more green plants

POWER PLANTS Encourage students to study the plant closely. After students have answered the question, ask volunteers to name the parts of the plant and to share what they know about how it gets its energy.

Read

Encourage students to highlight any sections that change their ideas about how choloroplasts function, especially the fact that they move. You can extend the reading by talking about the results of Wada's work. Tell students that Masamitsu Wada and his colleagues identified plants that had mutated copies of a gene. This specific gene codes for a protein in plants that detects blue light. When the protein detects blue light, it directs the movement of the choloroplasts. The scientists were intrigued. They already knew

By noting this response in the leaves of [a certain type of plant], Masamitsu Wada...and his [team] identified plants with...copies of a gene...that [lets the plant detect light and tells chloroplasts where to move in the cells].... With this knowledge, the researchers will try to determine [exactly how chloroplasts move]....

intense: strong or concentrated
convert: change
spherical: shaped like a ball
pigment: a colored substance
chlorophyll: a pigment needed for green plants to make food
gene: a section of DNA on a chromosome that determines a particular inherited characteristic

From: Netting, Jessica. "Gene Found For Chloroplast Movement." *Science News.*

NOTEZONE

Underline the substances plants need to make food.

Draw a box around the other substance that is produced when a plant makes food.

Explore

EXAMINE AN EQUATION A chloroplast has structures that look like stacks of coins. These flat, membrane-covered sacs contain the chlorophyll. Chlorophyll captures the energy in sunlight. The process by which green plants make their own food using the energy in sunlight is called *photosynthesis*. Photosynthesis is a series of chemical reactions that convert light energy into chemical energy contained in glucose. The chemical equation for photosynthesis looks like this.

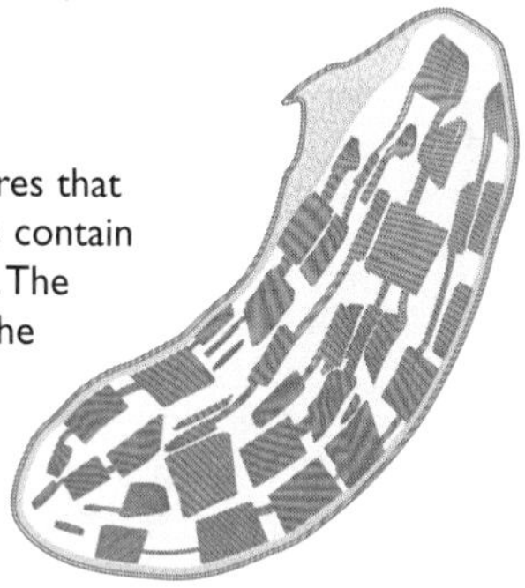

▲Chloroplast

$$6CO_2 + 6H_2O + \text{light energy} \rightarrow C_6H_{12}O_6 + 6O_2$$

carbon dioxide + water + light energy → glucose + oxygen

WHAT THE EQUATION MEANS During photosynthesis, carbon dioxide gas and water are combined to form glucose. This process requires energy from light. The light energy is changed to chemical energy in glucose. Some of the chemical energy in glucose is released by the plant's mitochondria and used right away, and some of it is stored in other molecules.

MAKE COMPARISONS With their chloroplasts, plants can do something that animals cannot do. What is it?

Plants can make their own food.

FIND OUT MORE

SCIENCESAURUS

Plant Cell 078
Cell Processes 079
Plant Physiology 107

SCILINKS. THE WORLD'S A CLICK AWAY

www.scilinks.org
Keyword: Cell Energy
Code: GSLD03

25

(continued from page 24)

Materials

Gather the materials needed for ***Before You Read*** (p. 24), ***Science Scope Activity*** (p. 20B and p. 25), and ***Experiment*** (p. 26).

Science Scope Activity

(continued from page 20B)

4. Glue on buttons or plastic eyes.
5. Pull the stocking to make a nose and ears. Fix the shapes with rubber bands.
6. Add wire glasses, hair, a hat, earrings, or other trimmings to give the grasshead a personality.
7. Cut the bottom half off the plastic bottle to make a clear dome.
8. Sprinkle the grasshead with water and put it under the dome.

Make a grasshead of your own. Then assign students places in the classroom to set their grassheads. Place your own in complete darkness, and have students place theirs in either full sunlight or dim light. Tell students to observe their grassheads every day for two weeks and to record their observations on the Data Collection Sheet. The grassheads placed in full sunlight will grow the longest hair in the shortest time. The grasshead placed in the darkness may not grow any hair.

about a similar gene that directs plants to turn their leaves toward sunlight or away from it. Wada said that his discovery might help genetic engineers who work with photosynthesis. Ask students to suggest ways in which other scientists could use Wada's discovery.

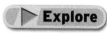

Explore

EXAMINE AN EQUATION Make sure students understand the numbers and letters in the equation.

WHAT THE EQUATION MEANS Remind students that the left side of the equation shows the substances a plant starts with, and the right side shows what the plant produces as a result of photosynthesis.

MAKE COMPARISONS After students write their answers, ask them to note how the mitochondria help the plant use the food it makes for itself during the process of photosynthesis.

CHECK UNDERSTANDING
Skill: Making and using models
Have students draw and label a diagram that shows what happens during photosynthesis. (Diagrams should include the sun, chloroplasts, chlorophyll, water, carbon dioxide, glucose, and oxygen.)

More Resources

The following resources are also available from Great Source and NSTA.

SCIENCESAURUS

Plant Cell	078
Cell Processes	079
Plant Physiology	107

SCILINKS. THE WORLD'S A CLICK AWAY

www.scilinks.org
Keyword: Cell Energy
Code: GSLD03

Connections

SOCIAL STUDIES Explain to students that after Masamitsu Wada and his colleagues discovered the gene for blue-light receptors, they were able to copyright the gene. This means that scientists who work with this gene must receive permission from Wada. Have small groups discuss this process and work together to write an opinion article that answers the following questions: *Do you think scientists should own the rights to a plant gene? Why or why not? How do you think this practice might affect people around the world?*

Experiment

A LOT O' STOMATA

Plant leaves have tiny openings called *stomata* that take in carbon dioxide and release oxygen. Learn about stomata by doing the following experiment.

FORM A HYPOTHESIS In the experiment, petroleum jelly will clog the stomata on some leaves.

► ***What do you think will happen to those leaves? Write your hypothesis as an "if / then" sentence.***

If the petroleum jelly clogs the leaves' stomata, then the leaves will not be able to take in carbon dioxide and release oxygen, and will die.

What You Need:

- 1 healthy plant
- petroleum jelly

What to Do:

1. Rub a thick layer of petroleum jelly on the top side of three leaves.
2. Apply the jelly to the underside of three other leaves.
3. Leave all the other leaves uncoated as the control.
4. Place the plant in a sunny location for one week.
5. Each day, turn the plant one-quarter turn.
6. Keep the soil moist, but be sure not to overwater the plant.
7. Record your observations each day for one week.

What Do You See?

Day	Leaves with petroleum jelly on top side	Leaves with petroleum jelly on underside	Leaves with no petroleum jelly
1	*look the same*	*Students should notice*	*look the same*
2	*look the same*	*gradual changes day*	*look the same*
3	*look the same*	*by day.*	*look the same*
4	*look the same*		*look the same*
5	*look the same*		*look the same*
6	*look the same*		*look the same*
7	*look the same*	*yellow and wilted; look dead*	*look the same*

26

TEACHING PLAN pp. 26–27

Experiment

Time: 15–20 minutes for initial setup; 10 minutes a day for examining the plant and recording observations
Materials: (for each group) 1 healthy plant, petroleum jelly

FORM A HYPOTHESIS

- ► You may want to have each group use a different type of plant to demonstrate that the process occurs in all broad-leafed plants.
- ► Remind students that a hypothesis is more than a guess. It is a statement that can be tested. Scientists develop a hypothesis, then perform an experiment to test it. Sometimes the hypothesis turns out to be wrong and a new hypothesis has to be developed and tested.
- ► Have students work in small groups. Each group should label its plant with the group members' names before placing it in the sunny location.
- ► Allow time each day for students to check the soil, turn the plant, and record their observations.

WHAT DO YOU SEE? Tell students that they should look for changes in the color, texture, and position of the leaves and record any changes from day to day.

Propose Explanations

DRAW CONCLUSIONS

► ***Based on your observations, where do you think the stomata are located on leaves? What is your evidence?***

Only the leaves that had the petroleum jelly on the bottom side died.

This is evidence that stomata are located on the underside of the leaves.

► ***Go back and look at your hypothesis. Do your results support your hypothesis? How can you tell?***

Students' answers will depend on their hypotheses. The results should support the hypothesis that the leaves with the clogged stomata would not be healthy.

INVESTIGATING FURTHER Could the rubbing of the leaves have destroyed the stomata? To test this idea, repeat the activity using water instead of petroleum jelly on some leaves. Compare the results of the two activities.

The leaves that were rubbed with water stayed healthy. The water did not clog the stomata. This is evidence that the leaves died as a result of the petroleum jelly, not the rubbing.

27

Assessment

Skill: Recognizing Cause and affect

Use the following question to assess each student's progress:

What role do stomata play in photosynthesis and the survival of the plant? (Stomata allow carbon dioxide to enter the plant so it can be used in photosynthesis to produce glucose, which plant cells need for energy. The stomata also allow oxygen to leave the plant. Oxygen is a by-product of photosynthesis.)

Propose Explanations

DRAW CONCLUSIONS Ask students to explain why clogging the stomata kills the leaf. (The stomata can't let in carbon dioxide and release oxygen when they are clogged.)

As students review their hypotheses, be sure they understand that it is fine to be wrong about a hypothesis. Let students restate any wrong hypothesis so that it can be supported or refuted by the experiment results.

INVESTIGATING FURTHER Point out that scientists have to take variables into account when they perform experiments. Variables include their own actions—such as failing to control a variable that affects results—or factors that they cannot control, such as weather conditions.

You may want to invite students to study the underside and topside of the leaves with a magnifier. Ask if they can see anything on the leaves that may have affected the results of the experiment. (They will not be able to see anything because stomata are microscopic.)

Point of Lesson

Cellular respiration and photosynthesis are complementary processes.

Focus

- Systems, order, and organization
- Structure and function in living systems
- Regulation and behavior

Skills and Strategies

- Comparing and contrasting
- Communicating

Advance Preparation

Vocabulary

Make sure students understand these terms. Definitions can be found in the glossary at the end of the student book.

- cell
- cellular respiration
- chemical equation
- chloroplast
- energy
- glucose
- mitochondria
- molecule
- photosynthesis

Materials:

Gather the materials needed for *Explore* (p. 29).

Cells at Work

All Together Now

Now you can put it all together—the mitochondria and the chloroplasts.

Life is filled with many kinds of cycles. Chloroplasts and mitochondria are involved in a cycle that is necessary for the lives of plants and animals. Through the processes of cellular respiration and photosynthesis, plants and animals get materials they need from each other.

NOTEZONE

Underline the two ways glucose is used by plants.

Circle the two gases that are involved in both respiration and photosynthesis.

Read

A student wrote to a scientist to find out whether all plants need to respire. This is what the scientist had to say.

From Sugar-Making to Sugar-Burning

Question: Do all plants respire?

Answer: Yes, all plants must carry out respiration. There are two types of respiration processes in plants. One is similar to our breathing process—the plant takes in oxygen through its leaves and releases carbon dioxide. The second type of respiration, called cellular respiration, occurs in the plant cells' mitochondria. This process releases energy that the plant cells need in order to carry out life processes such as growth and reproduction. In the mitochondria, oxygen is combined with glucose, a form of sugar. Carbon dioxide, water, and energy are released.

Energy is also used for photosynthesis. In that process, plants capture the energy in sunlight and use it to convert carbon dioxide and water to glucose. Some of the glucose is transformed into energy through cellular respiration. The rest is used for the plant's life processes. Any "extra" glucose is stored in certain parts of the plant, such as the fruits and vegetables we eat.

Photosynthesis releases much more oxygen than the plant needs for cellular respiration, so the plant releases the "extra" oxygen into the air. We use the oxygen we breathe in our own cellular respiration.

From: *MadSci Network*. Washington University Medical School. (www.madsci.org)

FIND OUT MORE

SCIENCESAURUS
Cell Processes 079

SCI LINKS. THE WORLD'S A CLICK AWAY
www.scilinks.org
Keywords: Photosynthesis
Code: GSLD04
Cellular Respiration
Code: GSLD05

TEACHING PLAN pp. 28–29

INTRODUCING THE LESSON

This lesson introduces the connection between cellular respiration and photosynthesis. Ask students how they think cellular respiration and photosynthesis might be related. Tell them to think carefully about what they have learned in the two previous lessons of this chapter.

Some students may have the idea that plants give off oxygen so that we can breathe it. Point out that oxygen is a by-product of photosynthesis and there is no "intent" on the part of the plant.

Read

After students have read the excerpt, have them review the equation for cellular respiration on page 29. Then ask: *What substance do mitochondria need in order to break down glucose and release energy?* (oxygen) *Where do plants get the oxygen they need for this process?* (Both glucose and oxygen are released during photosynthesis; in other words, the plant creates what it needs for cellular respiration.) Then have students offer their experience tasting sugar in plants (eating apples, carrots, sweet corn, and so forth).

Explore

REEXAMINE THE EQUATIONS Review the chemical equations for cellular respiration and photosynthesis.

Cellular Respiration

$$C_6H_{12}O_6 + 6O_2 \rightarrow 6CO_2 + 6H_2O + \text{energy}$$

glucose + oxygen → carbon dioxide + water + energy

Photosynthesis

$$6CO_2 + 6H_2O + \text{light energy} \rightarrow C_6H_{12}O_6 + 6O_2$$

carbon dioxide + water + light energy → glucose + oxygen

MAKE A COMPARISON

▸ *How are the processes of cellular respiration and photosynthesis alike? How are they different?*

Alike: The same materials—carbon dioxide, water, glucose, and oxygen—are involved. Different: Photosynthesis takes in carbon dioxide and water, while cellular respiration gives off these materials. Cellular respiration takes in oxygen and glucose, while photosynthesis gives off these materials. Photosynthesis converts light energy to stored chemical energy. Cellular respiration releases stored chemical energy.

▸ *What products does cellular respiration release that are needed for photosynthesis?*

carbon dioxide and water

▸ *What products does photosynthesis produce that are needed for cellular respiration?*

oxygen and glucose

SHOW RELATIONSHIPS You are going to explain cellular respiration, photosynthesis, and the relationship between these two processes to another class. Make a poster to use as a visual aid. Include a chloroplast and a mitochondrion on the poster, and use arrows to show the relationship between their two processes. Write a brief paragraph outlining what you will say to the other students.

Students' posters and paragraphs will vary.

29

More Resources

The following resources are also available from Great Source and NSTA.

SCIENCESAURUS

Cell Processes 079

SCI LINKS. THE WORLD'S A CLICK AWAY

www.scilinks.org
Keywords:
Photosynthesis
Code: GSLD04
Cellular Respiration
Code: GSLD05

Enrichment

Ask students to write a brief description of what each of the following equations means.

$2H_2 + O_2 = H_2O$

$H_2O + CO_2 = H_2CO_2$

Assessment

Skill: Organizing Information

Use the following task to assess each student's progress:

Have each student write one sentence that explains cellular respiration and one that explains photosynthesis. (During cellular respiration, glucose and oxygen combine to produce carbon dioxide and water and release energy. During photosynthesis, carbon dioxide and water are combined in the presence of light energy to produce glucose and oxygen.)

Explore

RE-EXAMINE THE EQUATIONS
Emphasize that chemical equations can express complicated information using just a few symbols and numbers. Review with students how to read the equations. Remind them that letter groups show formulas for molecules. A subscript number after a letter symbol shows the number of atoms present. A number before a letter symbol indicates the number of molecules.

MAKE A COMPARISON If students have difficulty writing a comparison, work with small groups to organize the information in a Venn diagram. Ask volunteers to explain the comparison to the class in their own words.

SHOW RELATIONSHIPS
Time: 30 minutes
Materials: posterboard, markers

Provide students with art supplies. When the posters are complete, schedule a visit to another class so students can make their presentations.

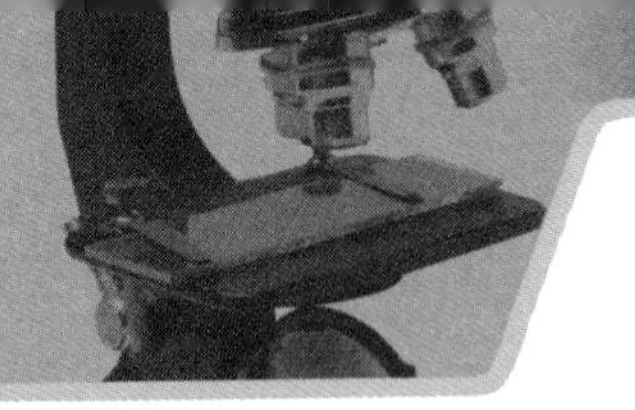

Cell Division

LESSON 7

One Becomes Two

Point of Lesson: ***During mitosis, a cell divides to produce two daughter cells, each with the same number of chromosomes as the parent cell.***

In this lesson, students interpret a diagram showing the steps that occur during mitosis. They then create their own models to show the five stages of division that the cell nucleus undergoes. Students also do research to find out the total number of chromosome pairs in various organisms, then draw conclusions about whether there is a relationship between the total number of chromosomes and the complexity of the organism.

Materials

Explore (p. 32), for each student or pair:

- students' choices, including yarn, construction paper, and other craft supplies

Take Action (p. 33), for the class:

- research sources such as biology and genetics textbooks

Laboratory Safety

Review the following safety guidelines with students before they do the Explore activity in this lesson.

- Be careful using sharp objects. Always cut in a direction away from yourself and away from others.
- Perform any skits or dances in a clear area, away from classroom traffic.

LESSON 8

The Sorcerer's Apprentice

Point of Lesson: ***Cell growth is exponential.***

Because each parent cell produces two daughter cells, and each daughter two more daughters, the process of cell growth can occur very quickly. In this lesson, students are introduced to the concept of exponential growth through a simple analogy involving money, then read a passage on the exponential growth of cells. They explore a model of exponential growth and compare it to the exponential growth of cells.

Materials

Before You Read (p. 34), for each student:

- calculator
- toothpicks or paper clips (optional)

Enrichment (p. 35), for the class:

- research sources such as life science and biology textbooks

Activity (p. 36), for each student:

- thin piece of paper, preferably tissue paper

LESSON 9

Cells Out of Control

Point of Lesson: ***Cancer is cell division out of control.***

The lesson begins with a scientist's explanation of cancer as unregulated cell division due to mutations in cancer cells. Students compare normal cell division with the division of cancer cells and research various types of cancer.

Materials

Take Action (p. 39), for the class:

- research sources about types of cancer

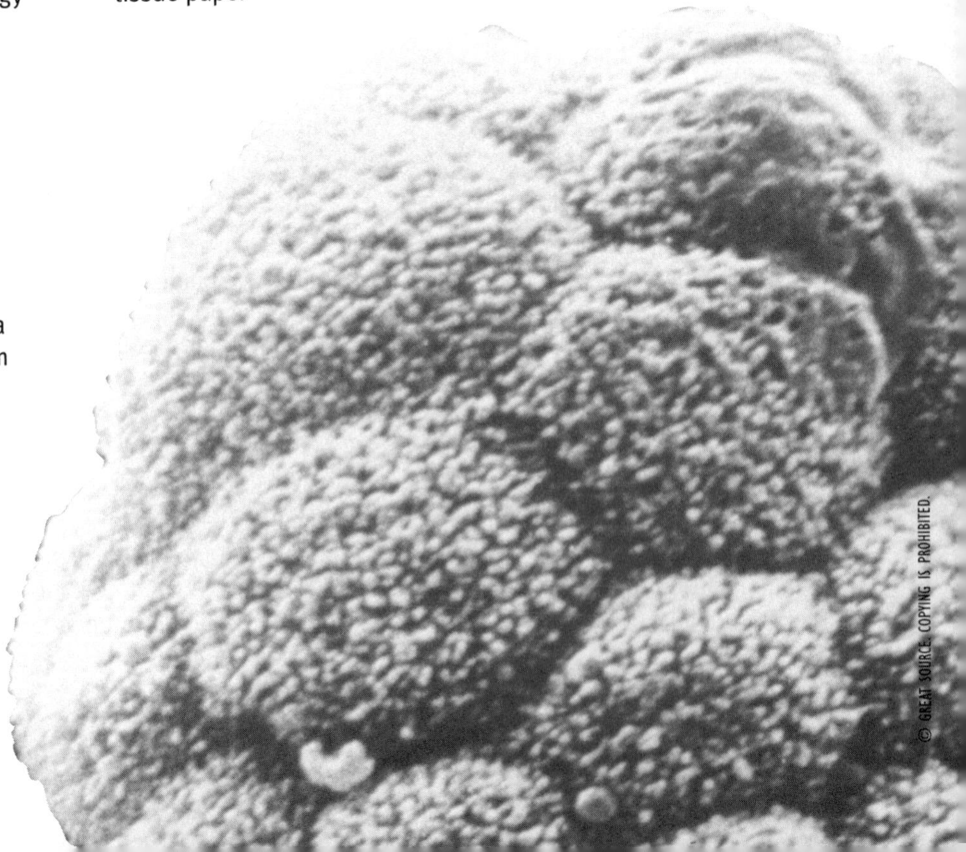

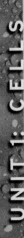

Background Information

Lesson 7

The cell cycle is a pattern of events—growth, DNA replication, growth, and cell division—that all dividing cells follow (except for egg and sperm cells, which undergo a different process: meiosis). When the cell is not dividing, it is said to be in interphase. Toward the end of interphase, before mitosis begins, DNA replication occurs in a phase called synthesis. Mitosis describes the series of events that follow, in which the nucleus of the cell divides.

Mitosis is generally divided into four stages: *prophase*—in which the nuclear envelope dissolves and cell structures prepare for division; *metaphase*—in which the chromosomes move to the equator of the spindle that formed during prophase; *anaphase*—in which the chromosomes are pulled to opposite poles of the spindle; and *telophase*—in which the chromosomes reach their destinations and uncoil and the nuclear envelope reforms. At this point, there are two smaller cells with the same genetic information as the larger original cell, but the cytoplasm must also be divided. The cytoplasm contains organelles such as the golgi, mitochondria or chloroplasts, endoplasmic reticulum, lysosomes, and peroxisomes. When mitosis is complete, the process of cytokinesis redistributes these organelles between the two daughter cells and causes the daughter cells to separate.

Lesson 8

Different types of cells divide at different rates. In the human body, red blood cells divide at a rate of 2.5 million per second. Other cells, such as nerve cells, may lose their ability to divide once they reach a mature stage. Some types of cells have the ability to divide but do not divide under normal conditions. Liver cells are one example of this type of cell; if part of the liver is removed, liver cells will divide until the liver returns to its original size.

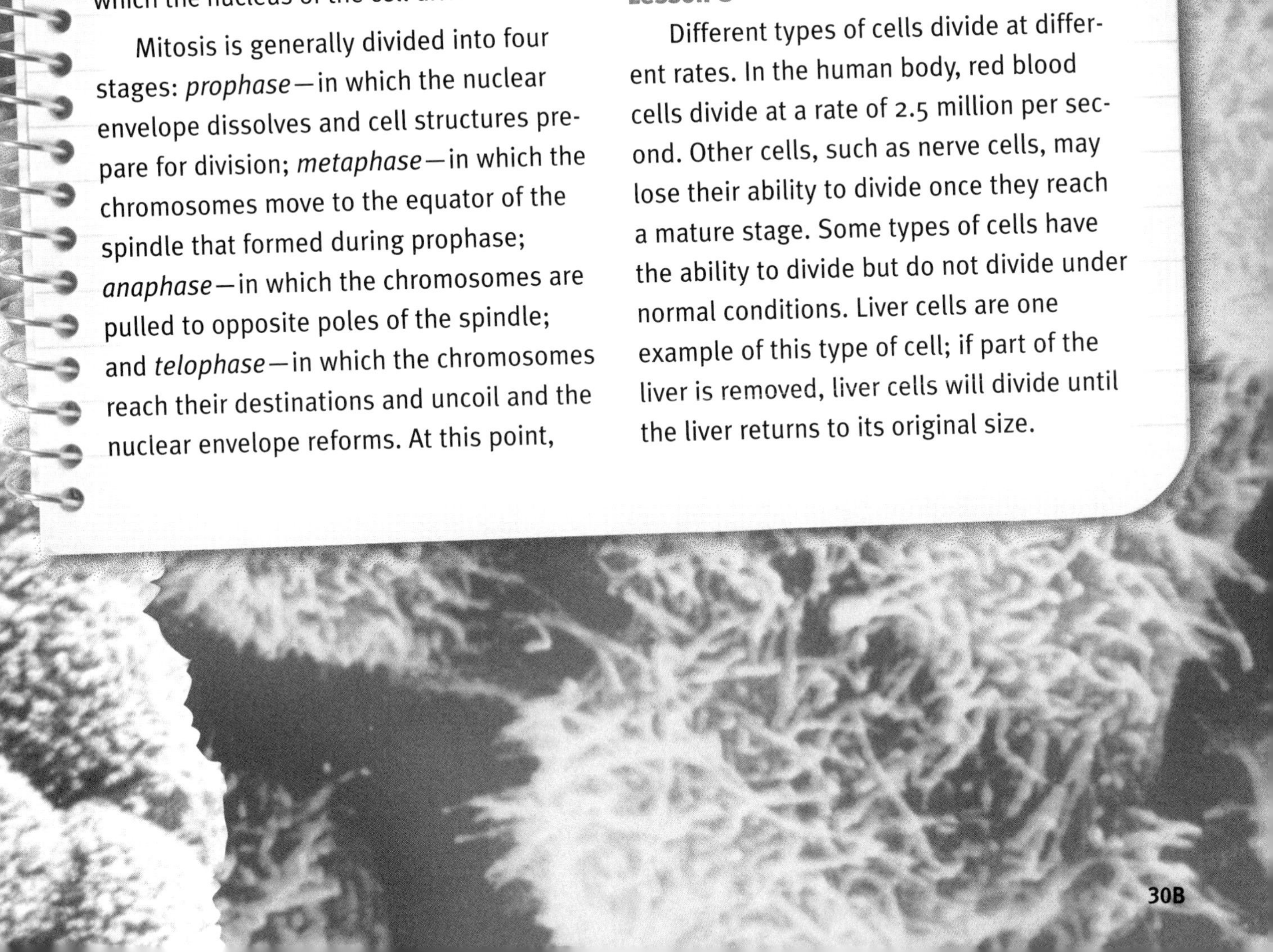

Point of Lesson

During mitosis, a cell divides to produce two daughter cells, each with the same number of chromosomes as the parent cell.

Focus

- Evidence, models, and explanation
- Change, constancy, and measurement
- Structure and function in living systems
- Reproduction and heredity

Skills and Strategies

- Making and using models
- Sequencing
- Communicating
- Collecting and recording data
- Comparing and contrasting

Advance Preparation

Vocabulary

Make sure students understand these terms. Definitions can be found in the glossary at the end of the student book.

- cell
- chromosome
- DNA
- egg
- nucleus
- organism
- reproduce
- species
- sperm

(continued on page 31)

One Becomes Two

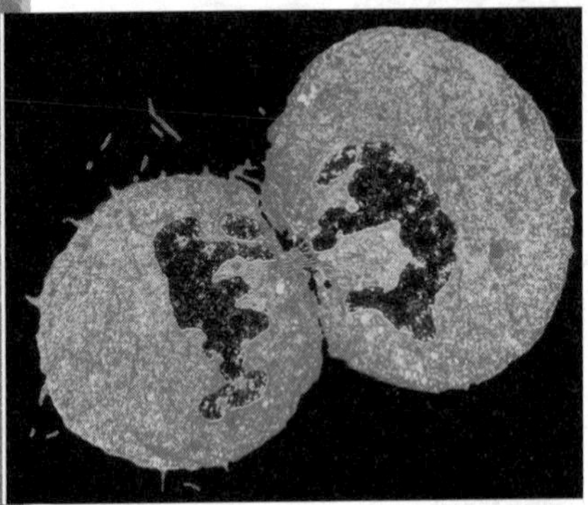

Every living thing begins as a single cell. But many organisms have lots of cells. Where do all the cells come from?

One characteristic of all living things is the ability to reproduce. This includes individual cells. If cells couldn't reproduce to make complete, new cells, life on Earth would cease to exist.

◄**Human kidney cell dividing**

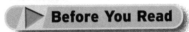

Before You Read

SPLIT IT Lots of things get divided in two. You cut a sandwich in half. You share a banana with your friend. You draw a line down a sheet of paper to make two columns.

► ***List 10 different things that get divided in two.***

Lists will vary.

TEACHING PLAN pp. 30–31

INTRODUCING THE LESSON

In this lesson, students learn that a cell reproduces by dividing in two. Ask students what it means to grow. Then focus the discussion by asking students how they think growth happens in the human body.

Some students may think that the growth process differs for different body structures and organs. Ask them how they think an arm grows as opposed to the heart. Explain that all growth happens through cell reproduction.

Before You Read

THINK ABOUT IT Ask students to complete their lists, and follow up the activity with a discussion of *how* things are divided. You may want to categorize things according to how they split: for example, by being measured and poured (soda), cut (banana), divided with a pencil line (paper), folded (paper), or divided by agreement (disputed land).

You can help students visualize division by asking them to sketch one or two items from their lists. Let them share their drawings with the class.

Read

All cells in your body contain identical sets of chromosomes. The chromosomes are made up of DNA (deoxyribonucleic acid) and proteins. The instructions for making all of your different proteins are in the DNA. Various proteins are needed for growth, reproduction, and cell functioning.

Where Do Cells Come From?

Whenever fresh cells are needed, a parent cell divides itself into two parts. Two new cells are formed, called daughter cells. What a great idea! Parents turn into children again!

Cell division is not…easy. The new daughter cells must be more or less identical to the parent cell. They need the same genes so that they can create the same proteins. Therefore, equal distribution of the DNA is key to cell division. The DNA wrapped up in the chromosomes must be doubled; each daughter cell can then receive its own copy of chromosomes. Here we can see how that works.

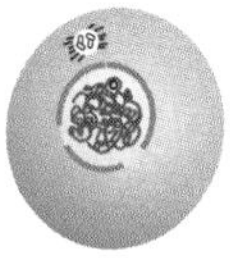

◀ **1. Each human cell has 23 pairs of chromosomes. When a cell gets ready to divide into two, each chromosome doubles.**

◀ **2. The nucleus gets ready to divide. The chromosome pairs are connected at the center and form an "X" shape.**

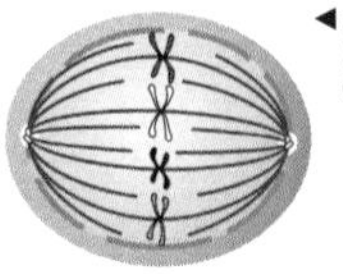

◀ **3. The chromosomes line up across the center of the cell.**

▼ **4. The chromosome pairs separate into two individual, identical chromosomes and move to opposite sides of the cell.**

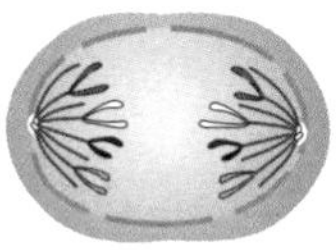

▼ **5. The cell splits into two. Each new cell has one full set of chromosomes.**

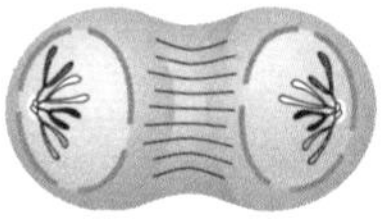

gene: a section of DNA on a chromosome that determines a particular inherited characteristic

proteins: substances that make up living things

distribution: division or "handing out" of something

From: Baeurele, Patrick, and Norbert Landa. *The Cell Works: An Expedition Into the Fantastic World of Cells*. Barron's Education Series, Inc.

NoteZone

Circle the part of the cell that contains the instructions for making proteins. *(Students could circle either "genes" or "DNA," or both.)*

Underline the structures that contain the DNA.

FIND OUT MORE

SCIENCESAURUS

Cell Division 080
Stages of Cell Division 081
DNA 115

SCILINKS
THE WORLD'S A CLICK AWAY

www.scilinks.org
Keyword: Mitosis
Code: GSLD06

31

(continued from page 30)

Materials

Gather the materials needed for ***Explore*** (p. 32) and ***Take Action*** (p. 33).

Enrichment

After students have completed the Explore activity on the next page, give them an opportunity to present their models to another class. Have the members of each group discuss and practice their presentations beforehand so the models will be clear to students who may be unfamiliar with cell division. Schedule time for students to present their models.

Read

Pronounce the term *deoxyribonucleic* for students. Call on volunteers to describe the steps of cell division shown in the diagram. Ask: *Why does the author say that cell division is not easy?* (The DNA must be equally distributed between the two daughter cells.) Be sure students understand that a person's complete DNA is present in each of his or her cells. (Some DNA is present in the mitochondria as well.) You may also want to tell the class that this type of cell division is called *mitosis*.

When students have completed the NoteZone task, ask them to reread the introduction above the excerpt. Ask: *What does it mean to have "the instructions for making all of your different proteins"?* (It has what is needed for growth, reproduction, and cell function.) *Why would having these instructions in every cell be necessary to an organism when it is growing?* (Proteins are necessary for growth and reproduction.)

CHECK UNDERSTANDING
Skill: Communicating
Ask students to explain how growth happens when they grow taller. (Cells divide to make more cells, and this makes all organs larger.)

More Resources

The following resources are also available from Great Source and NSTA.

ScienceSaurus

Cell Division	080
Stages of Cell Division	081
DNA	115

Reader's Handbook

Focus on Science Concepts	132
Elements of Textbooks: Charts	157

SciLinks
THE WORLD'S A CLICK AWAY

www.scilinks.org
Keyword: Mitosis
Code: GSLD06

Explore

DESIGN A MODEL Create a model to show the five steps in the division of a cell nucleus with six chromosomes. You and your classmates could represent the cell parts, or you could use materials such as yarn and construction paper. Draw and label your model below.

Models will vary but should include objects to represent the single parent cell with its nucleus containing six chromosomes; the doubling of the chromosomes to 12 before cell division; the alignment of the chromosomes; X-shaped chromosome pairs; the alignment of the chromosomes; the separation of the pairs; and a method of showing the parent cell splitting into two daughter cells, each with its own nucleus containing six chromosomes.

Propose Explanations

EXPLAIN YOUR MODEL

- ***What did you use to represent the six chromosomes?***

Students can use any six identical objects.

- ***How did you show the doubled chromosomes?***

Students could add another set of six objects or split the original ones in half.

- ***How did you show the movement of the chromosomes?***

Students should show the six pairs of objects first aligning in the center of the cell and then separating into two identical sets at opposite ends of the cell.

- ***How did you show the two new cells?***

The two new cells should contain identical sets of six chromosomes.

32

Teaching Plan pp. 32–33

Explore

Time: 30 minutes
Materials: students' choices, including yarn, construction paper, and other craft supplies.

DESIGN A MODEL Before students begin, you may want to ask them what they think happens to other organelles when a cell divides. Then explain that each cell already has several mitochondria, chloroplasts, and other organelles. These organelles are divided more or less equally between the two daughter cells during the final stage of cell division. Students may want to incorporate this information into their models.

Have students work in groups of three or four. Remind them to refer to the diagram on page 31 when they create their models. Encourage students to be creative—for example, use props such as rope or chairs or even choreograph a dance showing how the chromosomes double before the cell divides.

Propose Explanations

EXPLAIN YOUR MODEL Invite volunteers to demonstrate their models and explain exactly how they show the process of cell division. As you discuss the models, remind students that this process is occurring right now on a microscopic level in their own bodies as they grow.

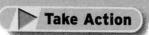

Take Action

DO RESEARCH The number of chromosomes in a cell is the same in all individuals of a species. All human body cells, except sperm and egg cells, contain 46 chromosomes. But different species of organisms have different numbers of chromosomes. Do research to find out the number of chromosomes in the cells of other species. Start with fruit flies and potato plants. Then add other organisms that you find in your research. Record your findings in the table.

NUMBER OF CHROMOSOMES PER CELL	
Species	Number of Chromosomes
Human	46
Fruit flies	8
White potato plants	48
Sweet potato plants	90
Answers will vary.	

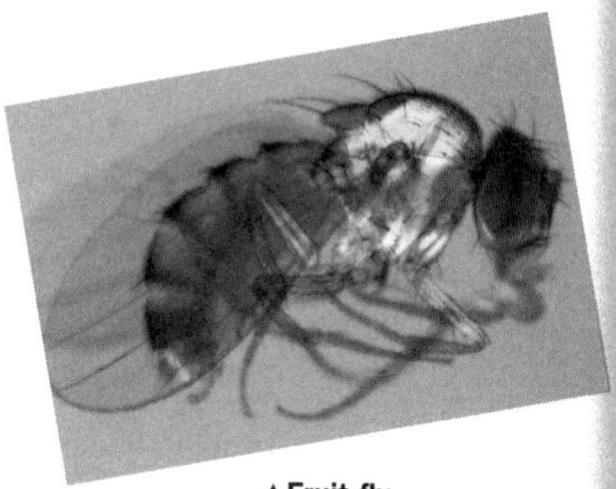

▲Fruit fly

▶ ***Based on your findings, do you think the number of chromosomes gives a clue about how complex an organism is? Explain your answer.***

Not necessarily. A white potato plant cell has 48 chromosomes, but a potato plant is not more complex than a human being.

Assessment

Skill: Drawing conclusions

Use the following task to assess each student's progress:

Remind students that detectives use DNA testing to determine exactly who perpetrated a crime. They are able, for example, to compare the DNA in skin cells found at a crime scene with DNA in cell samples taken from a suspect's inner cheek, hair follicle, or any other body part. This process helps them identify a person with nearly perfect accuracy. Ask students to explain how this is possible. (Since the chromosomes duplicate themselves each time the cells divide, an exact replica of a person's DNA is present in every one of his or her cells. Cells from all parts of the body have an identical DNA pattern and could be used to identify someone.)

Take Action

Materials: research sources such as biology and genetics textbooks

DO RESEARCH Let the class brainstorm a list of organisms, and have each student choose a few to research. Guide students to list names that are specific, such as "horned owl" rather than "owl."

Tell students they can find chromosome charts online at sites such as: www.kean.edu/~breid/chrom2.htm

Before they begin their research, ask students to look at the question that follows the activity. Ask how they can shape their research so that the question is easier to answer. (They can research species that are similar, such as polar bears and grizzly bears, as well as organisms they know are very simple or very complex.)

Point of Lesson
Cell growth is exponential.

Focus
- Evidence, models, and explanation
- Structure and function in living systems
- Regulation and behavior

Skills and Strategies
- Comparing and contrasting
- Making and using models
- Using numbers
- Creating and using graphs
- Using space/time relationships

Advance Preparation

Vocabulary
Make sure students understand these terms. Definitions can be found in the glossary at the end of the student book.

- cell
- cell division
- DNA
- egg
- fertilization
- model
- organism

Materials
Gather the materials needed for ***Before You Read*** (p. 34), ***Enrichment*** (p. 35), and ***Activity*** (p. 36).

The Sorcerer's Apprentice

Watch out! Those cells will take over before you know it!

You might think that when an organism grows, its cells increase in size. However, except for one-celled organisms, all organisms grow by producing new cells.

Before You Read

THINK ABOUT IT Suppose someone offered you a choice. You could get one penny the first day, two pennies the second day, four pennies the third day, eight pennies the fourth day, and so on for one month. The amount you get each day would be double the number you received the day before. Or you could get one million dollars. Which would you choose? Why?

I'd choose the pennies because I'd have more than a billion dollars on the last day of the month.

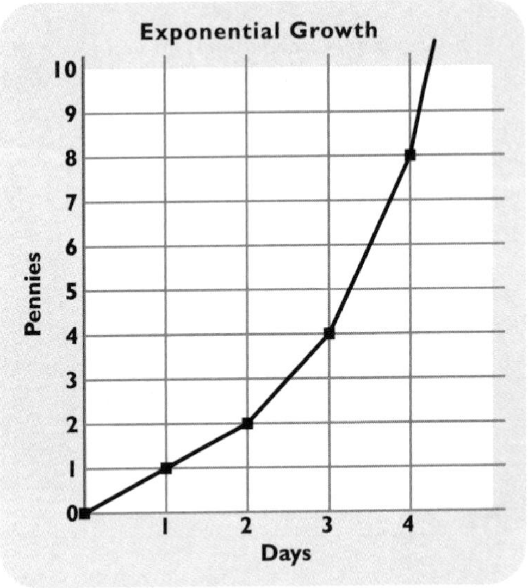

Teaching Plan pp. 34–35

INTRODUCING THE LESSON

This lesson introduces the concept of exponential growth. Ask students if they have ever seen the movie *Fantasia*. If they have, ask them what this lesson's title refers to (the Mickey Mouse character) and what happened to the broomsticks. (They kept multiplying uncontrollably.)

Ask students if they think that our cells continue to divide throughout our entire lives. Some students may think that cell division stops when the body reaches its full growth in early adulthood. Explain that all types of cells except nerve cells continue to reproduce throughout our entire lives.

Before You Read

Materials: calculators, toothpicks or paper clips (optional)

THINK ABOUT IT Let students use calculators to find the answer. You could supply counting objects such as toothpicks or paper clips and have students carry the calculations through one week and then continue with pencil and paper.

After students have answered the question, discuss the graph. They should note that the line has an extremely rapid increase in slope.

Read

Exponential Growth

All cells grow. They double their size by doubling everything they're made of. Then they exactly double their DNA and divide in half. Two completely new cells replace [the parent cell].

We each began as...a single cell. This cell divided, and then divided again, and then again. Doubling over and over—2 producing 4, producing 8, etc.—quickly leads to large numbers. If all these early cells divided at the same rate, it would take only about 30 divisions to make the many billions of cells of a newborn human....

Cell division is essential...to produce [a complete human being] from an egg. [It is also needed] to replace cells lost during an organism's lifetime by wear and tear and by...cell death.

essential: necessary
wear and tear: damage caused by ordinary activities

From: Hoagland, Mahlon, and Bert Dodson. *The Way Life Works: Everything You Need To Know About The Way All Life Grows, Develops, Reproduces, And Gets Along.* Times Books, a division of Random House, Inc.

NOTEZONE

Circle the number of cells present after two divisions.

FIND OUT MORE

SCIENCESAURUS

Kinds of Graphs 390
Line Graphs 394

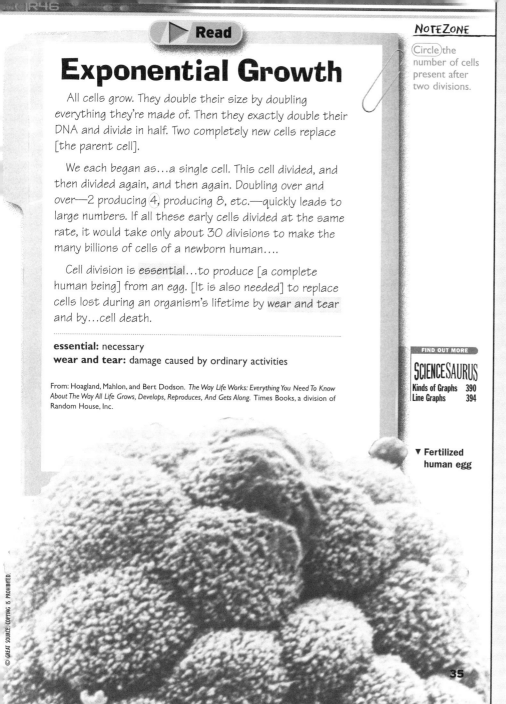

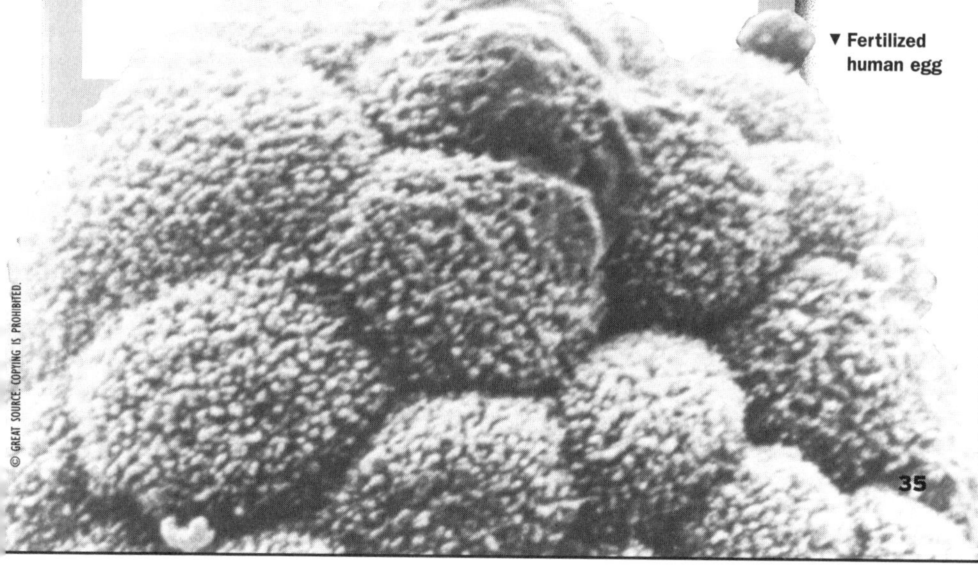

▼ Fertilized human egg

35

Enrichment

Time: will vary
Materials: research sources such as life science and biology textbooks

Encourage small groups of students to brainstorm a list of questions about cell reproduction and exponential growth. Then have them consult science textbooks and other sources to find additional examples of exponential growth—for example, information on bacteria, yeast, or fruit fly populations in laboratory experiments. Ask students to share what they have learned with the class. Encourage them to use graphs, diagrams, or other visuals to help explain what they have learned.

Read

After students finish the reading, discuss the connection between the penny exercise and cell growth. Make sure students understand that cell growth is exponential. You could have them draw a diagram to show the first three divisions mentioned in the reading.

Ask a volunteer to read the final paragraph aloud. Explain that cells throughout our bodies die on a regular basis but are continually replaced by new cells produced through cell division.

Invite students to ask questions about the reading. Some students may want to know how cells become specialized as bone cells, blood cells, and so on. Ask them to recall where the "instructions" are stored and to form their own hypotheses about how, in general, this process happens.

More Resources

The following resources are also available from Great Source.

ScienceSaurus
Kinds of Graphs 390
Line Graphs 394

Reader's Handbook
Comparison and Contrast 278
Note-taking 646

Math on Call
Slope 248
Exponential Growth 548

Connections

MATH Invite students to create math word problems based on exponential growth. Have them write their problems and test the solution themselves, then exchange problems with a partner and solve the partner's problems. Encourage students to use their imagination. For example, students could create a problem about business ventures that earn huge amounts of money. Or they might describe an imaginary, fast-growing plant with cells that divide every hour for a month.

Activity

THE GREAT DIVIDE

You can show how fast the number of cells increases when cells divide repeatedly. All you have to do is fold a sheet of paper.

What You Need:

- a thin sheet of paper, preferably tissue paper

What to Do:

1. Begin with a sheet of paper to represent the original parent cell.
2. Fold the sheet of paper in half. Each section represents one daughter cell. Record the number of "cells" in the table.
3. Fold the paper in half again. Record the number of daughter cells.
4. Repeat step 3 as many times as you can.

Fold #	Number of Cells
0	1
1	2
2	4
3	8
4	16
5	32
6	64
7	128
8	cannot do

What Do You See?

► ***How many times could you fold the paper? How many sections did you make?***

The maximum is 7 folds, 128 sections.

► ***Did you see a pattern? If so, what is it?***

The number of sections doubles with every new fold.

MAKE COMPARISONS If you could fold a sheet of paper 14 times, it would be as thick as you are tall. If you could fold it 30 times, its thickness would reach to the edge of the atmosphere, and it would have 1,073,041,824 sections. Fifty folds would create a thickness almost the distance to the sun. One hundred folds? Your paper's thickness would be about the same as the radius of the known universe!

36

Teaching Plan pp. 36–37

Activity

Time: 5–10 minutes
Materials: a thin sheet of paper, preferably tissue paper

- Tell students to make very careful folds that divide the paper exactly in half. This will make the final folds easier to complete.
- Students can unfold the paper each time to count the "daughter cells." Then they can carefully refold it along the original lines.

MAKE COMPARISONS Help students visualize what would happen if they could continue folding the paper. Write the following headings on the board: *Fold 7, Fold 8, Fold 9, Fold 10,* and so forth through *Fold 15*. Then place one example of the folded paper from the Activity on a desk, and ask a student to measure its total height in millimeters. Write this measurement on the board next to *Fold 7*. Then multiply this height by two and write the result next to *Fold 8*. Continue this way for the remaining folds. Students will quickly see how each fold extends the paper's height exponentially.

Propose Explanations

COMPARING MODELS A model is a useful tool for showing a complex process in a way that makes it more understandable. Each model has some parts that work the same way as the process it shows. Each model also has some parts that do not work quite the same way as the process.

Compare the paper-folding model you just made with the penny-multiplying model on page 34.

► ***In each model, how does the number of items (pennies or paper sections) change?***

In both models, the number of items doubles each time.

Compare the two models to the actual process of cell division.

► ***How is the penny model like cell division? How is it different?***

It is like cell division because the number of items doubles with each step. It is not like cell division because the pennies do not divide or grow, but the cells divide into smaller cells and then grow to full size before dividing again.

► ***How is the paper-folding model like cell division? How is it different?***

It is like cell division because the number of items doubles with each step, and also because each section divides in two, creating two new "daughters" that are half the size of the original. It is not like cell division because the sections do not grow after they divide.

► ***Starting with one parent cell, how many cell divisions are needed to produce more than one thousand daughter cells? Explain how you got your answer.***

10 divisions; starting with 1, keep multiplying the number of daughter cells by 2, and keep track of how many times you did the multiplication.

37

Assessment

Skill: Using numbers

Use the following task to assess each student's progress:

Imagine that your parents have just won a lottery. They have offered to increase your allowance for the next 12 weeks. You now get $3 a week. They have asked you to choose how you would like your raise. Would you like your allowance to double every week for 12 weeks? Or would you rather they raised it to $100 a week for 12 weeks? Explain your answer. (The choice that would result in the most money would be doubling the amount each week, which would produce a total of $12,288. If the allowance were raised to $100 a week, the total would be $1,200 for the same time period.)

Propose Explanations

COMPARING MODELS The questions in this section should help students compare and contrast the nonliving models they made with the process of cell division. You may want to create a Venn diagram on the board to help students visualize the similarities and differences between the models and actual cell division. Use the headings: *Model*, *Both*, and *Cells*. As students read aloud their answers to the questions on this page, fill in the diagram. Make sure the completed diagram shows all major differences and similarities.

CHECK UNDERSTANDING

Skill: Solving problems

Ask: *If you send an email joke to five friends who then send it to five of their friends, and so on, is that an example of exponential growth? How is it different from cell growth?* (Yes it is exponential growth. It is different from cell growth because the numbers are multiplied by five each time instead of being doubled.)

Point of Lesson

Cancer is cell division out of control.

Focus

- Change, constancy, and measurement
- Structure and function in living systems
- Regulation and behavior

Skills and Strategies

- Comparing and contrasting
- Generating questions
- Communicating

Advance Preparation

Vocabulary

Make sure students understand these terms. Definitions can be found in the glossary at the end of the student book.

- blood
- immune system
- nutrient

Materials:

Gather the materials needed for *Take Action* (p. 39).

Cells Out of Control

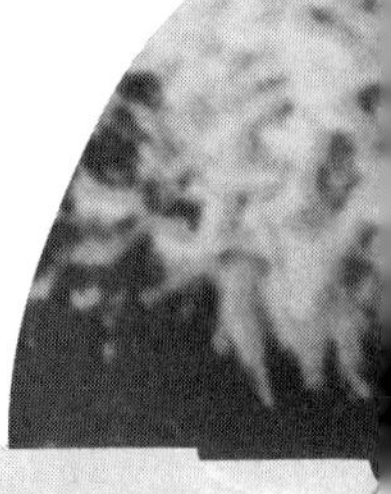

Cancer is not a modern disease. It has been around since ancient times.

Doctors want to help people who have cancer live longer. They are working hard to find ways to cure this disease. To do this, they need to know a lot about how cells divide and why.

Read

NOTEZONE

Number the ways that cell regulation can go wrong.

There is no signal that causes cancer to start. In fact, cancer starts because a signal that *should* happen *doesn't* happen.

Cell Activity Gone Wrong

Question: What exactly is cancer?

Answer: Think of cancer as uncontrolled cell division. Cell division is very important, such as when the body is growing or healing. Our cells have many controls in place to see that this process happens only when needed. Normal, healthy cells divide only when told to do so. Cancer cells divide without regulation and when they should not.

Why do cancers arise? Well, much work has been and continues to be done by scientists to answer this important question. Most cancer cells have gained mutations, or changes, in their genetic material that affect cell regulation. These mutations may [1]turn off normal controls or [2]leave cell division signals permanently on so the cell thinks it should always divide. Other mutations can [3]affect how quickly the cell divides, and whether it can [4]leave its current place and travel to other parts of the body to form new tumors. Some cancer cells are even [5]able to bring blood from the body to "feed" tumors oxygen and nutrients.

regulation: control

tumors: growths of cells that are not normal

From: *MadSci Network*. Washington University Medical School. (www.madsci.org)

FIND OUT MORE

SCIENCESAURUS

Cell Division	080
Immune System	098

TEACHING PLAN pp. 38–39

INTRODUCING THE LESSON

This lesson explains what happens when cell division is uncontrolled. Ask students what they know about cancer and cancer cells. Focus on the nature of the disease rather than individual case histories. Students may know certain cancers by their specific names, such as leukemia, brain tumors, or lung cancer.

Some students may think that cancer is incurable and that people always die from it. Explain that various treatments—chemotherapy, radiation therapy, and surgery—are used successfully to cure the disease by removing cancerous cells or killing them.

Read

If students are unfamiliar with the term *immune system*, tell them that this system fights disease. Explain that when our immune system functions normally, many bacteria, viruses, and other disease-causing organisms are destroyed before they can make us sick.

After students have read the passage and completed the NoteZone activity, have them make predictions based on what they read. Ask: *If cancer cells are able to bring blood to a tumor, what will probably happen to that tumor?* (It will continue to grow.) *What effect will this have on the surrounding parts of the body?* (They will be crowded or blocked and will not function correctly.)

Propose Explanations

MAKE COMPARISONS Cells have a built-in cycle that tells them how to grow, when to divide, when to stop dividing, and when to die. Sometimes a cell changes, or mutates, and its cycle doesn't work as it should. The reasons why this change occurs are not well understood, but it can cause the cell and its daughter cells to divide faster than in the normal cycle. The cells also don't get the signal to stop, and so they divide out of control. This is what happens in cancer.

▸ ***How are normal body cells and cancer cells alike?***

They both divide.

▸ ***How are normal body cells and cancer cells different?***

Normal cells divide more slowly than cancer cells. They don't suddenly mutate. They do not damage organs. They do not spread throughout the body.

Take Action

DO RESEARCH Use reference books, the library, or the Internet to find out more about one type of cancer. On a separate piece of paper, take notes on what we know about this cancer, its symptoms, how it progresses, and ways of treating it. Compare your findings with those of other students to identify differences between different kinds of cancers. On the lines below, write a question about cancer that you would like scientists to investigate.

39

More Resources

The following resources are also available from Great Source.

SCIENCESAURUS

Cell Division	080
Immune System	098

READER'S HANDBOOK

Reading Strategy: Note-taking	106
Search Engine	533

Enrichment

Encourage students to find out about recent developments in cancer research and treatment by visiting the following Web sites.

The National Foundation for Cancer Research: www.researchforacure.com

American Cancer Society: www.cancer.org

Assessment

Skill: Making inferences

Use the following question to assess each student's progress:

Why is cancer such a hard disease to treat and cure? (No one knows exactly what triggers cancer cells to divide at an abnormal rate, and there may be many causes.)

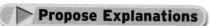

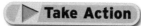

Propose Explanations

MAKE COMPARISONS Students should understand that a cancer cell can be *any* kind of cell that has mutated—skin cells, blood cells, lung cells, brain cells, bone marrow cells, and so forth.

Take Action

Materials: research sources about types of cancer

DO RESEARCH Help students locate sources for their research. You may want to bring in samples of cancer symptom brochures from a local hospital or the American Cancer Society. Students could also search the Internet using the names of specific cancers as keywords. Allow students enough time to discuss their findings with their classmates before they write their questions.

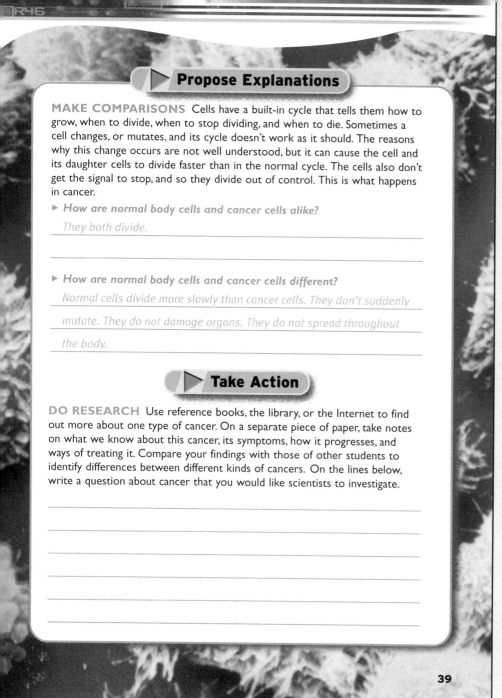

When Cells Get Together

LESSON 10

All Charged Up

Point of Lesson: ***Cells use electricity to communicate.***

In this lesson, a scientist's explanation about electricity in the human body introduces students to the transmission of impulses through nerve cells. Students interpret a diagram to relate the movement of ions across cell membranes to the transmission of electric signals through the body. They then consider the role of such signals in protecting the body.

Materials

Science Scope Activity (p. 40B and p. 41), for the class:

- current events journal (for each student)
- newspapers
- magazines

Explore (p. 42), for teacher demonstration:

- balloon

LESSON 11

Growing Tissue

Point of Lesson: ***Scientists have found a way to grow tissue from an adult's stem cells.***

Students read about a NASA experiment that uses a simulated weightless environment to encourage specialized tissues to grow from adult epithelial stem cells. Students compare diagrams showing the behavior of cells in a standard laboratory dish and in the "weightless" environment. They then interpret the reading to infer some of the leads scientists are pursuing as they seek to explain how the growth of adult stem cells is controlled.

Materials

none

LESSON 12

Organ Misfire

Point of Lesson: ***When an organ is not functioning normally, other organs are affected.***

In this lesson, students meet a fictional student named Janie whose behavior and other symptoms lead her teachers and parent to suspect a hormonal imbalance, which a doctor traces to hyperthyroidism. Students list Janie's symptoms and do research to discover the ways in which a malfunction in one organ—the thyroid gland—can have profound effects on other body organs and systems.

Materials

Enrichment (p. 49), for the class:

- research materials such as science and health textbooks
- roll of white packaging paper
- colored markers

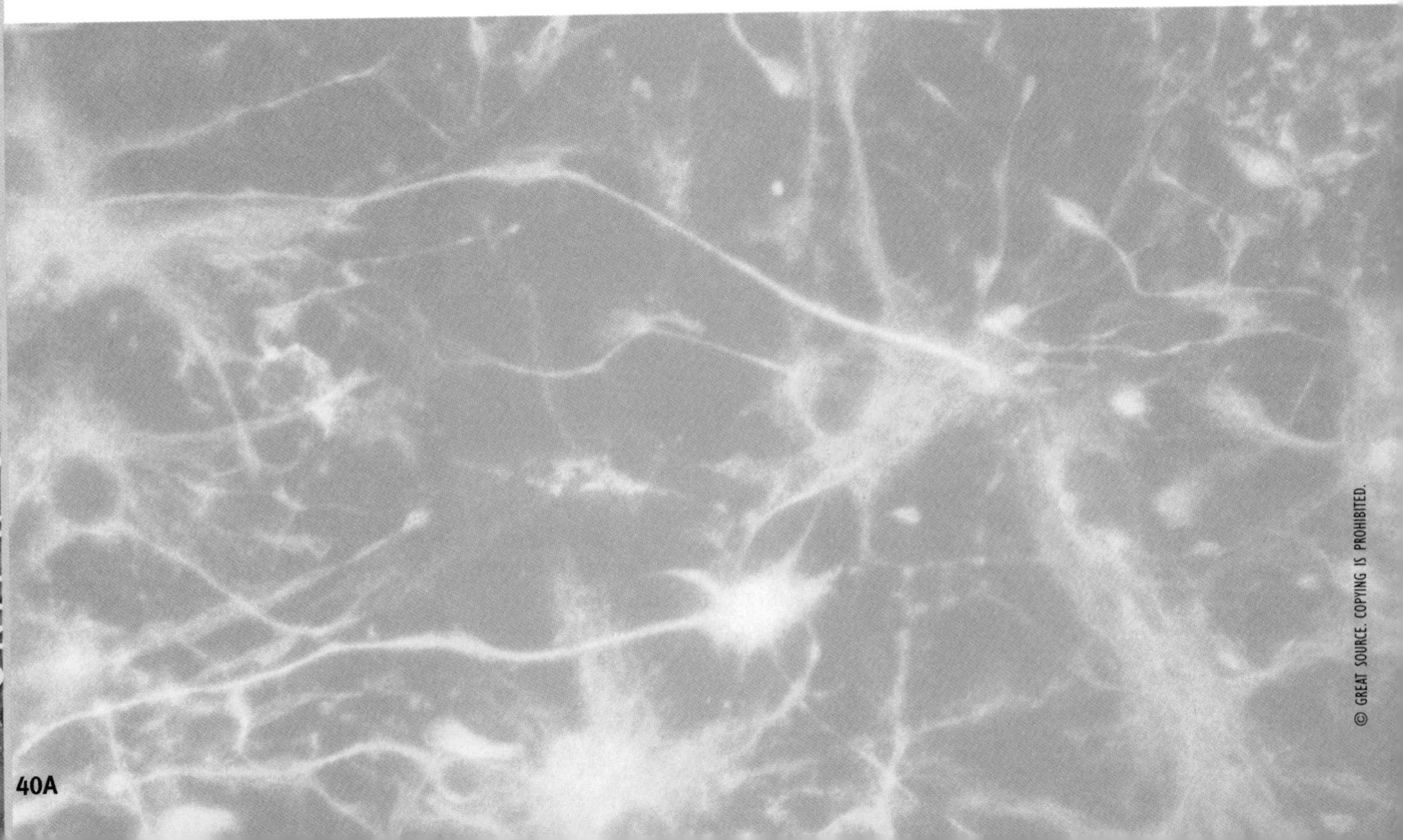

Science Scope Activity

Keeping Science Current

NSTA has chosen a Science Scope *activity related to the content in this chapter. The activity begins here and continues in Lesson 10, page 41.*

Time: ongoing

Materials: see page 40A

Current events can bridge the gap between students' knowledge of textbook science and real-world science. Have each student keep a current events journal in a bound notebook. Tell students to set up the journal as follows: Write your name and science class period on the cover page. On the second page, start a table of contents that lists the names of the articles in the order in which they appear in the journal.

(continued on page 41)

Background Information

Lesson 10

A synapse is the point of transmission between nerve cells or between a nerve cell and another type of cell. There are two basic types of synapses: electrical and chemical. At electrical synapses, cells communicate directly by means of ions that flow from one cell to another. At chemical synapses, chemicals called neurotransmitters deliver information from one cell to another.

Lesson 11

The controversy surrounding some stem cell research focuses on where the cells come from and how they will be used. Stem cells are undifferentiated cells that will develop into specialized cells that make up all the organs in the body. Stem cells are found in embryos, in the tissue of developing fetuses, and in adult tissue. Obtaining stem cells from human embryos and using stem cells in human cloning experiments are the most controversial aspects of stem cell research. The article presents research that involves a noncloning use of epithelial stem cells obtained from adult tissue.

Lesson 12

Hyperthyroidism can be treated with medication. Patients usually need to take the medication for their entire lives. In some cases, patients and their doctors decide to pursue other treatment to permanently keep the thyroid from overproducing thyroid hormone. In most cases, this involves taking a medicine by mouth that destroys the thyroid gland; in rare cases, most of the gland may be surgically removed.

Point of Lesson
Cells use electricity to communicate.

Focus
- Systems, order, and organization
- Structure and function in living systems
- Regulation and behavior
- Form and function

Skills and Strategies
- Making inferences
- Interpreting scientific illustrations
- Communicating

Advance Preparation

Vocabulary
Make sure students understand these terms. Definitions can be found in the glossary at the end of the student book.

- atom
- cell
- cell membrane
- electricity
- molecule
- organ
- spinal cord
- watt

Materials
Gather the materials needed for ***Science Scope Activity*** (p. 40B and p. 41), ***Explore*** (p. 42), and ***Take Action*** (p. 43).

All Charged Up

How do cells in the body communicate with each other?

All living things are made of cells. Cells join together to form tissues that perform different functions in the body. Muscles are one kind of human body tissue. Bones are another kind of tissue.

Cells that perform one function may not look exactly like cells that perform another function, but all cells have some things in common. One of those things is electricity. While we usually don't think of living things as being "electric," all cells generate electrical charges.

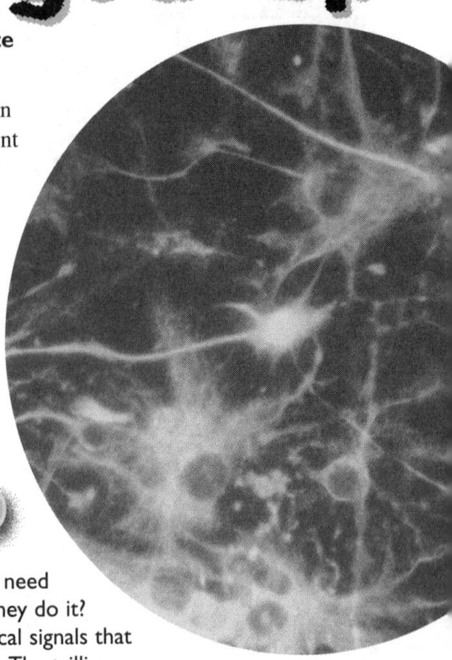

▲Human nerve cells

Before You Read

Imagine that two people in different towns need to plan and coordinate a trip. How could they do it? They could talk to each other using electrical signals that travel through telephone lines or by E-mail. The trillions of cells in your body are similar. Cells must work together so the body functions normally.

► ***How do you think the body's cells might use electricity to work together?***

Cells might use electricity to communicate with other cells.

TEACHING PLAN pp. 40-41

INTRODUCING THE LESSON

This lesson describes how cells use electricity to communicate with each other.

Ask students what they know about the functions of cells. List their responses on the board. Students may think that all body cells are identical. As students examine the list, lead them to understand that different types of cells perform different functions in the body. For example, there are muscle cells, bone cells, nerve cells, and so on. Point out the text statement that cells join together to form tissues.

Before You Read

Ask students to define *electricity* in their own words. If necessary, explain that electricity is the interaction of electrical charges. Electrical energy is the flow of an electric charge through a conductor such as wire—or a nerve cell.

Read

Jerry wanted to know where in the human body electricity was generated, so he asked Dr. Universe.

THE BODY ELECTRIC

Dear Dr. Universe,

How or where or what organs actually produce the electric[ity] that powers the human body?

Thank you,
Jerry

From: Ask Dr. Universe

Well, you're right about the body being "powered" by electricity. Actually, it uses electricity to communicate with itself. But there is no single organ in the body that produces [all] the electricity. Rather,...every cell in the body produces it. That's right—every single cell!

Some cells generate more [electricity] than others.... The amount depends on what the cells do and what they use the electricity for. Nerve cells and heart cells generate a lot of electricity. Nerve cells use it to transmit messages over long distances.

Suppose, for example, that you burn your finger. A nerve fiber (which is really one cell) uses electricity to send that pain signal all the way from your finger to your spinal cord. There, it makes a chemical signal to another cell, which sends another electrical signal to the brain. And there, somehow the signal gets interpreted as pain....

Other cells that use a lot of electricity are heart cells. They use electricity to control the beating of the heart.

[If you] add up the electricity generated by all the trillions of cells in the body...what you get is enough to light a 40 watt light bulb.

generate: produce
nerve cells: cells that send and receive information
transmit: send
interpreted: made sense of

From: "The BIG Questions." *Ask Dr. Universe.* Washington State University. (www.wsu.edu/DrUniverse/body.html)

NOTEZONE

Draw a diagram to show how a pain signal travels from your finger to your brain. Label the places where electricity is used.

Diagrams should show the pain signal traveling along one nerve fiber from the finger to the spinal cord, then along another nerve fiber to the brain. Electricity is used in the two nerve fibers.

FIND OUT MORE
SCIENCESAURUS

Cells 076
Tissues, Organs, and Systems 082
Nervous System 095

41

Science Scope Activity

(continued from page 40B)

Procedure

Give students the following instructions:

1. Each week, choose one article about a science topic that interests you.
2. Highlight important information in the article.
3. Circle five unfamiliar words in the article and find their definitions in a dictionary. List the definitions in your journal.
4. Insert the article in your journal. Record the article's source and date of publication.
5. On a separate page, write a paragraph that summarizes the article's content and main points.
6. Write another paragraph explaining why you chose the article and what makes the topic important to you or to society in general.

Check students' journals periodically to make sure they are following instructions and keeping their entries up to date.

Encourage students to present their articles to the class. Depending on the topic, articles will often generate questions, discussions, and lively debates.

Read

Have students share their NoteZone diagrams. Point out that nerve cells transmit signals throughout the body—both to and from the spinal cord and the brain. In order for a nerve cell to transmit a signal, it must first receive a stimulus (in this case, the burn). The nerve fiber transmits a signal to the spinal cord. The response occurs when the spinal cord sends signals to the muscles in the arm and hand. The muscles contract, pulling the finger away from the source of pain. You feel the pain when a signal travels from the spinal cord to the brain.

CHECK UNDERSTANDING
Skill: Sequencing
Ask students to draw a diagram showing the path that a pain signal and a response signal would take if you stepped on a sharp stone in bare feet. Tell students to label the diagram to show where electrical signals occur. (Diagrams should show the following sequence: nerve in foot spinal cord brain spinal cord foot. *Electricity* should be labeled below each arrow.)

More Resources

The following resources are also available from Great Source.

SCIENCESAURUS

Cells 076
Tissues, Organs, and Systems 082
Nervous System 095

READER'S HANDBOOK

How to Read a Diagram 602

Connections

MATH/LANGUAGE ARTS Tell students that it takes only a fraction of a second for a nerve impulse to travel to or from the spinal cord and brain. Ask students to use a dictionary to find the meanings of the terms *picosecond* (one trillionth of a second, or a factor of 10^{-12}) and *nanosecond* (one billionth of a second, or a factor of 10^{-9}). Ask them to also find the derivation of the prefixes *pico-* (Italian for "small") and *nano-* (Greek for "dwarf").

Explore

INTERPRET A SCIENTIFIC DIAGRAM How do cells generate electricity? They can't plug into electrical outlets or use batteries! Instead, they use atoms and molecules with negative and positive charges. These charged atoms and molecules, called ions, are found in some chemicals in the body.

To generate electricity, the cell first pumps out positive ions (+) through tiny spaces in the cell membrane. Now the inside of the cell has more negative ions (–) than positive ions. With more negative ions, the inside of the cell has a negative charge. The outside of the cell has more positive ions than negative ions, so the outside has a positive charge. This diagram shows where those charges are inside and outside the cell.

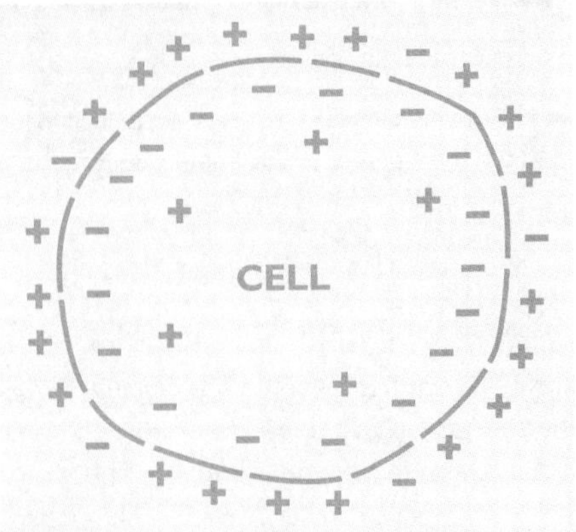

Objects that have positive and negative electric charges attract one another. If they are separated and given the chance to come back together, positive charges will rush toward negative charges. Electric current is the movement of electric charges.

► ***What happens to generate electricity?***

Positive charges move back through the membrane into the cell.

► ***The flow of electricity creates a signal. What kind of signal might a nerve fiber send from a burned finger to the spinal cord?***

a pain signal

A nerve cell's function is to send electrical signals to other parts of the body. A skin cell's function is to act as a barrier between the body and the outside world.

► ***Where do you think there is more electrical activity—in nerve cells or skin cells? Why?***

in nerve cells because they use electricity to send signals

42

TEACHING PLAN pp. 42–43

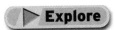

Explore

Time: 5–10 minutes
Materials: balloon

INTERPRET A SCIENTIFIC DIAGRAM Tell students that electrical charges are properties of the protons and electrons, the particles that make up atoms. Protons have a positive charge, and electrons have a negative charge.

To demonstrate an electrical charge, rub a balloon against a volunteer's hair. When you pull the balloon away, the hair is attracted to the balloon. Tell students that the balloon becomes negatively charged because it gains negatively charged particles (electrons) from the hair. The hair is now positively charged because it has lost negatively charged particles. The static electricity produced is caused by the movement of the negatively charged particles.

Call attention to the diagram on this page. Explain that the movement of positive and negative ions back and forth through the cell membrane is what causes the electrical current, much like the balloon demonstration.

Propose Explanations

MAKE INFERENCES Why do cells need to communicate? Think about what happens when you're in pain. You feel pain when nerve cells use electricity to send signals to cells in your spinal cord and then your brain.

- *Imagine you're climbing a tree and you scrape the skin of your hand on the bark. How would your body react?*

  My hand would pull away from the bark.

- *What purpose do you think pain serves?*

  Pain lets us know that our body is being injured and allows us to avoid the thing that is causing the pain.

- *What might happen if we didn't feel pain?*

  The thing that is causing the pain might injure us even more.

Take Action

RESEARCH REFLEXES A reflex is a reaction the body makes without thinking about it first. The electrical signal travels from the nerve cells of the body part that is in danger to the spinal cord. In a fraction of a second, the spinal cord sends an electrical signal back to the body part "telling" it to move away from the source of danger. A split second later, another electrical signal travels up the spinal cord to the brain. Then the brain interprets the signal as pain. If you've ever been to the doctor for a checkup, you know that one reflex you have is a "knee-jerk" when the front of your knee is tapped. What other reflexes do humans have? Do some research to find out about other reflexes. How does each reflex help humans survive in their environment?

Answers will vary. Examples: blinking when an object suddenly comes toward the face, pulling a hand away from a hot pan, coughing, and sneezing. Reflexes help protect the body from injury.

Assessment

Skill: Predicting

Use the following task to assess each student's progress:

Give students this problem: *A cell has an equal number of positive and negative ions inside the cell. The cell pumps out some of the positive ions through its cell membrane. When the positive charges move back through the cell membrane, what happens?* (The movement of the ions causes the cell to generate electricity.)

Propose Explanations

MAKE INFERENCES Explain to students that the structure of a nerve cell enables it to pass electrical signals along to another cell. Each nerve cell has a long, tail-like fiber that carries the signal away from the cell body. The signal "jumps" a gap between the two cells. The second cell has small, feathery fibers that receive the signal. The nerve that carries a signal from the hand, for example, to the spinal cord consists of the long fibers of single cells.

Take Action

Time: will vary
Materials: research sources about human reflexes

RESEARCH REFLEXES Point out that a reflex reaction does not involve the brain. The brain only becomes involved later. For example, if you touch a hot object, you immediately pull your hand away before your brain senses the pain. Draw a diagram on the board to illustrate the path of a reflex reaction. Have students compare your diagram with the ones they drew for the NoteZone task. Encourage students to include in their research the reflexes exhibited by infants but which fade as the infant matures. Have students share their research on reflexes.

Point of Lesson

Scientists have found a way to grow tissue from an adult's stem cells.

Focus

- Systems, order, and organization
- Structure and function in living systems
- Science as a human endeavor
- Abilities of technological design
- Understanding about scientific inquiry

Skills and Strategies

- Making inferences
- Interpreting scientific illustrations
- Comparing and contrasting
- Drawing conclusions
- Recognizing cause and effect

Advance Preparation

Vocabulary

Make sure students understand these terms. Definitions can be found in the glossary at the end of the student book.

- cell
- force
- nutrient
- organism
- tissue

Growing Tissue

How do cells "know" what kind of tissue to form? Scientists are beginning to find out.

Astronauts returning from space often have trouble walking on land. This is because in the "weightlessness" of space, their muscle tissue begins to break down. Scientists worried that astronauts traveling on long space missions might suffer severe tissue damage.

To study the effects of "weightlessness" on human body tissue, scientists at the National Aeronautics and Space Administration (NASA) developed the Bioreactor. This rotating can of liquid nutrients mimics the conditions experienced by astronauts in space. But scientists soon found a new use for the Bioreactor—growing new tissue from cells.

▲Bioreactor

Before You Read

TISSUE ISSUES Tissues are made of identical cells that joined together to perform a specific function.

▸ ***Why do you think scientists are interested in growing new tissue?***

Answers will vary. Example: The new tissue could be used to replace damaged or diseased tissue in patients' bodies or to test new medicines.

TEACHING PLAN pp. 44–45

INTRODUCING THE LESSON

This lesson explains one method that scientists are using to grow specific types of human body tissues from stem cells.

Ask students what they know about how tissues are formed. Some students may think that cells start out as different types from the beginning. Explain that all cells actually start out the same and become different only when they begin to form tissues.

Remind students that the space around Earth is not actually a "weightless" environment. A spaceship in orbit is essentially falling around Earth. Since the astronauts in the spaceship are freefalling in the same way and at the same rate as the spaceship, they feel as though they are floating.

Before You Read

TISSUE ISSUES Make sure students understand that a tissue is a group of identical cells that perform the same function. Ask them to identify different types of tissues in the body. (muscles, bones, nerves, blood) You may want to introduce the four basic types of tissue found in the human body: muscle tissue, epithelial tissue, nerve tissue, and connective tissue. Point out that epithelial tissue makes up part of our skin and the lining of certain organs, such as the intestines. Explain that connective tissue includes bone and cartilage.

Read

The Bioreactor is being used to grow human tissue.

Tissue Engineering

If you've ever seen a pile of ivy that has taken the shape of an old barn...it has overgrown, you've seen the principle that researchers are following in trying to grow replacement parts for bodies....

For many people, culturing cells means putting some small number into...a dish [with liquid nutrients]...and letting them grow. However, this kind of approach does not provide the...environment that supports tissue [formation]. Without a proper 3-D assembly, epithelial [stem] cells...lack the proper clues for growing into the [specific] cells that make up a particular tissue.

The Bioreactor was developed by NASA to simulate the ["weightless"] environment of space by putting cells in a [liquid-filled container] that constantly rotates and keeps the cells in endless free-fall.... In a rotating Bioreactor, the cells can be fooled into thinking they are in a body. With a plastic lattice to help direct their growth, cells can be encouraged to grow [into certain] shapes, just as the...barn gives shape to [the] vines [that cover it].

principle: a rule that determines how a process works
culturing: growing living cells or tiny organisms in a protected environment with nutrients
3-D: three-dimensional; having length, width, and depth
assembly: structure
epithelial stem cells: cells from an adult's skin that can specialize into different kinds of cells
free-fall: a falling motion that is affected only by gravity, not by a parachute or other object
lattice: a structure that something grows over and around

From: "Scientists Grow Heart Tissue In Bioreactor." *Science@NASA*. NASA. (science.nasa.gov/newhome/headlines/msad05oct99_1.htm)

NOTEZONE

What do you want to know more about after reading this?

FIND OUT MORE

SCIENCESAURUS
Cells 076
Tissues, Organs, and Systems 082

SCILINKS. THE WORLD'S A CLICK AWAY
www.scilinks.org
Keyword: Tissues and Organs
Code: GSLD07

45

Enrichment

Tell students that scientists have developed a way to treat burn victims by using artificial skin. After the outer layer of burned tissue is removed from the patient, surgeons apply a layer of artificial skin. This skin is made of protein fibers similar to those in human epithelial tissue. Invite students to contact the public affairs or community outreach office of a burn treatment center in your area and ask for information about this treatment. Have students share their findings with the rest of the class.

Read

After students have read the excerpt, discuss the meanings of any unfamiliar terms. Then ask: *Why is it important for the stem cells to be "fooled into thinking they are in a body"?* (If the cells did not "think" they were in a body, they would not grow into certain shapes to form tissue.)

Ask students to share the questions they wrote for the NoteZone task. You may want to have students form groups and choose one question to research.

CHECK UNDERSTANDING

Skill: Recognizing cause and effect

Ask students: *What does the plastic lattice inside the Bioreactor do?* (It provides a shape for the cells to grow into.)

More Resources

The following resources are also available from Great Source and NSTA.

ScienceSaurus

Cells 076
Tissues, Organs, and Systems 082

Reader's Handbook

Elements of Poetry 446
How to Read a Diagram 602

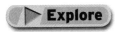

SciLinks

www.scilinks.org
Keyword: Tissues and Organs
Code: GSLD07

Connections

MATH Present this problem to students: *Suppose one milliliter of a fluid contained 5 million stem cells. How many stem cells would there be in 5 milliliters of fluid?* (25 million) *How many milliliters of fluid will contain 10 million stem cells?* (2 milliliters) Ask students to generate their own math problems using the above information and share their problems with classmates.

Explore

INTERPRET A SCIENTIFIC DIAGRAM The following diagram compares how cells act when they are grown in two different environments—a laboratory dish and the "weightless" environment of the Bioreactor. In both environments, the cells are placed in a liquid that contains nutrients they need in order to survive.

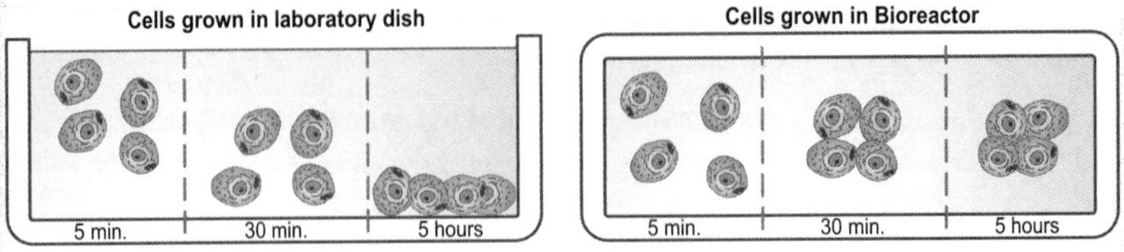

► ***After 30 minutes, how have the cells in the laboratory dish moved?***

They have started to sink to the bottom.

► ***What force is causing their movement?*** *gravity*

► ***After 30 minutes, how have the cells in the Bioreactor moved?***

They have clumped together.

► ***Compare how the cells in the two containers are arranged after five hours. What do you notice?***

The cells in the laboratory dish are lying in a single layer on the bottom of the dish. They seem to be just lying where they fell. The cells in the Bioreactor have grouped together in the middle of the fluid. Gravity isn't pulling them together, so there must be another reason for their joining.

DRAW CONCLUSIONS

► ***How does the Bioreactor encourage tissue growth more than the laboratory dish does?***

The Bioreactor takes away (most of) the effects of gravity. The cells are allowed to float in the liquid rather than settling to the bottom. When left to float, the cells can come together and start to form tissue.

46

Teaching Plan pp. 46–47

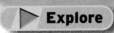

Explore

INTERPRET A SCIENTIFIC DIAGRAM Call attention to the diagram, and ask students which setup provides an environment similar to the human body. (the Bioreactor) Make sure students understand that when the cells group together in the Bioreactor, they form tissue.

DRAW CONCLUSIONS Ask students: *How might the formation of human body tissues in a laboratory be helpful to medical science?* (Tissues grown from stem cells could be used to replace tissues that are diseased, damaged, or functioning improperly or could be used for scientific research.)

Propose Explanations

MAKE INFERENCES There are many different kinds of cells. Cells that come together to form tissues are specialized to perform that tissue's function. For example, heart muscle cells form heart tissue. The muscles contract and relax to keep blood moving throughout the body.

Stem cells are cells that have not yet become specialized. Stem cells can become any kind of cell. Some stem cells, like the ones used in the experiment, are found in adults. Others are found in developing organisms, such as a fetus in its mother's uterus. When an organism is first forming, it has many stem cells. As the organism begins to form tissues, its stem cells become specialized. Some become skin cells. Others become heart cells. Still others become nerve cells. Scientists don't yet understand exactly how stem cells "know" which kind of specialized cells to become, but they are working on some ideas.

► ***Based on the reading, what can you infer about where stem cells get the clues to follow in order to become specialized cells?***

They must receive clues from their environment, just as the cells grown on the lattice formed tissue shaped like the lattice.

► ***How might scientists use this information to create different types of tissues? (Hint: Recall the example of the barn.)***

They could use different frame shapes to grow tissues of different shapes.

Take Action

WRITE A HAIKU A haiku is a form of poetry from Japan. The poem has only three lines, and each line has a set number of syllables: 5, 7, and 5. Unlike some poems, the words in a haiku do not rhyme. The following is an example of a haiku. Count the syllables in each line. Write the number at the end of each line.

Water falls in drops *5*
collecting in a smooth pool *7*
blue and green and white. *5*

Create your own haiku about how cells form tissues or how tissue grows in a Bioreactor. Make sure your haiku has three lines and that each line has the correct number of syllables. *Examples:*

Cells must follow clues
when deciding what to be
what tissue to form.

Spinning in free-fall
growing over a lattice
forming a tissue

Assessment

Skill: Recognizing cause and effect

Use the following question to assess each student's progress:

How has the Bioreactor enabled scientists to overcome the difficulties involved in growing tissues from stem cells? (The Bioreactor creates a weightless environment that fools the cells into "thinking" they are in a human body, so tissue formation occurs.)

Propose Explanations

MAKE INFERENCES Explain to students that a developing fetus has stem cells that become specialized as the fetus matures. Point out that the adult human body also contains stem cells and that these cells are constantly developing into the cells that make up the tissues in our body.

Take Action

WRITE A HAIKU Point out that a traditional Japanese haiku is usually about some aspect of nature. Allow students time to share their poems.

Point of Lesson

When an organ is not functioning normally, other organs are affected.

Focus

- Systems, order, and organization
- Structure and function in living systems
- Regulation and behavior
- Personal health

Skills and Strategies

- Observing
- Creating and using tables
- Classifying
- Drawing conclusions
- Recognizing cause and effect

Advance Preparation

Vocabulary

Make sure students understand these terms. Definitions can be found in the glossary at the end of the student book.

- cell
- endocrine system
- energy
- organ system
- tissue

Materials

Gather the materials needed for *Enrichment* (p. 49).

Organ Misfire

What happens when an organ stops functioning normally?

Tissues in the body join together to form organs. Organs perform specific functions, just as cells and tissues do. Organs work together in systems to carry out important life processes.

One system in your body is the endocrine system. The organs in this system are known as *glands*. Glands release substances called *hormones* that act as chemical messengers throughout the body.

One gland in the endocrine system is the thyroid gland. It controls growth and metabolism—the rate at which your body uses energy. People whose thyroid gland isn't working properly can experience many different problems.

Before You Read

FIND YOUR THYROID The thyroid is a butterfly-shaped organ located under the skin in the front of your neck. To find it, touch your "Adam's apple" with one finger and the top of your breastbone (just below the little depression at the base of your neck) with your thumb. The thyroid is in that space between your fingers.

Read

Janie hadn't been feeling well. After hearing about her symptoms and having some tests done, Janie's doctor was able to figure out that one of her organs wasn't working properly.

HYPERTHYROID BLUES

Janie didn't notice the changes very much at first—but her teachers did. Since starting sixth grade, Janie had become restless. She was squirmy and nervous, and it was hard for her to sit still in class. Paying attention was hard, too. Finally, Janie's teachers asked the school nurse to call her father.

Janie's dad had noticed some changes as well. She was eating more than usual. But instead of gaining weight, Janie was getting thinner. And even though it was almost December, she was sweating a lot.

FIND OUT MORE
SCIENCESAURUS
Tissues, Organs, and Systems 082
Endocrine System 097

TEACHING PLAN pp. 48–49

INTRODUCING THE LESSON

In this lesson, students are presented with a scenario in which the malfunction of the thyroid gland affects other organ systems.

Ask students to name various body systems (nervous system, digestive system, circulatory system, and so on). Some students may not be aware that the thyroid gland is part of the endocrine system and is responsible for regulating the body's growth and metabolism. Point out the term *metabolism* and its meaning in the student text. Explain that the body uses energy to carry out all life processes—growth, breathing, digestion, and so on.

Before You Read

FIND YOUR THYROID Some students may have difficulty locating their "Adam's apple." Point out your own "Adam's apple" and demonstrate the technique described in the student text.

Read

As students read through the excerpt, have them underline words that describe Janie's symptoms. Let students share their responses to the NoteZone question.

Tell students that hyperthyroidism can be detected through blood testing and can be treated with medication. Patients usually need to take the medication for the rest of their lives. They also need to have blood tests regularly to make sure that blood levels of thyroid hormones are within normal range.

He decided it was time for Janie to have a checkup. It didn't take Janie's doctor long to discover what was wrong. Janie had [an overactive] thyroid gland.

Kids with hyperthyroidism can feel jumpy and have trouble concentrating. Like Janie, their hearts might beat fast and their hands may tremble. They can sweat a lot and have trouble sleeping. And even though they might have more of an appetite, they often lose weight or stop gaining it as they grow.

hyperthyroidism: a condition in which the thyroid gland produces too much of its hormone

tremble: shake

From: "Thyroid Disorders." *KidsHealth*. The Nemours Foundation. (kidshealth.org/kid/health_problems/gland/thyroid.html)

NOTEZONE

Before you read that Janie had an overactive thyroid, what did you think was wrong with her?

Answers will vary but might include personal problems, an eating disorder, or a learning disorder.

Propose Explanations

In the chart below, list the symptoms of hyperthyroidism. Then use a science or health textbook or another reference to decide which organs or organ systems are affected by hyperthyroidism.

Symptom	Organ or Organ System Affected by Condition
squirmy and nervous	*nervous system*
can't pay attention	*nervous system (brain)*
eating more and getting thinner	*digestive system*
heart beats fast	*circulatory system*
hands tremble	*nervous system, muscular system*
sweat a lot	*excretory system, circulatory system*
have trouble sleeping	*nervous system (brain)*

▸ **What does this chart tell you about how organs and organ systems in the human body are connected?**

The thyroid is only one gland. Yet when it wasn't working right, it affected many parts of Janie's body. Organs have effects on other organs within the body, so if one is malfunctioning, others might be, too.

49

More Resources

The following resource is also available from Great Source.

SCIENCESAURUS

Tissues, Organs, and Systems 082
Endocrine System 097

Enrichment

Time: will vary

Materials: research materials such as science and health textbooks; roll of white packaging paper; colored markers

Ask students to find out more about the different glands that make up the endocrine system—the pituitary, hypothalmus, thymus, parathyroids, adrenal glands, pancreas, ovaries, and testes. Students could share their findings by drawing a life-size outline of the human body on a large sheet of paper cut from a roll. Tell students to draw the organs in their correct locations and label each one with its name and function.

Assessment

Skill: Recognizing cause and effect

Use the following question to assess each student's progress:

Why did Janie's hyperthyroidism affect so many organs and systems in her body? (The thyroid's hormones travel throughout her body.)

Propose Explanations

To complete the chart's left column, students can refer to the words that they underlined earlier in the reading. If necessary, list organ systems on the board to help students complete the second column. Briefly discuss the function of each system and the names of the organs in it.

Make sure students understand that when one organ in the body malfunctions, other organs and systems are affected. Stress that it is important to have regular check-ups to make sure the body is functioning normally.

CHECK UNDERSTANDING

Skill: Organizing information

Have students list the symptoms of hyperthyroidism. (nervousness, inability to pay attention, eating more but losing weight, increased heart rate, trembling hands, sweating, difficulty sleeping)

About the Photo

The double-helix shape and base-pair structure of a DNA molecule was discovered by Francis Crick, James Watson, and Rosalind Franklin in 1953. Students may be interested to know that Watson and Crick established the shape and structure by using a large three-dimensional wire model. The model shown in this photo is far more complex than Watson and Crick's wire model. When Watson and Crick published the paper announcing their discovery, they could not decide whose name would come first, so they flipped a coin. Watson won.

About the Charts

A major goal of the *Science Daybooks* is to promote reading, writing, and critical thinking skills in the context of science. The charts below describe the types of reading selections included in this unit and identify the skills and strategies used in each lesson.

UNIT 2

Heredity, Diversity, and Change

How does a species change over time?

You may think that one type of animal will look exactly the same forever. But in fact species change over the course of generations. Why would a species change? If the species' environment changes, the species may change to survive in the new environment.

There's a code inside cells that determines what an organism will become, what it will look like, and why it will be different from another: the genetic code. In this unit, you'll explore how differences in this code can change the size of a cob of corn or the color of a pea plant's flowers. You'll also find out how scientists use genes to help group and identify organisms. And you'll learn that genes determine a lot about you...but not everything.

50

SELECTION	READING	WRITING	APPLICATION
CHAPTER 5 • HOW GENES WORK			
13. "The Book of Life" (nonfiction science book)	• Formulate questions	• Compare and contrast	• Write analogies
14. "In the Garden" (biography)	• Compare and contrast • Draw a diagram • Read a diagram	• Make inferences • Analyze data • Cite supporting evidence	• Use figurative language
15. "How People Changed Corn" (nonfiction science book)	• Graphic organizer • Read for details	• Brainstorming • Make connections • Make inferences	• Write a research report
CHAPTER 6 • GENES AND PEOPLE			
16.		• Make inferences • Graphic organizer	• Interpret a chart • Defend your answer
17. "The Blue People" (science news magazine)	• Make connections • Make inferences	• Interpret a diagram	• Write a dialogue
18. "Who We Are" (museum Web site)	• Make a list • Read for details	• Compare and contrast • Make inferences	• Conduct an interview • Draw a diagram • Draw conclusions

THE CHAPTERS IN THIS UNIT ARE . . .

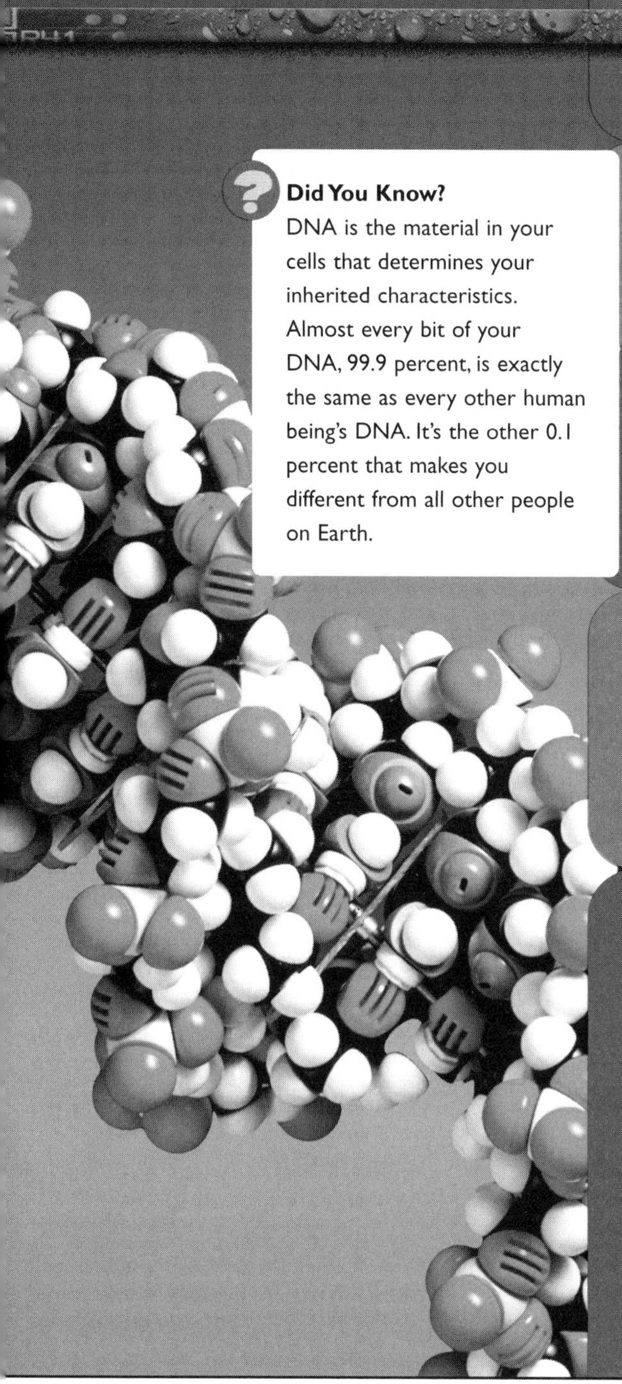

Did You Know?
DNA is the material in your cells that determines your inherited characteristics. Almost every bit of your DNA, 99.9 percent, is exactly the same as every other human being's DNA. It's the other 0.1 percent that makes you different from all other people on Earth.

CHAPTER 5:
How Genes Work
Find out: How did Native Americans create corn with longer cobs?

CHAPTER 6:
Genes and People
Find out: Why do certain people in Kentucky have blue-tinged skin?

CHAPTER 7:
Most Likely to Survive
Find out: Why is the gene to grow tusks disappearing from some elephant populations?

CHAPTER 8:
One Hundred Million Kinds of Things
Find out: What happens when scientists discover a brand-new organism?

51

Answers to *Find Out* Questions

Chapter 5
They used corn with longer cobs as parents generation after generation. (p. 59)

Chapter 6
They have a rare blood disorder that is inherited as a recessive trait. Because the community is small, recessive gene forms are often paired, and the trait shows up frequently. (pp. 64–65)

Chapter 7
Illegal hunting of male Asian elephants for their ivory tusks leaves a higher proportion of male elephants that have a recessive gene form for not growing tusks. The tuskless elephants pass this trait to their offspring. (pp. 77–78)

Chapter 8
They first figure out how the new organism fits into the scientific classification system. If it does not fit into an existing category, a new category must be created. (pp. 82–83)

SCILINKS. THE WORLD'S A CLICK AWAY

www.scilinks.org
Keyword: Developing Classroom Activities
Code: GSSD05

SELECTION	READING	WRITING	APPLICATION
CHAPTER 7 • MOST LIKELY TO SURVIVE			
19. "Successful Variations" (newspaper article)	• Use prior knowledge • Read for details	• Compare and contrast • Draw conclusions	• Creative thinking • Draw and label a diagram
20. "More Tuskless Elephants Than Ever" (news service article)	• Formulating questions	• Write an explanation • Use a model	• Hands-on activity • Generate and analyze data • Write a research report
21.	• Read information in photographs	• Draw conclusions	• Create a compare/contrast chart
CHAPTER 8 • ONE HUNDRED MILLION KINDS OF THINGS			
22. "New Order of Insects Discovered" (science magazine article)	• Read for details • Classifying • Organizing ideas	• Classifying • Make comparisons • Draw conclusions	• Hands-on activity • Write field notes • Record research findings
23. "The 'Bear Facts'" (museum Web site)	• Read for details • Read a chart	• Draw conclusions • Cite supporting evidence	• Compare and contrast
24.	• Drawing a diagram		• Use a specialized chart (dichotomous key)

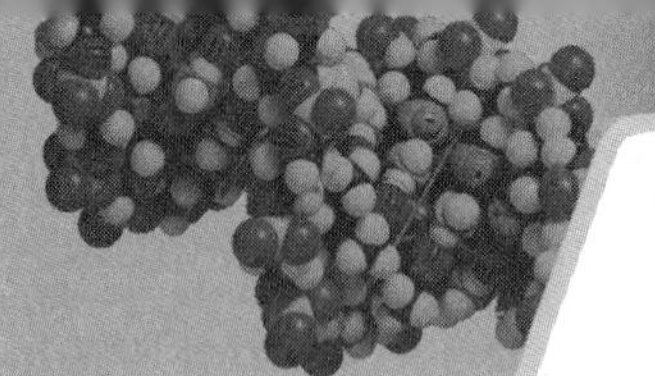

How Genes Work

LESSON 13

Your Genes and Chromosomes

Point of Lesson: ***DNA contains the instructions for all of an organism's physical traits.***

An excerpt from the book *Genome: The Autobiography of a Species in 23 Chapters* uses the analogy of a book to convey the sheer complexity of the human genome. Students compare and contrast the genome to a book and carry the analogy further by comparisons with a cookbook. They end the lesson by constructing their own analogy to make a science concept more understandable.

Materials

none

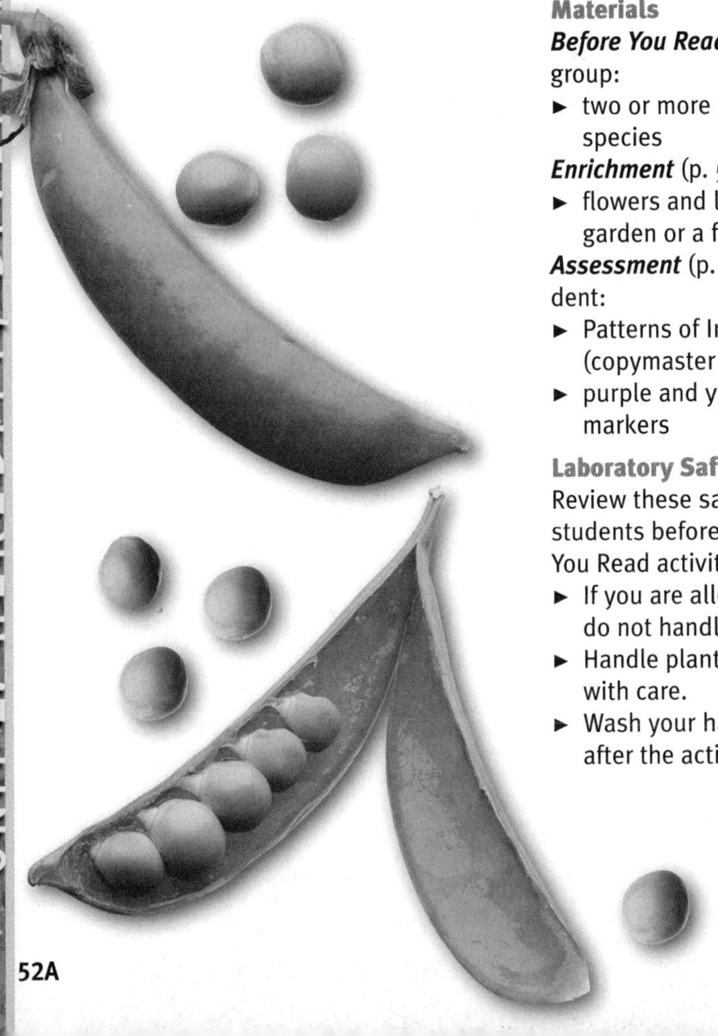

LESSON 14

In-gene-ius!

Point of Lesson: ***Gregor Mendel investigated inherited traits in pea plants.***

This lesson introduces the work of Gregor Mendel. Students begin by observing similarities and differences between individuals of the same plant species. A description of Mendel working in his "garden laboratory" then sets the stage for student analysis of data drawn from Mendel's work. After students are introduced to Mendel's hypothesis about dominant and recessive traits, they revisit the data to determine dominance of a trait in pea plants. An exercise on similes and metaphors, as used in the excerpt describing Mendel in his garden, rounds out the lesson.

Materials

Before You Read (p. 54), for each group:

- two or more plants of the same species

Enrichment (p. 55), for each group:

- flowers and leaves from a home garden or a florist

Assessment (p. 57), for each student:

- Patterns of Inheritance diagram (copymaster page 227)
- purple and yellow pencils or markers

Laboratory Safety

Review these safety guidelines with students before they do the Before You Read activity in this lesson.

- If you are allergic to any plant, do not handle it.
- Handle plants and living things with care.
- Wash your hands thoroughly after the activity.

LESSON 15

Custom Corn

Point of Lesson: ***Selective breeding produces organisms with desirable traits.***

Today's corn is the result of thousands of years of selective breeding. Students read about the origin of corn, then compare the work Native Americans did to develop corn with the discoveries Mendel made, as described in Lesson 14. They then consider whether there are limits to the length a corn cob can grow and why Native Americans would pay so much attention to corn in the first place. The lesson ends with an opportunity to research selective breeding as it relates to the origin of dog breeds.

Materials

Before You Read (p. 58), for the class:

- fruits and vegetables containing seeds (optional)

Read (p. 59), for teacher demonstration:

- cob of blue corn

Explore (p. 60), for the class:

- different varieties of corn (on the cob)

Connections (p. 60), for each group:

- seed catalogs that advertise both conventional and heirloom varieties of fruits and vegetables (available from the companies "Seeds of Change" and "Burpee Seed Company" on the Internet or at a local nursery)

Take Action (p. 61), for the class:

- research sources about breeds of dogs

Laboratory Safety

Review these safety guidelines with students before they do the Before You Read and Explore activities in this lesson.

- Do not taste any substance in the laboratory.
- Wash your hands thoroughly after the activity.

Background Information

Lesson 13

The Human Genome Project is an international scientific research project managed by the U.S. Department of Energy. The project was begun in October 1990 and was planned to last for 15 years; however, advances in technology have allowed the work to progress more quickly than planned, and the project should be finished two years early in 2003. One of the goals of the project is to map the human genome—in other words, to identify every gene on every chromosome of the human genome.

Four chemical bases, which occur over and over again in pairs, make up the DNA of every living thing. The human genome contains about 3 billion pairs of these chemical bases. Although the number of base pairs in the human genome is essentially known, there is debate over the number of genes, or functional units, that determine human genetic traits. A gene is a section of DNA on a chromosome that determines a particular inherited characteristic.

In February 2001, special issues of the journals *Science* and *Nature* published the working draft of the human genome sequence. At that time, the number of human genes was estimated at about 35,000. This number came as a surprise to many people because previous estimates called for about 100,000 genes. However, another team of scientists working on the human genome claim that the number of genes is between 65,000 and 75,000. In contrast, the nematode worm has 18,000 genes, and the fruit fly has 13,000 genes. One question scientists are interested in is how humans can be so much more complex than other organisms when we have only two or three times as many genes as those organisms. Some scientists speculate that human genes may work differently, with more complex controls governing how the genes work to determine traits.

For more information on the Human Genome Project, see the following Web site: www.ornl.gov/TechResources/Human_Genome/home.html

Point of Lesson
DNA contains the instructions for all of an organism's physical traits.

Focus
- Systems, order, and organization
- Reproduction and heredity

Skills and Strategies
- Comparing and contrasting
- Generating ideas

Advance Preparation
Vocabulary
Make sure students understand these terms. Definitions can be found in the glossary at the end of the student book.

- cell
- chromosome
- DNA
- gene
- molecule
- nucleus
- organism
- trait

More Resources
The following resources are also available from Great Source and NSTA.

ScienceSaurus

DNA	115
Genes	116
The Human Genome	117
Heredity	121

(continued on page 53)

Your Genes and Chromosomes

What makes you "you" and different from your friends or even the other members of your family? Three letters say a lot: DNA.

Who you are depends on lots of things, including how you are brought up and the choices you make. But each of us has a "book of life" in our cells that tells most of the story about who we are and how we grow. That "book," the book of *your* life, is given to you by your biological parents. It helps determine how your body looks, functions, and responds to the things around you. Your "book of life"—your genome—is coded in something called deoxyribonucleic acid, or DNA.

NoteZone

What else would you like to know about your genome?

Read

Here is how science writer Matt Ridley describes the genome.

The Book of Life

Imagine that the genome is a book. There are twenty-three chapters, called chromosomes. Each chapter contains several thousand stories called genes.

There are one billion words in the book, which makes it longer than 5,000 volumes. If I read the book out loud to you for eight hours a day, it would take me a century. This is a gigantic document, an immense book and it all fits inside the microscopic nucleus of a tiny cell that fits easily upon the head of a pin.

Instead of being written on flat pages, genomes are written on long chains called DNA molecules. Each chromosome is one pair of (very) long DNA molecules.

genome: all the genes of an organism
chromosomes: strands of DNA in a cell's nucleus that carry the code for the organism's inherited characteristics
gene: a section of DNA on a chromosome that determines a particular inherited characteristic
DNA: the material in a cell's nucleus that determines the organism's genetic traits
molecules: groups of atoms linked together

FIND OUT MORE

ScienceSaurus

DNA	115
Genes	116
The Human Genome	117
Heredity	121

SciLinks
www.scilinks.org
Keyword: DNA
Code: GSLD09

From: Ridley, Matt. *Genome: The Autobiography of a Species in 23 Chapters.* HarperCollins Publishers, Inc.

Teaching Plan pp. 52–53

INTRODUCING THE LESSON
This lesson describes DNA and the human genome. Discuss inherited traits with students. Ask them to identify basic physical traits, such as hair and eye color, that they share with other people in their biological families.

Students may think that scientists know exactly how genes affect our personalities and behavior. Bring up the subject of twins who look similar but have different interests and behavior. This will help students understand how genetics are actually only part of the "Book of Life." Explain that scientists debate how much of our personality is genetic and how much is learned.

Read

Be sure students understand that 1 billion is 1,000 times larger than 1 million. Then ask them what the author means by "long chains" and "very long" DNA molecules. (The chains are slender and look long compared with the nucleus of the cell. In reality, they are microscopic.)

Ask students to explain how the analogy of the book helps them understand the enormous amount of complex information stored on each chromosome. Remind them that each chromosome carries the same genetic information.

Talk about the NoteZone question with the class. Use students' questions to spark discussion about the genome.

Explore

MAKE COMPARISONS DNA is a very long molecule that carries the information needed to produce an organism and keep it functioning. All the information makes up the organism's genome. The information is organized into genes, which code for (give instructions for) individual physical characteristics, or traits. Genes are gathered together on chromosomes. Science writer Matt Ridley compared this information to a book.

► *In what ways is the human genome like a book? In what ways is it different?*

Both store large amounts of information. The book is printed on paper and is big, while the genome is a series of DNA molecules and is microscopic. A book is easy to see and read but a genome is not.

► *If your genome were compared to a cookbook, what "recipes" would it include?*

"recipes" for my hair color, my body shape, the color of my eyes and skin, and so on

Take Action

USE ANALOGIES Matt Ridley used a book as an analogy for the human genome. An analogy uses an everyday, familiar example to help explain a more complex and less familiar topic. One example of an analogy is *The circulatory system is like a network of major highways, main roads, and small streets.* Create your own analogy to explain a complex science process or structure. Write your analogy below.

Analogies will vary. Example: Cell division is like a square dance.

53

(continued from page 52)

READER'S HANDBOOK

Analogies 586, 636

WRITE SOURCE 2000

Analogy 138
Metaphor 139
Simile 140

SCI LINKS. THE WORLD'S A CLICK AWAY

www.scilinks.org
Keyword: DNA
Code: GSLD09

Assessment

Skill: Organizing information

Use the following task to assess each student's progress:

Write the following terms on the board in this order: *DNA molecules, chromosomes, human genome, physical traits, genes.* Have each student draw a simple flowchart to show how the terms are related, beginning with the largest category and continuing to the smallest. *(human genome → chromosomes → genes → DNA molecules → physical traits)*

Explore

MAKE COMPARISONS Students should understand that the genome is "read" by the body in ways that do not require thinking. Discuss the idea of variation. Ask: *Why do you think there are so many genes? How does the large number of genes allow for so many differences in people's looks and personalities?* (Human genetics is complex because combinations of genes determine almost all of our traits.)

Take Action

USE ANALOGIES Write the following on the board: *school lunchroom, basketball game,* and *taking a test.* Ask students to think of analogies that describe these events or processes. Then ask them to explain how their Take Action analogies represent scientific processes or structures. Invite other students to comment on how each analogy makes it easier for them to understand the scientific concept being described.

CHECK UNDERSTANDING

Skill: Making and using models

Have each student create a table of contents for his or her own "Book of Life." Tell students to write the titles and summaries for several chapters that explain which genetic traits they inherited from a parent or a grandparent. For example, a student might invent the chapter title "Running" and write as a summary: "I have long legs like my dad, and when I run I look exactly like him."

Point of Lesson
Gregor Mendel investigated inherited traits in pea plants.

Focus
- Systems, order, and organization
- Reproduction and heredity
- Structure and function in living systems
- Diversity and adaptation of organisms

Skills and Strategies
- Observing
- Comparing and contrasting
- Interpreting data
- Generating ideas

Advance Preparation

Vocabulary
Make sure students understand these terms. Definitions can be found in the glossary at the end of the student book.
- gene
- ovary
- species
- trait

Materials
Gather the materials needed for *Before You Read* (p. 54), *Enrichment* (p. 55), and *Assessment* (p. 57).

IN-GENE-IUS!

How can garden peas help explain why a father and daughter both have red hair and freckles?

Gregor Mendel was a monk who lived in Austria in the mid-1800s. Mendel spent most of his time in the monastery garden, tending to the pea plants he grew there. He was interested in different physical traits of the plants. For example, he studied how tall they were, what their seeds looked like, and what color flowers they produced. In particular, Mendel was interested in how these traits were inherited, or passed from one generation of plants to the next. Did all pea plants look exactly like their parents? To find out, Mendel conducted experiments over many years.

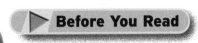

Before You Read

MAKE COMPARISONS Examine two or more plants that are the same species. Are the plants identical in every way? Look for differences in color, shape, and size of leaves or flowers, and so on. What do you notice?
- ***Sketch the plants in the box below. Label any differences you found.***

While members of the same species generally resemble one another, many small differences should be discernable.

TEACHING PLAN pp. 54–55

INTRODUCING THE LESSON
In this lesson, students explore inherited traits through Gregor Mendel's discoveries with pea plants. Discuss differences in family traits. Have students describe people who have the same biological parents but look very different from one another. Ask students how they think this phenomenon happens.

Ask students what they know about reproduction in plants. Students will probably suggest that plants reproduce by seeds, but they may not realize that plants reproduce through sexual reproduction. Explain that in plants with cones or flowers, both female and male reproductive organs are needed in order to produce seeds. Students need to know this information for later reference in this lesson when they read about "crossing" plants.

Before You Read

Time: 40 minutes
Materials: (for each group) two or more plants of the same species

MAKE COMPARISONS Give small groups of students two or more plants of the same species, and ask them to sketch what they see. Suggest that students sketch parts of the plants, such as the leaves or stems, as well as making a smaller sketch of the entire plant. Encourage students to talk about their observations as they draw. Explain that scientific drawings must be clear and accurate. Students who are not skilled at sketching can use extra labels to explain what they have observed. Allow students time to share their drawings. Discuss the differences that the groups observed.

Read

Scientific breakthroughs require a lot of hard work. Mendel spent many long hours working in his "garden laboratory."

In the Garden

In a corner of the monastery garden, Mendel huddled...over rows of greening [pea] plants. These were functional little vegetable plants, but they held a strange beauty. Climbing along sticks and strings, they twirled and twisted gracefully as they arched toward the...sunshine....

As he moved from one row of pea plants to another, Mendel carefully lifted the leaves away from the slim stalks, pulling at the flowers hidden beneath like coy little butterflies. The leaves were smooth ovals, [reminding him] of cupped hands enclosing something precious; as they gradually unfurled, they revealed a flower, either white or a variation of purple, shaped like a tiny bonnet. These flowers, like those of most plants, were the plant's ovaries. Over time the petals faded and the calyx toughened and elongated, becoming the long, leathery pea pods we recognize easily. Within each pod were six or seven peas, the offspring of the plants on which they grew....

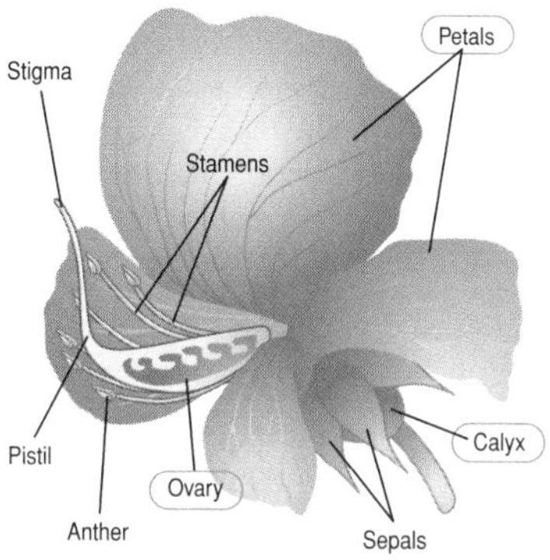

▲ **Pea plant flower**

monastery: the building where a community of monks live
coy: shy
unfurled: opened up
ovaries: the female reproductive parts of plants that produce seeds
calyx: the outermost ring of petals on a flower
offspring: the young of an organism

From: Henig, Robin Marantz. *The Monk in the Garden.* Houghton Mifflin.

NOTEZONE

Study the diagram of a pea plant flower. On the diagram, circle the names of the flower parts that are mentioned in the reading. Where do the peas form?

in the ovary

FIND OUT MORE

SCIENCESAURUS

Sexual Reproduction 114
Genes 116
Heredity 121
Dominant and Recessive Alleles 122

SCILINKS. THE WORLD'S A CLICK AWAY

www.scilinks.org
Keyword: Mendelian Genetics
Code: GSLD08

55

Enrichment

Time: 30 minutes
Materials: flowers and leaves from a home garden or a florist

Ask students to bring in flowers or, if it is not flowering season, leaves from home gardens. Bring in some varieties of flowers or leaves from a florist as well. (Be sure that plants from the florist have not been dyed.) Have students organize the flowers and/or leaves into groups that look like they are related. Then ask students to list characteristics they think are controlled by genetics. For example, students might list the number of petals and number of parts inside a flower as well as the shape, size, and color of the plant parts. Then talk with students about the variety of plants overall and the variety within groups that look alike or nearly alike. Relate this information to what students learned about Gregor Mendel. Ask students what their observations tell them about the variety of genetic traits.

Read

As students begin the NoteZone activity, ask: *When you look at the diagram at the bottom of the page, can you imagine how the calyx will change to a pea pod?* Have students describe this process in their own words.

After students complete the NoteZone activity, ask them to relate this new information to their observations of the classroom plants in Before You Read. Explain that the process described in the reading is similar to the process in all flowering plants. Encourage students to use a magnifier to study any flowers on the plants. Discuss their observations.

Finally, ask students what the author meant by calling the garden a "garden laboratory." (Mendel's studies and experiments took place in his garden.)

CHECK UNDERSTANDING
Skill: Drawing conclusions
Ask: *Why did Mendel investigate pea plants? What was he trying to find out?* (He wanted to find out how the plants' traits were passed down from one generation to the next.)

More Resources

The following resources are also available from Great Source and NSTA.

SCIENCESAURUS
Sexual Reproduction 114
Genes 116
Heredity 121
Dominant and Recessive Alleles 122

READER'S HANDBOOK
Elements of Textbooks: Charts 157
Examining Figurative Language 426
How to Read a Diagram 602

WRITE SOURCE 2000
Metaphor 139
Simile 140

MATH ON CALL
Ratio 424

SCI LINKS. THE WORLD'S A CLICK AWAY
www.scilinks.org
Keyword: Mendelian Genetics
Code: GSLD08

Explore

ANALYZE DATA Mendel crossed pairs of pea plants to see what their offspring would look like. One cross he did was between pea plants with purple flowers. Here are the results Mendel got when he crossed purple-flowered plants with each other.

MENDEL'S DATA: CROSSING PURPLE-FLOWERED PLANTS	
Flower Color of Offspring Plants	Number of Plants
Purple	705
White	224

▶ ***What is the ratio of purple to white flowers in the offspring plants? (In other words, about how many purple-flowered plants are there for every white-flowered plant?)***

3.15 : 1 or about 3 : 1

▶ ***Does anything about these results seem odd to you? If so, explain.***

Yes. Pairs of purple-flowered plants produced some white-flowered plants.

Mendel hypothesized that pea plants must receive one instruction for flower color from one parent and another instruction for flower color from the other parent. We now know that these instructions are genes. Each parent pea plant contains two genes for the trait of flower color. Each parent gives one gene for flower color to each of its offspring, so each offspring also has two genes for that trait.

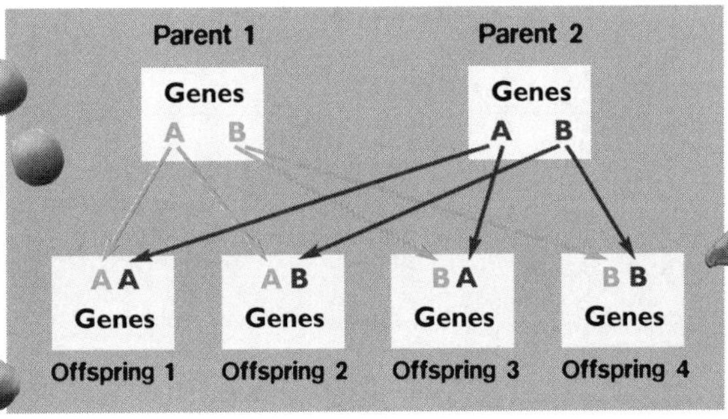

56

TEACHING PLAN pp. 56–57

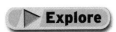

Explore

ANALYZE DATA Tell the class that the term "crossed" refers to the process of cross-fertilization. In nature, fertilization—the distribution of pollen from the male parts of a flower to the female parts of the same or another flower—is accomplished by birds, insects, bats, or wind. Mendel controlled his experiment by hand-pollinating his pea plants. He gathered pollen from the male part of one flower and placed it on another flower.

After students answer the second question, ask them to explain *why* it seems odd that purple-flowered plants produced white-flowered plants. (You'd expect the offspring of purple-flowered plants to be purple-flowered, too.)

Review the diagram with the class. Explain that A and B do not represent any particular trait. Ask volunteers to explain each of the combinations shown—for example, Offspring 1 gets gene A from Parent 1 and gene A from Parent 2. If students have difficulty following the diagram, let them work out the combinations using labeled squares of colored construction paper or colored toothpicks.

Propose Explanations

BLOOMING GENES Mendel noticed that even when a pea plant had parents with two different flower colors, only one color was seen in the offspring plant. Mendel concluded that the other gene must be in the parent plant but not be shown. The trait controlled by the hidden gene he called the *recessive trait.* The trait shown by the plant he called the *dominant trait.* Mendel reasoned that recessive traits weren't seen as often as dominant traits because a plant must have two genes for the recessive trait in order for the trait to show.

▸ ***Which flower color do you think is dominant in pea plants? Support your answer with evidence from the chart of Mendel's data.***

Purple must be the dominant color trait. There are about three times as many plants with purple flowers as there are plants with white flowers.

▸ ***How do you think plants with white flowers could have come from two parent plants with purple flowers?***

The purple-flowered parent plants must have carried recessive genes for white-flowered plants. White-flowered offspring plants must have received one gene for the recessive trait from each parent plant.

Take Action

USING FIGURES OF SPEECH Similes and metaphors are figures of speech used to explain how something acts or looks by comparing it to how something else unrelated to it acts or looks. A simile uses the word "like" or "as" to compare two things—for example, "a flower shaped like a tiny bonnet." A metaphor compares two things without using "like" or "as"—for example, "leathery pea pods."

▸ ***Circle the similes and metaphors in the reading. Then create your own similes or metaphors to describe a simple action you perform every day, such as brushing your teeth or taking out the trash. See how using similes and metaphors can make a description of an ordinary task more interesting.***

Similes and metaphors in the reading: "the flowers hidden beneath like coy little butterflies," "The leaves were smooth ovals, [reminding him] of cupped hands enclosing something precious," "a flower...shaped like a tiny bonnet," and "leathery pea pods." Students' similes and metaphors will vary.

57

Connections

SOCIAL STUDIES/LANGUAGE ARTS Show students a video or film on Gregor Mendel and his discoveries. Then students can share what they have learned by writing monologues from Mendel's point of view. Tell them to explain in their writing what Mendel was looking for, how he went about his research, and what he discovered. Invite volunteers to read their monologues to the class.

Assessment

Skill: Interpreting scientific illustrations

Time: 15 minutes
Materials: Patterns of Inheritance diagram (copymaster page 227); purple and yellow pencils or markers

Use the following task to assess each student's progress:

Give each student a copy of the diagram. Tell students to color-code the diagram to explain Mendel's results, indicating the flower colors and the dominant and recessive traits in the two parent plants and in the offspring. Tell them to decide which form of the gene is dominant and label it on the diagram. Tell students to use yellow to represent white. (Students' diagrams should show that three of the four offspring have the dominant color trait and one has the recessive trait.)

Propose Explanations

BLOOMING GENES Explain to the class that the diagram on page 56 is a simplified version of what actually happens. Most traits are determined by a combination of genes, not just two forms of one gene.

If students have difficulty answering the two questions in this section, let them use colored paper squares or toothpicks to work out the gene combinations, as suggested for Explore.

Take Action

USING FIGURES OF SPEECH You may want to review figures of speech in *Reader's Handbook*. Give students several examples before they begin circling similes and metaphors. After students have written their descriptions, ask if the writing helped them understand the process more clearly themselves. Then invite students to share and talk about their metaphors and similes.

Point of Lesson

Selective breeding produces organisms with desirable traits.

Focus

- Systems, order, and organization
- Structure and function in living systems
- Reproduction and heredity
- Diversity and adaptations of organisms

Skills and Strategies

- Recognizing cause and effect
- Generating ideas
- Predicting

Advance Preparation

Vocabulary

Make sure students understand these terms. Definitions can be found in the glossary at the end of the student book.

- gene
- seed
- species
- trait

Materials

Gather the materials needed for ***Before You Read*** (p. 58), ***Read*** (p. 59), ***Explore*** (p. 60), ***Connections*** (p. 60), and ***Take Action*** (p. 61).

How Genes Work

CUSTOM CORN

Can a working knowledge of genes help us create a "super vegetable"? It already has.

A tiny potato would be hard to make into a pile of French fries. But what if you crossed two parent plants that produce big potatoes, and then took the offspring with the biggest potatoes and crossed them with other plants that produce big potatoes, and so on for several generations? What kind of potato plant would you get?

Before You Read

THINK ABOUT SEEDS Most plants produce seeds that grow to become new plants. In nature, this happens when the seeds fall from the parent plant and take root in the soil. Gardeners often collect seeds from one year's harvest and plant them the following spring to produce new plants.

► ***If you wanted to get seeds from a certain kind of garden plant, which parts of the mature plant would you collect? Describe where you think the seeds are found in the following fruit and vegetable plants.***

Fruit or Vegetable Plant	Location of Seeds
Tomato plant	*inside tomato*
Corn stalk	*on cob*
Cucumber vine	*inside cucumber*
Pea plant	*inside pea pods*
Apple tree	*in apple core*

TEACHING PLAN pp. 58–59

INTRODUCING THE LESSON

This lesson describes how an understanding of inheritance can be used as the basis for selective breeding. Talk with the class about the variety of fruits and vegetables available in the United States. Have students identify several different varieties of apples. Ask them to use what they learned about genes and inheritance to explain how the varieties could have been developed.

Students may think that controlling the traits of edible plants is a very recent development. Explain that people have been changing the traits of fruits and vegetables for a very long time. For example, the large baking potato, called the Idaho potato, was developed by horticulturist Luther Burbank over 100 years ago.

Before You Read

Time: 20–30 minutes (if optional materials are used)
Materials: fruits and vegetables containing seeds (optional)

THINK ABOUT SEEDS Students should be familiar with seeds from their elementary science experiences. Remind them that a seed contains the embryo of a new plant. In other words, seeds carry the genetic information needed to grow the next generation of plants.

You may want to bring in examples of fruits and vegetables so students can observe the location, size, and shape of the seeds. Ask students to bring in examples as well.

Read

When you butter up that big ear of summer corn, you can thank ancient Native Americans.

How People Changed Corn

Did you know that the first cobs of corn weren't that long...? In fact, scientists have found five-thousand-year-old corncobs that are less than one inch long!

What changed corn? People did.

Native Americans first began growing corn about seven thousand years ago in what is now New Mexico. Soon they noticed many differences between different cobs of corn....

The Native Americans made great use of the differences they observed. In particular, they made use of the differences in length. They found that when they used only longer cobs as parents, the offspring corn tended to be longer. If they were careful to use only the longest cobs as parents generation after generation, the corn got longer and longer. They were changing the species of corn itself!

Now, centuries later, the average cob of corn is ten times longer than its ancient ancestor. Thanks to centuries of this process, you can butter and salt a long cob of corn!

generation: one set of offspring
century: 100 years
ancient: very old
ancestor: a related organism in the past

From: Aronson, Billy. *They Came From DNA.* Henry Holt and Company.

NoteZone

Corn plants produce seeds every year. How many generations of corn have been grown since Native Americans first began growing corn?

about 7,000 generations

FIND OUT MORE

SCIENCESAURUS

Genes 116
Heredity 121
Dominant and Recessive Alleles 122

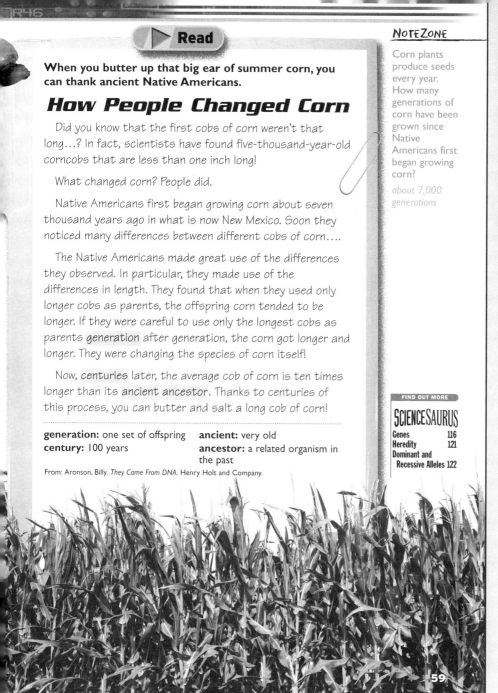

Enrichment

Ask students to develop a new breed of animal. Tell them that the breed will take four or five generations to develop, so there can be several chances to breed for specific traits. Ask students to write several sentences that describe their choices of parents and the traits they hope to produce reliably in the following generations. Ask what recessive or undesirable traits they would like to eliminate from the breed.

Read

Time: 5 minutes
Materials: cob of blue corn

Show students an example of blue corn and explain that it is similar to native corn. Explain that Native Americans were using a technique called *selective breeding* to create a type of corn that had the characteristics they desired.

After students complete the NoteZone activity, point out that this kind of selective breeding can take a very long time. Ask: *Can you think of any way that scientists might speed up this process?* (They could use artificial light and hand-pollinate to make plants produce more than one generation every year.)

Discuss the author's comment that the Native Americans were "changing the species of corn." Emphasize that corn with naturally short cobs is genetically different from corn with naturally long cobs.

CHECK UNDERSTANDING
Skill: Drawing conclusions
Ask students: *How are plants able to pass on their traits?* (The genetic information is located in a plant's seeds. When new plants sprout from the seeds, the offspring have the parent plant's traits.)

More Resources

The following resources are also available from Great Source.

SCIENCESAURUS

Genes 116
Heredity 121
Dominant and Recessive Alleles 122

READER'S HANDBOOK

Elements of Textbooks: Charts 157

WRITE SOURCE 2000

Brainstorming for Ideas 10

Connections

Time: 40–45 minutes
Materials: seed catalogs that advertise both conventional and heirloom varieties of fruits and vegetables (available from the companies "Seeds of Change" and "Burpee Seed Company" on the Internet or at a local nursery)

SOCIAL STUDIES Invite small groups to read about varieties of corn, tomatoes, or other fruits and vegetables and to make a list of the various characteristics listed in the catalogs. Then have students explain to the class what characteristics are valued in different varieties of these crops and why.

Explore

THINK ABOUT IT Members of a species share most of their physical traits—but not all of them. There is natural variety among individuals. For example, all humans share a basic body plan, but individuals have different hair and skin colors, heights, facial features, and other physical traits. These differences make each of us unique.

► ***What variation between corn plants did the Native Americans find?***

the lengths of their cobs

► ***How did the Native Americans use this variation to change the corn?***

They selected parent plants with longer cobs and crossed the plants to produce offspring with longer cobs.

► ***Think back to the discoveries Mendel made in his garden. How did the Native Americans use the natural laws of inheritance that Mendel later discovered in his experiments?***

Like the genes for flower color, the genes for cob length are passed from parent to offspring. By selecting long-cobbed parents generation after generation, Native Americans produced corn plants with longer and longer cobs.

Propose Explanations

GENERATE IDEAS

► ***Could even longer cobs be produced? How would you do it?***

Yes. You could repeatedly select the parent plants with the longest cobs and cross them.

TEACHING PLAN pp. 60–61

Explore

Time: 15 minutes
Materials: different varieties of corn (on the cob)

THINK ABOUT IT Explain that all cultivated corn—known as *Zea mays Linnaeus* to scientists and as "maize" throughout most of the world—is the same species and is a member of the grass family. Within this species there are many kinds of corn. If possible, bring in varieties of corn, and invite students to examine them to observe variations in color and texture. If students have eaten any of the varieties, they can describe differences in taste as well. After students answer the questions in this section, ask which corn varieties they would want to breed selectively because of their desirable characteristics.

Be sure students understand that Native Americans followed the same process as Mendel. When they planted seeds from the longest cobs, these seeds grew into new plants. The new plants cross-pollinated naturally in the field and produced a new generation of corn plants with slightly longer cobs. Over many generations, the cobs got larger until they were the size they are today.

Propose Explanations

GENERATE IDEAS Students should understand that plants with long cobs carry the genetic traits for long cobs, so when seeds from only the longest cobs were used, the following generations developed increasingly longer cobs. Although you could keep producing longer cobs with this process, it might take a very long time to make a measurable difference. The plant would probably not support a 1-meter long cob, although it is possible the stalk would strengthen as the plant changed.

▶ ***Do you think it would be possible to produce plants with cobs that were 1 meter long and had a mass of 20 kilograms? Why or why not?***

Probably not. The cobs would be too heavy for the plant to support, so they would bend and break the plant. It may be possible if the stalks also increased in size.

CONSIDER THE BENEFITS

▶ ***Why do you think Native Americans put time and effort into developing corn plants that produced longer cobs? What advantage would longer cobs give the Native Americans?***

Longer cobs would produce more food with less effort.

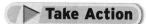

Take Action

DO RESEARCH Vegetables are not the only living things that can be changed by people. All the dogs we see today are actually members of the same species. Different breeds were produced by crossing parents with desirable traits.

▶ ***What is your favorite dog breed? Do some research to find out what traits your favorite breed was bred to have. Why were these traits desirable to the breeder? What task was the dog bred to do? How long has this dog been recognized as a breed?***

Answers will vary.

61

Assessment

Skill: Generating ideas

Use the following task to assess each student's progress:

Ask students to choose one fruit or vegetable they like. Have them describe its characteristics and explain which traits they would selectively breed for if they were farmers who wanted to improve the crop. (Answers will vary. For example, students may choose to plant the seeds of the biggest, sweetest, pinkest grapefruit and allow or help those plants cross-pollinate, then harvest the fruit and repeat the process.)

CONSIDER THE BENEFITS Ask students: *Considering the total length of time the Native Americans put into developing corn, what does this tell you about corn's importance to Native American culture?* (Example: Corn must have played a key role in the diet of Native Americans or in their ceremonies.)

Take Action

Time: will vary
Materials: research sources about breeds of dogs

DO RESEARCH Help students find library books and Internet sites that provide information on breeds of dogs. Provide an opportunity for students to share their research. When students have finished writing, you could have them present oral reports, or you could assemble the reports in a class binder so all students can read them. Talk with students about breeds that have developed undesirable genetic traits (such as weak hips and other medical conditions) as well as desirable traits.

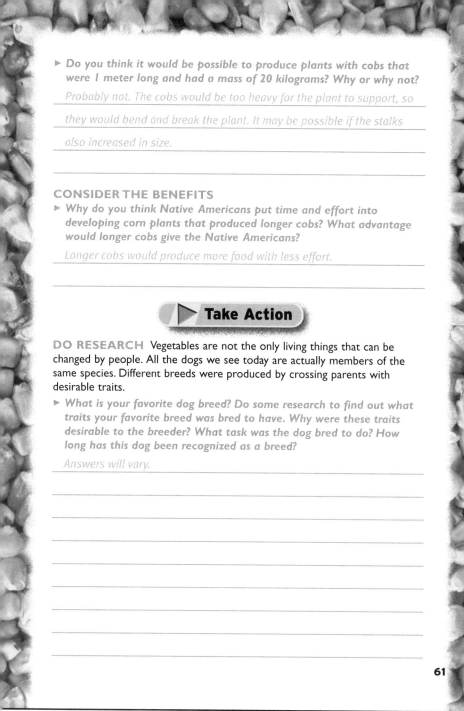

CHAPTER 6
Overview

Genes and People

LESSON 16

Single-Gene Human Traits

Point of Lesson: ***Some human physical traits are controlled by a single gene.***

Students learn that some traits are controlled by only one gene and that the gene's appearance in a human depends on the inheritance of its dominant or recessive form. Students identify their own traits and determine which gene combination they may have for each trait. They then evaluate the traits of an imaginary student and identify her biological parents from a profile of their traits.

Materials
none

LESSON 17

The Blue People of Kentucky

Point of Lesson: ***Blue-tinged skin is caused by the recessive form of a gene.***

Students evaluate a case study of a Caucasian family that carries a recessive trait, blue-tinged skin, caused by a rare hereditary blood disorder. Using a family tree, students trace the inheritance of the trait through six generations and determine whether men or women or both can be carriers of the gene. Students use their knowledge of inheritance to explain why one child exhibited the blue-tinged skin trait even though his parents did not. Students then apply this knowledge to explain how another recessive trait, sickle-cell anemia, can be passed along by parents who do not have the disease themselves.

Materials
Enrichment (p. 65), for the class:
- research sources about hereditary genetic disorders

LESSON 18

More Than Just Genes

Point of Lesson: ***Genes alone do not determine all of a person's characteristics.***

Students explore the role of environment in shaping an individual. Through consideration of various physical and nonphysical characteristics, they discover that although genetic inheritance may control some characteristics, it is the interaction between genetics, the environment, and the choices people make that determine who they become, physically and intellectually.

Materials
Connections (p. 70), for the class:
- research sources about DNA "fingerprinting"

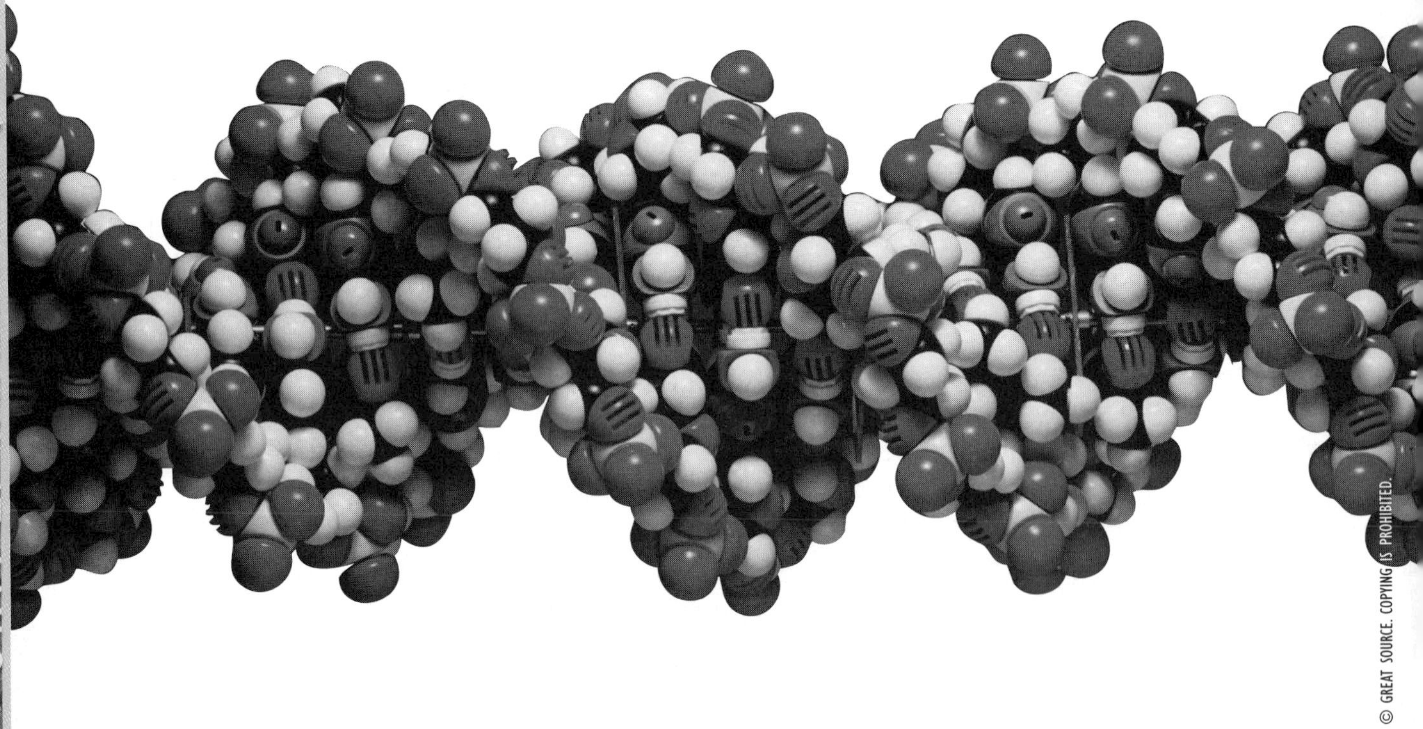

Background Information

Lesson 17

As noted in the reading, the blue people of Kentucky do not inherit a pigment for blue skin; they inherit a condition that causes their normally pink (white) skin to appear blue. The condition, methemoglobinemia, was diagnosed by a hematologist named Madison Cawein. He took blood from members of the family who had blue-tinged skin to try to determine the cause.

Methemoglobinemia can be caused by abnormal hemoglobin formation, an enzyme deficiency, or by taking too much of certain drugs, including vitamin K. The tests for abnormal hemoglobin came back negative. Then the doctor found an earlier report that described hereditary methemoglobinemia among Alaskan Eskimos and Native Americans. In this case, the condition was caused by a deficiency of the enzyme diaphorase. Blood tests confirmed that the cases in Kentucky were also caused by enzyme deficiency.

Lesson 18

The Minnesota Twin Family Study was established to investigate whether traits are determined by genes, by environment, or by a combination of factors. Because identical twins share 100 percent of their genes, any differences between them are thought to be due to environment, while their similarities are thought to be due to genes.

Scientists investigated whether identical twins raised together have more similarities than identical twins separated at birth and raised separately. Initial findings show that identical twins raised together were about 50 percent similar in personality assessments, and identical twins raised apart were also about 50 percent similar. Scientists concluded that environmental factors play a role in the development of personality and other psychological traits.

Point of Lesson

Some human physical traits are controlled by a single gene.

Focus

- Evidence, models, and explanation
- Reproduction and heredity

Skills and Strategies

- Collecting and recording data
- Interpreting data
- Drawing conclusions

Advance Preparation

Vocabulary

Make sure students understand these terms. Definitions can be found in the glossary at the end of the student book.

- gene
- trait

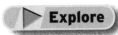

Single-Gene Human Traits

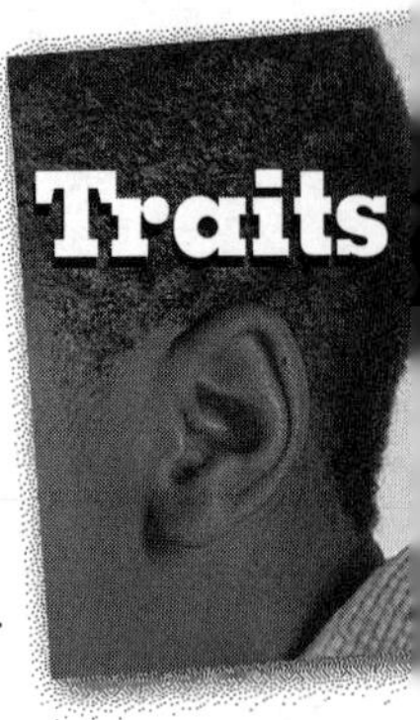

Are your earlobes loose from the side of your head? If they are, then your earlobes show a dominant trait.

Most human traits are determined by a combination of several genes. This makes trying to figure out which gene controls which trait very complicated! But a few human traits are determined by a single gene.

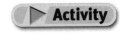

Explore

GENE COMBINATIONS Since everybody has two biological parents, everybody has two sets of genes—one set from the mother and another set from the father. Each gene in one set pairs up with one gene in the other set. Both genes in each pair control the same trait. But the two genes in the pair might be different forms. For example, one gene in the pair might code for detached earlobes, and the other gene might code for attached earlobes. Or both genes might code for detached earlobes, or both for attached earlobes.

- ***Can a person have more than two genes for a single trait? Explain.***

  No. For any trait, the person receives only one gene from one parent and one gene from the other parent.

One form of the two genes in a pair might override the other form of the gene. The form that shows up in the person is called the *dominant* form of the gene. The form that shows up only when a dominant form is not present is called the *recessive* form. Detached earlobes are produced by the dominant form of the gene. Attached earlobes are produced by the recessive form of the gene.

- ***What are the possible combinations of dominant and recessive forms of a gene?***

  dominant/dominant, dominant/recessive, recessive/recessive

- ***Which of these combinations would show the dominant trait? Which would show the recessive trait?***

  Both dominant/dominant and dominant/recessive would show the dominant trait. Recessive/recessive would show the recessive trait.

TEACHING PLAN pp. 62–63

INTRODUCING THE LESSON

This lesson gives students an opportunity to determine whether they have the dominant or recessive form of several single-gene traits.

To determine whether students know that a trait may be present in an offspring even when the mother and father do not show that trait, ask: *Would it be possible for a father with brown hair and a mother with brown hair to have a child with red hair?* (yes) *How could that happen?* (Students may not be able to explain this in terms of dominant and recessive forms of a gene, but they will most likely be able to reason that a grandmother, grandfather, or other close relative must have had red hair.) If students think that two brown-haired parents could not have a red-haired child, tell them to remember their answer and think about it again when they have completed this lesson and the next.

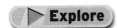

Explore

GENE COMBINATIONS Tell students that very few human traits are determined by just one pair of genes. Emphasize that the questions in this section refer to single-gene traits that follow this simple model. You may also want to tell students that the different forms of a gene are called *alleles*.

Activity

Time: 10–15 minutes

- Have each student work with a partner.
- Tell students that the bent little finger trait is easier to see if they hold their three middle fingers down with the thumb.
- To clarify the description of the bent thumb trait, show students how large a 60° angle is in comparison with a 90° angle.

Activity

STATE YOUR TRAIT The chart below lists human traits that are determined by a single gene. Do you show the dominant or recessive form of each trait? Fill in the boxes to show which form you have. In the last column, write the gene combination you might have for each trait.

Trait	Description	Dominant or Recessive	Do I have this trait?	Possible Gene Combination
Detached earlobes	Earlobes hang free from the side of the jaw.	dominant		
Curved little finger	When hand is flat on table, the little finger curves toward other fingers.	dominant		
Thumb on top	When hands are clasped with fingers interlaced, the left thumb is on top.	dominant		
Bent thumb	The end segment of the thumb can be bent back more than 60 degrees.	recessive		
Dimpled chin	The middle of the chin has a dimple or cleft.	dominant		

Take Action

MATCHING TRAITS A girl named Jeanie Trate has a straight little finger, detached earlobes, and a dimpled chin. The chart below lists the gene forms that each possible parent has. Select which mother and father are Jeanie's parents. Explain your answer.

Mother A		Mother B		Father A		Father B	
Curved little finger	Curved little finger	Curved little finger	Straight little finger	Straight little finger	Straight little finger	Curved little finger	Straight little finger
Detached earlobes	Attached earlobes	Attached earlobes	Attached earlobes	Detached earlobes	Attached earlobes	Attached earlobes	Attached earlobes
Dimpled chin	Dimpled chin	Dimpled chin	Undimpled chin	Undimpled chin	Undimpled chin	Dimpled chin	Dimpled chin

Mother B and Father A are the parents. Jeanie has a straight little finger (recessive), so each parent must carry at least one gene for it. Detached earlobes is dominant, so at least one parent must carry at least one gene for it. A dimpled chin is dominant, so at least one parent must carry at least one gene for it.

FIND OUT MORE

SCIENCESAURUS

Genes 116
Heredity 121
Dominant and Recessive Alleles 122

More Resources

The following resources are also available from Great Source.

ScienceSaurus

Genes 116
Heredity 121
Dominant and Recessive Alleles 122

Math on Call

Angles: Measuring Angles 330
Probability and Odds: Combinations 460

Reader's Handbook

Elements of Graphics: Table 559

Assessment

Skill: Predicting

Use the following questions to assess each student's progress.

Call students' attention to the Take Action chart. Ask: *Suppose Mother B were paired with Father B. What possible traits would Jeanie have?* (She would have either a curved or straight little finger, attached earlobes, and a dimpled chin.) *What if Mother A and Father A were paired?* (She would have a curved little finger, either detached or attached earlobes, and a dimpled chin.)

Take Action

MATCHING TRAITS On the board, list the possible gene combinations for each trait Jeanie shows. Let students select a pair for each trait, then ask volunteers to explain their choices.

Since Jeanie has a straight little finger (recessive), either Father A or B could be her parent. However, only Mother B could pass on to her the matching form of the gene for this recessive trait. Jeanie also has detached earlobes (dominant), so she needs only one parent to pass on that form of the gene for the trait. Only Father A has the dominant form of the gene for detached earlobes. Thus, Mother B and Father A must be Jeanie's parents.

CHECK UNDERSTANDING

Skill: Recognizing cause and effect

Tell students that the ability to roll your tongue is the dominant form of a single-gene trait. Ask: *If you cannot roll your tongue, could either of your parents have the trait? Explain.* (Yes. Both parents must have one dominant form and one recessive form of the gene. You could inherit a recessive form from each parent.)

Point of Lesson

Blue-tinged skin is caused by the recessive form of a gene.

Focus

- Evidence, models, and explanation
- Reproduction and heredity
- Personal health

Skills and Strategies

- Recognizing cause and effect
- Drawing conclusions
- Interpreting scientific illustrations

Advance Preparation

Vocabulary

Make sure students understand these terms. Definitions can be found in the glossary at the end of the student book.

- dominant
- gene
- recessive
- trait

Materials

Gather the materials needed for *Enrichment* (p. 65).

The Blue People of Kentucky

Some people inherit blue eyes from their parents. But a group of people in Kentucky inherit blue skin.

A recessive trait can lie hidden in a family's genes for generations before it shows up again. That's because each offspring has to receive the recessive gene from both parents, not just one. Blue-tinged skin is one such recessive trait. It is found among a group of people living in eastern Kentucky. Because the group is relatively small, recessive forms of genes are often paired, and the trait shows up frequently.

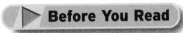

Before You Read

WHO AM I? Take a look at your classmates. Does anyone look just like you? No—unless your identical twin is in your class! Does anyone share something in common with you? Well, yes—most have the same basic body features. But does everyone have hair just like yours? What about the shape of your eyes?

- ***Why do you think people often look like other members of their family?***

Physical traits are passed from one generation to the next.

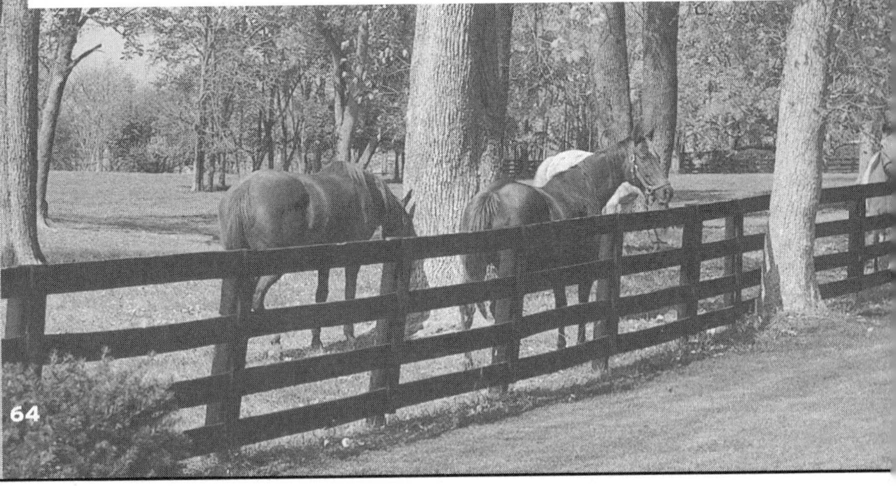

TEACHING PLAN pp. 64–65

INTRODUCING THE LESSON

This lesson uses an unusual family trait to illustrate the inheritance of dominant and recessive forms of a gene.

To find out what students know about genes, ask: *If dominant traits override recessive traits, why do recessive traits pop up in later generations of offspring?* (The recessive form of the gene is hidden in the person who shows the dominant trait but can be passed to the next generation.)

Students may think that every human trait is controlled by only one pair of gene forms. Explain that in humans, very few traits are single-gene traits. The traits discussed in the previous lesson and the trait discussed in this lesson are exceptions, not the rule.

Before You Read

WHO AM I? Ask students: *What makes each of us unique?* Student answers should reflect the idea that except for identical twins, each of us has a unique combination of physical traits that makes us different from any other person, yet we may also resemble our parents, siblings, or other close family members. We look like our family members because we inherited a set of "blueprints" for traits in the form of genes from each parent.

Read

Traits make their way through generations as they are passed from parents to offspring.

THE BLUE PEOPLE

Six generations after a French orphan named Martin Fugate settled on the banks of eastern Kentucky's Troublesome Creek with his redheaded American bride, his great-great-great great grandson [Ben Stacy] was born in a modern hospital not far from where the creek still runs.

The boy inherited his father's lankiness and his mother's slightly nasal way of speaking. What he got from Martin Fugate was dark blue skin. "It was almost purple," his father recalls.

Ben lost his blue tint within a few weeks, and now he is about as normal looking a seven-year-old boy as you could hope to find. His lips and fingernails still turn a shade of purple-blue when he gets cold or angry.

▲Martin and Elizabeth Fugate

After ruling out heart and lung diseases, the doctor suspected methemoglobinemia, a rare hereditary blood disorder.... [The doctor] also concluded that the condition was inherited as a simple recessive trait. In other words, to get the disorder, a person would have to inherit two genes for it, one from each parent. Somebody with only one gene would not have the condition but could pass the gene to a child.

lankiness: being tall and thin
nasal: related to the nose

From: Trost, Cathy. "The Blue People of Troublesome Creek." *Science 82.*

NOTEZONE

How could Benjy Stacy have blue skin?

Both parents must have carried the gene form for blue skin.

FIND OUT MORE

SCIENCESAURUS
Genes 116
Heredity 121
Dominant and Recessive Alleles 122

SCILINKS. THE WORLD'S A CLICK AWAY
www.scilinks.org
Keyword: Genes and Traits
Code: GSLD10

65

Enrichment

Time: will vary
Materials: research sources about hereditary genetic disorders

Suggest that students research other hereditary genetic disorders, such as cystic fibrosis, hemophilia, Tay-Sachs disease, and certain types of deafness and dwarfism. Tell them to focus on the impact of genetic disorders in real-life situations, treatments, support groups, and high-risk populations as well as data about the inheritance patterns of the disease. Students could share their findings by preparing educational pamphlets on the disorders they researched.

Read

Emphasize that the family members' blue skin is merely tinged pale blue, not a deep blue like Smurf dolls. Point out that it is not a gene for blue skin tone that is being passed down. Rather, as pointed out in the reading, the blue skin tone is a result of a hereditary blood disorder called methemoglobinemia. The gene for this disorder has been passed down through the Fugate family for more than 150 years.

CHECK UNDERSTANDING
Skill: Recognizing cause and effect

Ask: *Why does blue-tinged skin show up so frequently in the Fugate family?* (The group of people in the area is small, so recessive forms of genes pair up more frequently than they would if the population were large.)

More Resources

The following resources are also available from Great Source and NSTA.

ScienceSaurus

Genes 116
Heredity 121
Dominant and Recessive Alleles 122

Reader's Handbook

Focus on Dialogue 360
Elements of Graphics: Diagram 552

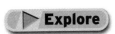

SciLinks
THE WORLD'S A CLICK AWAY

www.scilinks.org
Keyword: Genes and Traits
Code: GSLD10

Explore

INTERPRET A DIAGRAM A recessive trait shows up only when someone has two recessive forms of the gene. A person who has only one recessive form of the gene is a carrier of the recessive trait but does not show that trait.

The following diagram shows how the recessive trait that results in blue skin tone is passed down through generations in Troublesome Creek, Kentucky. The dominant gene is for white (non-blue) skin.

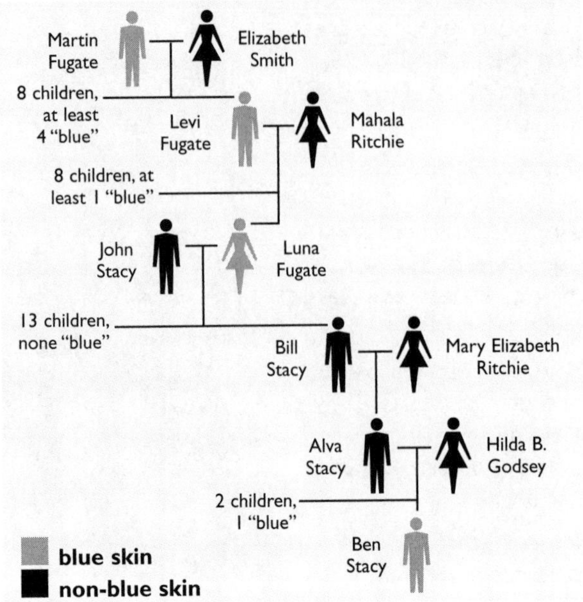

Use the diagram to answer the following questions.

- ***Can men carry the gene form for blue skin tone? Explain.***

Yes. Martin Fugate and Levi Fugate both had blue skin. John Stacy, Bill Stacy, and Alva Stacy must have been carriers because the trait showed up again in Ben Stacy.

- ***Can women carry the gene form for blue skin tone? Explain.***

Yes. Luna Fugate had blue skin. Elizabeth Smith, Mahala Ritchie, Mary Elizabeth Ritchie, and Hilda B. Godsey must have been carriers because the trait showed up again in Ben Stacy.

Teaching Plan pp. 66–67

Explore

INTERPRET A DIAGRAM Tell students that the diagram is a "family tree" showing the observable form and the carriers of the blue-skin disorder through five generations of offspring. Make sure students understand that the diagram should be read from top to bottom. Ben Stacy, the child described in the reading, is shown at the bottom. Also point out to students that the names Bill Stacy and Ben Stacy are similar, and they should be careful not to confuse them when they answer the questions on this page and the next.

To answer the questions in this section, students will need to find specific people on the diagram. Draw their attention to the diagram's key. Explain that they should use the key in order to understand the inheritance pattern.

Propose Explanations

THINK ABOUT IT

▸ *Why didn't Bill Stacy have blue skin even though his mother did?*

His father, John Stacy, didn't have it, so John must have had at least one dominant form of the gene, which he passed on to his son. Even though Bill's mother passed the recessive form of the gene on to him, he didn't have blue skin because the dominant form from his father overrode the recessive form from his mother.

▸ *How could Ben Stacy have had blue skin when neither of his parents did?*

Both his parents were carriers of the recessive gene form and passed it on to Ben, so he had two recessive forms.

▸ *Most people in the small Troublesome Creek community are carriers of the recessive blue-skin trait. They also tend to marry within their own community. How do these facts explain why blue-skinned children keep appearing in the population?*

In a small community of carriers whose members intermarry, there's a much higher chance that a child will inherit two recessive forms of the gene.

Take Action

WRITE A DIALOGUE Imagine that a husband and wife have just returned from being tested by a doctor, who discovered that they are both carriers of the recessive gene form for sickle-cell anemia. Sickle-cell anemia is a disease of the red blood cells. Instead of being round like normal blood cells, sickle cells are shaped like half-moons. These cells can get stuck in small blood vessels and cause dangerous swellings.

Although neither of the parents has sickle-cell anemia, the doctor explains that there's a one-in-four chance that any child of theirs would have the disease. The husband doesn't understand how his child could possibly inherit a life-threatening disease from him when he doesn't have the disease himself.

▸ *On a separate piece of paper, write a dialogue between the husband and wife in which the wife explains to her husband how recessive genes can be passed down by parents who are carriers.*

Students' dialogues will vary but should include information about carriers of recessive gene forms.

67

Assessment

Skill: Recognizing cause and effect

Use the following questions to assess each student's progress.

Which form of the blue-skin trait will appear if someone has a dominant and a recessive gene pair? (white or nonblue skin) *When does the recessive form appear?* (only when a person has inherited two recessive forms of the gene)

Propose Explanations

THINK ABOUT IT To answer the questions in this section, students will need to make inferences based on what they already know about dominant and recessive traits and what they have learned in this lesson about the Fugate family and the role of carriers of recessive traits. After students have written their responses, call on volunteers to read aloud their answers and explain their reasoning.

Explain to students that the custom of marrying within a small community was a common and accepted practice in nineteenth century America.

Take Action

WRITE A DIALOGUE Remind students to use quotation marks, a speech tag ("the husband said," for example), and a new paragraph each time a different speaker begins talking. Encourage students to do research about this genetic disorder so that they can include basic information on risk groups, treatment, and genetic screening methods. Direct interested students to the Sickle Cell Society Web site at www.sicklecellsociety.org/scsinfo.htm as a starting point for the research. Successful dialogues will show that students have integrated concepts about carriers of recessive traits and why observable forms of recessive traits keep recurring in the general population.

Point of Lesson

Genes alone do not determine all of a person's characteristics.

Focus

- Evidence, models, and explanation
- Reproduction and heredity
- Populations, resources, and environments
- Abilities necessary to do scientific inquiry

Skills and Strategies

- Comparing and contrasting
- Making inferences
- Generating ideas

Advance Preparation

Vocabulary

Make sure students understand these terms. Definitions can be found in the glossary at the end of the student book.

- cell
- DNA
- environment
- gene
- molecule
- trait

Materials

Gather the materials needed for *Connections* (p. 70).

MORE THAN JUST GENES

Is there more to us than long strings of DNA molecules? You bet!

Genes are made of DNA, and DNA provides the "recipe" for every cell in your body. So we are simply what our genes make us, right? Think again! Human beings are more than just what is spelled out by DNA. Many of our characteristics are not controlled by genes.

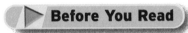

Before You Read

WHO ARE YOU? There are a lot of different ways to describe yourself. Some of these ways have to do with your personality and your likes and dislikes. Other ways have to do with what you look like and how your body functions.

► ***Write down ten words that describe you.***

Answers will vary.

▼ Model of a DNA molecule

TEACHING PLAN pp. 68–69

INTRODUCING THE LESSON

This lesson introduces the idea that human beings can vary a great deal within the basic body plan written in their genes.

Ask students what other factors besides genes help determine a person's characteristics. If they have difficulty answering the question, suggest that they consider the influences of personal health, education, experiences, and the society in which we live.

Some students might think that all of our physical traits—eye color, body shape, height, and so forth—are determined by our genes, while our behavior, skills, talents, and other nonphysical characteristics are not influenced by genes. Emphasize that each person's unique characteristics result from a *combination* of genetic and environmental influences.

Before You Read

WHO ARE YOU? Many variations in human characteristics are largely the result of life experiences and are not controlled by genes. Ask students to suggest physical traits in which human beings are alike and different. Also ask them to name skills, personality traits, or talents at which people excel, such as sports or drawing. Make a class list on the board to which students can refer as they compile their personal inventories.

Read

Genes direct part of the story of your life—but not the whole story.

Who We Are

"Creativity runs in the family." "I inherited this bad back." "All the women in my family live past 80." People often wonder how they acquire their traits, from talents to ailments. Genes we inherit from our parents do indeed guide how the body develops and functions. But where we live, what we do—our individual environment, starting in the womb—also plays a large role in determining the outcome.

Nutrition, exercise and education are some of the influences on our health and behavior. Identical twins, for example, share the same genes. But twins develop unique personalities, disabilities, skills, and sometimes looks based on environmental factors.

Researchers are now finding connections between genes and human characteristics ranging from athletic ability to aging. But for the most part, our genes are not our ultimate fate. Instead, we are a product of interactions between genes *and* our environment....

ailments: mild illnesses

womb: uterus; the female organ in which a baby develops

ultimate: final

From: "Our Genetic Identity." *The Genomic Revolution.* American Museum of Natural History. (www.amnh.org/exhibitions/genomics/1_identity/nature.html)

NOTEZONE

Circle the things in our environment that influence who we are.

FIND OUT MORE

SCIENCESAURUS

Genes	116
The Human Genome	117
Heredity	121

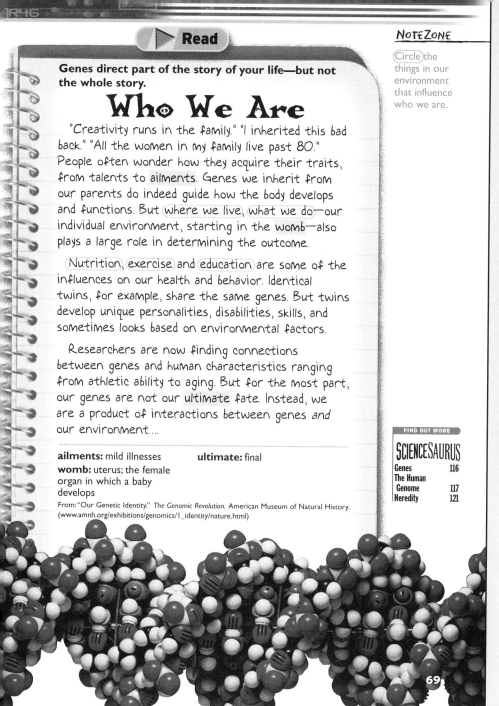

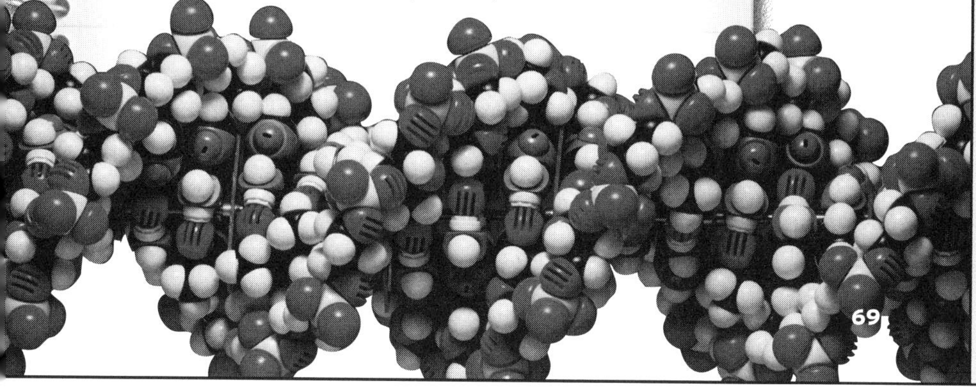

Enrichment

Time: 40–45 minutes

Divide the class in half. Call one of the groups *Heredity* and the other *Environment*. Tell students that the two groups will have a debate. The *Heredity* group must argue that human behavior is determined by genetic factors, while the *Environment* group must argue that human behavior is determined by environmental factors. Give both groups a few minutes to meet and brainstorm their arguments.

Have the *Heredity* group begin by describing a human trait that is controlled by genes. Next, ask the *Environment* group to respond by describing how the trait is influenced by the environment. Then the *Environment* group should describe a trait controlled by environmental factors, and the *Heredity* group must respond by explaining how the trait is influenced by genetic factors. Continue this way for several traits.

Read

You may want to explain that many studies of human variation have focused on identical twins. Since they started life as one cell, they share the same genes. Thus, any differences in their characteristics must be due to environmental influences.

Suggest that students take notes to summarize the main idea and the supporting details in the reading. You may want to tell them to add a statement explaining ways in which people are the products of interaction between their genes and their environment.

CHECK UNDERSTANDING

Skill: Recognizing cause and effect

Ask students to list aspects of athletic performance that might be influenced by *both* genes and the environment. (Examples: strength, endurance, speed, coordination)

More Resources

The following resources are also available from Great Source.

SCIENCESAURUS

Genes 116
The Human Genome 117
Heredity 121

READER'S HANDBOOK

Elements of Nonfiction:
Comparison and Contrast 278

Connections

Time: will vary
Materials: research sources about DNA "fingerprinting"

SOCIAL STUDIES/FORENSIC SCIENCE Students could research how forensic scientists use DNA "fingerprints," sequences in the genetic code that are unique to every person. DNA can be derived from saliva, blood, hair follicles, or bits of skin to link a suspect to the scene of a crime or to eliminate a suspect. Students might be particularly interested in recent cases of wrongly convicted people being released from prison as a result of DNA testing.

Explore

WHO'S IN CONTROL? In the previous lesson, you learned about some physical traits that are controlled by genes. What other physical traits do you think are controlled by your genes?

Answers will vary. Examples: height, body shape, skin color, hair color

You also learned that there is usually more than one gene involved in determining a physical trait. More than just genes are involved, too.

Look at the following table. The traits in the left column are controlled by your genes. The traits in the right column are controlled by more than just your genes.

Traits Controlled by Genes	Traits Controlled by More Than Genes
Hair color	Athletic ability
Eye color	Personality
Thickness of beard	Tendency to get sick
Shape of fingernails	Response to frustration

► ***What similarities are there among the traits in the left column? The traits in the right column?***

The traits in the left column can't be changed permanently. The traits in the right column can be influenced by a person's environment and experience.

► ***How might the traits in the right column be influenced by genes? How might they be influenced by a person's environment?***

Answers will vary. Example: Genes may give me good coordination, but athletic ability is also determined by things such as how often I practice and what my coach teaches me.

70

TEACHING PLAN pp. 70–71

Explore

WHO'S IN CONTROL? To identify additional physical characteristics that might be controlled by their genes, students could refer to the class list you compiled in Before you Read. Have students examine the table, then ask: *Are any of the traits you listed on the board included on the table?*

The questions in this section encourage students to look for similarities and differences between the inherited traits and the traits that are not entirely inherited. Prompt students to suggest ways in which our genes and the environment interact to shape the whole person. For example, hair color and fingernail shape are influenced, but not controlled, by environmental factors such as hair dyes and manicures. Exposure to an illness in childhood might leave the person's immune system permanently weakened. Susceptibility to certain diseases, such as breast cancer, is strongly influenced by genetic factors.

Propose Explanations

THINK ABOUT IT Take another look at the traits you listed on page 68. Which traits do you think are determined by your genes? Write *Yes* next to those. Which do you think are not determined by your genes? Write *No* next to those.

► ***Were some traits difficult to put into one category or the other? Why?***

Students will probably find that some traits seem to be affected by both genes and environmental influences.

► ***Look at the traits you wrote No next to. What might affect these traits?***

Answers will vary. Examples: how you were raised, interactions with other family members, school environment, exposure to different events or ideas

Take Action

TALENT INTERVIEW Do you have a friend who is very good at something? Maybe it's sports or playing a musical instrument. Maybe it's drawing or singing or telling stories. Interview your friend and try to find out whether other people in your friend's family also have that ability. Create a diagram of your friend's family that shows which relatives share that particular ability. Did any family members ever use their ability in this area professionally? What sort of training did they have to develop their ability? Do they think that talent or hard work was more important to their success? Or were they equally important?

► ***Based on what you learned from the interview, do you think that talent might be determined by the family members' genes? What other factors might have influenced the development of the talent?***

Answers will vary, but students may find that talents such as a singing voice, athletic ability, and others do seem to run in families.

71

Assessment

Skill: Making inferences

Use the following task to assess each student's progress.

Name a talent or skill, such as musical ability. Ask students to identify genetic factors and environmental factors that determine or influence various traits involved. (For musical ability, for example, environmental factors could include how often you practice and whether you have a good teacher. Genetic factors could include having perfect pitch and certain physical features, such as long fingers for playing the piano.)

Propose Explanations

THINK ABOUT IT Ask students to explain their reasoning in deciding which traits are determined by their genes and which are not. Ask them what, if any, aspects of what they have learned so far helped them to decide. Let students share their responses to the first question.

Take Action

TALENT INTERVIEW Refer students back to the class list of skills and talents for ideas about whom they might interview. Before they conduct the interviews, help them prepare a list of questions to ask. Tell them they can tape the interview to use later for analyzing the responses. (Remind them to get the person's permission before taping.)

After completing the interviews, students could use the Fugate family tree on page 66 as a model for their diagrams. Have students share any interesting anecdotes or stories from their interviews. Finally, ask them to evaluate whether the particular talents they investigated are largely inherited, a product of environmental factors, or a combination of both.

Most Likely to Survive

LESSON 19

The Right Stuff

Point of Lesson: ***Adaptations enable a species to survive in its environment.***

The article excerpted in this lesson uses the example of giraffes to explain the process of natural selection. Students compare how the adaptations of the giraffe and of another animal, the platypus, enable these species to survive in their respective environments. Students then consider how a change in the environment might affect the survival of a bird species. Finally, students summarize their understanding by inventing a fanciful creature that would thrive in a familiar environment.

Materials

Enrichment (p. 73), for the class:

- PBS video "Tall Blondes" (available from www.pbs.org/wnet/nature/shop/tallblondes.html)

LESSON 20

Tall, Gray, and Tuskless

Point of Lesson: ***In some populations of Asian elephants, the gene for growing tusks is being lost due to illegal hunting.***

In this lesson, students consider the situation of Asian elephants on the island of Sri Lanka. Due to ivory poaching, male elephants that do not have tusks are becoming much more common than those that do. Students perform an activity that models the effect of ivory poaching on an elephant population, relate their results to what is happening in Sri Lanka, and research the uses of ivory and materials that can be used in its place.

Materials

Activity (p. 78), for each pair:

- 20 white jellybeans
- 30 red jellybeans
- small paper bag

Laboratory Safety

Students with food allergies, diabetes, or other conditions requiring them to avoid sugary foods or the food additives found in jellybeans should not eat the jellybeans in the Activity. Instead, they can do the Activity with colored marbles, setting aside the white marbles at the end of each round. Review these safety guidelines with students before they do the Activity.

- Do the activity in a clean area that is free of chemical residues and other hazardous substances.
- Use new, food-safe bags to hold the jellybeans.
- Do not lick your fingers when you eat the jellybeans. If you do, wash your hands before the next round to avoid contaminating the rest of the jellybeans.
- Wash your hands thoroughly after the activity.

LESSON 21

New and Improved

Point of Lesson: ***Adaptive radiation and convergent evolution are two results of natural selection.***

Students further consider the role of environment in shaping species by examining the concepts of convergent evolution and adaptive radiation. After reading an introduction with examples of each type of evolution, they consider adaptive radiation by studying the similarities and differences between two species of spiders. The lesson ends with a research exercise involving convergent evolution of species in the Sahara desert.

Materials

Take Action (p. 81), for the class:

- research sources about Sahara desert animals

Background Information

Lesson 19

The process of natural selection was first described in a paper Charles Darwin wrote with Alfred Wallace. While on an expedition to the South Seas, Darwin had noticed that differences between individuals within a species often determined which individuals would be more successful in competing for resources. He hypothesized that individuals with more successful traits would be more likely to reproduce and pass those traits to their offspring. In this way, advantages would be multiplied from generation to generation, while disadvantages would not be perpetuated.

Lesson 20

Although human poachers are involved in the decrease in tusked elephants in Sri Lanka, the change is an example of natural selection, not artificial selection. In artificial selection, humans select for desirable traits by cross-breeding individuals that have those traits. The poachers are not cross-breeding the elephants; they are removing individuals with a certain trait (tusks) from the breeding population. In doing so, they are actually selecting for the less desirable (to them) trait of tusklessness.

The Activity on page 78 may remind students of other activities that model Mendelian inheritance. If this comes up, point out that although the activity does involve genetic inheritance, the jellybeans represent individuals in a population, not traits in the genotype of an individual. You may also want to note that the jellybean model is not completely accurate since tusklessness is a recessive trait and not likely to appear in all the offspring of the individual.

Lesson 21

For Take Action, you might suggest the alternative topic of the Kaibab squirrels of the Grand Canyon. These squirrels, which differ on the North and South Rims of the canyon, are a classic example of adaptive radiation. Also note that for the Sahara desert, many of the adaptations students will discover in their research are behavioral rather than structural—for example, animals burying themselves in sand to avoid strong sunlight. You may want to introduce the concept of behavioral adaptation before students begin their research.

Point of Lesson

Adaptations enable a species to survive in its environment.

Focus

- Form and function
- Evolution and equilibrium
- Diversity and adaptations of organisms
- Reproduction and heredity
- Structure and function in living systems

Skills and Strategies

- Comparing and contrasting
- Making inferences
- Predicting
- Generating ideas

Advance Preparation

Vocabulary

Make sure students understand these terms. Definitions can be found in the glossary at the end of the student book.

- environment
- gene
- habitat
- nutrient
- organism
- predator
- reproduce
- species

Materials

Gather the materials needed for *Enrichment* (p. 73).

Most Likely to Survive

The Right Stuff

◄ Ruby-throated hummingbird

Plants and animals that are well-adapted to their environment are most likely to survive.

For animals, survival means finding food, escaping predators, and adjusting to environmental changes. Plants also face survival challenges, such as getting enough water, nutrients, and sunlight. Some organisms are better equipped for survival in their environment than others. The characteristics that improve an organism's chances of survival are called *adaptations*. Adaptations are passed down from one generation to the next in genes.

Before You Read

IDENTIFY STRUCTURES

- *Name one of your favorite kinds of wild animals and describe its habitat (the area in which it lives).*

Answers will vary. Example: a deer; lives in forests and meadows

- *Identify three body structures that enable the animal to survive in its environment. Briefly describe the function of each structure and how you think it helps the animal survive.*

Example: A deer's light brown hair blends in with its background.

Its long, strong legs enable it to run away quickly from predators.

It also has large, movable ears that help it detect predators nearby.

Teaching Plan pp. 72–73

INTRODUCING THE LESSON

This lesson discusses animal adaptations and gives examples of adaptations that help different animals survive in their environments. Ask students to give examples of adaptations that are passed down from one generation to the next in genes.

Students may think that individual animals develop adaptations within a single generation. Explain that animals inherit adaptations from their parents. Animals with successful adaptations are more likely to live long enough to reproduce and pass those adaptations on to their young.

Before You Read

IDENTIFY STRUCTURES To help students answer the questions, talk about how the features of an animal's habitat affect the animal's chances for survival. Prompt students to think about the climate and weather, vegetation, other animals, geological features, and human activity in their chosen animals' habitats. Then ask students how the animals find food, escape predators, raise and protect their young, and adjust to environmental changes. Point out that the body structures that help the animals do these things are adaptations that help the animals survive in their environment.

Read

How did giraffes get their long necks?

Successful Variations

Giraffes have the longest necks of any mammal, which is why they're so tall.... At one time, people imagined that giraffes [evolved] their long necks as they stretched to eat higher leaves. We now know that changes in animals and plants over generations don't occur that way. [Today's] idea, developed by scientists such as Charles Darwin, is that evolution [begins with] variation.

Variation means that sometimes, by accident, an animal will be born that is somehow different from the others of its species. Maybe its legs are built a little differently and it can run faster. Or maybe it's [extremely] slow. Variations aren't necessarily good or bad. They just happen in nature.

...The better [adapted] an animal is to the area it lives in, the better its chances of living a long life and having [offspring]. And the [offspring] may inherit whatever variation made the animal so successful in its environment.

Something like this probably happened with the shorter-necked ancestors of modern giraffes. Those that by chance were born with somewhat longer necks could [reach] farther up into the trees and find more food—a definite survival advantage. So over generations, longer-necked giraffes gradually crowded out shorter-necked ones.

From: Wollard, Kathy. "The Long and Short of Giraffes." *Newsday.*

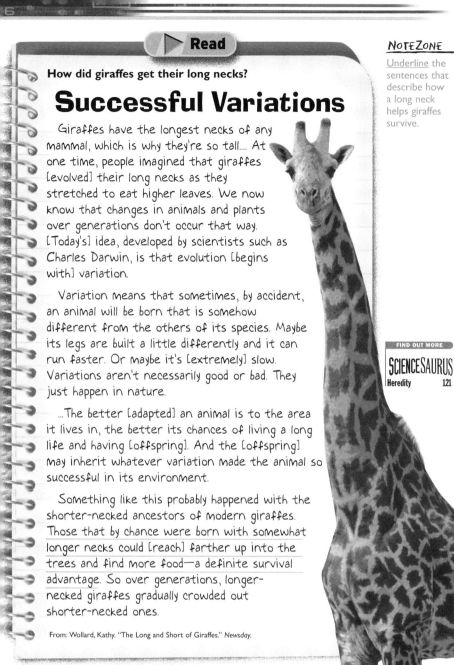

NOTEZONE

Underline the sentences that describe how a long neck helps giraffes survive.

FIND OUT MORE

SCIENCESAURUS

Heredity 121

73

Enrichment

Time: 40 minutes

Materials: PBS video "Tall Blondes" (available from www.pbs.org/wnet/nature/shop/tallblondes.html)

You may want to show the PBS Nature program "Tall Blondes" to help students learn more about giraffes. Point out that having a longer neck than other animals makes it necessary for the giraffe to be different in other ways as well. Ask students to speculate about what other special structures the giraffe has evolved along with a long neck. Explain that the giraffe has an exceptionally large heart to pump blood up its long neck. Its elastic blood vessels have valves that prevent blood from draining away from its brain when it lifts its head suddenly. Giraffes also have a special gait, unique in the animal world, and they move their necks as they run, which helps them keep their balance.

Read

Encourage students to identify any unfamiliar terms as they read. Have them use a dictionary to find the meaning of the unfamiliar terms and then rewrite the sentences containing those terms in their own words.

After students have completed the NoteZone activity, ask volunteers to read the sentences they underlined.

CHECK UNDERSTANDING

Skill: Comparing and contrasting

Ask: *How did people once think that giraffes evolved their long necks?* (by stretching to reach higher leaves) *How do scientists now know that giraffes evolved their long necks?* (Some giraffes happened to be born with longer necks, which enabled them to reach more food. This allowed them to survive longer and pass along the variation to their offspring.)

More Resources

The following resource is also available from Great Source.

READER'S HANDBOOK

Classification Notes 669

Connections

LANGUAGE ARTS Tell students that many myths, folk tales, and stories have been written to describe how different animals developed unusual traits. Have students write a fanciful story that tells how the giraffe got its long neck. Encourage students to include drawings with their stories, and provide time for students to share their stories and drawings with the class. In a class discussion, compare the explanations given in students' stories with factual scientific explanations. As an extension, interested students may want to read a similar story, such as Rudyard Kipling's *How the Leopard Got His Spots,* or you may want to read it to the class.

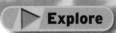

Explore

COMPARE ADAPTATIONS Two animal species that are well-adapted to their environment are the duck-billed platypus and the giraffe. Read the photo captions to learn about each animal's habitat, diet, predators, and adaptations.

PLATYPUS
Habitat: Australia's rivers, lakes, and streams; when not swimming, they live in burrows along the banks of these bodies of water
Diet: includes worms, small shellfish, frog and fish eggs, and other animals from the bottom of streams
Predators: include hawks, eagles, crocodiles, and water-rats
Adaptations: broad tail similar to a beaver's; thick, brown fur; claws on its feet; webs on its front feet that can extend beyond the claws; a duck-like bill

GIRAFFE
Habitat: open grasslands south of the Sahara desert in Central Africa
Diet: tree leaves
Predators: lions; young giraffes are also hunted by leopards, cheetahs, hyenas, and crocodiles
Adaptations: long neck; long, strong legs; patchlike markings on its body; large heart; long tongue; long eyelashes

▸ ***Compare the adaptations that the platypus and giraffe use to move around in their habitats. How do these adaptations help them survive?***

Both the platypus and giraffe have adaptations that help them move quickly to escape predators. The platypus's webbed feet and flat tail help it swim quickly through the water. The giraffe's long, strong legs help it run very fast.

▸ ***What adaptations do the platypus and the giraffe have that help them get food?***

The platypus has claws on its feet that can dig and a duck-like bill that can search through mud for food. The giraffe has long legs, a long neck, and a long tongue that help it reach leaves on trees.

74

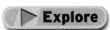

TEACHING PLAN pp. 74–75

Explore

COMPARE ADAPTATIONS To help students identify and compare adaptations, have them create two Classification Notes graphic organizers, one for the platypus and one for the giraffe. Have students label the columns *Habitat, Food,* and *Defense,* as shown at right, and then list the related adaptations for each animal. Point out that some adaptations may belong in more than one column.

PLATYPUS		
Habitat	Food	Defense

▸ *What adaptation do you think would help an adult giraffe defend itself if lions attacked? What adaptation would help a platypus avoid a hawk?*

giraffe: long, strong legs for running and kicking; platypus: able to dive underwater and use its webbed feet to swim away

Propose Explanations

CONSIDER CHANGES Adaptations that are useful in one environment may not be useful in another. For example, birds with long, slender beaks have a survival advantage over birds with shorter beaks in an area where nectar is plentiful. But suppose that a disease killed off all the plants in the area that produced flowers with nectar.

▸ *How would this change affect the bird populations in the area?*

The birds with long, slender beaks wouldn't be able to survive in that area anymore. Birds that had beaks adapted for eating other kinds of food in that area would then have the survival advantage.

Take Action

INVENT A SPECIES Choose one location you know really well, such as your gym locker, a local movie theater, a computer store, a shopping mall, or a skateboard park. On a separate piece of paper, describe the place you chose. Be as detailed as you can. Then create an imaginary animal with adaptations that would enable it to survive in that environment. How does the animal find food? How does it protect itself from predators? How does it stay warm (or cool)? How does it move around? Which of its senses is the strongest? In the space below, draw a picture of your animal. Label its structures to explain how each one enables the animal to survive in its environment.

Assessment

Skill: Predicting

Use the following task to assess each student's progress.

Suppose that a major climate change occurred in Australia. The areas where platypuses now live experienced long-term drought, and over time the rivers, lakes, and streams dried up. What adaptations might the platypus species evolve to enable it to survive in dry conditions, and how would each adaptation be useful?

(Examples: longer legs and smaller feet with shorter claws and pads instead of webs for moving quickly on dry land; a sharp, pointed bill for digging in dry soil; thinner fur that would not overheat the animal; a thin tail that would not be so heavy to carry around)

Propose Explanations

CONSIDER CHANGES Point out to students that their answers to the question in this section apply to differences between species, as well as to differences between individual birds within a species. In other words, the entire species of long-beaked birds would not necessarily die out in that area. Instead, the individuals with shorter beaks might be able to survive and reproduce. Gradually their numbers would increase, and over time birds of that species living in that area would have shorter beaks.

Take Action

INVENT A SPECIES Before students start drawing their invented species, have them organize their thinking by answering each question. In addition to the questions listed in the text, ask students to consider the size of their animal, the type of shelter it will use, the time of day when it is most active, and how it interacts with others of its own species. Remind them to keep the habitat in mind as they design their animal's various body structures. Provide time for students to share their creations with the class. If several students chose the same environment, you may want to have them extend the activity by working together to develop a food web that includes all the invented animals.

Point of Lesson

In some populations of Asian elephants, the gene for growing tusks is being lost due to illegal hunting.

Focus

- Evolution and equilibrium
- Diversity and adaptations of organisms
- Reproduction and heredity
- Science and technology in society

Skills and Strategies

- Making and using models
- Recognizing cause and effect
- Collecting and recording data
- Communicating

Advance Preparation

Vocabulary

Make sure students understand these terms. Definitions can be found in the glossary at the end of the student book.

- environment
- gene
- model
- population
- recessive
- reproduce
- species
- trait

Materials

Gather the materials needed for *Activity* (p. 78).

Tall, Gray, and Tuskless

Due to illegal hunting, some Asian elephant populations may be losing the gene for tusks.

When we think of an elephant, we think of a big, gray animal with large ears and long, curved, white tusks. These physical traits are determined by the elephant's genes.

An animal inherits its genes from its parents. Its genes determine which traits the animal has. Its traits can either help the animal survive in its environment or make it difficult or even impossible for the animal to survive. Animals with "helpful" traits have a much better chance of surviving long enough to produce offspring and pass on their genes. Animals with "unhelpful" traits often don't survive long enough to reproduce. Over time, the "unhelpful" traits disappear from the population. Only the "helpful" traits are still passed from one generation to the next. This process is called *natural selection*. Scientists think they are seeing a kind of natural selection in action in certain Asian elephant populations in Sri Lanka.

▲ Asian elephant

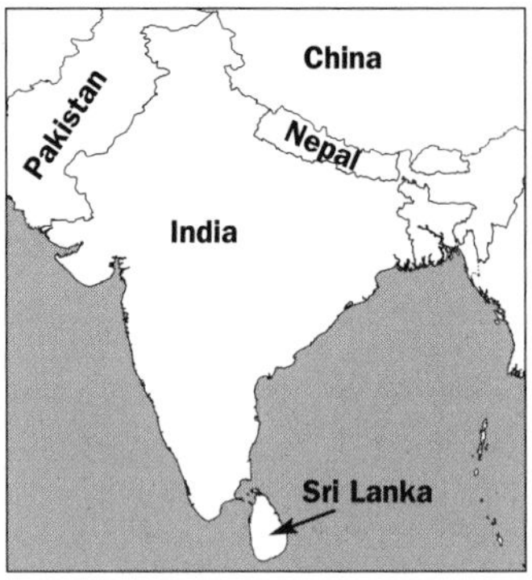

Teaching Plan pp. 76–77

INTRODUCING THE LESSON

This lesson introduces the process of natural selection as it is occurring today in some Asian elephant populations. Ask students what they know about genes. Then have them give some examples of genetic traits that elephants pass on to their offspring.

Students may think that environmental conditions cause changes in traits or that animals develop new traits in order to survive in a particular environment. Explain that a population's traits change when individuals with that trait reproduce more successfully than individuals without that trait.

Read

Hunters that kill elephants for their tusks may be unintentionally removing the "tusk gene" from some Asian elephant populations.

More Tuskless Elephants Than Ever

In a woeful version of natural selection, ivory poaching may be causing Asian elephants to lose the gene that allows them to develop tusks....

In contrast to the African species, not all male Asian elephants grow tusks. "The ones that do are the ones being hunted by ivory poachers, so the tusk gene may well disappear from the population," [say] leading international conservationists.

About 40 to 50 percent of [Asian elephants] are normally tuskless, but [on the island of] Sri Lanka, more than 90 percent of the population is not growing tusks.

"When you have ivory poaching, the gene that selects for whether an elephant has tusks or not will be removed from the population," said Paul Toyne, a species conservation officer of the World Wildlife Federation. "Animals that don't have tusks must have some sort of recessive gene, which might normally be shown in the next generation. But once the males with tusks are removed, they will not have the opportunity to pass on these genes. It is an alarming situation."

▲ Tusks from elephants killed by poachers

woeful: full of sadness

ivory poaching: the illegal killing of elephants to obtain their tusks, which are made of ivory

gene: segment of DNA that determines the inheritance of a particular trait

conservationist: a person who protects endangered species and their habitats

recessive gene: one of a pair of genes that is masked if a dominant gene is present

From: "Poaching Creates Tuskless Elephants," *United Press International.*

NOTEZONE

If you could interview conservationist Paul Toyne, what's one question you would ask him?

FIND OUT MORE

SCIENCESAURUS

DNA 115
Genes 116
Heredity 121
Dominant and Recessive Alleles 122
The Theory of Evolution 126
Natural Selection 127

SCILINKS. THE WORLD'S A CLICK AWAY

www.scilinks.org
Keyword: Natural Selection
Code: GSLD11

77

Enrichment

Explain that illegal hunting is not the only threat to the Sri Lankan elephant population. In fact, according to the Sri Lanka Department of Wildlife Conservation, conflicts between humans and elephants are a major problem in Sri Lanka. Have students review the following problems, and then have a class discussion to brainstorm solutions.

- Many wildlife preserves are too small for elephants, so they wander beyond the borders of the protected area and into farmlands.
- Elephants can completely destroy small farms. Many elephants are killed by farmers each year.
- The habitat once available to elephants has been greatly reduced by human population growth, deforestation, and clearing of lands for farming.
- Gunshot wounds account for most wild elephant deaths. Other causes include electrocution from illegal fences, poisoning, land mines, falling into wells and abandoned gem mines, and collisions with vehicles.

After the brainstorming session, you may want to tell students that solutions to these problems have been discussed or implemented in Sri Lanka. The solutions include scaring elephants away from farmlands, connecting smaller wildlife preserves to create a larger preserve, relocating elephants to larger preserves, and compensating farmers for damage.

Read

To help students understand the reading, have them underline phrases or sentences that are confusing or unclear to them or about which they have questions. Then have students work in pairs to figure out the meaning of the sentences they underlined. Suggest that students paraphrase the sentences in their own words. After students have worked in pairs, ask if there are any unresolved questions about the text that you can help answer.

When students have completed the NoteZone task, use students' questions as the foundation for a class discussion. Read each question aloud, and lead the class in a discussion. Have students look for answers in the reading, and also encourage them to share any other knowledge, information, or opinions they may have.

CHECK UNDERSTANDING

Skill: Using numbers

Ask: *If there were 100 male Asian elephants in a population, how many of them would normally have tusks?* (about 50 to 60) *If there were 100 male elephants in a population that was exposed to illegal hunting, how many of them would have tusks?* (about 10)

More Resources

The following resources are also available from Great Source and NSTA.

SCIENCESAURUS

DNA	115
Genes	116
Heredity	121
Dominant and Recessive Alleles	122
The Theory of Evolution	126
Natural Selection	127

SCILINKS. THE WORLD'S A CLICK AWAY

www.scilinks.org
Keyword: Natural Selection
Code: GSLD11

Connections

MATH Tell students that Sri Lanka's land area is 65,610 km^2. According to the Sri Lanka Wildlife Conservation Society, there were 20,000 elephants in Sri Lanka in the year 1900 but less than 3,500 elephants by the year 2000. Have students calculate the number of elephants per km^2 in the year 1900 and in the year 2000. (1900: 0.30 elephants/km^2, or 1 elephant per 3.33 km^2; 2000: 0.05 elephants/km^2, or 1 elephant per 20 km^2)

Activity

ELEPHANT WALK

In this simplified model, you'll see how some Asian elephant populations are changing as a result of ivory poaching. In this model, white jellybeans will represent adult elephants with tusks. Red jellybeans will represent adult elephants that never developed tusks.

The natural selection of genetic traits sometimes happens over a long period of time, even millions of years. But other times, a species' genes are altered in only a few years. What is causing the tusk gene to disappear from Asian elephant populations? To understand the answer, consider two important factors.

- The poachers usually kill only elephants that have tusks. Tuskless elephants aren't killed because they are not a source of ivory.
- Adult male elephants that don't have tusks do not have the gene for growing tusks.

What You Need:

- 20 white jellybeans
- 30 red jellybeans
- small paper bag

What to Do:

1. Select a partner. Decide which one of you will represent a forest where Asian elephants live and which one will represent an ivory poacher. (You'll change places each round.)
2. Put 20 white and 20 red jellybeans into the paper bag and mix them up. Give the bag to the "forest."
3. The "ivory poacher" reaches into the bag without looking and removes one jellybean.
   - If the jellybean is white (tusks), the "poacher" eats it. This represents a poacher killing the elephant.
   - If the jellybean is red (no tusks), the "poacher" puts it back in the bag and adds two more red jellybeans to represent the tuskless elephant's offspring.
4. Repeat step 3 four more times, switching roles with your partner each time.

TEACHING PLAN pp. 78–79

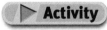

Activity

Time: 35–40 minutes
Materials: 20 white jellybeans; 30 red jellybeans; small paper bag

- Before students perform the activity, use the two important factors listed in the text as the basis for a class discussion. Ask students to explain why each factor is important.
- Make sure students understand that it is possible for an animal to have a form of a gene for a trait that the animal does not show. In this case, the gene form must be recessive. Point out that the gene for growing tusks is dominant, not recessive. Adult male elephants that do not grow tusks have *two* recessive forms of the tusk gene. They cannot pass the gene form for growing tusks to their offspring.
- Depending on which jellybeans were pulled from the bag, the final results will be somewhere between 15 white jellybeans and 20 red jellybeans to 20 white jellybeans and 30 red jellybeans. In any combination, the results will show that there are more red jellybeans than white.

What Do You See?

With your partner, count the white jellybeans (elephants with tusks) and the red jellybeans (elephants without tusks). Record your results in the following chart. Compare these results with the number of white and red jellybeans you started with.

	RED JELLYBEANS	WHITE JELLYBEANS
Start	20	20
End		

WHAT DO YOU THINK?

▶ ***Explain what happened to the numbers of white and red jellybeans after you repeated step 3 five times.***

The number of red jellybeans increased, and the number of white jellybeans decreased.

▶ ***How does this model show what is happening to some Asian elephant populations in Sri Lanka?***

Poachers kill off the elephants with the tusk gene (white jellybeans). The elephants without the tusk gene (red jellybeans) continue to survive and produce offspring that also do not have tusks. Over time, not having tusks becomes more common in the population.

Take Action

WHY IVORY? Even though the international ivory trade was outlawed in 1989, elephants continue to be hunted for their tusks. Research some of the products that ivory has been used for over the years. Then find out what alternative materials are used instead of ivory.

Students' research results will vary.

79

Assessment

Skill: Predicting

Use the following question to assess each student's progress:

What do you think would happen to an elephant population in Sri Lanka if ivory poachers stopped killing the elephants for their ivory? (The number of male elephants with tusks would increase, and the percentage of male elephants with tusks would eventually return to what was once considered normal, 40–50 percent.)

WHAT DO YOU THINK? Let each pair of students share their final numbers with the class. Ask: *What do all the results have in common?* (There are more red jellybeans than white jellybeans.) *What does this mean for the elephant population?* (The number of male elephants with tusks is decreasing while the number of male elephants without tusks is increasing.)

Encourage students to speculate about how this change in the elephant population will affect the Asian elephant's chances for survival. Explain that male elephants use their tusks to dig for food, strip trees, move things, and fight. Ask: *Do you think having tusks is a helpful trait for Asian elephants? Why or why not?* (Examples: Tusks are not a helpful trait because they attract poachers. Tusks are a helpful trait because they enable the elephants to behave normally.)

Take Action

WHY IVORY? Among other things, people have used ivory to make figurines, jewelry, piano keys, billiard balls, and pool cues. The nut from the ivory palm (sometimes called vegetable ivory, tagua, and ivory nut) is often used in place of actual ivory. There is also an artificial ivory called mycarta that can be sketched on and used as a substitute for ivory.

Allow time for students to present their findings. Encourage them to find pictures or draw examples of real ivory and its substitutes.

Point of Lesson
Adaptive radiation and convergent evolution are two results of natural selection.

Focus
- Evolution and equilibrium
- Structure and function in living systems
- Populations and ecosystems
- Diversity and adaptations of organisms

Skills and Strategies
- Comparing and contrasting
- Making inferences
- Creating and using tables

Advance Preparation

Vocabulary
Make sure students understand these terms. Definitions can be found in the glossary at the end of the student book.

- adaptation
- biodiversity
- environment
- evolution
- mammal
- natural selection
- organism
- population
- species

Materials
Gather the materials needed for ***Take Action*** (p. 81).

◂Fruit bat

New and Improved

Through the process of natural selection, an amazing number of different species of organisms have evolved on Earth.

Don't be fooled by appearances. Just because two different animals have similar structures doesn't mean they're related. Bats and birds both have wings and fly, but they are not closely related. They don't share a common ancestor. How did bats and birds both end up with wings? Long ago, the first ancestors of bats and the first ancestors of birds to be born with winglike structures stood a better chance of surviving in their environment than those that did not have these structures. As a result, both bat ancestors and bird ancestors with winglike structures were naturally selected. When organisms that are not related evolve similar structures in order to survive in similar environments, the process is called convergent evolution.

Sometimes natural selection works the other way around. Kangaroos and koalas look very different, but they are closely related. They share a common ancestor that lived millions of years ago. Why do they look so different today? Over many generations and many genetic changes, this ancient ancestor evolved into different kinds of animals. The kangaroo's ancestors evolved powerful legs to travel quickly over wide stretches of land. The koala's ancestors evolved a shape that enables it to climb trees easily. When organisms that are closely related evolve different structures in order to survive in different environments, the process is called adaptive radiation.

◂Koala

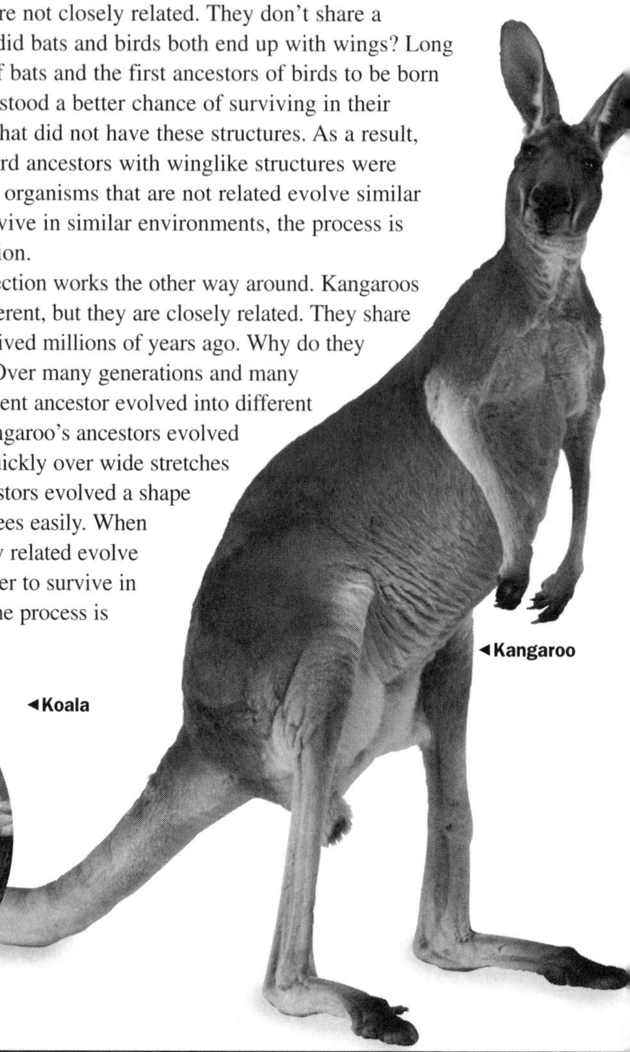
◂Kangaroo

Teaching Plan pp. 80–81

INTRODUCING THE LESSON
In this lesson, students explore convergent evolution and adaptive radiation. Briefly review what students learned about natural selection in the previous two lessons. Make sure they understand that a change in a species occurs when some individuals with "helpful" traits survive more successfully than individuals without those traits and pass the traits on to their offspring, *not* when all the individuals in a population gradually change.

Students may think all animals that look alike are related and animals that do not look alike are not related. Emphasize that some animals are related but look nothing alike, and other animals have very similar adaptations but are not related at all.

To help students remember the meanings of the two terms *convergent evolution* and *adaptive radiation,* have them first define the words *radiate* and *converge*. (*Radiate*: to extend in straight lines from a center; *converge:* to come together) Knowing these terms can make understanding each concept easier. Have students use the definitions of the words to explain each concept. (Example: In convergent evolution, unrelated species "come together" by sharing similar structures. In adaptive radiation, closely related organisms move out from a "common center" by evolving different structures.)

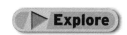

Explore

ADAPTIVE RADIATION: SPIDERS After students read the captions and examine the photographs, discuss similarities and differences between the two species. If any students have seen these two types of spiders—in either a zoo or a natural setting—ask them to describe the spiders.

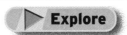

Explore

ADAPTIVE RADIATION: SPIDERS All of the 35,000 known species of spiders evolved from a common ancestor that lived many millions of years ago. Through many generations and genetic changes, different kinds of spiders became adapted to different environments.

Look at these photos and facts about two different kinds of spiders, then answer the question below.

▲ **The red-kneed tarantula *(Megaphobema mesomelas)* is large and hairy. It feeds on insects and other spiders.**

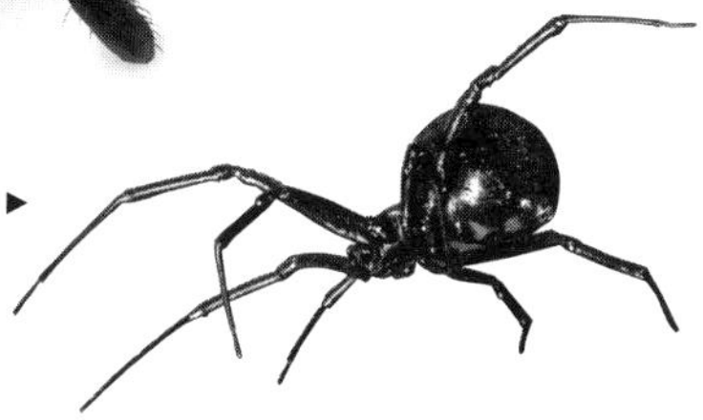

The black widow ▶ *(Latrodectus mactans)* is considered the most venomous spider in North America.

▶ *How do the physical adaptations of each spider help it survive?*

Answers will vary. Examples: The tarantula's large size could help it scare away predators that eat smaller spiders. The black widow's venom paralyzes its prey.

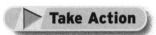

FIND OUT MORE

SCIENCESAURUS

Recognizing Common Ancestors 125
The Theory of Evolution 126

SCILINKS THE WORLD'S A CLICK AWAY

www.scilinks.org
Keyword: Evolution
Code: GSLD12

Take Action

CONVERGENT EVOLUTION IN THE DESERT Many different species make their home in the Sahara desert of Africa. Some examples include the horned viper, the desert monitor, the desert hedgehog, the elephant shrew, and the barbary leopard. Research three different animals that live in the Sahara. Create a chart that shows how the shape and structure of each animal have adapted for survival in hot, dry, sandy conditions. In what ways are these adaptations similar?

Students' animal choices and charts will vary.

81

More Resources

The following resources are also available from Great Source and NSTA.

ScienceSaurus

Recognizing Common Ancestors 125
The Theory of Evolution 126

SCILINKS THE WORLD'S A CLICK AWAY

www.scilinks.org
Keyword: Evolution
Code: GSLD12

Assessment

Skill: Comparing and contrasting

Use the following question to assess each student's progress:

What is the difference between adaptive radiation and convergent evolution? (Adaptive radiation occurs when different species evolve from a common ancestor. Convergent evolution occurs when different species evolve similar structures that enable them to survive in a particular environment.)

Point out that these photographs do not accurately represent the actual sizes of the spiders: Tarantulas are very large and can have a leg span of up to 14 cm (5.5 inches), whereas black widows have a leg span of only about 4 cm (1.5 inches). If students have access to a photocopier that enlarges and reduces images, suggest that they make a life-size copy of each photo.

Take Action

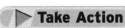

Time: will vary
Materials: research sources about Sahara desert animals

CONVERGENT EVOLUTION IN THE DESERT You might want to provide the following list of other Sahara animals for students to research:

- fennec fox
- sand cat
- desert jerboa
- dorcas gazelle
- addax
- striped hyena
- caracal
- Barbary macaque
- mouflon
- desert eagle owl
- scarab beetle

Students may find helpful information at the following Web site: www.pbs.org/sahara
Provide time for students to share their findings.

CHECK UNDERSTANDING
Skill: Classifying
Ask students to give one example of convergent evolution and one of adaptive radiation. (Students may cite the examples in the text—bats and birds for convergent evolution, tarantulas and black widow spiders or kangaroos and koalas for adaptive radiation—or other examples they have learned about elsewhere.)

One Hundred Million Kinds of Things

LESSON 22

What's in a Name?

Point of Lesson: ***When scientists discover a new organism, they must determine how it fits into the scientific classification system.***

A news item about the discovery of a new order of insects, the gladiators (Mantophasmatodea), introduces students to the workings of the taxonomic system of classification. Students compare the characteristics of insects belonging to the new order with the characteristics of insects in related orders. They consider the importance of both field observations and DNA analysis in the classification of living things. They then collect insects and classify them using reference materials.

Materials

Introducing the Lesson (p. 82), for teacher-led discussion:
- pictures of lion, leopard, housecat, wolf, dog, coyote

Science Scope Activity (p. 83), for the class:
- reference books and field guides that describe animal orders

Explore (p. 84), for teacher-led discussion:
- picture of a mountain lion *(Felis concolor)*

Take Action (p 85), for the class:
- field guides
- Insect Structure sheet (copymaster page 228)

LESSON 23

We Are Family

Point of Lesson: ***Organisms are sometimes reclassified based on new evidence.***

In this lesson, students consider the classification—and reclassification—of the giant panda. They compare and contrast the characteristics of the giant panda and its three most likely relatives (the red panda, the raccoon, and the spectacled bear) and come to their own conclusions about the giant panda's classification. Students then consider the recent DNA data that have led scientists to reclassify the giant panda with the spectacled bear rather than with the raccoon.

Materials

Enrichment (p. 87), for the class:
- field guides

Connections (p. 88), for the class:
- globe or world map
- geography textbooks, field guides, and other resources

LESSON 24

It's Classified!

Point of Lesson: ***A dichotomous key helps identify organisms by presenting a series of choices.***

Students use a dichotomous key to identify eight different species of sharks. They examine pictures of the sharks and identify features of each species. By comparing each shark's features with descriptions on the dichotomous key, they identify the name of each shark species.

Materials

none

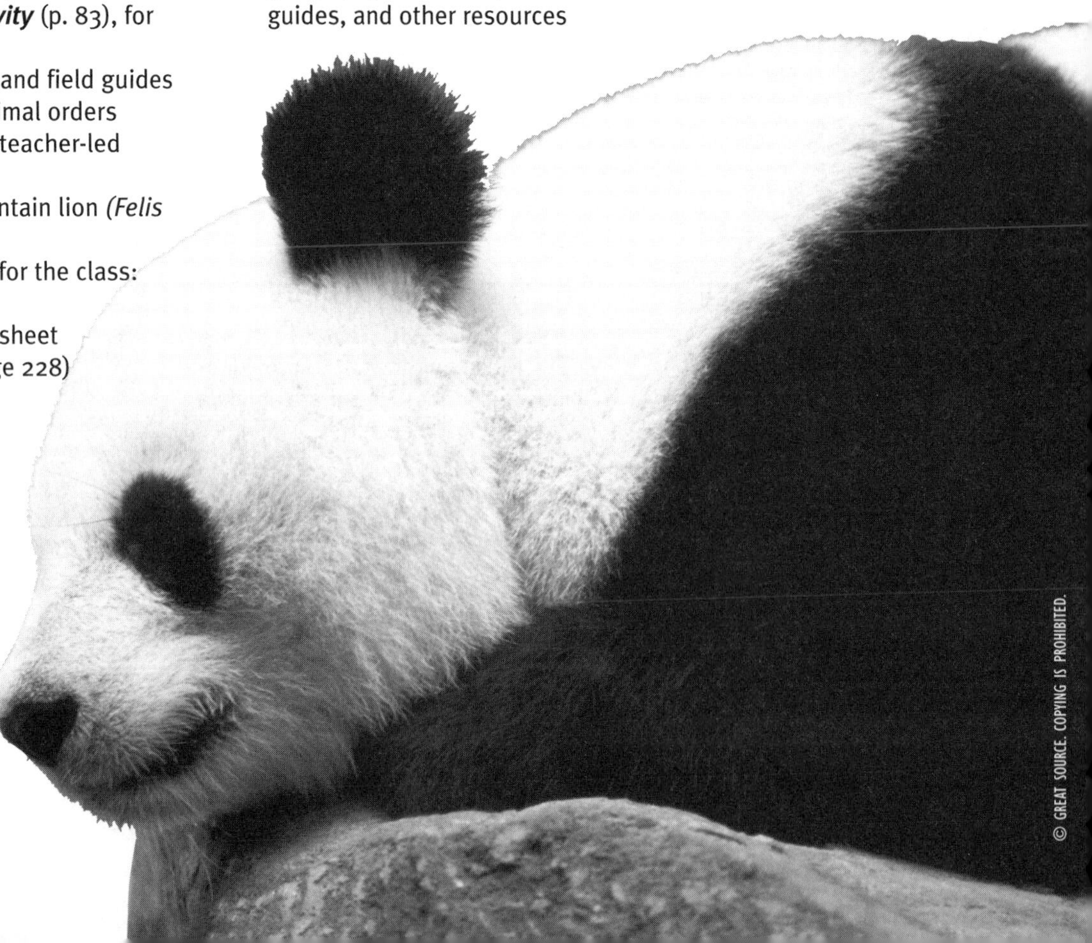

Science Scope Activity

Classification of Animals

NSTA has chosen a Science Scope *activity related to the content in this chapter. The activity begins here and continues in Lesson 22, page 83.*

The mnemonic device "King Philip Came Over For Great Spaghetti" is often used to teach students the modern classification system of Kingdom, Phylum, Class, Order, Family, Genus, and Species. In this activity, students gather classification information about a single animal order from Internet sites, CD-ROMs, and other resources. Studying a specific order in depth rather than observing a variety of animals from different orders will enable students to focus on specific questions that interest them. It will also be easier for students to determine what the animals in the order have in common and to identify the range of differences between animals in the same order.

(continued on page 83)

Background Information

Lesson 22

The modern taxonomic system is based on the work of the Swedish scientist Linnaeus, who developed the system and set out rules for its use, including the use of Latin names, in the 1700s. As new species were identified and classified by different scientists around the world, the number of names grew quickly. By the late 1800s, many organisms' names had become confused within the system. Since then, international scientific committees have formulated rules to reduce such confusion.

Lesson 23

The diagram on page 89 showing relationships among raccoons, pandas, and bears is an example of a *cladogram*, which belongs to the classification method known as *cladistics*. Scientists using cladistics seek to classify organisms on the basis of evolutionary relationships. This is in contrast to earlier methods of classification, which relied on structural similarities and differences among organisms. The increasing availability of DNA analysis has driven a surge in reclassification, including the reclassification of the giant panda.

Point of Lesson

When scientists discover a new organism, they must determine how it fits into the scientific classification system.

Focus

- Systems, order, and organization
- Diversity and adaptations of organisms
- Science as a human endeavor
- Nature of science
- Understanding about scientific inquiry

Skills and Strategies

- Classifying
- Comparing and contrasting
- Making inferences
- Interpreting data
- Creating and using tables

Advance Preparation

Vocabulary

Make sure students understand these terms. Definitions can be found in the glossary at the end of the student book.

- carnivore
- DNA
- extinct
- fossil
- organism
- species

(continued on page 83)

What's in a Name?

A discovery led to a new category of insects.

▲Honeybee

Scientists use a classification system to identify every known organism on Earth. There are nine categories in the system—domain, kingdom, phylum, class, order, family, genus, species, and subspecies. Domain is the broadest category, and subspecies is the smallest. The classification of one of the most common kinds of honeybees is given in the chart below.

The scientific classification system shows how organisms are related. For example, all insects are grouped in the same class, Insecta. This class is divided into smaller groups called orders. All butterflies belong to the same order. All beetles belong to another order.

Honeybee Classification	
Domain	Eukarya
Kingdom	Animalia
Phylum	Arthropoda
Class	Insecta
Order	Hymenoptera
Family	Apidae
Genus	Apis
Species	mellifera
Subspecies	ligustica

When scientists discover a new organism, they must figure out how it fits into the classification system. Finding a new genus or species is not unusual for scientists, but finding a new order or family is a rare and exciting event. In 2002, entomologist Oliver Zompro found an insect that didn't fit into any of the 30 existing orders of insects.

Before You Read

CLASSIFY IT Think of a collection you have—CDs, books, or stamps, for example. Select one of the items in that collection, and classify it according to the scientific categories above. (For example, domain: Recordings; kingdom: CDs; phylum: Music; class: Classical Music, and so on.)

- ***If you added a new item to the collection, would it fit easily into your system? Explain.***

Yes, it would fit easily. For example, if I added a jazz CD to my collection, it would fit into the same domain, kingdom, and phylum but would be in a different class.

Teaching Plan pp. 82–83

INTRODUCING THE LESSON

Time: 15 minutes

Materials: pictures of lion, leopard, housecat, wolf, dog, coyote

This lesson describes how one scientist determined that a newly discovered insect constituted a new order in the scientific classification system. Many students may think that all animals can be easily classified into one category. To demonstrate this point, display the pictures and ask: *What do these animals have in common?* (All are mammals, have fur or hair, have four legs, give birth to live young, and nurse their young.) Then ask: *Which animals would you classify together in subgroups? Why?* (Students may group the leopard, lion, and housecat together as cats and the wolf, dog, and coyote together as dog-like animals. Some may group the domestic pets and the other animals separately.)

Before You Read

CLASSIFY IT Tell students that classification systems based on physical characteristics have been used since the ancient Greeks. As new technologies help scientists learn more, classification systems are often modified to accommodate new information. For example, some scientists now use a category above kingdom—the domain. In this system, organisms are classified into three domains—Bacteria, Archaea, and Eukarya.

Call on volunteers to share their classification system for the objects they chose. Then ask students if they can think of other classification systems that are commonly used to organize types of objects. (Examples: Libraries use the Dewey decimal system to organize books; supermarkets classify foods and nonfood items into smaller, more specific groups; scientists classify

Read

Entomologist Oliver Zompro thought a certain insect had been extinct for millions of years. Then he found living specimens in Africa.

New Order of Insects Discovered

For the first time [since 1915], researchers have discovered an insect that **constitutes** a new order of insects. Dubbed "the gladiator" [for the movie] **entomologist** Oliver Zompro...said it resembles "a cross between a stick insect, a **mantid**, and a grasshopper...." The discovery of the new insect order... increases the number of insect orders to 31. "This discovery is [like] finding a **mastodon** or **saber-toothed tiger**," said [one scientist].

Zompro, a specialist in stick insects, was studying... fossils...when he began to suspect he was seeing a new type of insect.... When Zompro dissected [one] **specimen**...he found the remains of insects in its **gut**.... [This showed] that the stick-like insect was a carnivore. All other known stick-like insects are plant eaters. "At this point, I was sure I had found an absolutely new order of insects," said Zompro. He set out to [see] whether the insect—which [scientists thought was] extinct—might still be found in the wild.

He joined an expedition to [Namibia in Africa].... The scientists were dropped onto a mountain peak in the remote area.... After a night of shaking grass bushes, a scientist... found the first of the live insects that came to be known as "the gladiator." During the trip, Zompro collected a dozen of the insects, which he carried back to his lab...to study....

constitutes: makes up
entomologist: a scientist who studies insects
mantid: a large, green insect; one type is known as a "praying mantis"
mastodon: a woolly mammoth, an extinct relative of modern elephants
saber-toothed tiger: a huge lion-like animal, now extinct
specimen: an individual example of an organism
gut: digestive system

From: Trevedi, Bijal P. "New Insect Order Found in Southern Africa." *National Geographic Today.*

NOTEZONE

Underline the sentences that explain why "the gladiator" did not belong in the same order as stick insects.

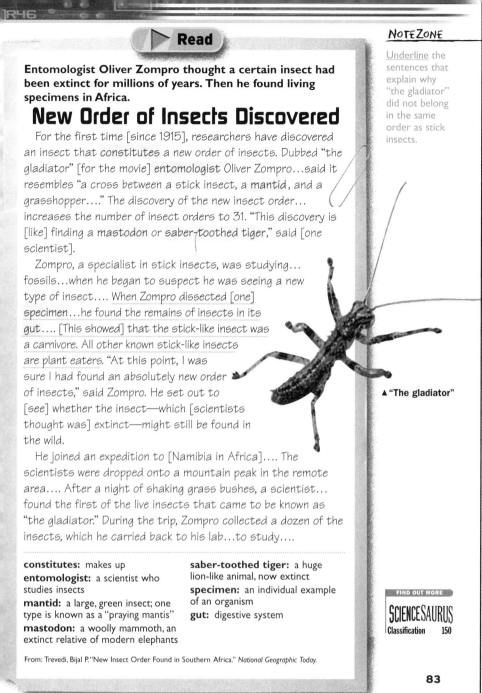

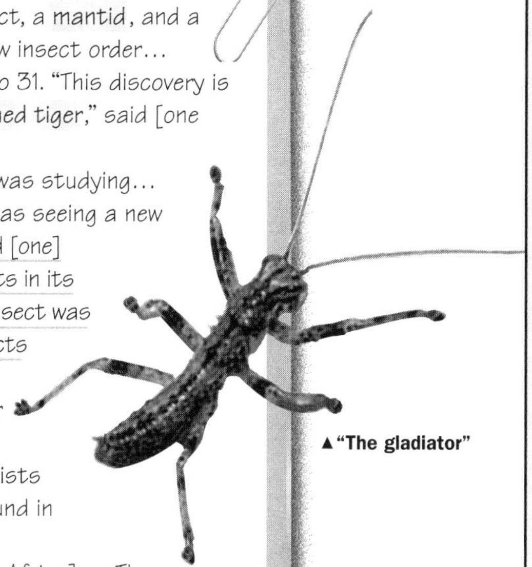

▲ **"The gladiator"**

FIND OUT MORE
SCIENCESAURUS
Classification 150

83

(continued from page 82)

Materials

Gather the materials needed for ***Introducing the Lesson*** (p. 82), ***Science Scope Activity*** (p. 82B and p. 83), ***Explore*** (p. 84), and ***Take Action*** (p. 85).

Science Scope Activity

(continued from page 82B)

Time: 10–15 minutes per group for oral presentations
Materials: reference books and field guides that describe animal orders

Procedure

1. Have students work in small groups. Each group should choose one order of animals and generate a list of questions about it.
2. Tell students to research the order's structural characteristics, reproduction, behavior, and other common traits. Explain that they could use print resources or visit a "virtual zoo" at one of these Web sites: library.thinkquest.org/11922/ www.nationalgeographic.com/ animals
3. Allow students several days to gather information and create an oral presentation for the class. Tell them each group will have 10–15 minutes for its presentation.

rocks and minerals into different subgroups.) Point out that by using a classification system for living things, scientists are better able to understand similarities and differences between organisms.

Read

After students finish the reading, have them find Namibia on a map of Africa. Explain that scientists think there are many species of plants and animals that have yet to be discovered in remote parts of the world, particularly the tropical rain forests of South America. Ask: *How might the discovery of a new order affect the scientific classification system?* (A new order would have to be added to the system.)

Point out that comparing the gladiator's characteristics with the characteristics of insects in other orders enabled Zompro to quickly determine that he had discovered a new order of insects. Emphasize that without the classification system, it would be difficult to determine if a newly discovered organism represents a new species (or other classification category) or one that is already known.

CHECK UNDERSTANDING
Skill: Classifying
Ask: *What is the broadest category in the scientific classification system?* (domain) *What is the smallest category?* (subspecies) *Which category includes the most types of organisms?* (domain)

More Resources

The following resource is also available from Great Source.

SCIENCESAURUS
Classification 150

Connections

LANGUAGE ARTS Arrange for a librarian to visit the class and explain the 10 categories of subject matter used in the Dewey decimal system. Then present students with several books, and have them classify the books using the system. Ask: *How is this classification system helpful to people?* (It makes it easier to find books on a particular subject.)

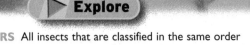

Explore

COMPARE ORDERS All insects that are classified in the same order share many characteristics. The chart below provides information about the four orders of insects that are mentioned in the reading.

Order	Type of Wings	How It Moves Around	Diet	How It Catches and Holds Its Prey
Gladiators (Mantophasmatodea) 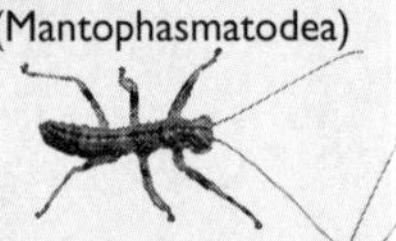	no wings	walks	insects, including other gladiators	uses front and middle pair of legs
Walking sticks (Phasmatodea) 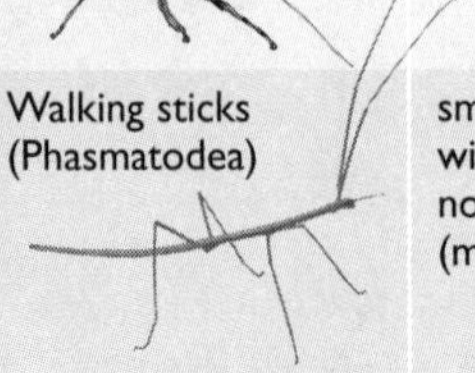	small, useless wings or no wings (most species)	walks	plants	
Mantids (Mantodea) 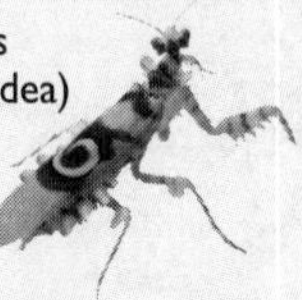	thickened front wings, long hind wings	walks, flies some	insects such as crickets	uses front pair of legs
Grasshoppers (Orthoptera) 	thickened front wings protect long, thin hind wings	walks, jumps, flies short distances	plants (most species)	

► ***Examine the characteristics listed in the chart. Which insects besides gladiators are carnivores? Why didn't Zompro classify gladiators in the same order as those insects?***

Mantids; mantids have wings, but gladiators do not.

► ***Why did Zompro's discovery lead to the creation of a new insect order?***

The gladiator's characteristics did not fit all the characteristics of any one of the existing orders.

84

TEACHING PLAN pp. 84–85

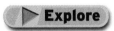

Explore

Time: 15 minutes
Materials: picture of a mountain lion *(Felis concolor)*

COMPARING ORDERS Show students a picture of a mountain lion, and ask them to identify the animal. (Students may use different names.) Explain that people in different regions often refer to this animal by different names, such as mountain lion, puma, panther, cougar, or wildcat. Explain that all scientists worldwide use organisms' scientific names so there is no confusion about which specific species or subspecies is being referred to. Point out that most scientific names are Latin words.

Ask students to highlight the gladiator's traits where they are included in the descriptions of the other orders. Students will be able to see that the gladiator does not share all its traits with any other order.

Propose Explanations

An organism's traits are determined by its DNA. Every species has a unique DNA pattern. By comparing DNA patterns, scientists can determine whether one species is related to other species, even species that are now extinct.

▸ ***How would comparing the DNA of the gladiator and walking sticks help scientists classify the gladiator?***

Scientists could learn whether the two kinds of insects are closely related and whether the gladiator should be classified in the same order as walking sticks.

Michael Whiting is a biologist doing DNA research on the gladiator. He said, DNA "is one more piece of a large and complex puzzle. It's exciting to have the piece, but it's not going to provide the answer by itself."

▸ ***DNA can tell scientists a lot about a species, but not everything. What kinds of information can be learned only by observing a live gladiator in natural surroundings?***

Answers will vary. Examples: how the insect moves, how it catches prey, how it defends itself against predators

Take Action

INTO THE FIELD Entomologists spend part of their time collecting specimens in the wild to bring back to the lab for more study. With another student, go outside with two small, clear containers with lids (be sure to poke airholes in the lids) and a flat wooden stick or plastic coffee stirrer. Use the stick or stirrer to help place one insect in each jar. (When you are finished observing the insects, return them unharmed to the area where you found them.) Avoid capturing any insects that you think might sting or bite. Take notes to identify features of each insect, such as wings or no wings, coloring, and so on. Use the library or Internet to research the classification of each of the two insects—from its kingdom down through its phylum, class, order, and (if possible) its family.

Insects and classifications will vary.

Assessment

Skill: Concept mapping

Use the following task to assess each student's progress:

Have students create a concept map that identifies the types of evidence that scientists use when they classify organisms. Tell students to put the term *Evidence for Classification* in the center of the map. A sample concept map is shown below.

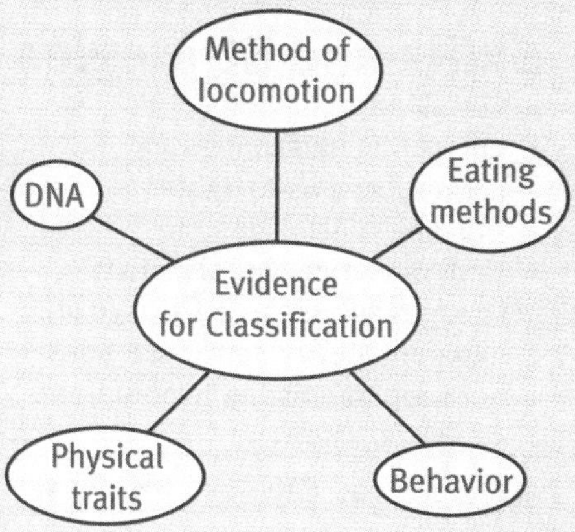

Propose Explanations

Explain to students that early classification systems were based on observable physical characteristics. DNA analysis provides a new kind of tool for classifying organisms. Ask: *How do you think DNA analysis might affect the classification system that scientists use now?* (DNA patterns might show that a species is more or less closely related to another species than scientists thought.) Emphasize that the more closely related two species are, the more similar their DNA patterns (their genes) are. But almost all organisms share these patterns. Tell students that humans share 99.9 percent of their genes with each other, 98 percent with chimpanzees, and even 23 percent with yeast.

Take Action

Time: 40 minutes
Materials: field guides, Insect Structure sheet (copymaster page 228)

Caution: Before students go outdoors, find out if any of them are allergic to bee venom or have any other related allergies. Alert students to any biting and stinging insects that live in your area. Also warn them if disease-carrying insects or ticks are a health hazard in your area, and review appropriate safety precautions.

INTO THE FIELD Before students start collecting, distribute copies of the Insect Structure sheet and review the distinguishing characteristics of insects: three body parts, six jointed legs, one pair of eyes, one pair of antenna, and so forth. If necessary, supervise the collecting to make sure students do not collect non-insects such as spiders or centipedes. Allow students class time to share their findings.

Point of Lesson

Organisms are sometimes reclassified based on new evidence.

Focus

- Systems, order, and organization
- Diversity and adaptations of organisms
- Nature of science
- Understanding about scientific inquiry

Skills and Strategies

- Classifying
- Comparing and contrasting
- Creating and using tables
- Drawing conclusions
- Understanding that scientists change their ideas in the face of experimental evidence that does not support existing hypotheses

Advance Preparation

Vocabulary

Make sure students understand these terms. Definitions can be found in the glossary at the end of the student book.

- classify
- species
- DNA

(continued on page 87)

WE ARE FAMILY

Should giant pandas be classified with bears or with raccoons? Scientists have debated this question for more than 100 years.

The giant panda is famous for its black and white fur and big, bear-shaped body. It spends about 12 hours a day eating. Its diet is made up almost entirely of one food—bamboo. Giant pandas make their home high in the isolated mountain forests of central China. Another species of panda, the red panda, is found in forested mountains of western China. These remote locations make it difficult for scientists to study pandas.

NOTEZONE

Number the different ways that the giant panda has been classified.

Read

Sometimes, classifying an organism is not so easy.

The "Bear Facts"

One of the world's rarest animals, the giant panda, lives in the subalpine forests in the west central region of China. The classification of the panda has long been a matter of controversy among zoologists.[1] Originally classified with the bears,[2] it was later grouped with raccoons. The weight of evidence that has accumulated over the years, however, now supports the view that[3] it is related to bears. Its closest relative is the spectacled bear of South America.

subalpine: just below the highest places that trees will grow on a mountain

zoologist: a scientist who studies, observes, and classifies animals

From: "Giant Panda," *Canadian Museum of Nature* (www.nature.ca/notebooks/english/gpanda.htm)

FIND OUT MORE

SCIENCESAURUS
Classification Hierarchy 151

SCILINKS. THE WORLD'S A CLICK AWAY
www.scilinks.org
Keyword: Taxonomy
Code: GSLD13

▲ Giant panda

TEACHING PLAN pp. 86–87

INTRODUCING THE LESSON

This lesson presents the history of the giant panda's classification and the recent use of DNA analysis to reclassify the species. If any students have seen a panda in a zoo or in a video or television program, ask them to describe its characteristics. How big was it? What was it doing? Did it eat any food and if so, what kind of food? Did the animal make any sounds? What kind?

Many students think that classifying a known organism is an easy task. Tell students that many controversies exist over the classification of certain animals and that the panda is one of those animals.

Read

Call attention to the pictures of the giant panda on these two pages. Take a class poll to determine whether students think the panda should be classified with bears or with raccoons and to explain their reasoning. Review their ideas after they complete the Explore section.

Point out that due to human destruction of the panda's natural habitat, fewer than 1,000 giant pandas survive in the wild today.

Explore

IDENTIFYING FAMILIES Compare the giant panda's characteristics with the characteristics of the other animals listed in the chart.

Appearance and Behavior	Giant panda	Red panda	Raccoon	Spectacled bear
has dark, mask-like fur around eyes	yes	yes	yes	yes
eats bamboo plants	yes	yes	no	no
has long wrist bones covered with skin that function like human thumbs	yes	yes	no	no
has ringed tail pattern	no	yes	yes	no
is bear-like in size and weight	yes	no	no	yes
has bear-like teeth	no	no	yes	yes
can walk on hind legs	no	no	no	yes

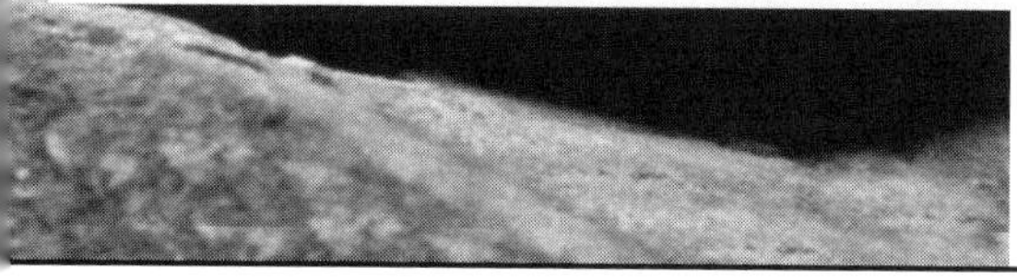

87

(continued from page 86)

Materials

Gather the materials needed for ***Enrichment*** (below) and ***Connections*** (p. 88).

Enrichment

Time: 20 minutes per group for presentations
Materials: field guides

Tell students to imagine that a scientist has discovered a living specimen of a mythical creature such as the Loch Ness Monster, Sasquatch (Big Foot), a Yeti (Abominable Snowman), a unicorn, a dragon, or the Jersey Devil. Let students work in small groups to write, rehearse, and present a television panel discussion about the discovery with students representing scientists who disagree about how the creature should be classified. Each group should also include a moderator.

Tell students that each group should first agree on the broadest classification category for the creature—its phylum, class, order, family, or genus. Provide field guides so each group can find out the scientific classifications of animals they think would be most closely related to their creature. Each "scientist" on the panel should obtain pictures of those related animals. Let each group present its panel discussion to the rest of the class.

Explore

IDENTIFYING FAMILIES Ask students to examine the chart and identify the number of different species represented. (four) Then have students use the chart to name similarities and differences between the giant panda and each of the other animals. To elicit this information, ask: *How are the giant panda and the (name the other animal) similar?* After students' responses, ask: *How are they different?* To conclude the activity, ask: *Why do you think scientists were unsure about how to classify the giant panda?* (The giant panda's characteristics are both similar in some ways and different in some ways from each of the other animals' characteristics.)

CHECK UNDERSTANDING
Skill: Making inferences
Ask: *Which animal do scientists now think is the giant panda's closest relative?* (the spectacled bear) *Why do you think scientists grouped the giant panda with the raccoon in the past?* (The giant panda and raccoon have several obvious characteristics in common.)

More Resources

The following resources are also available from Great Source and NSTA.

SCIENCESAURUS

Classification Hierarchy 151

SCILINKS
THE WORLD'S A CLICK AWAY

www.scilinks.org
Keyword: Taxonomy
Code: GSLD13

Connections

Time: 30 minutes
Materials: globe or world map; geography textbooks, field guides, and other resources

GEOGRAPHY Have students review the lesson's introductory paragraph and the reading to identify where giant pandas live. (mountain forests in west-central China) Help them locate this area on a globe or world map. Provide geography textbooks, field guides, and other resources so students can find out more about the panda's natural habitat—specific locations and their sizes, physical terrain, temperature, elevation, vegetation, other indigenous animals, and

(continued on page 89)

Explore

▸ ***Which of the other animals does the giant panda seem most closely related to? What evidence from the chart led you to that conclusion?***

The red panda. Even though the red panda is smaller than the giant panda, they both have dark mask-like fur around their eyes, both eat bamboo, both have long wrist bones that function like thumbs, and both do not have bear-like teeth and cannot walk on their hind legs.

▸ ***The giant panda was first classified in the Ursidae family with bears. During the mid-1900s, it was reclassified in the Procyonidae family with raccoons. What characteristics of the spectacled bear are not shared by giant pandas?***

The giant panda can't walk on its hind legs, but the spectacled bear can. The spectacled bear has bear-like teeth, but the giant panda does not. The giant panda feeds on bamboo plants, but the spectacled bear does not.

NEW EVIDENCE, NEW CLASSIFICATION Just when scientists thought the giant panda would remain in the raccoon family, they discovered a new tool to help classify animals—DNA analysis. Scientists assume that closely related animals will have more DNA (genes) in common than animals that are distantly related. By comparing different animals' DNA, scientists can find out about the animals' ancestors.

Scientists analyzed DNA samples from the giant panda, the red panda, the raccoon, and the spectacled bear. They discovered that all four animals have some DNA in common. This meant that they all evolved from one common ancestor in the distant past. But the giant panda and the spectacled bear have more DNA in common with each other than they have in common with the raccoon and red panda. And the red panda and raccoon have more DNA in common with each other than they have in common with the giant panda and spectacled bear. Based on this DNA analysis, scientists developed the "family tree" shown on the next page.

88

TEACHING PLAN pp. 88–89

Explore *(continued)*

Ask students to share their answers to the first question on this page. Pay particular attention to the evidence they cited, particularly for those students who did not choose the red panda. Let students refer back to the chart on page 87 to answer the second question.

NEW EVIDENCE, NEW CLASSIFICATION Ask students if they have ever seen a diagram of a family tree. If not, refer them to the one on page 66 of Chapter 6. Ask: *What does a family tree show?* (how people in the same family are related to one another) Explain that the diagram on page 89 is a family tree for the giant panda based on the genetic relationships between it and the other three animals. Have students refer to the diagram as they read the last paragraph on this page.

These diagrams, often called *cladograms*, show that different organisms evolved from a common ancestor. They also show the evolutionary relationship among a group of organisms and the point at which they diverged from each other. Tell students to notice where the lines split in the diagram. Then ask: *According to the diagram, is the giant panda related to the raccoon?* (Yes; they share a common ancestor.)

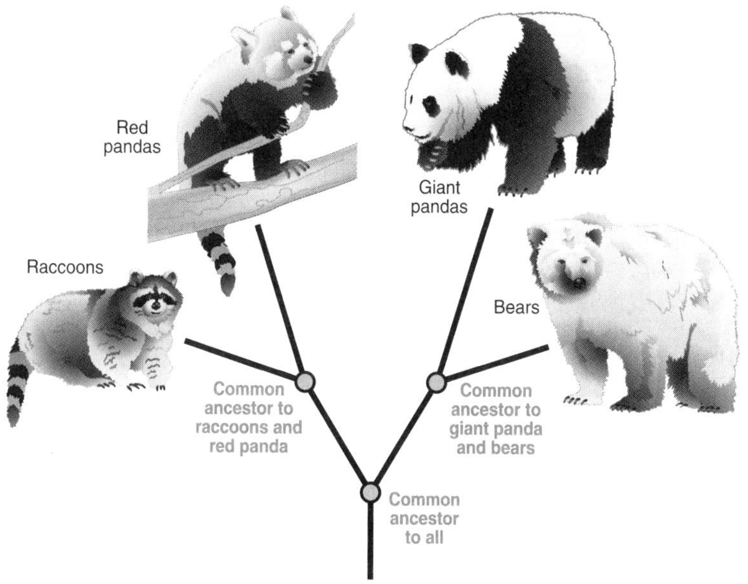

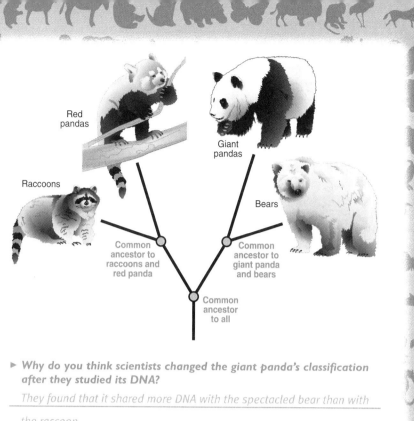

► ***Why do you think scientists changed the giant panda's classification after they studied its DNA?***

They found that it shared more DNA with the spectacled bear than with the raccoon.

► ***How is classifying animals based on their physical characteristics different from classifying them based on DNA evidence? Which evidence do you think is more useful to scientists? Explain why.***

Answers will vary. Example of difference—Many animals that have similar physical characteristics are not closely related. DNA analysis shows whether the animals have any of the same inherited genes. Usefulness—Accept either position as long as the student supports it.

(continued from page 88)

the proximity of human settlements, logging activities, and the like. Students could create posters displaying the information they have gathered about the giant panda's habitat.

Assessment

Skill: Classifying

Use the following question to assess each student's progress:

How did DNA evidence lead scientists to reclassify the giant panda? (The DNA evidence showed that the giant panda has more DNA in common with the spectacled bear than it has with the raccoon or the red panda. The more DNA two species have in common, the more closely related they are.)

Point of Lesson

A dichotomous key helps identify organisms by presenting a series of choices.

Focus

- Systems, order, and organization
- Diversity and adaptations of organisms
- Nature of science
- Abilities necessary to do scientific inquiry

Skills and Strategies

- Classifying
- Interpreting scientific illustrations
- Comparing and contrasting

Advance Preparation

Vocabulary

Make sure students understand these terms. Definitions can be found in the glossary at the end of the student book.

- organism
- species

It's Classified!

▲Caribbean reef shark

With more than 350 shark species to choose from, identifying one particular shark can be a challenge!

Scientists sometimes use a dichotomous key to help identify organisms. The key presents a series of choices between two characteristics. By choosing one characteristic at each step, they can identify the organism.

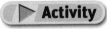

Activity

SHARK, SHARK! WHO'S THERE?

Eight different shark species are pictured on the next page. Use the dichotomous key below to identify each kind of shark.

What to Do:

Choose one of the shark pictures. Go to step 1 on the key. Decide whether **a** or **b** fits the shark you chose. If **b** fits, go to step 2 on the key. Again, decide which choice fits the shark. Continue through the key until you reach the shark's name. Write the name below the shark's picture. Repeat the steps until you have identified all eight sharks.

DICHOTOMOUS KEY

1	**a.** mouth at front of snout **b.** mouth underneath snout	African angel shark Go to 2
2	**a.** no anal fin **b.** has anal fin	Go to 3 Go to 4
3	**a.** very long snout **b.** short snout	Japanese saw shark Cookie-cutter shark
4	**a.** two dorsal fins **b.** one dorsal fin	Go to 5 Broadnose seven-gill shark
5	**a.** mouth ends in front of eyes **b.** mouth continues beyond eyes	Go to 6 Go to 7
6	**a.** barbels (fleshy whiskers) on lower jaw **b.** no barbels on lower jaw	Nurse shark Whale shark
7	**a.** nictitating eyelid (membrane that moves over eye to protect it) **b.** no nictitating eyelid	Smooth hammerhead shark Great white shark

TEACHING PLAN pp. 90–91

INTRODUCING THE LESSON

In this lesson, students use a dichotomous key to identify eight species of sharks. Ask students to describe sharks they have seen on television, in movies, or in an aquarium. Ask: *What features of sharks might help scientists identify a particular kind of shark?* (Examples: size, shape of head, shape of tail and fins, feeding habits) Based on the portrayal of sharks in movies such as the *Jaws* series, students most likely think that all sharks are vicious predators that readily attack humans. Explain that sharks rarely attack humans. Also emphasize that sharks do not intentionally target humans but instead confuse humans with their natural prey.

Activity

Time: 15–20 minutes

- Tell students that *dichotomous* means "divided into two parts." Ask students to explain why this term is used for the key on this page. (Each step offers two choices.)
- Explain that a dichotomous key describes the physical appearance of related organisms. It is not based on DNA analysis or any other "hidden" (internal) characteristics.
- Point out the text statement that there are more than 350 species of sharks. A key that worked for identifying every shark species would have many more paired steps and choices than this key does.

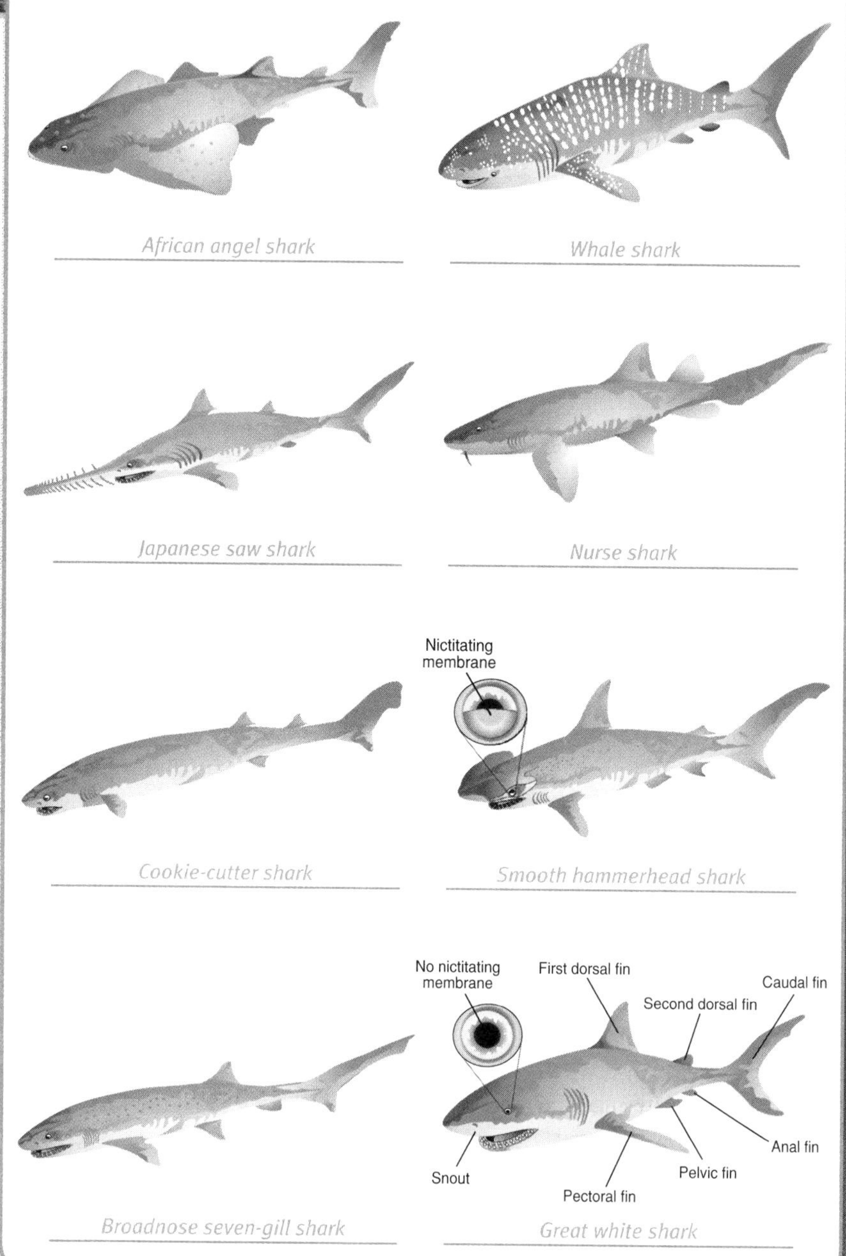

Enrichment

Have students create a dichotomous key to identify six or more foods in a particular food group. For example, students' keys could be used to identify specific vegetables—broccoli, cauliflower, asparagus, spinach, lettuce, and tomato. Emphasize that the key must be based on observable physical characteristics such as color, size, texture, and shape and must not include subjective personal opinions such as "tastes awful!" Remind students that the key should include illustrations of all the items being identified. Allow class time for students to share their keys.

Assessment

Skill: Classifying

Use the following question to assess each student's progress:

How does a dichotomous key help identify organisms? (It focuses on specific physical characteristics that enable you to distinguish between related organisms that are similar in many ways.)

- Tell students to use the labeled illustration at the bottom right of page 91 to help them identify structures.
- Explain to students that in some cases, they may need to skip a step to properly identify a shark. For example, in step 2, if the shark has an anal fin, skip step 3 and go directly to step 4.
- To make the decisions between choices less difficult, have students work in pairs so they can check and verify or correct each other's choices.

CHECK UNDERSTANDING
Skill: Observing

Ask students to list the physical characteristics that are used to identify sharks in this dichotomous key. (placement of mouth, presence or absence of anal fin, size of snout, number of dorsal fins, length of mouth, presence or absence of barbels, and presence or absence of nictitating eyelid)

About the Photo

Killer whales often swim quickly to the surface of the water, thrust themselves up out of it, then fall back with a large splash—an activity known as *breaching*. Scientists do not know why killer whales breach. Explain to students that the killer whale is not a whale at all but is a member of the dolphin family.

About the Charts

A major goal of the *Science Daybooks* is to promote reading, writing, and critical thinking skills in the context of science. The charts below describe the types of reading selections included in this unit and identify the skills and strategies used in each lesson.

UNIT 3 Living Things

All living things on Earth come into contact with other living things.

That's when it gets interesting for scientists who study these relationships. They observe things such as how insects can get to plants they can eat, and how plants catch insects they can eat.

In this unit, you'll learn how organisms—from bacteria to bugs to birds—get around and interact with each other. Sometimes when two organisms interact, it's a little like a fight; one must harm the other in order to survive. Other times, such as when a bird eats a plant's seeds and drops them somewhere else, both organisms benefit. You'll also learn how insects escape certain interactions and how whales interact with other whales in their groups.

92

SELECTION	READING	WRITING	APPLICATION
CHAPTER 9 • BACTERIA			
25. "Dirty Money" (science news magazine)	• Make predictions • Directed reading	• Make connections to own experience	• Creative problem solving
26. "Killer Germs" (nonfiction science book)	• Make predictions • Directed reading • Map reading	• Draw diagram • Make inferences	• Research report or poster
27. "Bacteria Good Guys" (student essay)	• Generate questions	• Opinion statement	• Draw conclusions
CHAPTER 10 • HOW INSECTS GET AROUND			
28. "Insect March" (children's science book)	• Visualizing • Directed reading	• Write from experience • Draw conclusions	• Design a model
29. "Leaping Insects" (children's science book)	• Make a list • Draw a diagram • Read critically	• Make predictions	
30. "Flight of the Dragonfly" (children's science book)	• Record prior knowledge • Visualizing	• Label a drawing • Defend answer	• Create new text from well-known text • Anthropomorphism

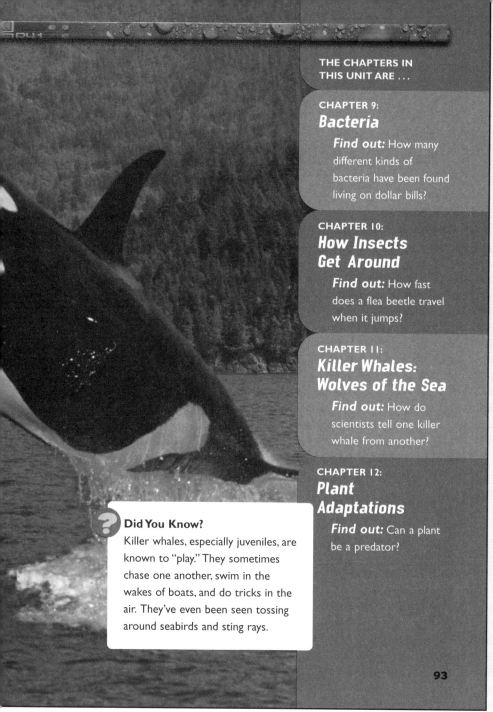

THE CHAPTERS IN THIS UNIT ARE . . .

CHAPTER 9:
Bacteria

Find out: How many different kinds of bacteria have been found living on dollar bills?

CHAPTER 10:
How Insects Get Around

Find out: How fast does a flea beetle travel when it jumps?

CHAPTER 11:
Killer Whales: Wolves of the Sea

Find out: How do scientists tell one killer whale from another?

CHAPTER 12:
Plant Adaptations

Find out: Can a plant be a predator?

Did You Know?
Killer whales, especially juveniles, are known to "play." They sometimes chase one another, swim in the wakes of boats, and do tricks in the air. They've even been seen tossing around seabirds and sting rays.

93

Answers to *Find Out* Questions

CHAPTER 9
93 different types in the study cited in Lesson 25 (p. 95)

CHAPTER 10
faster than 9 miles (14 km) per hour (p. 109)

CHAPTER 11
Scientists differentiate between killer whales by the nicks and scars on each whale's dorsal fin and the saddle patch at the base of the fin. (p. 122)

CHAPTER 12
Yes; carnivorous plants are predators. They catch and digest insects. (p. 128)

SCILINKS. THE WORLD'S A CLICK AWAY

www.scilinks.org
Keyword: Science Fair
Code: GSSD03

SELECTION	READING	WRITING	APPLICATION
CHAPTER 11 • KILLER WHALES: WOLVES OF THE SEA			
31. "Clicks, Calls, and Whistles" (nonfiction science book)	• Make predictions • Read critically	• Read a diagram • Draw conclusions	• Observe and record information • Make a drawing
32. "An Encounter" (nonfiction science book)	• Complete a graphic organizer • Visualizing • Generate questions	• Make predictions • State opinion based on information given	• Analyze information to make conclusion • Compare and contrast
33. "Snapshot ID" (nonfiction science book)	• Visualizing • Read critically	• Make predictions • Classifying	
CHAPTER 12 • PLANT ADAPTATIONS			
34. "The Sticky Seeds of the Mistletoe" (nonfiction science book)	• Classifying • Visualizing • Read a graph	• Organize information graphically • Defend answer	• Predict possible outcomes
35. "A Mean, Green Predator" (nonfiction science book)	• Use prior knowledge • Visualizing • Directed reading	• Make inferences	• Create your own carnivorous plant
36.	• Read critically	• Chart findings • Compare data • Cite evidence to support answer	• Hands-on activity • Create a model

Bacteria

LESSON 25

More Bacteria for Your Buck

Point of Lesson: ***Bacteria thrive on paper money.***

Money is dirty, and some high school students helped scientists prove it! An article about an investigation into bacteria on paper money introduces students to the conditions that bacteria require to thrive. After reading the article, students compare the properties of a dollar bill with the properties of other objects in their homes to identify places likely to harbor the most bacteria. Finally, students consider why most people do not become ill from handling money, since bacteria are so common.

Materials

Science Scope Activity (p. 94B and p. 95), for each group:

- petri dish
- nutrient agar
- masking tape
- magnifier
- wax pencil
- Bacteria Samples Data Collection Sheet (copymaster page 229)

Explore (p. 96), for each pair:

- dollar bill
- microscope or magnifier

Laboratory Safety

Review these safety guidelines with students before they do the Science Scope activity in this lesson.

- Do not taste any substance in the laboratory.
- Do not remove the tape sealing the petri dishes. Do not open the petri dishes.
- If a petri dish breaks open accidentally, do not handle it. Do not inhale the contents of the petri dish.
- Wash your hands thoroughly after the activity.

LESSON 26

The Bad Guys

Point of Lesson: ***Some bacteria are deadly.***

An excerpt from a book describes the symptoms of the bacterial infection known as bubonic plague and its devastating march across the Middle East, Northern Africa, and Europe in A.D. 540. After reading the passage, students learn how plague is spread, describe ways to prevent the transfer of the deadly bacteria, and learn why plague does not pose the threat it once did. Students follow up by researching a bacterial disease that is still a threat to humans.

Materials

Read (p. 99), for the class:

- world map

Enrichment (p. 99), for the class:

- research sources about bubonic plague

Connections (p. 100), for each student:

- calculator (optional)

LESSON 27

Bacteria at Work

Point of Lesson: ***Some bacteria help keep us healthy.***

An award-winning student essay informs students of many beneficial uses of bacteria. They then consider bacteria as a life form and evaluate the practice of judging bacteria as "good" or "bad." Students then analyze the results of a medical experiment involving bacteria that can be helpful to people.

Materials

none

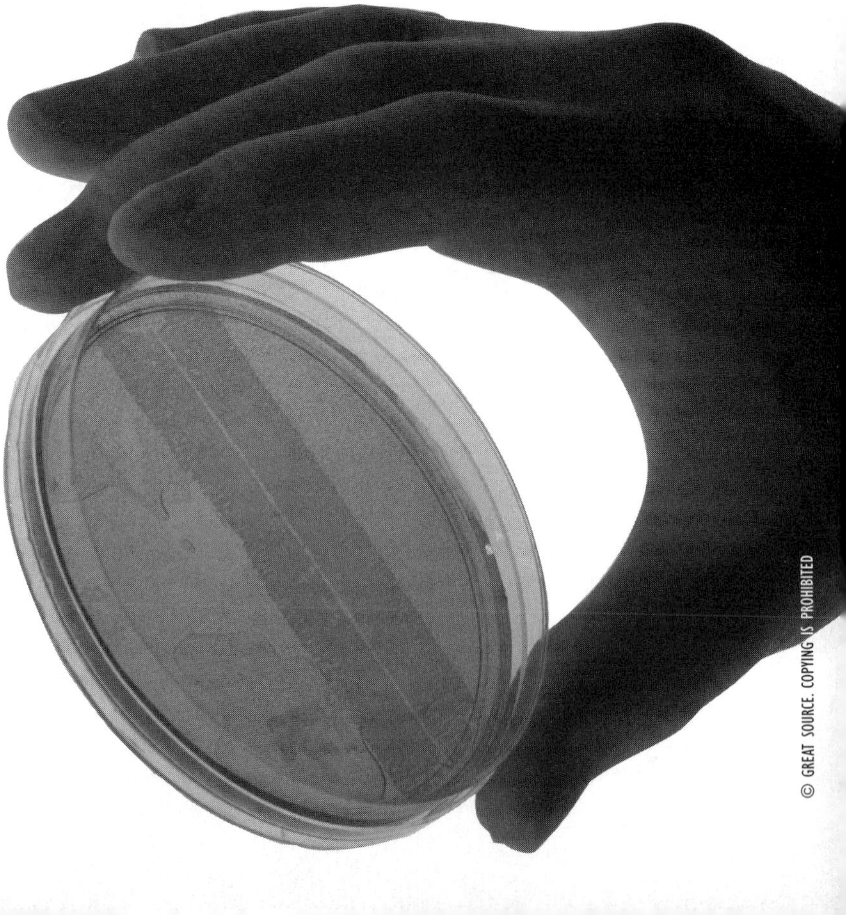

Science Scope Activity

Classifying Microorganisms

NSTA has chosen a Science Scope *activity related to the content in this chapter. The activity begins here and continues in Lesson 25, page 95.*

Time: 8 days (partial use of class time)

Materials: see page 94A

Materials note: Petri dishes and nutrient agar are available from science supply houses. Mix the nutrient agar and add it to each petri dish well before students start this activity.

Safety note: To dispose of the petri dishes, first heat them in a microwave oven to kill the bacteria and mold. Then double-bag the dishes in plastic bags tied securely closed.

In this activity, students sample organisms in the air, culture their samples, and generate ideas about how to classify the colonies of microorganisms they observe. Students should record the number of different types of colonies they observe in their petri dishes as well as the size of each colony. Encourage students to evaluate their results and resolve any inconsistencies in their classification methods.

Procedure

1. Divide the class into groups of two to four, and give each a petri dish filled with agar, a roll of masking tape, and a copy of the Bacteria Samples Data Collection Sheet. Have each group label its dish with the group members' initials.
2. Take the groups outdoors. Have them place the petri dishes on a table or other raised surface and remove the lids. After 10 minutes, have them replace the lids and tape the dishes closed.

(continued on page 95)

Background Information

Bacteria and Disease

Louis Pasteur (1822–1895) was among the first to investigate the relationship between disease and bacteria. His work led to the development of vaccines as well as to the process of pasteurizing food products by heating them to kill the bacteria living in them.

Knowledge of the role of bacteria in illness has led to better sanitation, vaccines against some bacterial diseases, and antibiotics. However, in recent years antibiotic-resistant strains of some bacteria have brought increased cases of some infectious diseases; their resistance to antibiotics makes these diseases difficult to treat.

Point of Lesson

Bacteria thrive on paper money.

Focus

- Change, constancy, and measurement
- Personal health
- Diversity and adaptations of organisms
- Understanding about scientific inquiry

Skills and Strategies

- Comparing and contrasting
- Sequencing
- Making inferences
- Recognizing cause and effect
- Drawing conclusions
- Generating ideas

Advance Preparation

Vocabulary

Make sure students understand these terms. Definitions can be found in the glossary at the end of the student book.

- bacteria
- cell
- experiment
- immune system
- nutrient

Materials

Gather the materials needed for *Science Scope Activity* (p. 94B and p. 95) and *Explore* (p. 96).

More Bacteria for Your Buck

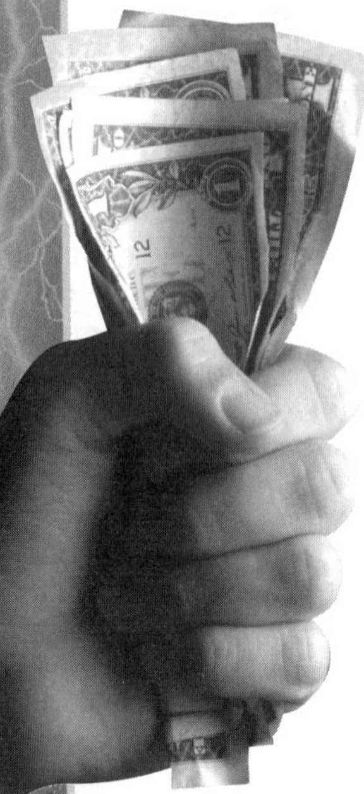

Should you be washing your money as well as your hands?

All bacteria have just one cell and are some of the smallest forms of life on Earth. Where can you find bacteria? Just about everywhere. One group of researchers found that even the dollar bills that most people carry around with them are perfect homes for all kinds of bacteria. The bills—and the bacteria—travel from person to person with every purchase, and some of these germs are even quite dangerous!

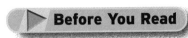

Before You Read

THINK ABOUT IT Did your parents ever warn you not to play with money when you were little? "Don't put that near your mouth. You don't know where it's been!" People usually worry about coins because they often fall on the ground. But as you know, money comes in two varieties. The surface of coins is hard and smooth, while bills are soft and somewhat rough.

- ***Do you think more bacteria live on dollar bills or on coins? Why?***

On bills, the soft, rough surface provides protected places for bacteria to live and reproduce, but the hard, smooth surface of coins does not provide protected places.

TEACHING PLAN pp. 94–95

INTRODUCING THE LESSON

This lesson presents a science-fair study that investigated the incidence of bacteria living on paper money. Point out that *bacteria* is the plural form of the word and that the singular form is *bacterium*.

Ask students: *What are bacteria, and where are they found?* Students may know that bacteria are living organisms, that each bacterium consists of only one cell, and that the cell does not have a true nucleus. Bacteria are found virtually everywhere.

Many students may think that bacteria and viruses are the same thing. Explain that viruses are not considered living organisms. They consist of only genetic material (DNA, RNA) surrounded by a protective coating of protein. Viruses are much smaller than bacteria and must attack and enter other cells in order to reproduce.

Before You Read

THINK ABOUT IT Ask students if they think paper money has more bacteria on it than other common objects that people put in their mouth, such as pencil tips, toothpicks, and toothbrushes, and to explain their reasoning. (Paper money probably does have more bacteria on it because it is handled by so many different people, whereas the other objects are not.)

Read

Here is what researchers found in the cracks and crevices of your cash.

Dirty Money

Dollar bills support a rich flora of bacteria, some of them infectious, say research physicians Theodore W. Pope and Peter T. Ender of the Medical Center of Wright-Patterson Air Force Base in Ohio.

They worked with Michael A. Koroscil at Beavercreek (Ohio) High School, who originated the idea for a science-fair project.[1] The group counted the [kinds of] bacteria living on 68 dollar bills collected from people in line at a high school sporting event and a grocery store.

[2] The researchers incubated each bill in nutrient broth for up to a day and [3] then grew any bacteria in culture dishes to identify them. More than half the bills hosted bacteria that commonly infect people in hospitals or those who have depressed immune systems, the team reported. Five of the bills contained a bacterium that can sicken healthy people, either *Klebsiella pneumonia* [which causes pneumonia] or *Staphylococcus aureus* [which can cause deadly infections]. The researchers identified a total of 93 different types of bacteria living on the bills, and two-thirds of the bills had at least one type.

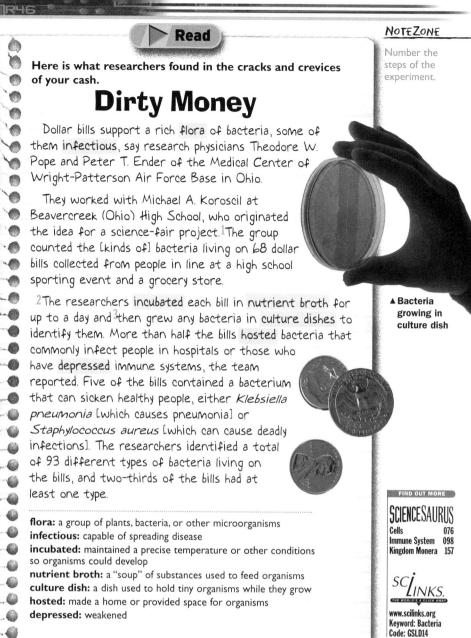

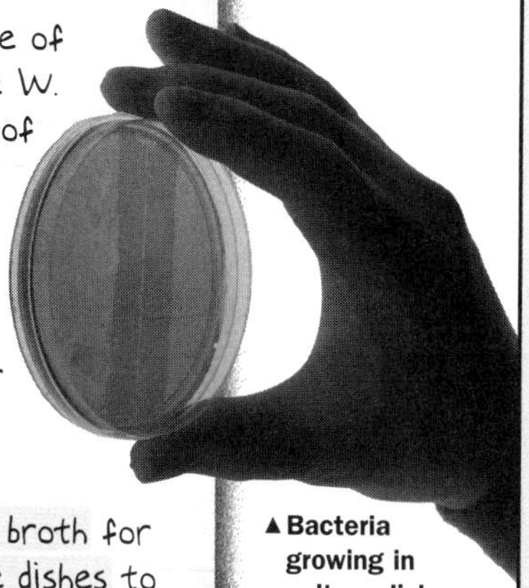

flora: a group of plants, bacteria, or other microorganisms
infectious: capable of spreading disease
incubated: maintained a precise temperature or other conditions so organisms could develop
nutrient broth: a "soup" of substances used to feed organisms
culture dish: a dish used to hold tiny organisms while they grow
hosted: made a home or provided space for organisms
depressed: weakened

From: Netting, Jessica. "Dirty Money Harbors Bacterial Dangers." *Science News*.

NOTEZONE

Number the steps of the experiment.

▲ **Bacteria growing in culture dish**

FIND OUT MORE

SCIENCESAURUS
Cells 076
Immune System 098
Kingdom Monera 157

SCILINKS. THE WORLD'S A CLICK AWAY
www.scilinks.org
Keyword: Bacteria
Code: GSLD14

95

Science Scope Activity

(continued from page 94B)

3. In the classroom, have students place the dishes in a warm, dark place to allow the microorganisms to grow. Tell students that this process is called *incubation*.
4. Let groups observe the dishes with a magnifier every day for at least one week and record any changes they see. Students could also use a wax pencil on the lid to trace around the edge of the growth so they can observe changes in size. **Caution:** Warn students not to remove the tape or open the dish.
5. Let the groups exchange dishes and compare their results. Discuss the changes that students observed. Make sure they understand that the growth in the dishes was produced by living organisms.
6. Ask students: *Where did the organisms come from?* (They were present in the air.) *Why couldn't you see the organisms in the dishes when you started?* (They are too small to be seen without a microscope.) *What do you think the microorganisms are?* (bacteria) If mold also grew in the dishes, point that out as well.

Read

Ask a volunteer to read the third paragraph's first sentence aloud. Ask: *Why did the researchers have to incubate the bills in order to identify the bacteria?* (Bacteria are microscopic, so the researchers had to let them grow.) Point out that bacteria are single-celled organisms. The bacteria themselves did not grow—i.e., become larger. Rather, the bacteria reproduced by dividing in half repeatedly until the entire bacteria population was large enough to see.

After students have identified the steps of the experiment in the NoteZone task, ask: *What other steps in an experiment are not mentioned in the reading?* (developing a hypothesis, designing the experiment, identifying and controlling variables, interpreting data, reporting results)

CHECK UNDERSTANDING

Skill: Recognizing cause and effect

Ask: *What does it mean to incubate bacteria?* (to provide bacteria with the right temperature and other conditions they need)

More Resources

The following resources are also available from Great Source and NSTA.

SCIENCESAURUS

Cells 076
Immune System 098
Kingdom Monera 157

READER'S HANDBOOK

Making Inferences 40
Drawing Conclusions 41
Reading Science 100

MATH ON CALL

Gathering Data 263

SCILINKS. THE WORLD'S A CLICK AWAY

www.scilinks.org
Keyword: Bacteria
Code: GSLD14

Explore

WHAT BACTERIA NEED Because paper money is woven, it offers plenty of nooks and crannies where bacteria can make their homes.

► ***Name three other objects in your home that have tiny crevices where bacteria could grow.***

Answers will vary. Examples: carpets and rugs, tile floor, sofa

Like all living things, bacteria also need water to survive. Paper absorbs moisture from the air or objects around it—another reason bacteria thrive on dollar bills.

► ***Would the three objects you named also provide moisture for bacteria? If not, name three other objects in your home that would provide a moist environment for bacteria.***

Answers will vary. Examples: towels, cleaning rags, sponges

Bacteria also need nutrients to survive. This is why food spoils—bacteria are making both a meal and a home of the food. Bacteria can get their nutrients from many sources. It might be from the same things that we eat, or from the things we throw away, from the skin oil on our hands, or even from our waste products.

► ***Protected places, water, and nutrients—these are the three things that bacteria need. Knowing this, where do you think would be the best places to find bacteria in your home? List three.***

Answers will vary. Examples: exercise clothes, shoes, bath mat

Propose Explanations

GERMY MONEY

► ***Why do you think the researchers were so interested in studying the bacteria on dollar bills? Why would bacteria that live on money be more dangerous to people than bacteria that live inside your sneakers, for example?***

The bacteria on money are passed around to a large number of people. Bacteria in your sneakers stay in one place. Also, people touch their eyes, hair, nose, mouth, and other surfaces before and after handling money.

96

TEACHING PLAN pp. 96–97

Explore

Time: 10 minutes
Materials: dollar bill; microscope or magnifier

WHAT BACTERIA NEED Have students examine a dollar bill with a microscope or magnifier. Encourage them to think of the bill's surface from the perspective of bacteria. Then ask: *Why is paper money such a good place for bacteria to grow?* (The surface of paper money has cracks and crevices that provide protected places for bacteria.) Explain that bacteria can be less than 1 micron (0.001 mm or 0.00004 in.) in diameter and that hundreds of thousands of them could fit on the period at the end of a sentence. Remind students that bacteria are visible only when they reproduce and form a large population.

Propose Explanations

GERMY MONEY Have students brainstorm places where humans would come into contact with harmful bacteria. To prompt their ideas, ask them to think of their favorite restaurant and then identify all the surfaces in it where germs might be encountered. Some surfaces, such as the countertop, may be cleaned regularly, but the money used to pay for the food would carry bacteria. The table, handrails, door handles, and chairs are also potential sources of bacteria.

Ask students to suggest ways to avoid infection by bacteria. Also ask them how the workers who prepare the food can avoid passing bacteria along.

Remind students about the danger of using antibacterial soaps and cleaners, since bacteria may become resistant to the antibacterial chemicals in them. Focus instead on the use of warm water and ordinary soap to remove bacteria.

The bacteria that live on paper money are usually not a great threat to our health. However, over 50 percent of the bills in the research study carried bacteria that could cause disease. Even so, most people do not get sick from handling paper money. The people most at risk are those who are already sick or who have a weakened immune system.

▸ ***Why do most people stay healthy after handling money? Why are the bacteria on paper money more dangerous to people who are already sick?***

Usually a healthy person's immune system can fight off the bacteria. The immune system of someone who is already sick may not be strong enough to fight off another infection.

▸ ***Describe ways that we can avoid spreading germs on dollar bills.***

Answers will vary. Examples: by washing the money, washing your hands after handling money, using a credit card or check instead of dollar bills

▶ Take Action

HEALTH IS WEALTH Using what you've learned about bacteria, design a new type of money to replace dollar bills. The new money should not give bacteria a good place to live and grow. Draw your new money and explain why it would avoid the problems of paper money.

Answers will vary. Possible answers; coins to replace dollar bills, smooth bills made of hard plastic, a credit card or debit card to replace all cash transactions

97

Connections

HEALTH Explain to students that the overuse of antibiotics may be lessening the drugs' effectiveness. Tell students that when someone uses an antibiotic, it kills most of the bacteria, but some bacteria have natural resistance and survive. These bacteria reproduce, and their "offspring" are also resistant to the antibiotic. Over time, that entire species of bacteria becomes resistant to the antibiotic, and researchers have to try to develop a new antibiotic against it. The fear is that some antibiotics may cease to be effective at all. For this reason, doctors avoid over-prescribing antibiotics.

Assessment

Skill: Drawing conclusions

Use the following question to assess each student's progress:

Why can bacteria live on paper money as well as on other surfaces such as food, dead leaves, and dirty clothes? (Bacteria need moisture, nutrients, and protected places to survive. Paper money and other surfaces provide an environment with those basics.)

▶ Take Action

HEALTH IS WEALTH Encourage students to give imaginative responses and futuristic possibilities such as self-cleaning money or money baths used at banks and other money collection points. Have students explain why their new money would be more resistant to bacteria growth. Let students share their ideas. Students could also discuss the uses of electronic transactions they are familiar with.

Point of Lesson
Some bacteria are deadly.

Focus
- Systems, order, and organization
- Personal health
- Diversity and adaptations of organisms
- Populations, resources, and environments

Skills and Strategies
- Predicting
- Making and using models
- Making inferences
- Recognizing cause and effect

Advance Preparation

Vocabulary
Make sure students understand these terms. Definitions can be found in the glossary at the end of the student book.

- antibody
- bacteria
- continent
- infectious
- organism
- population

Materials
Gather the materials needed for ***Read*** (p. 99), ***Enrichment*** (p. 99), and ***Connections*** (p. 100).

Bacteria

THE BAD GUYS

These guys are small, but deadly!

Some bacteria are deadly. One of the best known is *Yersinia pestis*, the bacterium responsible for the bubonic plague, or "Black Death" as it was commonly called. Over the course of history, bubonic plague has killed hundreds of millions of people around the world.

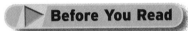

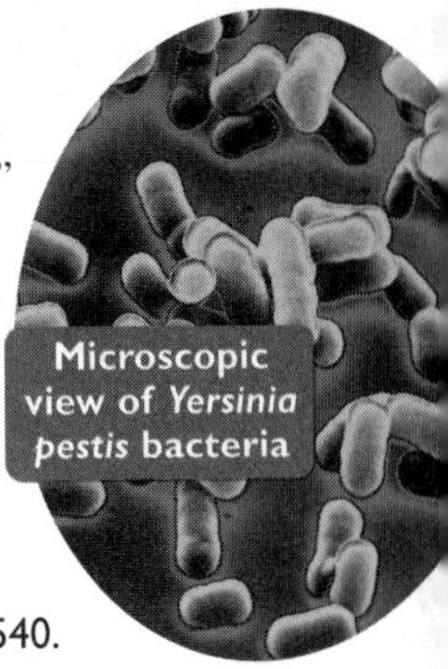
Microscopic view of *Yersinia pestis* bacteria

Before You Read

MAKE A PREDICTION One way humans get the bacterium that causes bubonic plague is from the bite of a flea that usually lives on rats. The bubonic plague spread across the world in A.D. 540.

- ***How do you think it could have traveled from one continent to another?***

Answers will vary. Example: It may have traveled in fleas that were living on rats that boarded boats going to other continents.

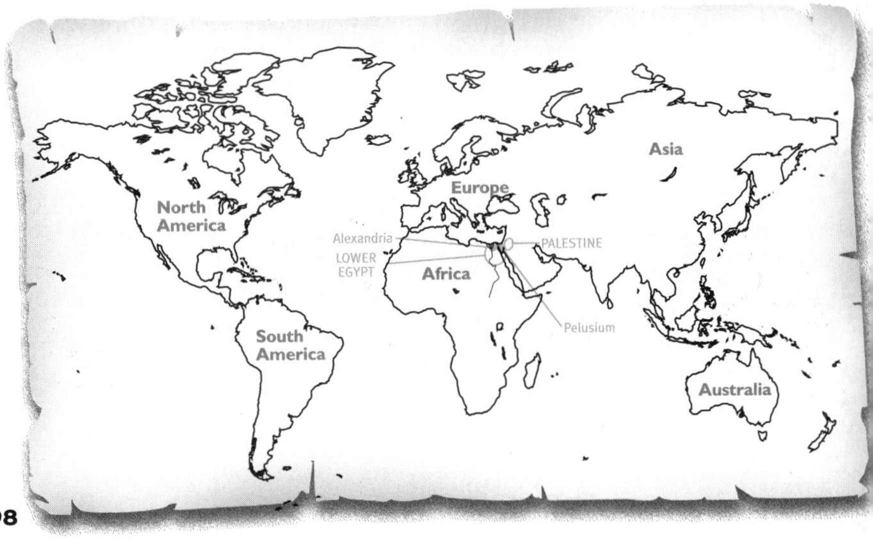

TEACHING PLAN pp. 98–99

INTRODUCING THE LESSON
This lesson describes bubonic plague as one deadly disease caused by a bacterium. Students may not realize that some of the diseases that can be treated successfully today were once a serious threat to huge numbers of people worldwide. They also may not be aware that diseases now rare in this country remain threats throughout the world. Explain that medicines to treat these diseases and medical facilities to care for the first victims and prevent the disease from spreading are not always available in other parts of the world. Also tell students that international, national, and private agencies work to improve medical care throughout the world.

Before You Read

MAKE A PREDICTION After students have answered the question, ask: *How do you think diseases spread from country to country today?* (Students should realize that airplanes carrying infected passengers make the spread of disease easier and faster than in the past.) Explain that today, the international medical community distributes information about outbreaks and available treatments and provides assistance to control the spread of disease.

Read

Here is how one of the smallest life forms wiped out entire populations of people.

KILLER GERMS

The bubonic form [of the plague] is characterized by large buboes, [which are] swollen lymph nodes in the neck, armpits or groin.... Bubonic plague victims characteristically flex and extend their arms in attempts to lessen the pain of the buboes. Infection of the blood can lead to bleeding beneath the skin, which causes the characteristic black splodges on the skin. These symptoms are accompanied by a very high fever, headache, shaking chills, and delirium and are followed by death in fifty to sixty percent of cases when left untreated.

...In A.D. 540, during the reign of Emperor Justinian, a pandemic (an epidemic that spreads across whole continents) broke out in Pelusium, Lower Egypt, and spread throughout Alexandria and on to Palestine. From there it traveled the world. At the peak of the crisis, estimates suggest that ten thousand people were dying each day. Maybe one hundred million people died in all. Historians say this scourge contributed to the fall of the Roman Empire.

NoteZone

Underline the places where the plague broke out in A.D. 540 and first spread. Use a world map to find those places and mark them on the map on page 98.

lymph nodes: small structures in the body that remove and kill bacteria and other microorganisms
flex: bend
extend: straighten
splodges: patches or large, uneven spots
delirium: mental confusion
scourge: a source of widespread suffering

From: Moore, Pete. *Killer Germs: Rogue Diseases of the Twenty-First Century.* Carlton Books Limited 2001.

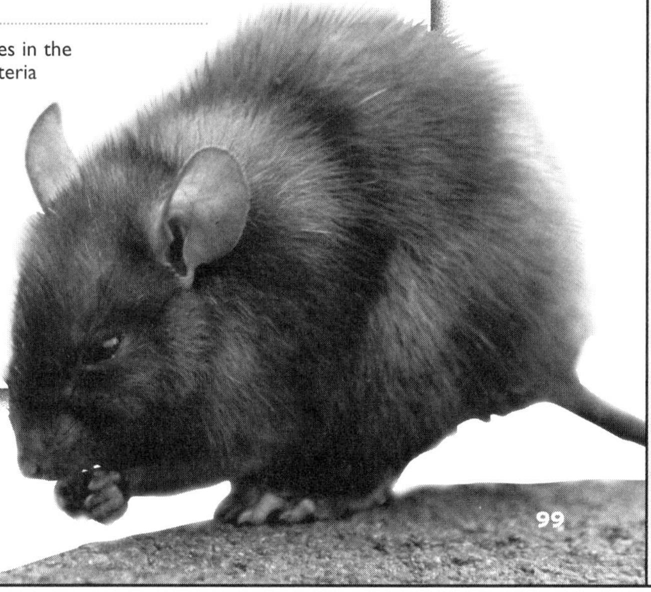

Rat ▶

99

Enrichment

Time: will vary
Materials: research sources about bubonic plague

Tell students to imagine the reaction of people living in a town in the ancient world when an unknown disease suddenly struck the citizens and caused the symptoms described in the reading. (Examples: People would be frightened. They might panic and flee the town, carrying the infectious bacteria with them.) Note that when the first cases of AIDS appeared in the U.S. in the 1980s, many people were equally fearful and panicked. Students could research the superstitions that arose to explain where the plague came from and how it might be cured. (Earthquakes and "fire from the sky" were considered to be causes.) Tell students to think about how daily interactions between people and travel from town to town would be affected. After they have identified some of the superstitions, have students compare them with the actual causes of and cures for the plague.

Read

Time: 10 minutes
Materials: world map

Provide a world map for students' reference in the NoteZone task.

Students may wonder where the term "bubonic plague" came from. Explain that it derived from the Greek word *boubon*, meaning "swelling." Ask students to explain why this term was used. (Victims had swollen lymph nodes in the neck, armpits, or groin.) Also ask students why the disease was known as the "Black Death." (There were black splodges on the victims' skin.)

Point out the statement in the reading that maybe 100 million died in the A.D. 540 pandemic. To help students comprehend the great loss of life, explain that at that time the world population was about 200 million people, compared with today's population of about 6 billion. The deaths of 100 million people in A.D. 540 means that half the world's population died.

CHECK UNDERSTANDING

Skill: Recognizing cause and effect
Tell students that cities and towns in A.D. 540 were infested with rats. Ask: *What does this have to do with the spread of bubonic plague?* (The bacterium that causes plague is carried by fleas that usually live on rats.)

More Resources

The following resource is also available from Great Source.

READER'S HANDBOOK

Drawing Conclusions	41
Concept Map	137
Elements of Graphics: Map	555
Looking for Cause and Effect	644

Connections

Time: 10 minutes
Materials: calculators (one per student, optional)

MATH Have students calculate the approximate number of deaths from the plague in 1665 London. (500,000 ÷ 3 = almost 167,000 people) Students could also calculate the number of people that could be infected through an initial single case. Tell students to suppose that one infected person can infect two other people in a 24-hour period. *How many people would be infected in two days?* (4) *In three days?* (8) *In one week?* (128) Students may know that this rate of increase is called exponential growth. (See Chapter 3, pages 34–35.)

Explore

HOW THE PLAGUE TRAVELS Deadly bacteria often travel through animals before reaching human beings. The first organisms bubonic plague bacteria infect are fleas that live on rats. The bacteria do not kill the fleas. When the infected fleas bite the rats, they pass the bacteria to them, and soon the rats die. If the fleas cannot find another rat, they may then move to a human and bring the deadly bacteria with them.

► ***Suggest some ways that people could keep the plague from spreading.***

Get rid of all of the rats; kill fleas where they breed; keep homes very clean; exterminate fleas and rats from homes, offices, and public buildings.

► ***Draw a diagram to show how Yersinia pestis bacteria usually travel to humans.***

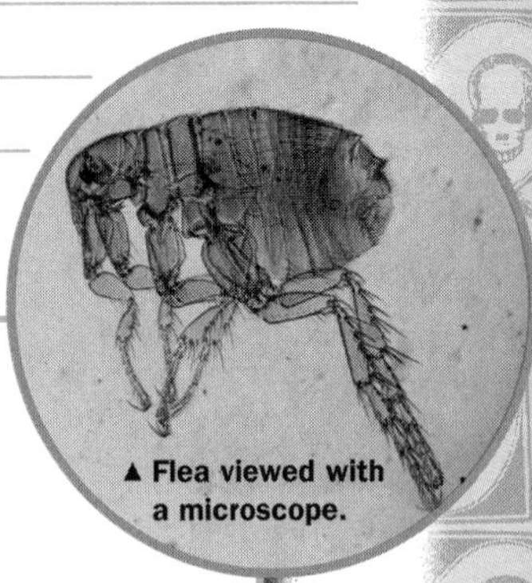

▲ Flea viewed with a microscope.

Diagram should show that Yersinia pestis travels from fleas to rats to humans or directly from fleas to humans.

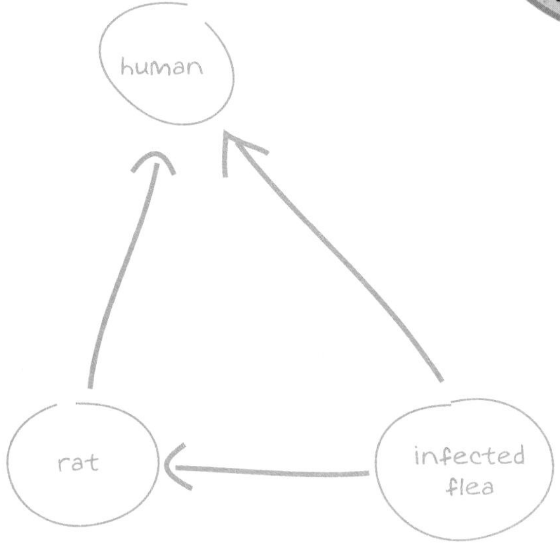

TEACHING PLAN pp. 100–101

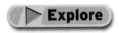

Explore

HOW THE PLAGUE TRAVELS Have students explain how the plague is physically passed from fleas to rats, making sure they understand that a flea bite passes the bacteria to the rat. The disease is then spread to humans in two ways. The flea can leave the rat and go on to bite a human, thus spreading the bacteria into the person's bloodstream. Or an infected human can spread the bacteria through droplets sprayed in a cough; another person inhales the droplets, and the bacteria spread from the lungs throughout the body. Contact with contaminated skin, clothing, food, dead rats, or other objects also spreads the disease.

Tell students that scientists theorize the plague all but ended when black rats, the original carriers, either died out or became immune to the disease or were replaced in their habitats by the larger brown rats, which are not carriers of the disease.

After students draw their diagrams, have them add transmission from one human to another human.

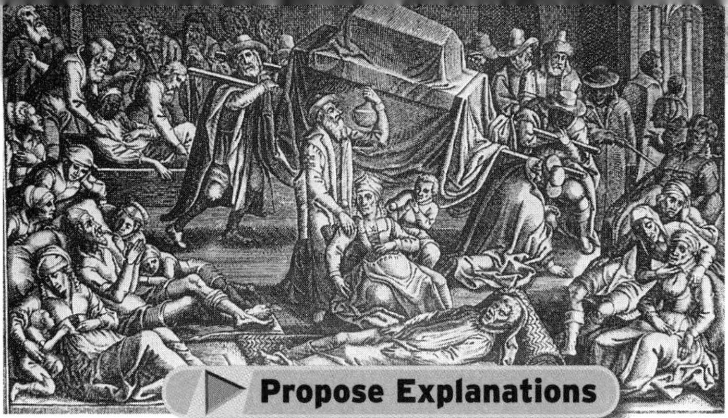

◂ Plague victims in an engraving by J. Orlers, 1674

Propose Explanations

THINK ABOUT IT In 1665 the Black Death attacked London and killed about one third of the city's population of 500,000 before dying out.

- ***What do you think would have happened to Yersinia pestis bacteria if the plague had wiped out the entire city?***

If the bacteria had wiped out all of the fleas' hosts (humans, rats, and other mammals), then the fleas couldn't survive, and neither could the bacteria.

- ***The plague often spread in cities. What is it about cities that makes them such good homes for infectious bacteria? What are some of the ways you can protect yourself from bacteria wherever you live?***

In cities many people live close together, and there are more rats with fleas living near people. The bacteria are quickly and easily spread from organism to organism. You can protect yourself by keeping your home clean and exterminating any insects and rats in your home.

Take Action

GERM-INATE AWARENESS Bubonic plague is no longer a major health threat. Cities today are cleaner, and doctors can recognize plague symptoms quickly and treat the disease with antibiotics.

However, other infectious diseases caused by bacteria do threaten humans today. Choose one such infectious disease to research. Some examples are food poisoning, Lyme disease, staph infections, tuberculosis, and typhus. Find out how the disease is transmitted to people, what the symptoms are, where the disease is most common, and how to prevent it from spreading. Present your findings on a poster or in a brief oral report.

Assessment

Skill: Generating ideas

Use the following question to assess each student's progress:

Why didn't people in A.D. 540 realize that rats and fleas were spreading the plague? (People then didn't know about bacteria and how diseases are spread.)

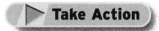

Propose Explanations

THINK ABOUT IT Ask students to suggest reasons why the plague did not kill the entire population of London. (Examples: Not every person was exposed to the bacteria; not every exposed person became infected; not every infected person died.)

Take Action

GERM-INATE AWARENESS Students could do this activity individually or in small groups.

Review students' selections of diseases. If they select a disease not mentioned in the second paragraph, make sure that it is one caused by a bacterium, not a virus.

Encourage students who choose to do an oral report to include charts, illustrations, and other graphics. Point out that clever and eye-catching graphics will make these presentations more effective.

Point of Lesson

Some bacteria help keep us healthy.

Focus

- Evolution and equilibrium
- Personal health
- Diversity and adaptations of organisms
- Understanding about scientific inquiry

Skills and Strategies

- Comparing and contrasting
- Recognizing cause and effect
- Interpreting data
- Making inferences

Advance Preparation

Vocabulary

Make sure students understand these terms. Definitions can be found in the glossary at the end of the student book.

- antibody
- bacteria
- experiment
- hormone
- hypothesis
- intestines

More Resources

The following resource is also available from Great Source.

SCIENCESAURUS

Kingdom Monera 157
Renewable Material Resources 330

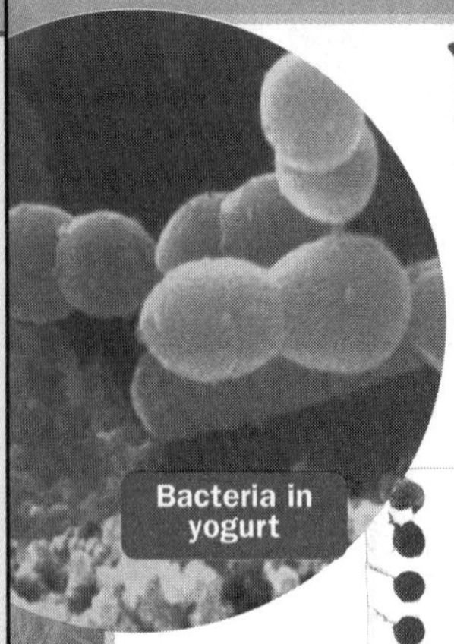
Bacteria in yogurt

Bacteria at Work

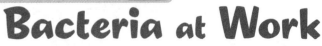

Is "bacteria" just another word for disease? Not at all!

Most of the bacteria we hear about are harmful to humans, but that's just because bad guys always make the headlines. Most bacteria are not harmful to us at all. There are many different kinds of bacteria living inside our bodies that help keep us healthy.

Read

A 13-year-old student named Rachel wrote an essay about bacteria and won the Young Naturalist Award from the American Museum of Natural History for her work.

BACTERIA GOOD GUYS

Bacteria are responsible for much more than just diseases. There are thousands of kinds of bacteria. Most of them are harmless to humans.

Vast numbers of bacteria live in our bodies. One example is found in the intestine. The bacteria help us with digestion and to produce vitamins. In exchange, they soak up a little extra food for themselves. Neat. Huh? Most dairy products are made by or with the help of bacteria. Some dairy foods are cheese, buttermilk, yogurt, and sour cream. Some other kinds of foods that involve bacteria in their production are pickles and high fructose corn syrup. Can you imagine our soda without high fructose corn syrup? A hamburger with no cheese or pickles?

Bacteria are very important in medicine. Doctors and scientists have figured out how to use dead or weakened bacteria to prevent other bacterial diseases. This process is called vaccination. Vaccination has helped us all become a lot healthier than we were a hundred years ago.... Bacteria do so much for us, where would we be without them?

fructose: a sugar found in fruit and honey

From: Mock, Rachel. "Bacteria." *Young Naturalist Awards.* American Museum of Natural History. (www.amnh.org/nationalcenter/youngnaturalistawards/1998/bacteria.html)

NOTEZONE

What else would you like to know about helpful bacteria in our bodies?

FIND OUT MORE

SCIENCESAURUS

Kingdom Monera 157
Renewable Material Resources 330

TEACHING PLAN pp. 102–103

INTRODUCING THE LESSON

In this lesson, students learn that some bacteria are helpful to humans and in some cases necessary for good health. Ask students: *Are any bacteria helpful to humans?* Students may think of bacteria only in terms of causing disease. Explain that many types of bacteria neither help nor harm humans, some harm humans, and some are helpful to us. Then ask: *Do you know of any helpful bacteria?* Explain that bacteria are necessary to produce yogurt and buttermilk. Some students may be aware that bacteria help our bodies digest food and also produce vitamins. Bacteria perform an essential function in ecosystems by breaking down waste matter such as leaves, animal wastes, and dead organisms into nutrients that plants and other organisms can use.

Read

Tell students that in addition to the benefits mentioned in the reading, helpful bacteria in the intestines can prevent harmful bacteria from living there by taking the nutrients and places that the harmful bacteria would need in order to survive. Helpful bacteria also produce substances that kill harmful bacteria. To learn more about the types of bacteria commonly found in humans, students can visit the following Web site: www.bact.wisc.edu/Bact303/Bact303normalflora

Explore

"GOOD" OR "BAD"? Bacteria are doing the same thing we're doing—trying to stay alive. Unfortunately, what some bacteria do to stay alive means harm to us. For example, some bacteria that cause food to spoil do not harm people. But when those bacteria break down food, they give off chemicals that are poisonous to us. However, there are also bacteria that help us while they help themselves, such as the bacteria in our intestines. Bacteria are also what turn milk into yogurt and cabbage into sauerkraut. One scientist has even found sewer bacteria that release a gas that may someday be able to be used as a fuel!

- ***Is there really such a thing as "good" bacteria and "bad" bacteria? Why do we call bacteria "good" or "bad"?***

Bacteria are not "good" or "bad." They're just organisms trying to survive. We call bacteria "good" when they help us and "bad" when they harm us.

Propose Explanations

HELPFUL BACTERIA A group of scientists did an experiment using the following hypothesis: A daily dose of certain intestinal bacteria may keep children who are in hospitals from getting diarrhea so they won't have to spend extra time in the hospital. The diarrhea is usually caused by a virus that the children catch while they are in the hospital.

The scientists tested their hypothesis by giving one group of children a dose of beneficial bacteria called *Lactobaccillus GG* twice a day during their hospital stay. Another group was given a placebo, a pill that doesn't have any effect. The scientists found that the risk of getting diarrhea was 80 percent lower in the group that received the bacteria than in the group that didn't.

- ***Based on what you know about "good" intestinal bacteria, suggest a possible reason for these results.***

Answers will vary. Example: The bacteria may have formed a protective barrier against the virus or crowded it out.

Enrichment

Encourage students to make yogurt at home. Instructions can be found at the following Web site, or students may prefer to locate recipes on their own. www.billstclair.com/DoingFreedom/000623/df.0600.ff.yogurt.html

Emphasize to students that they should obtain permission before using an oven. Let students bring in samples of their homemade yogurt to share with the class. **Caution:** Make sure students who are allergic to dairy products do not participate in the yogurt tasting.

Assessment

Skill: Organizing information

Use the following question to assess each student's progress:

What are some ways that bacteria are beneficial to humans? (Bacteria in our intestines help digest food and produce vitamins. Bacteria are needed to produce some foods. Vaccines are made using dead or weakened bacteria.)

Explore

"GOOD" OR "BAD"? Ask students to explain what the text means when it says that bacteria are simply "trying to stay alive." (Bacteria do not intentionally help or hurt humans. The benefit or harm to humans is just a by-product of the bacteria's life processes—obtaining air, water, and nutrients, reproducing, and so forth.)

Propose Explanations

HELPFUL BACTERIA Ask students to suggest why the placebo—the pill that did not contain the bacteria—was used for one group of children. (The researchers had to make sure that it was not something besides the beneficial bacteria that was keeping children from getting diarrhea. The children who got the placebo were the control group in the experiment.)

CHECK UNDERSTANDING

Skill: Making inferences

Ask: *People who have been taking antibiotics for an infection are often told to eat yogurt. Why would this be beneficial to them?* (The antibiotics may have killed helpful bacteria in their intestines. Since yogurt contains helpful bacteria, eating it could replace bacteria that were killed.)

How Insects Get Around

LESSON 28

Walk Like an Insect

Point of Lesson: ***An insect's body structure makes it stable as it walks.***

Students in groups of three first attempt to coordinate six legs while walking, then learn how insects move their six legs to walk. Students consider the importance of walking as a structural adaptation that helps insects survive. They also compare the stability of different insects by observing their legs.

Materials

Enrichment (p. 105), for the class:

- drawing paper
- colored pencils or markers
- field guides
- globe or world map

LESSON 29

Jump!

Point of Lesson: ***Structures for jumping help insects survive.***

Students read an article about various body structures that enable different insects to jump. They also compare the energy used in jumping versus walking and consider how jumping helps some insects function in their environment.

Materials

Enrichment (p. 109), for each student:

- Insect Structure sheet (copymaster p. 228)
- drawing paper
- colored pencils or markers

LESSON 30

Flights of Fancy

Point of Lesson: ***Flying and migration are structural and behavioral adaptations of some insects.***

An excerpt from a fiction book about dragonflies introduces some structural and behavioral adaptations of these amazing insects. Students consider how the body parts of a green darner dragonfly coordinate as it flies and how its skill as a flier helps it hunt and migrate successfully. The lesson ends with an exercise on what constitutes anthropomorphism and identifying anthropomorphism in familiar stories.

Materials

Enrichment (p. 111), for the class:

- research sources about migratory insects

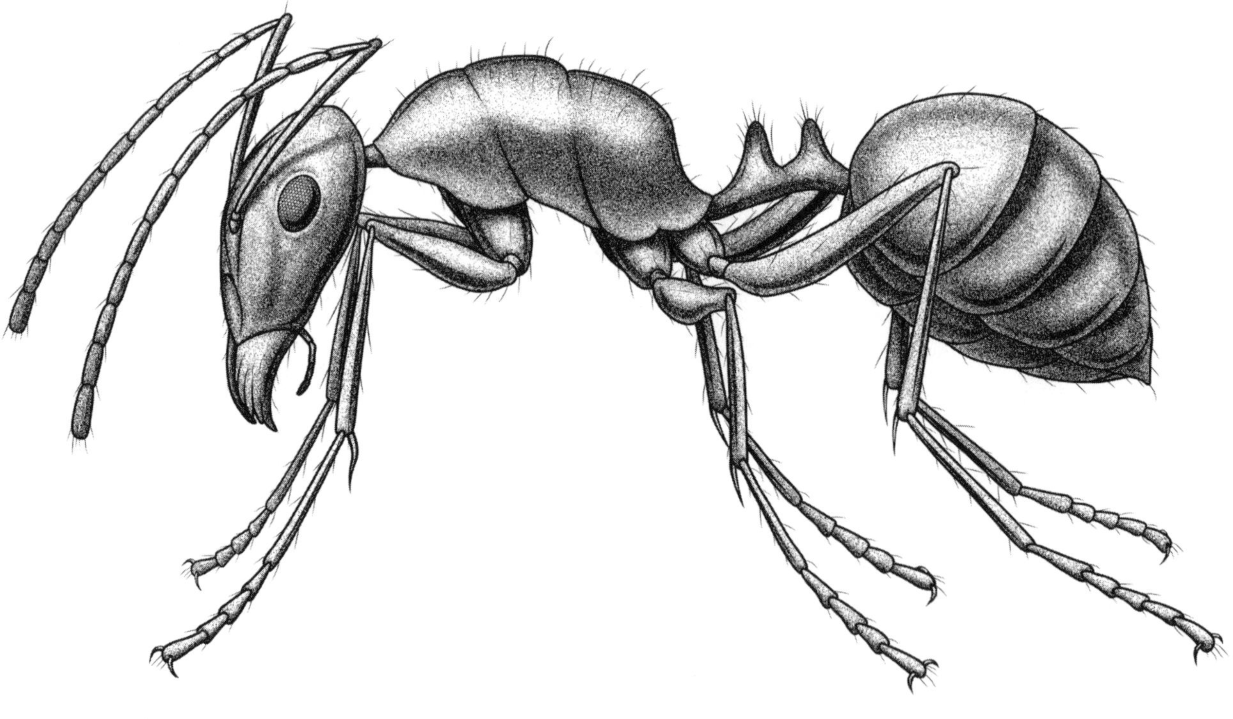

Background Information

Lesson 28

Robot design engineers often study insects because many insects' body structures make them highly stable and mobile. Additionally, by creating robots that are modeled after insects, engineers provide an opportunity for entomologists to test their hypotheses about how insects coordinate their movements. Engineers videotape an insect walking and then analyze the tape frame by frame to learn how the insect moves in a variety of situations. Modeling walking robots after insects has enabled engineers to build robots that can walk on uneven terrain and that can recover from stepping in a hole or meeting an obstacle. This is accomplished through sensors built into the robots' legs, which mimic the cells in an insect's leg that signal pressure and stress.

Lesson 30

The green darner dragonfly species described in the lesson migrates seasonally, but not all dragonfly species do. Green darner dragonflies lay their eggs on aquatic plants. When the egg hatches, the larval stage—called a nymph—lives in the water. The longest part of a dragonfly's life cycle, which can be several years for some species, is spent in this nymph stage. During this stage, the nymph molts its skin several times as it grows to its adult size. When the dragonfly reaches the adult stage, it leaves the water and flies over land. The adult stage of a dragonfly's life lasts only a few weeks. A particular adult green darner dragonfly may or may not migrate, depending on the time of year that it reaches the adult stage.

Point of Lesson
An insect's body structure makes it stable as it walks.

Focus
- Form and function
- Structure and function in living systems
- Diversity and adaptations of organisms

Skills and Strategies
- Making and using models
- Making inferences
- Comparing and contrasting

Advance Preparation

Vocabulary
Make sure students understand these terms. Definitions can be found in the glossary at the end of the student book.

- gravity
- mass
- species

Materials
Gather the materials needed for *Enrichment* (p 105).

CHAPTER 10 / LESSON 28

How Insects Get Around

Walk Like an Insect

Walking seems easy, but what if you had six legs?

There are more kinds of insects than any other kind of animal on Earth. Scientists have identified about 800,000 species of insects, and they know that there are many more yet to be found!

All adult insects have a body made up of three parts, with six legs attached to the middle part. Beyond that, insects are very different. One way insects differ from each other is in how they get around. Many insects get around just by walking on their six legs. That's a lot of legs to coordinate!

Before You Read

HOW DO THEY DO IT? We all know how people with two legs walk—after all, most do it every day. One leg goes forward, then the other, then the first leg again, and so on. But how does a six-legged insect walk? By moving one leg at a time? All three on one side and then all three on the other?

Find out what method works best by teaming up with two classmates to form a six-legged "insect." Stand one in front of the other, and put your hands on the shoulders of the person in front of you.

- ***Now try to get your "insect" to move forward. First try to walk without talking to your "other legs." Then try planning with your teammates how you will move. What did you learn?***

Answers will vary. Answers should describe the difficulty of coordinating the movement of six legs and explain that it is harder to coordinate movement when the "legs" cannot communicate than when they can.

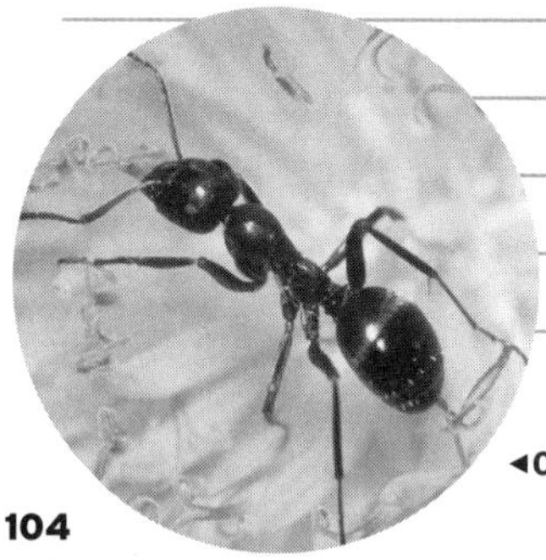

◀Carpenter ant

UNIT 3: LIVING THINGS

104

TEACHING PLAN pp. 104–105

INTRODUCING THE LESSON
This lesson discusses the structural adaptations of insects that walk. Ask students to tell you what all insects have in common. (six legs, a pair of compound eyes, a pair of antennae, and three segmented body parts—head, thorax, and abdomen)

Ask students to name animals they would classify as insects. Students may think that spiders are insects. Explain that spiders are arachnids, not insects. They have eight legs, not six, and no antennae. Spiders also have more than one pair of eyes.

Before You Read

HOW DO THEY DO IT? After students have done the Before You Read activity, ask them to describe the different ways they tried to walk. Which way was the most successful? Which was the least successful? Have them describe the sequence of their six legs and explain why it was the best method. If not all groups were successful, let the other groups demonstrate their methods.

Ask students what kinds of insects they have observed walking and where they observed them. What were the similarities and differences in the insects' overall body shape and appendages?

Read

Amazingly, insects are able to move their six legs without ever getting them tangled. Here's how they do it.

Insect March

Insects have six multi-jointed legs that make them very stable. They can (start fast) and (stop suddenly) without falling over. They are also very light, making it easy for them to maneuver....

When an insect (walks,) it (moves three legs at a time.) The first and third legs on one side and the middle leg on the other side all (step forward together.) Then it's the turn of the other three legs to (step out.) The end result is a (slightly zigzagging walk.)

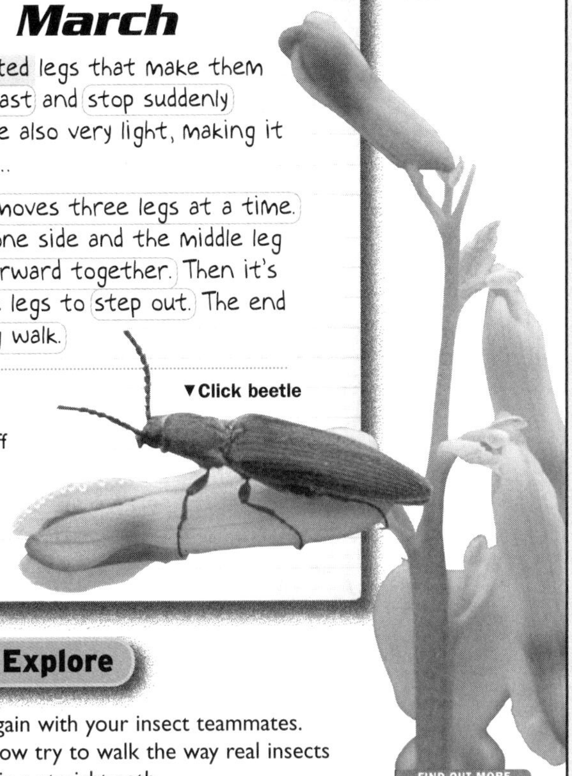

▼Click beetle

multi-jointed: having many places that bend

stable: steady and hard to throw off balance

maneuver: change direction and position

From: Robertson, Matthew. *Reader's Digest Pathfinders: Insects and Spiders.* Reader's Digest Children's Publishing, Inc.

NOTEZONE

(Circle) all the phrases that describe insect actions.

Explore

SHAKE A LEG! Get together again with your insect teammates. Stand in a line as you did before. Now try to walk the way real insects walk. Try walking across the room in a straight path.

► ***Descibe the path you made across the room. Explain what happened when you tried to walk in a straight line. Why do you think a single insect walks more easily than three two-legged people walking together?***

The path was zigzagged. It was impossible to walk in a straight line. In an insect, one brain controls all six legs.

FIND OUT MORE

SCIENCESAURUS
Structure and Function 075
Vertebrates and Invertebrates 161

SCILINKS. THE WORLD'S A CLICK AWAY
www.scilinks.org
Keyword: Insects
Code: GSLD15

105

Enrichment

Time: 40–45 minutes

Materials: drawing paper, field guides, colored pencils or markers, globe or world map

Insects are one of the most adaptable classes of animals in the animal kingdom. They are found in every climate on Earth, from deserts to frozen tundra. Ask each pair of students to choose one insect species found in a hot climate and one found in a cold climate—for example, red harvester ants in the deserts of New Mexico and springtails in Antarctica. Supply field guides for students to use in making their choices.

Have students look up information about their insects on the Internet or in a library. Instruct them to make two columns on a sheet of paper, one for each insect, and list the physical adaptations that enable each insect to survive in its environment. Direct students to draw their insects and label the specialized structures. Then ask students to share the information about their insects, including locating on a map or globe where their insects live. Discuss similarities and differences in the insects' adaptations.

Read

As students read, have them keep in mind the ways they walked as an "insect" during the Before You Read activity. Encourage them to mentally revise their ideas while reading. Then have them compare their own six-legged walks with the reading's description of how an insect walks. Did they walk in a similar manner? Did they feel stable while they walked?

Explore

SHAKE A LEG! While walking, an insect always has three legs firmly on the ground, the first and third on one side and the middle leg on the other (a tripod) while the other three are moving. When the three that were standing begin moving, the other three stay on the ground and form a tripod. This gives the insect balance and stability. Ask students to think of reasons why an insect might need more stability than an animal with four legs. (An insect's small size and light weight make it more susceptible to being blown over by the wind than a larger animal with four legs.)

CHECK UNDERSTANDING

Skill: Recognizing cause and effect

Ask: *What characteristics of insects make them able to walk around so well?* (Their six legs make them stable so they don't fall over. They are also very light, so they can change direction easily.)

More Resources

The following resources are also available from Great Source and NSTA.

SCIENCESAURUS

Structure and Function	075
Insects	106
Vertebrates and Invertebrates	161

READER'S HANDBOOK

Read with a Purpose	108
Visualizing and Thinking Aloud	664

SCILINKS. THE WORLD'S A CLICK AWAY

www.scilinks.org
Keyword: Insects
Code: GSLD15

►*How does walking help an insect survive? List three things an insect needs to do to survive that walking helps it do.*

find food; move into shelter to protect itself from the weather; escape predators

►*How does the structure of an insect allow it to walk and therefore survive?*

Six multi-jointed legs that move well together let the insect walk or run quickly. The legs help it find food and shelter, and escape predators.

►*Think of a situation where an insect's six legs do not help it survive.*

Accept any answer that shows an understanding that the adaptation of legs will not always ensure survival. Possible answers: if someone steps on it, if it falls in water and drowns

Propose Explanations

DON'T KNOCK ME OVER When most of an object's mass is near the ground, it is said to have a low center of gravity. Objects that have a low center of gravity are harder to knock over than objects whose center of gravity is higher. Legs that are spaced far apart also help.

►*Identify two things that help make an insect's body stable.*

six multi-jointed legs spaced far apart; a low center of gravity

106

TEACHING PLAN pp. 106–107

Explore *(continued)*

Ask students: *What advantage does an insect with six legs have over an animal with only four legs?* (A six-legged animal is more stable than a four-legged one.) Make sure students do not confuse the issue of six legs with the advantages an insect's specialized legs and feet may have—for example, sticky pads on the bottom of the feet.

Propose Explanations

DON'T KNOCK ME OVER Ask students to describe the leg and body positions of the three insects show on page 107. (All three insects' legs are spaced apart, but the weevil's legs project farther outward from its body than the mantis's and mosquito's legs do. In addition, the weevil's body is low to the ground, while the mantis's and mosquito's long legs keep them high off the ground.)

Ask students: *Why would a more stable position be an advantage to a weevil?* (Having a low center of gravity helps it climb trees and plants without being blown off.) *Why would it be an advantage for a praying mantis to be higher off the ground?* (Being higher helps a praying mantis see the movement and judge the distance of its prey.) *Why do you think a mosquito requires less stability than a weevil?* (A mosquito flies more than it walks. It does not need as much stability on a surface.)

►*Now look at the following insects. Which one do you think is the most stable when it walks? Explain how that insect's structure makes it more stable than the other insects.*

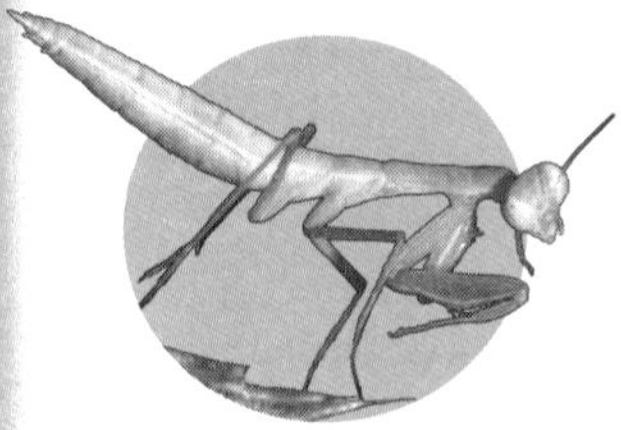

▲**Praying mantis**

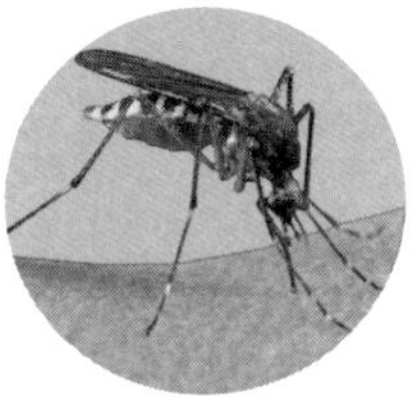

▲**Mosquito**

▲**Green weevil**

The green weevil is the most stable. Its lower center of gravity helps keep it from being knocked or blown over. The other insects' bodies are higher from the ground, making them less stable.

►*Imagine an insect walking along a tree branch in the wind. How does being stable help the insect survive in these conditions?*

The insect's low center of gravity helps keep it from being knocked over or blown away.

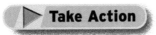

Take Action

WALK THE WALK Imagine that you work at a science museum in the Hall of Insects. It's your job to explain to visitors how an insect walks. How could you show which legs move when? Draw and label a diagram of an insect's footprints as it walks.

Students' diagrams will vary but should have some kind of coding to show which legs move together.

107

Connections

TECHNOLOGY Lead a class discussion about the new types of robots that engineers have created based on the way insects walk. These robots can be sent into places that are too small for people to fit into or too dangerous for people. Among other tasks, the robots have been tested to find and dismantle land mines and to explore the surface of other planets, such as Mars. Ask students why a robot with insectlike legs might be more useful in some situations than a robot with wheels. Also ask them to suggest other uses for insectlike robots.

Assessment

Skill: Communicating

Use the following task to assess each student's progress:

Have each student write a brief paragraph describing how an insect walks. (First it steps forward with the first and third legs on one side and the middle leg on the other side. Then it alternates and steps forward with the other three legs—two on one side and one on the other side.)

Take Action

WALK THE WALK Suggest that students try to visualize an insect's footprints as they might appear if it had walked through a puddle of ink. Encourage them to refer back to the reading as they draw their diagrams. Does the diagram illustrate the description? What changes could be made so the diagram more closely represents the description? Let students compare their diagrams.

Point of Lesson

Structures for jumping help insects survive.

Focus

- Form and function
- Structure and function in living systems
- Diversity and adaptations of organisms

Skills and Strategies

- Making inferences
- Generating ideas

Advance Preparation

Vocabulary

Make sure students understand these terms. Definitions can be found in the glossary at the end of the student book.

- energy
- predator
- environment
- species

Materials

Gather the materials needed for *Enrichment* (p. 109).

More Resources

The following resource is also available from Great Source.

SCIENCESAURUS

Structure and Function	075

How Insects Get Around

Jump!

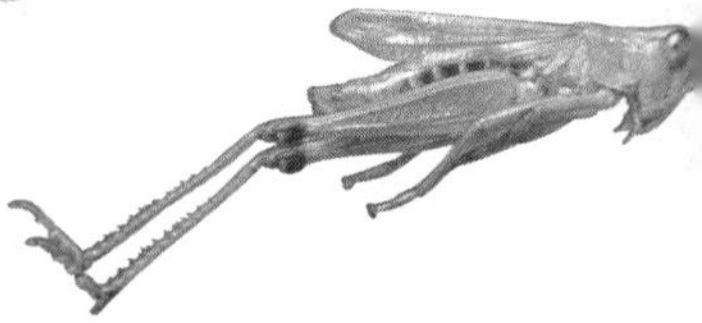

Why walk when jumping gets you there so much faster?

Have you ever tried to catch a grasshopper, only to have it jump away? Grasshoppers can walk, but mostly they jump. Many other insects that can do both also jump more than walk. Why? They can travel faster by jumping. Traveling faster makes the insect better able to escape a predator. For fleas, jumping is the best way to quickly get from the ground onto the body of a passing animal, where it will find food and shelter.

◄ Meadow grasshopper

Before You Read

JUMPING GEAR Many animals have special body parts that allow them to "spring into action."

► ***Make a list of animals that can jump. What body parts do they have that are specially adapted for jumping? How is jumping helpful to each animal's survival? Draw and describe your ideas below.***

Answers will vary. One possible answer:

Flying squirrels

Strong back leg muscles and flaps on the sides of their bodies help them travel farther when they jump from tree branch to tree branch.

This enables them to find shelter in trees, get to food sources more quickly, and escape predators that can' t leap as far.

TEACHING PLAN pp. 108–109

INTRODUCING THE LESSON

This lesson introduces insects' ability to jump as an adaptation that helps them survive in their environment. Ask students to name some animals that use jumping as their primary means of locomotion. (kangaroos, grasshoppers, fleas, and so on) Ask: *How do you think jumping might benefit an animal?* (Jumping lets the animal move any distance more quickly than walking does. The animal also might be able to jump up onto something that it couldn't climb.)

Some students may think that jumping is not a particular survival advantage. Explain that jumping can increase an animal's chances of obtaining food and escaping predators.

Read

JUMPING GEAR Encourage students to study the legs of the grasshoppers shown on these two pages. Have them compare the front legs with the back legs. Make sure students recognize that the back legs are longer and more muscular than the front legs. Ask: *Why are the back legs so different from the front legs?* (The back legs are used for jumping.)

Read

Jumping is a good way to go—and there's more than one way to do it!

Leaping Insects

Some [insect] species...have developed [body parts] made just for jumping. Grasshoppers have such powerful back legs that they can make leaps many times higher than their bodies. Some jumpers don't use legs at all—tiny springtails flick a special "tail," while click beetles use a peg-like spring to propel themselves....

When [the] flea beetle makes a jump, it shoots through the air at speeds greater than 9 miles [14km] per hour, spinning head-over-claws 70 times in a single second. [And it] still manages to land feet first. The enlarged back legs hold a special jumping [muscle]...that lets the beetle leap at such speeds and always land where it wants.

propel: move forward

From: Robertson, Matthew. *Reader's Digest Pathfinders: Insects and Spiders*. Reader's Digest Children's Publishing, Inc.

NoteZone

Circle all the words related to structures that help insects jump.

Propose Explanations

AT HOME IN THE GRASS Grasshoppers live among tall grasses. Eating grass and other plants gives grasshoppers energy. Moving uses energy. It takes less energy for the grasshopper to jump than it does for it to walk the same distance because it has specially adapted back legs.

► ***How might jumping help the grasshopper survive in its environment?***

The grasshopper can jump from one blade of grass to another without having to climb down one and up another. Jumping uses less energy than walking the same distance, so the grasshopper gets to a new food source with less effort than walking.

FIND OUT MORE
SCIENCESAURUS
Structure and Function 075

Enrichment

Time: 40-45 minutes
Materials: Insect Structure sheet (copymaster page 228), drawing paper, colored pencils or markers

Let students design their own versions of jumping insects. Distribute copies of the Insect Structure sheet, and review the basic body structure of all insects: head, thorax, abdomen, and six legs. Tell students that they can give their insects any special structures they want so long as the basic body structures are included. Also emphasize that the structures used for jumping must be shown. Display students' designs in the classroom.

Assessment

Skill: Organizing information

Use the following task to assess each student's progress:

Write *cricket* and *flea* on the board. Ask: *What behavior do these insects have in common?* (They both jump.) *How do these insects use this behavior in different ways?* (The cricket jumps to find food while conserving the additional energy involved in walking; it also jumps to escape predators quickly. The flea jumps to move onto a host's body.)

Read

Set a purpose for reading by asking students to look for the ways in which different insects are able to jump. Also have students infer why being able to jump is essential for some insects.

When students complete the NoteZone task, let them compare the words they circled with a partner.

Propose Explanations

AT HOME IN THE GRASS Remind students that all animals use energy from food to stay alive. The more an animal moves around, the more energy it uses and the more food it needs to eat. Make sure students understand that animals use the most efficient movement to get from one place to another in order to conserve energy. Help students conclude that in this way, jumping is essential for a grasshopper's survival.

Point of Lesson

Flying and migration are structural and behavioral adaptations of some insects.

Focus

- Form and function
- Structure and function in living systems
- Diversity and adaptations of organisms

Skills and Strategies

- Making inferences
- Creating and using tables
- Interpreting scientific illustrations
- Drawing conclusions
- Evaluating source material
- Communicating

Advance Preparation

Vocabulary

Make sure students understand these terms. Definitions can be found in the glossary at the end of the student book.

- adaptation
- migration
- organism
- predator
- scientific name

How Insects Get Around

Flights of Fancy

Look! Up in the sky! What is it? A bird? A plane? No, it's a dragonfly!

Imagine that you're sitting by a pond on a warm summer day. If you look along the surface of the water, you'll notice many different kinds of insects moving around. Some seem to be floating in the air. But others, such as dragonflies, are expert fliers that can do amazing acrobatics.

The book *A Dragon in the Sky* tells the story of a male green darner dragonfly named Anax that lives in the northeastern U.S. The name Anax comes from the scientific name of the green darner dragonfly, *Anax junius*. Anax's two pairs of wings move independently, allowing him to fly expertly. Like the other green darners in his area, Anax will migrate to areas in the southern state of Florida when the weather gets colder.

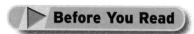

Before You Read

MIGRATION Most animals move around for several hours each day as they search for food, water, shelter, and mates. Some animals go on even longer journeys called migrations. Some animals migrate to better feeding grounds every summer, others to a watering hole every dry season, still others to a warmer place in winter. Other animals make only one migration in their lifetime—a journey to where they will lay their eggs and then die.

- ***Which animals can you think of that migrate? Where do they go? Do they fly, walk, or swim? What benefit do you think they gain from migrating? Record that information in the chart below.***

Answers will vary. Examples are given below.

Animal	Where It Migrates	How It Travels	Benefit Gained
Pacific salmon	*from ocean to freshwater stream where it hatched*	*swims*	*reproduction in a more protected location*
Canada goose	*from south to north and back, seasonally*	*flies*	*warmer weather in south, more food in summer in north*

TEACHING PLAN pp. 110–111

INTRODUCING THE LESSON

This lesson introduces flight as an adaptation that helps insects survive. Begin by asking students to define the term *migration* in their own words. Find out what they already know about migration in the insect world by asking: *Can you name any insects that migrate?* (some species of bees and dragonflies; over 200 species of butterflies; locusts) *Do you think flying insects can migrate across an ocean?* (Some insects do in fact travel very long distances.)

Students may think that insects are too small and delicate to make long migrations. Explain that although many insects look fragile, they can travel hundreds or even thousands of kilometers in a migratory season. For example, the desert locust travels over 4,500 kilometers (2,800 miles) through several countries in Africa and then across the Atlantic Ocean.

Before You Read

MIGRATION Review the answers that students recorded in the chart. Make sure they understand that animals migrate for other reasons besides escaping the cold climate of a northern winter to find warmth in more southern latitudes. Ask students to suggest other reasons why it would be beneficial for an animal to migrate. If necessary, explain that animals, including insects, also migrate to find more abundant sources of food or water during a certain time of the year or to return to the area where they normally reproduce.

Read

Like all dragonflies, Anax can fly with great skill.

FLIGHT OF THE DRAGONFLY

His wings were strong but flexible. They could not only beat up and down but also twist and bend.... Fine hairs on the upper surface of Anax's wings measured the airflow. His eyes kept track of his surroundings, including the horizon. All of this information was sent to his brain. Without thinking, Anax made dozens of changes in his wing and body positions every minute....

Anax could hover in midair, then beat all four wings together and, in a few seconds, accelerate to thirty miles [48 km] per hour. He could dart to the side, fly backward for a short distance, and even turn an aerial somersault. Flying swiftly, he could stop in an instant by lowering his abdomen and hind legs....

◄ **Green darner dragonfly**

Now [Anax] sensed it was time for a change. He was not yet a fully developed [dragonfly], but he was ready to begin migration. One morning in late September, Anax ate several mosquitoes and a robber fly.... Then he lifted into the air and began to fly south.

airflow: the flow of air over a surface

horizon: the line where Earth and sky appear to meet

accelerate: speed up

aerial: in the air

abdomen: the rear body section of an insect

From: Pringle, Laurence. *A Dragon in the Sky: The Story of a Green Darner Dragonfly.* Orchard Books, a Division of Scholastic, Inc.

NOTEZONE

What did Anax do to prepare for his migration? *ate insects to get energy*

FIND OUT MORE

SCIENCESAURUS

Animal Life Cycles 106
Behavior 109
Animal Behavior 110

111

Materials

Gather the materials needed for ***Enrichment*** (below).

Enrichment

Time: will vary

Materials: research sources about migratory insects

Scientists do not fully understand what prompts migration in certain insect species. The trigger that starts an insect on its annual journey sometimes is temperature, but more often it is the position of the sun and the resulting angle of its light shining on the insect's sensory organs. Scientists are also studying whether insects rely more on landmarks or on their internal compass to guide them once their migration begins.

Encourage interested students to research an insect that migrates. Ask them to find out the insect's migration path and the reasons for migrating. Students can research an insect from the list below or an insect of their choosing.

- Corn earworm *(Helicoverpa zea)*
- Monarch butterfly *(Danaus plexippus)*
- Birch aphids *(Euceraphis betulae)*
- Armyworm *(Helicoverpa armigera)*
- Migratory locust *(Locusta migratoria capito)*

Read

After students have read the passage and completed the NoteZone task, tell them to re-read the passage, this time highlighting words that identify the body parts that the dragonfly used when flying. (wings, fine hairs on the wings, eyes, brain, abdomen, hind legs) Tell them to use another color to highlight words and phrases that describe ways in which the dragonfly moved. (hover in midair, accelerate, dart to the side, fly backward, turn a somersault, lower his abdomen and hind legs, lift into the air)

CHECK UNDERSTANDING

Skill: Drawing conclusions

What are three reasons an insect would migrate? (to find food, water, or warmer weather)

More Resources

The following resources are also available from Great Source.

ScienceSaurus

Animal Life Cycles 106
Behavior 109
Animal Behavior 110

Reader's Handbook

Note-taking 106
Reading Science: Connect 113
How to Read a Chart or Table 600

Math on Call

Displaying Data in Tables and Graphs 284

Write Source 2000

Kinds of Paragraphs 55

Explore

ADAPTED FOR FLIGHT An adaptation is a characteristic that enables an organism to survive in its environment. Flying is one adaptation that helps insects like the dragonfly survive.

► ***Many body structures must work together for an insect to fly. Label the drawing to explain how Anax's body structures coordinate so he can fly.***

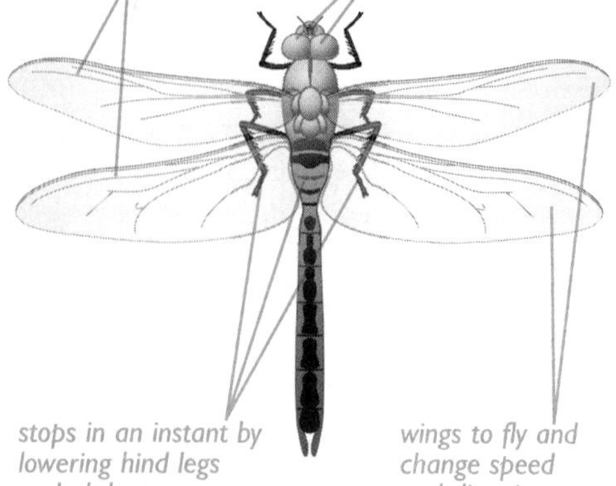

► ***Herbivores are animals that eat plants. Carnivores are animals that eat other animals. Are dragonflies herbivores or carnivores? How can you tell?***

Carnivores; the reading says that Anax ate mosquitoes and a robber fly.

► ***Think about a time you tried to slap a mosquito. Do you think mosquitoes would be easy for a predator to catch? Explain.***

No; mosquitoes are very fast, and a predator would also have to be fast to catch one.

► ***How does a dragonfly's flying skill make it a successful predator?***

It can move very fast and change direction quickly when it goes after prey.

► ***What environmental change triggered Anax's migration?***

The weather was getting colder.

112

Teaching Plan pp. 112–113

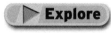

Explore

ADAPTED FOR FLIGHT The labeling task and questions in this section require students to make inferences based on the reading. To help students answer the first question, have them refer back to the reading's description of the body parts they highlighted in Read.

Explain that not all species of dragonflies migrate. Ask: *What benefits does a dragonfly that migrates to the northeastern part of the United States in the springtime have over a different kind of dragonfly that stays in the Southeast throughout the year?* (The dragonfly that went north might have better feeding grounds and less competition for food.)

Take Action

DESCRIBING CHARACTER When writers create a story, they sometimes use anthropomorphism to make the story's characters more interesting. *Anthropomorphism* means describing animals or objects as having human feelings, thoughts, and reasons for doing things.

► ***Review the reading in this lesson. Is the description of Anax an example of anthropomorphism? Why or why not?***

No; dragonflies don't have names, but the reading does not give Anax human thoughts, feelings, or reasons for his actions.

Recall a story you enjoyed when you were young that was about the make-believe adventures of an animal or object. *The Little Engine That Could, Corduroy,* and *The Three Little Pigs* are three examples. Write two or three sentences from the story that use anthropomorphism to describe the nonhuman characters. Then rewrite each sentence so it is not anthropomorphic.

Answers will vary.

113

Connections

SOCIAL STUDIES Explain to students that when locusts migrate in swarms, they can devour thousands of acres of crops. Tell them that in China, some farmers use locust-eating "duck soldiers" to combat invasions of locusts. The ducks are environmentally friendly, and each duck can eat up to 0.5 kg (about 1 lb) of the insects each day. They also eat the locusts' eggs. Ask: *Are there any disadvantages to using ducks in the fight against locusts?* Ask students to suggest other ways to kill or control insects without using pesticides.

Assessment

Skill: Drawing conclusions

Use the following question to assess each student's progress:

How do an insect's adaptations for flight help it survive? (Flying helps it find food and water, escape from predators, find mates, and migrate.)

Take Action

DESCRIBING CHARACTER After students complete the Take Action task, point out to them that an important part of studying science is evaluating any material they are reading and deciding whether it is factual or fictional. *A Dragon in the Sky*—the book from which the Read excerpt was taken—accurately describes the body structure and behavior of a green darner dragonfly and does not use anthropomorphism. However, it is not considered scientific writing because it is not an account of actual observations made by the author. Instead, the author used his knowledge of green darner dragonflies to write realistic fiction. Emphasize that even though realistic fiction uses many facts to tell a story, it is still fiction.

Killer Whales: Wolves of the Sea

LESSON 31

Sounds of the Sea

Point of Lesson: ***Killer whales use sound to navigate and to communicate underwater.***

A passage from the book *Killer Whales* introduces the topic of echolocation. In this lesson, students learn about the variety of sounds that killer whales can produce. They then explore how killer whales use these sounds to navigate by echolocation and to communicate with other killer whales in their pods.

Materials
none

LESSON 32

The Hunters

Point of Lesson: ***Killer whales show cooperative behavior when hunting.***

This lesson begins with students recalling a predatory animal that is familiar to them and identifying the methods that animal uses to hunt. Students then read a gripping eyewitness account of a pod of killer whales attacking a sea lion and identify the cooperative behaviors of the killer whales during this unsuccessful hunt. Students then review data about the mass and teeth of two of the killer whale's prey species and relate those characteristics to the hunting methods killer whales use for each type of prey. Finally, students contrast the pod size and communication habits of killer whales that live in different groups and relate those differences to the preferred food of each group.

Materials
none

LESSON 33

Name That Whale

Point of Lesson: ***Marine biologists use a system to identify individual killer whales.***

Students learn how researchers use photographs of killer whales to identify individuals by unique features of their dorsal fins and why this method has been so important to the study of killer whales. Students then compare photos of killer whale fins and saddle patches. In a final activity, students suggest reasons why it is helpful to biologists to use the same system for identifying individual killer whales.

Materials
Enrichment (p. 123), for each student or group:
- posterboard
- markers

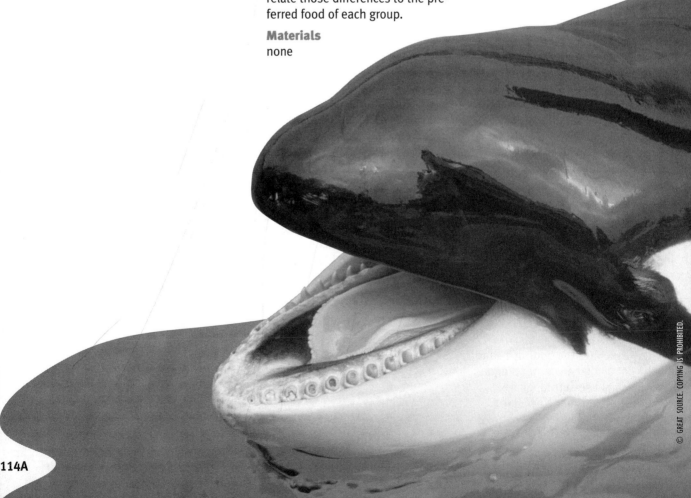

Background Information

Lesson 31

Researchers have discovered that killer whales have calls that they repeat the same way over and over again. Each pod has a distinct dialect, made up of the calls used by that pod to communicate. Pods can actually be identified by the sounds they make, even though pods that interact do have some calls in common.

Lesson 32

Some groups of killer whales live in a small home range, usually near coastal headlands, and are known as *residents*. Other groups travel over a much larger range, often changing direction and sometimes moving into small bays, and are known as *transients*. Observations suggest that killer whales belong to one type of group or another their entire lives. There are differences between these two types of killer whales. For example, resident pods can have between 5 and 50 whales, while transient pods are smaller and have only 1 to 7 whales. Resident killer whales usually eat a diet of fish and squid, while transients are hunters that prey on mammals such as seals, sea lions, and true whales. Residents are also more communicative; they vocalize frequently and use more calls than transients.

Lesson 33

Observers can tell a lot about killer whales just by looking at them. Newborn whales are 2.1 to 2.5 m (7 to $8\frac{1}{2}$ ft) long and usually weigh about 180 kg (395 lb). Adults range from 5.5 to 9.8 m (18 to $32\frac{1}{4}$ ft) in length and weigh between 2.6 and 9 tons. Males are larger than females, with an average length of 7.3 m (24 ft) compared with about 6 m (20 ft) for females. The dorsal fins of male killer whales are also much taller and straighter than the fins of females.

Point of Lesson

Killer whales use sound to navigate and to communicate under water.

Focus

- Evidence, models, and explanation
- Populations and ecosystems
- Regulation and behavior
- Nature of science
- Understanding about scientific inquiry

Skills and Strategies

- Comparing and contrasting
- Interpreting scientific illustrations
- Using space/time relationships
- Observing
- Making inferences

Advance Preparation

Vocabulary

Make sure students understand these terms. Definitions can be found in the glossary at the end of the student book.

- behavior
- echolocation
- mammal
- sound

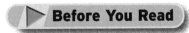

Sounds of the Sea

If you were a killer whale, how would you stay in touch with other killer whales?

Killer whales are found in all oceans of the world. The groups we know the most about are found along the west coast of North America. That's where killer whale biologist John Ford and his colleagues conduct their studies about whale biology and behavior. Scientists know that killer whales form groups called pods in which they live and hunt. They also know that a pod of whales can be a noisy group.

Before You Read

NOISY WHALES Whale biologists have recorded a wide variety of sounds made by killer whales under water.

- ***Why do you think the whales make sounds? What functions do you think the sounds serve?***

Answers will vary. Examples: Sounds might be used to locate other killer whales or communicate with them about getting food or meeting other needs.

TEACHING PLAN pp. 114–115

INTRODUCING THE LESSON

This lesson shows students how the sounds that killer whales make help them keep in contact with one another. Ask students if they have ever heard a recording of sounds produced by whales and if so, to describe the sounds.

Students may not realize that killer whales are mammals, not fish. Point this out, and explain that like other mammals, killer whales breathe oxygen from the air and give birth to live young. Introduce the term "orca" as another name for killer whales.

Before You Read

NOISY WHALES The sounds whales make function to maintain social structure and hunting methods. The sounds are also used to distinguish different whales and whale groups. Ask students to suggest ways in which they keep in contact with family and friends, such as by telephone, e-mail, and face-to-face conversation.

Students can visit the following Web sites to hear killer whale vocalizations:
www.whalelink.org/orcafm/pre.html
www.earthisland.org/immp/orca/index.htm

Students can see if they can tell the difference between types of whale calls. Point out that scientists use special microphones called hydrophones to record these underwater sounds.

Read

Whale biologist John Ford has discovered a lot about the different sounds that killer whales make under water.

Clicks, Calls, and Whistles

Killer whales rely heavily on underwater sound for both navigation and communication, and with good reason. Sound is by far the most efficient and reliable [way to collect] sensory information about a whale's surroundings and for social communication with other whales....

The echolocation signals produced by the whales are [called] "click trains," which are short-duration pulses given in [repeated] series that may last for 10 seconds or more. Echoes from these clicks allow the animals to form an acoustical image of their surroundings....

The signals used for social communication within and between pods consist of calls and whistles. Calls are more common than whistles.... Typically less than two seconds long, calls are made up of bursts and pulses [produced] at rates of up to several thousand per second. Such pulse bursts produce high-pitched squeals and screams, not unlike the sounds made by rusty hinges on a quickly closing door. By varying the timing and [pitch]...of these bursts, the whales can generate a variety of complex signals.... These calls appear to serve generally as contact signals, coordinating group behavior and keeping pod members in touch when they are out of sight of each other....

navigation: finding one's way
efficient: getting the best result for the least amount of effort
reliable: dependable
sensory: related to sight, hearing, and the other senses
echolocation: a system of using bounced sounds to determine the location of objects
short-duration: lasting for a short amount of time
acoustical: related to sound
pitch: how high or low a sound is

From: Ford, John K.B., Graeme M. Ellis, and Kenneth C. Balcomb. *Killer Whales.* UBC Press.

NoteZone

What are the functions of clicks and calls in echolocation?

Clicks are used to locate objects; calls are used for communicating with other whales.

FIND OUT MORE
SCIENCESAURUS
Animal Behavior 110

SCILINKS. THE WORLD'S A CLICK AWAY
www.scilinks.org
Keyword: Whales
Code:GSLD16

115

Enrichment

To help students appreciate the way killer whales communicate with sound, have students create their own vocabulary of sounds to communicate with each other. If students have listened to recordings of whale sounds, they can imitate the types they have heard. If recordings are not available, students can make up their own sequences of sounds. Stress that each student should create an identifying pattern of sounds that is unique to him or her. The sounds can then be used to identify the individual making them. Have students communicate with each other using their signature sounds as well as by creating other sounds that will serve as social contacts and hunting information. Have volunteers record a dictionary of these sounds and their meanings.

Read

Have students locate the definitions and functions of clicks and calls in the reading. The reading contains many descriptions of these sounds, and students' understanding can be increased by having them imitate click trains, whistles, squeals, and screams that sound like rusty hinges on a quickly closing door.

Briefly discuss how sound waves move through water. Explain that both air and water transfer sound waves across distances. For example, when two rocks are clinked together under water in a swimming pool, the sound is easily heard far across the pool, even more so than if the rocks were clinked above water in the air.

Explain the term *acoustical image*: the interpretation of reflected sound waves as images of objects. Sonar, fish finders, and medical sonograms all use sound waves to form images of objects. Note that marine mammals such as whales and dolphins and land mammals such as bats use echolocation.

CHECK UNDERSTANDING

Skill: Comparing and contrasting

Ask: *How could whales use communication to determine which pod an individual whale belongs to? What characteristics of the sounds might a killer whale from the same pod recognize?* (The sounds' frequency, pattern, and duration may give an "accent" to an individual whale or pod of whales. Other whales could recognize these characteristics.)

More Resources

The following resources are also available from Great Source and NSTA.

SCIENCESAURUS

Animal Behavior 110

WRITE SOURCE 2000

Writing Observation Reports 209

READER'S HANDBOOK

Reading Science 100

Elements of Graphics: Diagram 552

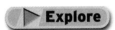

SCILINKS
THE WORLD'S A CLICK AWAY

www.scilinks.org
Keyword: Whales
Code: GSLD16

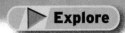

Explore

NAVIGATING UNDER WATER The following diagram shows how echolocation works. The lines represent sound waves. Sound waves move away from their source and spread out in all directions. When the sound waves hit an object, they bounce off and travel back to the source.

▸ ***Look at the diagram. Explain how the killer whale uses sound waves to locate an object.***

The whale makes sounds that travel in waves. When the waves hit an object, they bounce off and return to the whale. The whale hears the echo and knows where the object is.

▸ ***How do you think the killer whale can tell the direction of the object?***

The sound waves leave the whale and then bounce back to the whale from the direction of the object.

▸ ***How do you think the killer whale can tell how far away the object is?***

The longer it takes for the sound waves to bounce back to the whale, the farther away the object is.

116

TEACHING PLAN pp. 116–117

Explore

NAVIGATING UNDER WATER Work with students to interpret the diagram. Point out that the sound waves from the killer whale are directed toward the fish. Ask students to identify the waves that struck the fish and are bouncing back. (the waves that are between the whale and the fish with the convex sides pointing toward the whale) Be sure students understand that these sound waves are reflected by the fish's body, not generated by the fish itself. Ask why there are no sound waves behind the fish. (The fish's body blocked the sound waves.)

Explain that whales do not vocalize as humans do, by passing air through the windpipe. They create sounds by passing air through nasal sacs in their blowhole, the opening through which they exhale air. The whale that picks up the sounds does so through a mass of fatty tissues in its forehead that go to a fat-filled area in the lower jaw, which transmits them to the inner ear. The distance and direction of the sound source is also detected. Point out that scientists are not sure that a whale can time the return of a sound wave from an object, but sonar machines use this method to judge distance.

Propose Explanations

THINK ABOUT IT

▸ *What do most land mammals use to navigate?*

their eyes, their sense of smell, sense of touch (moles, for example)

Bats, which hunt at night, also use echolocation. But both bats and whales have eyes.

▸ *Why do you suppose killer whales and bats use echolocation instead of sight to find their way?*

It would be hard for whales to see very far under water and for bats to see in the dark.

▸ *Think about common land mammals, such as squirrels, dogs, and cats. What do most land mammals use to communicate?*

sounds, body movements, touching

▸ *Communication helps killer whales survive in their environment. How might communicating with other members of its pod help a killer whale survive?*

Answers will vary. Examples: Communication could help a whale stay in touch with its pod members and not get lost, learn where a good food source is, and warn other pod members of danger.

Take Action

PET PROJECT Do you have a pet at home? If not, maybe a close friend has one. Think about how the animal communicates with members of its own species and with people. How does it communicate? What parts of its body does it use? How does it combine sounds and movements to get its message across? What do you think it is trying to communicate? How does communicating help the animal? How well can a person understand the pet's messages?

▸ *Record your ideas and observations on a separate sheet of paper. Make a drawing that shows how the animal communicates.*

Answers will vary.

117

Connections

LANGUAGE ARTS Ask students to think of examples of how humans can convey different messages using the same words. Show how ordering someone to "Come here!" uses a threatening tone and delivery. Yet if you are trying to entice someone to join you, you might say, "Come here..." with a beckoning, gentle delivery. Let students suggest other examples. Then explain that whale sounds also seem to have a wide variety of ranges and interpretations, even though their exact meanings are unclear to scientists.

Assessment

Skill: Comparing and contrasting

Use the following question to assess each student's progress:

What is the difference between how killer whales find prey and how they locate other killer whales in the open ocean? (Killer whales use a series of click trains to find prey. They use other calls and whistles to locate and identify other killer whales.)

Propose Explanations

THINK ABOUT IT Work with the class to compare the communication methods of land animals and killer whales. Have students give examples of means of navigation, such as a keen sense of smell or sight. Ask: *Why would whales use sounds to communicate instead of fin gestures or other body language?* (Sounds can be easily heard under water, but it's hard to see visual signals. Dark ocean depths or murky water would block sight but would not affect sounds.) Ask students how darkness, fog, or long distances would affect their own eyesight. *What have people done to help communication in those circumstances?* (Sample answer: They have created foghorns, lighthouses, radar, and the telegraph.)

Take Action

PET PROJECT Have students describe their pets' behaviors. They will most likely mention different combinations of vocalizations and body movements that are requests for food and expressions of emotion. Ask students if their animals use these same methods to communicate with other animals. Have students explain how they know what their pets are trying to communicate. As students describe their pets' behaviors, ask them to compare pet behavior to that of wild animals. Help students understand that killer whales communicate among themselves, just as dogs or cats do.

Point of Lesson

Killer whales show cooperative behavior when hunting.

Focus

- Systems, order, and organization
- Populations and ecosystems
- Nature of science
- Regulation and behavior
- Understanding about scientific inquiry

Skills and Strategies

- Making inferences
- Observing
- Comparing and contrasting
- Communicating

Advance Preparation

Vocabulary

Make sure students understand these terms. Definitions can be found in the glossary at the end of the student book.

- adaptation
- mammal
- predator
- prey

Materials

Gather the materials needed for ***Take Action*** (p. 121).

The Hunters

If you're a killer whale, your choice could be teamwork or going hungry.

Killer whales are not really whales at all. They are classified as members of the dolphin family. However, dolphins and whales are closely related. Early fishermen who watched killer whales hunt and kill whales called them "whale killers." But over time, the words were reversed and the animals came to be known as "killer whales." But killer whales hunt more than just whales. They also eat seals, sea lions, and porpoises.

Before You Read

ORGANIZING INFORMATION Like other predators, killer whales hunt for their food. Different animals have different ways of hunting and catching their prey.

► ***Think of a predator you know of. How does the animal hunt? Does it hunt alone or in a group? Is its prey bigger or smaller than it is, or the same size? Record your ideas below.***

Answers will vary. Examples are shown.

Prey Animal
field mouse

Does the predator hunt alone or in groups?
alone

Is the prey bigger, smaller, or the same size as the predator?
smaller

Predator
hawk

How does the predator hunt?
spots the prey from the air, then swoops down and grabs it with claws

TEACHING PLAN pp. 118–119

INTRODUCING THE LESSON

This lesson investigates the hunting behavior of killer whales. Ask students if they know what killer whales eat and how they find their food. Answers may include that they are vegetarians or solitary feeders on larger animals. Point out the food needs of an animal that size. Some students might think that because they are called "whales," they might be filter feeders that eat plankton, like the much larger baleen whales. Have students look at the teeth visible in the photograph on page 114. Ask: *What kind of food would teeth like those be suited for?* (meat, fish)

Before You Read

ORGANIZING INFORMATION Point out that killer whales, which live in groups called *pods*, also hunt cooperatively. Have students discuss the advantages of teamwork in group activities like hunting or protection of the young.

The organizational chart is a convenient way for students to see how the size of the predator somewhat determines the prey it pursues. Trace the lines of relationships shown in the chart by indicating how each box relates to the other.

When considering the killer whale, point out that males can reach 30 feet (9.5 m) in length and weigh over 8 tons. Note that their size enables killer whales to prey on many sea creatures, but through group hunting, they can prey on even larger animals, such as whales.

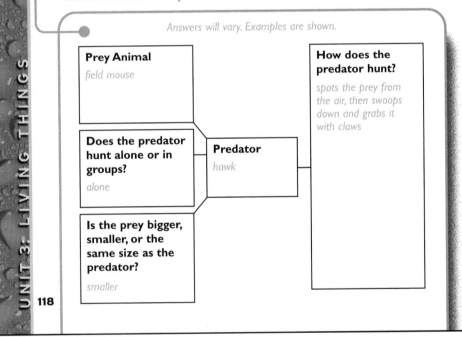

Read

Michael Bigg, a pioneer of modern killer whale research, recalls the day he watched a group of killer whales attack a sea lion.

An Encounter

The sea lion slowly made his way toward the shore about 200 yards [189 m] away. The [killer] whales were not concerned by our presence and continued to search for him. Suddenly, when the sea lion was about 100 yards [91 m] from shore, the whales apparently detected him with their sonar. They dove in unison, accelerating toward him. We saw nothing for about 30 seconds, then the water exploded around him. One after another, the whales charged the sea lion, diving around, under, and over him, smashing him from below and above with their flukes, and ramming him with their heads. Despite this fearsome assault, the sea lion resurfaced every minute or so and continued his slow progress toward shore. The episode lasted about 10 minutes in all. When the sea lion was within about 50 feet [15 m] of shore, the whales abruptly abandoned him and headed rapidly northward.

sonar: an echolocation system
in unison: all together
accelerating: speeding up
flukes: the two flattened parts of a whale's tail
assault: attack
episode: event
abandoned: left

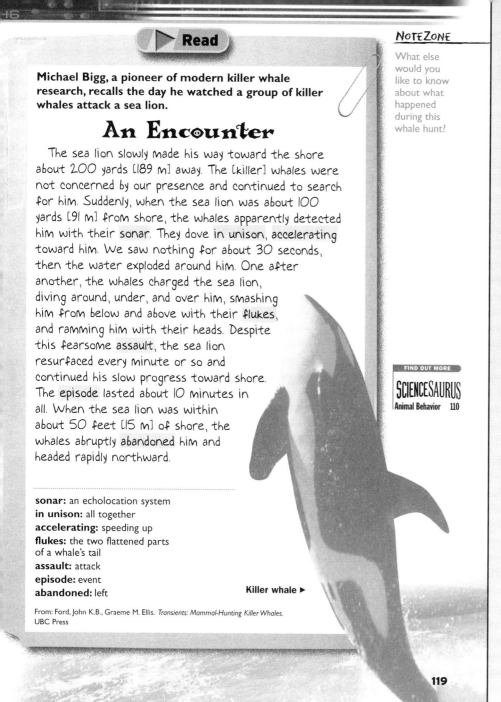

Killer whale ▸

From: Ford, John K.B., Graeme M. Ellis. *Transients: Mammal-Hunting Killer Whales.* UBC Press

NOTEZONE

What else would you like to know about what happened during this whale hunt?

FIND OUT MORE
SCIENCESAURUS
Animal Behavior 110

Enrichment

After students read about the encounter between the killer whales and the sea lion, have them rewrite the same sequence of events from the point of view of the sea lion—the prey. Students may research the behavior patterns of sea lions, but the reading contains enough detail for students to make reasonable inferences as to what the sea lion might have been doing during this encounter. Ask students to suggest why the killer whales abandoned their attack.

Read

Encourage students to form a mental image of the events described in the reading. The NoteZone task will prompt students to think about what is not described in the reading. Ask: *Why couldn't the scientists note everything that was happening during the attack?* (They couldn't see what was happening under water or at too great a distance.)

Ask students to consider the sounds that the whales may have been making during this hunt. *What types of whale sounds might an underwater diver have heard?* (clicks, calls, and whistles)

CHECK UNDERSTANDING

Skill: Making inferences

Ask students to explain why killer whales attack Steller sea lions if harbor seals are easier for them to catch and kill. (The sea lions are much larger and provide a larger meal. The availability of sea lions could also be a factor.)

More Resources

The following resources are also available from Great Source.

ScienceSaurus
Animal Behavior 110

Write Source 2000
Writing Research Papers 223
Writing Guidelines 224

Reader's Handbook
Reading Science 100
Focus on Science Concepts 132
Using Graphic Organizers 139
Elements of Textbooks: Charts 157

Connections

PHYSICAL EDUCATION

Compare a successful animal hunt by predators to the group coordination required to win in team sports such as soccer, basketball, and lacrosse. These sports involve an attack on a goal much like a group hunt on an individual animal. Have students review the strategies and rules of the games, then describe the communication between team members and the role of individuals working for the success of the group. Discuss the role of planning, previous experience, and strength and stamina.

Explore

WORKING TOGETHER

► *How did the killer whales cooperate when they attacked the sea lion?*

They attacked it one after another.

► *How might hunting in a group help make an attack like this successful?*

By surrounding the sea lion, the whales make it hard for the sea lion to escape. With the whales attacking it from different directions, the sea lion cannot fight back.

► *Do you think a single killer whale might have been more successful attacking the sea lion? Why or why not?*

Probably not. The sea lion might have been able to get away even more easily from a single attacker, or may have fought back.

A FORMIDABLE FOE Harbor seals and stellar sea lions are two prey animals that killer whales hunt for food. Study the information in the table. Notice the differences between harbor seals and sea lions.

Predator Species	Weight	Features
Killer whales	up to 5,443 kg	large, cone-shaped teeth
Prey Species	**Weight**	**Features**
Harbor seals	up to 115 kg	no large canine teeth
Stellar sea lions	up to 1,000 kg	large canine teeth

A single killer whale can chase a harbor seal, grab it in its mouth, and eat it.

► *Why can't killer whales use this hunting method with sea lions? Why is a group attack better?*

Sea lions are much larger and have bigger teeth than harbor seals, so they are more dangerous to attack. If the whales attack as a group, there is less chance that any of them will be injured by the sea lion.

120

Teaching Plan pp. 120–121

Explore

WORKING TOGETHER Have students review the reading and find specific references made by the observer to back up their response to the first question. Students should understand that the killer whales coordinated their attack on the sea lion by approaching it one after another.

Ask students whether causing the sea lion to become confused might also have been part of the killer whales' strategy. Students should be able to see that a flustered prey is more likely to make a mistake and be easier to capture. Mention that most predators try to avoid serious combat to prevent injuring themselves.

A FORMIDABLE FOE Review the information in the data table with the class, and have them note the size differences and the type of teeth each prey animal has. Guide students to use facts from the table to answer the questions.

Propose Explanations

WHALE GROUPS Ask: *How might the size of these whale groups be best suited to the type of prey they pursue?* (A smaller whale group could carry out a strategy that a larger group could not execute.)

As a way of explaining the term *behavioral adaptation*, mention that Galapagos marine iguanas feed on algae and moss in the cold ocean because they are ready sources of food, even though the cold water greatly lowers the iguanas' body temperature. Tell students that animals develop hunting strategies that increase their rate of survival by providing a steady source of energy.

Propose Explanations

WHALE GROUPS Killer whales that hunt sea lions and other marine mammals usually travel together in pods of three, four, or five whales. Killer whales that feed on fish travel together in much larger pods—20 or more whales. Whales that feed on fish do not need to cooperate to attack the fish.

► ***How might being in a larger pod make cooperative hunting more difficult?***

Answers will vary. Examples: Being in a larger pod would require more communication. It would be harder for a large pod to surprise a large prey animal.

A behavioral adaptation is something an animal does that helps it survive.

► ***How does cooperative hunting help some killer whales survive?***

The whales are able to attack and capture larger prey.

Take Action

GROUP BEHAVIOR Whale biologists have identified two major types of killer whale social groups. One group is called "transients," which means "move from place to place." The other is called "residents," which means "stay in the same place." These terms refer to the types of pods killer whales form and where they live in the ocean. Research the social structure and feeding habits of each type of group. How do they differ? How is each type of social structure suited to the group's feeding habits?

Answers will vary. Example: Resident whales form permanent pods. They feed mainly on fish. Resident pods are large, with up to a couple hundred members. Transients do not form permanent pods but switch pods periodically. They hunt marine mammals in deeper waters. They form smaller pods, usually 3–6 individuals. Because transients rely on surprise for their attacks, smaller pods are easier to coordinate. Because many fish travel in large schools, fish-eating resident killer whales can form larger pods and still obtain enough food for all.

121

Assessment

Skill: Making inferences

Use the following question to assess each student's progress:

Why would communication and cooperation among a group of killer whales be essential to their survival as hunters? (A group of killer whales would need communication to keep each other informed of events during a hunt. Their ability to coordinate their activities would also prevent the prey from escaping.)

Take Action

Time: will vary
Materials: research sources about killer whales

GROUP BEHAVIOR Divide the class into six groups to research the questions posed in this task. Two groups could look into the social structure of each type of killer whale pod. Two other groups could investigate the feeding habits of each type. The remaining two groups could research the pods' social structures. Then have the groups meet to note differences and similarities. The class could work with guidance to create a statement that relates a killer whale group's social structure to its feeding habits. To strengthen their conclusions, students should also find observations by scientists of each type of killer whale group.

Point of Lesson

Marine biologists use a system to identify individual killer whales.

Focus

- Systems, order, and organization
- Populations and ecosystems
- Science as a human endeavor
- Understanding about scientific inquiry

Skills and Strategies

- Observing
- Making inferences
- Comparing and contrasting
- Understanding that scientists share their results to form a common core of knowledge

Advance Preparation

Vocabulary

Make sure students understand these terms. Definitions can be found in the glossary at the end of the student book.

- behavior
- mammal
- population

Materials

Gather the materials needed for *Enrichment* (p. 123).

Name That Whale

How can you identify an animal that spends most of its life under water?

Usually, killer whales are completely under water. But like other marine mammals, killer whales must come to the surface to breathe air. They can also come up out of the water while they play and hunt. As the whales swim near the water's surface, whale biologists make observations of their behavior and movements. The more information biologists can gather about the whales' behavior, the better they can understand and protect them.

Read

NOTEZONE

Circle the physical characteristics used to identify individual killer whales.

Whale researcher Michael Bigg developed a system that all scientists can use to identify individual killer whales.

SNAPSHOT ID

In 1970, Mike Bigg took on the task of determining the population status and dynamics of killer whales in British Columbia.... Early in his study, Mike Bigg devised a technique that would become by far the most important tool in the field research on killer whales—photographic identification of individuals. Mike determined that every whale could be positively identified from naturally occurring nicks and scars on its dorsal fin and the grey "saddle patch" at the base of the fin. By photographing and cataloging every whale, the population could be accurately counted, rather than just estimated, and other important [facts about the whales'] life history could be documented.

status: the condition of a thing
dynamics: movements and changes
dorsal fin: the fin on a whale's back
cataloging: classifying according to an organized system
documented: supported with evidence

From: Ford, John K.B., Graeme M. Ellis. *Transients: Mammal-Hunting Killer Whales.* UBC Press.

TEACHING PLAN pp. 122–123

INTRODUCING THE LESSON

This lesson introduces students to the system that scientists use to identify whales. Ask students to describe any individual differences among killer whales they have seen in aquariums, in TV documentaries, in movies, or on a whale watch. Ask them if they think all killer whale markings are the same. Have they noticed different fin shapes or features, coloration, or other markings?

Read

Ask: *What changes might occur in the whale population that Mike Bigg studied?* (increases or decreases in the population due to disease, environmental changes, predation, food shortages, and so on) *How would an identification system help determine population changes?* (By identifying individual whales, scientists could make accurate counts of the population rather than rough estimates. They could recognize the loss of an individual whale from the pod and could track new offspring and other additions to the population.)

Ask: *If scientists couldn't distinguish one killer whale from another, how would they be able to keep track of a population?* (Students may mention tagging, banding, or attaching electronic tracers.) Discuss the costs and logistics of these methods.

When students have completed the NoteZone task, discuss the possible causes of nicks and scars. Ask them what they think the origin of the term "saddle patch" might be and how the term relates to horses.

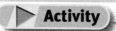

Activity

WHALE IDENTIFICATION Look at the pictures of dorsal fins below. What features could be used to identify each whale?

fin size and shape, pattern of nicks and scars, shape of saddle patch

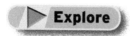

Give each whale a name based on the unique physical characteristics of its dorsal fin. Write the name below the whale's picture.

Explore

FIELD TECHNIQUES Whale biologists give each whale a code that tells when it was identified, what pod the whale is in, and whether it was the offspring of another whale in the pod.

- ***Why might it be important for all whale observers to use the same system of identification?***

They can tell whether they're talking about the same whale and can combine their observations and data.

- ***What do you think scientists can learn about whale populations by tracking and studying individuals?***

Answers will vary. Examples: They can learn which whales are in a particular pod, whether whales ever change pods, and whether a whale has died or given birth. They can also track the movement of pods.

123

More Resources

The following resource is also available from Great Source.

READER'S HANDBOOK

Reading Science	100
Elements of Graphics: Photograph	557

Enrichment

Time: 20 minutes
Materials: posterboard, markers

Killer whales spend much of their time under water and out of sight. Have students think of techniques and devices that could help scientists observe and study killer whales—for example, underwater photography by a remote-controlled robot. Encourage students to sketch and explain their ideas on posters to display in the classroom. Remind students that an undisturbed environment is important for accurate observation of animals in their natural environment.

Assessment

Skill: Drawing conclusions

Use the following question to assess each student's progress:

Why have researchers developed a coding system to identify killer whales rather than just giving each whale a nickname? (A coding system tells when the whale was identified, what pod the whale is in, and whether it was the offspring of another pod member. A nickname wouldn't supply that information.)

Activity

Time: 15 minutes

- Have students work in groups of two or three.
- Tell the groups to discuss what might have made these dorsal fins appear so different. (for example, inherited traits, disease, or injury) Have them list their ideas on paper.
- Then have each student group generate a list of adjectives that describe each dorsal fin pictured.
- Each group could then use its list to come up with a name for each of the whales.
- Ask a volunteer in each group to report the names they decided on for the three whales. Discuss similarities and differences in the names.

Explore

FIELD TECHNIQUES Discuss how biologists share information and observations with each other. Ask: *Why would a coding system be helpful?* (Codes would identify whales, particularly transients, that might be seen by more than one researcher.)

CHECK UNDERSTANDING
Skill: Comparing and contrasting
Have students create rough sketches of three different, imaginary killer whales. (Students should illustrate differently shaped dorsal fins with unique nicks and scars, and variations in the shape of the saddle patches.)

CHAPTER 12 Overview

Plant Adaptations

LESSON 34

Mistletoe, Birds, and Trees

Point of Lesson: ***Mistletoe plants depend on symbiotic relationships with other organisms to survive.***

In this lesson, students learn about three different types of symbiotic relationships and read a description of the relationship between the mistletoe bird and the plant for which it is named. Students organize their ideas about the relationships between the bird, the plant, and the trees on which it grows. They then analyze data from an experiment that tests a hypothesis about the cause for the declining number of mistletoe plants in New Zealand. Students also suggest ways in which the experiment could be made more conclusive.

LESSON 35

Not Your Usual Carnivores

Point of Lesson: ***Some plants have adaptations that enable them to capture and consume insects.***

This lesson engages students with a colorful description of a carnivorous plant capturing and ingesting a fly. Students learn how the adaptation of ingesting insects is helpful to the survival of carnivorous plants. They then explore the various methods by which pitcher plants, sundews, and butterworts attract and capture insects. Finally, they apply their knowledge by designing their own carnivorous plants.

Materials

Read (p. 129), for the class:
- plant fertilizer packaging

Enrichment (p. 129), for each group:
- carnivorous plants in their original soil
- clear glass or plastic containers for use as terrariums
- reference sources about growing carnivorous plants

Connections (p. 130), for the class:
- *Little Shop of Horrors* videotape

Laboratory Safety

Review the following safety guidelines with students before they do the Enrichment activity in this lesson.
- Handle plants and other living things with care.
- Wash your hands thoroughly after constructing the terrarium.

LESSON 36

What Attracts Insects to Flowers?

Point of Lesson: ***Flowers have features that attract insects.***

In this lesson, students conduct a controlled experiment to explore flower features—color, pattern, and nectar—that attract pollinating insects. They analyze the data they have collected to determine which feature is most important in attracting insects.

Materials

Activity (p. 132), for each group:
- cardboard
- pink and white construction paper
- scissors
- thin black marker
- 8 skewers
- honey (small jar)

Laboratory Safety

Review the following safety guidelines with students before they do the Activity in this lesson.
- Do not taste any substance while doing an activity unless instructed to do so.
- Handle plants and living things with care.
- If you are allergic to insect stings, do not participate in the observation phase of the Activity (step 8).
- Inform your teacher immediately in the event of an insect sting or any other type of injury.
- Wear light-colored clothing and do not wear scented products on the day of the observation phase.
- Check yourself for ticks and remove any before returning indoors.
- Wash your hands thoroughly after the activity.

Background Information

Lesson 34

Mistletoe grows by sending its roots into trees, especially hardwood trees such as oak and apple. In the United States, mistletoe can be found in a range of latitudes extending from Florida to New Jersey. Although it is mostly found on trees, mistletoe is able to live on its own. It is also common for one mistletoe plant to grow on another. Mistletoe is easiest to see in the winter because its leaves stay green all year.

Many species of birds eat and spread mistletoe berries. The species that is called the mistletoe bird *(Diacaeum hirundinaceum)* is native to Australia and New Zealand.

Lesson 35

Despite the fact that they are found in a small geographic area, Venus flytraps are world-famous. Because these plants are so rare, some early botanists believed that stories of flesh-eating plants were invented. The overwhelming popularity of these extremely rare plants has led to the over-harvesting of Venus flytraps. They are now listed as an endangered species, and it is illegal to collect them in the wild in most if not all places where they grow naturally.

Lesson 36

Many plants are pollinated by animals, including insects, birds, and bats. The amazing diversity of flowering plants indicates that different pollinators are attracted by different flower characteristics. It is beneficial to a plant to attract specific pollinators because an insect that visits only one type of flower is more likely to cross-pollinate that species than an insect that visits many types of flowers. Scientists are currently studying how different flower features such as color, pattern, and scent attract insects and other pollinators.

Point of Lesson

Mistletoe plants depend on symbiotic relationships with other organisms to survive.

Focus

- Systems, order, and organization
- Diversity and adaptations of organisms
- Structure and function in living systems
- Understanding about scientific inquiry

Skills and Strategies

- Creating and using graphs
- Drawing conclusions
- Concept mapping
- Interpreting data
- Predicting

Advance Preparation

Vocabulary

Make sure students understand these terms. Definitions can be found in the glossary at the end of the student book.

- experiment
- nectar
- nutrient
- organism
- pollen
- predator
- reproduce
- seed

Mistletoe, Birds, and Trees

Mistletoe plant growing on a tree ▼

Mistletoe plants have symbiotic relationships with both birds and trees.

When one organism affects the survival of another organism, scientists say the organisms have a symbiotic relationship. The word *symbiosis* means "living together." Three types of symbiotic relationships are mutualism, parasitism, and commensalism. In mutualistic relationships, both organisms benefit from their interaction with each other. In parasitic relationships, one organism benefits from the interaction while the other is harmed. In commensal relationships, one organism benefits while the other organism is not helped or harmed.

Before You Read

WORKING TOGETHER Three symbiotic relationships are described below. Decide if each one is an example of parasitism, mutualism, or commensalism.

- *Clownfish live among sea anemones. The anemone's stinging tentacles protect the clownfish from predators. The clownfish cleans the anemone's tentacles by eating material that clings to them.*

  mutualism

- *Fleas bite a dog's skin and feed on its blood. Many dogs are allergic to flea saliva, which irritates their skin.*

  parasitism

- *Ivy grows up the trunk of a tree. The ivy receives more sunlight high in the tree. The ivy does not take anything from the tree or block the tree's leaves from light.*

  commensalism

TEACHING PLAN pp. 124–125

INTRODUCING THE LESSON

This lesson presents three different types of symbiotic relationships—parasitism, mutualism, and commensalism—using the example of relationships between mistletoe plants, trees, and mistletoe birds.

Ask students to name the parts of a typical plant and describe each part's function. Students may think that all plants grow in soil. Explain that plants manufacture their own food from elements in water and air and that many plants can grow without soil as long as they have these substances.

Before You Read

WORKING TOGETHER Find out what students already know about symbiotic relationships. Ask them to identify any examples they know of in which two different species live closely together. (Answers will vary but could include ticks on a dog, bees and flowers, cleaner fish on large fish in the ocean, and so forth.) Ask students to describe the interaction in each relationship and identify the type of symbiosis it represents.

Read

As the mistletoe bird flies from tree to tree, it spreads the mistletoe's seeds.

The Sticky Seeds of the Mistletoe

The mistletoe bird on the tree branch has something hanging from its rear end. What is it? An odd little white packet, dangling by threads. The bird seems to know the hanger-on is there. It rubs its bottom against the branch and the thing comes off. Now it's stuck on the branch! But the sticky threads remain attached to the bird, stretching out as the bird hops away. Finally they break and the bird is free.

The mistletoe bird will go through this undignified procedure many times a day. Every day. The little package that was stuck to its hind end was a mistletoe seed.... The sticky threads and the constant wiping are the price the bird must pay for the tasty seeds [inside the mistletoe berries] that it loves.

For the wiped-off seeds, life is just beginning. The seed is now in a prime location to begin its vicious attack on the tree!

undignified: not respectable; embarrassing

hind: rear

prime: top quality

From: Kneidel, Sally. *Skunk Cabbage, Sundew Plants & Strangler Figs: And 18 More Of The Strangest Plants On Earth.* John Wiley & Sons, Inc.

NOTEZONE

The second sentence in the reading asks what the white packet is. Underline the sentence that answers the question.

▼**Mistletoe birds**

FIND OUT MORE

SCIENCESAURUS

Natural Selection 127
Relationships Between Populations 132

SCILINKS. THE WORLD'S A CLICK AWAY

www.scilinks.org
Keyword: Adaptation of Plants
Code: GSLD17

125

Enrichment

Have students write a short story or creative dialogue about the relationships between trees, mistletoe, and mistletoe birds from the point of view of one of the organisms. Students could model their stories after television shows, movies, magazine features, advice columns, or other media that dramatize relationships. For example, students might write a scene for a soap opera or a dating show describing the symbiotic relationships. Tell students to use facts from the lesson to provide details for their stories.

Read

Explain that like all other producers, mistletoe can make its own food. However, it usually exists as a parasite. The mistletoe's roots behave in a remarkable way. A sticky mistletoe seed is left by a bird on a tree branch. When the seed begins to sprout, a threadlike root begins to grow and pierces the bark of the branch. The root then absorbs nutrients produced by the tree that are circulating in the tree's sap. Over time, the mistletoe plant can kill the branch on which it grows, but it rarely kills the entire tree.

Point out the reading's last sentence, and ask students: *Do you think the mistletoe's attack on the tree is vicious? Is this sentence a scientific statement?* (Students should understand that the plant is not behaving in a vicious manner. It is merely surviving with the adaptations it has. It means no harm to the tree.)

CHECK UNDERSTANDING

Skill: Sequencing

Ask students: *What are the two organisms the mistletoe has relationships with during its life cycle?* (the mistletoe bird and the tree) *How does its relationship with the mistletoe bird work?* (The mistletoe has a seed package with sticky threads that attaches to the bird. The bird then flies to a tree and rubs it off. There the seeds will be able to root.) *How does its relationship with the tree work?* (The mistletoe seeds end up on a tree branch, where they can take root on the tree.)

More Resources

The following resources are also available from Great Source and NSTA.

ScienceSaurus

Natural Selection 127
Relationships Between Populations 132

Reader's Handbook

Elements of Graphics: Bar Graph 549
How to Read a Graph 603

SCILINKS. THE WORLD'S A CLICK AWAY

www.scilinks.org
Keyword: Adaptation of Plants
Code: GSLD17

Explore

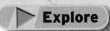

GIVE AND TAKE When a mistletoe plant blooms, birds feed on the sweet nectar inside the flowers. The plant benefits from this interaction, too. As the bird goes from flower to flower feeding on nectar, it scatters the mistletoe's pollen. This enables the plants to reproduce.

When a bird transfers mistletoe seeds to a tree, the seeds' roots grow into the tree. The new mistletoe plants take water and nutrients from the tree. This can weaken the tree but usually doesn't kill it.

USE GRAPHIC ORGANIZERS Create a graphic organizer that explains all the symbiotic relationships between mistletoe plants, the birds that feed on mistletoe berries, and the trees that the mistletoe plants grow on. Identify each relationship as parasitic, mutualistic, or commensal.

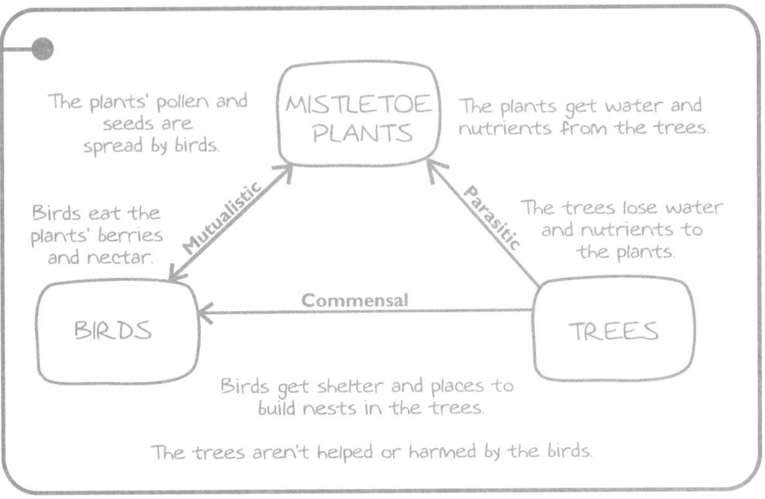

USING GRAPHS Since the mid-1800s, several species of mistletoe in New Zealand have been decreasing in number. Dr. Dave Kelly and his team of scientists investigated the cause for this decline. They found that there is nothing wrong with the mistletoe plants. But over the years, people introduced predators into the region, including cats and rats. The scientists hypothesized that these predators kill the birds that spread the mistletoe's seeds and pollen. Gradually, the number of birds is decreasing. However, from one year to the next, the number of birds does not change very much.

In the 1990s, Dr. Kelly's team studied the number of mistletoe berries produced each year. During the first season, 1994–1995, scientists pollinated the mistletoe plants by hand. This tested whether the mistletoe plants were able to reproduce. During the second season, 1995–1996, the mistletoe was left to be pollinated naturally.

126

Teaching Plan pp. 126–127

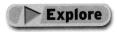

Explore

GIVE AND TAKE Tell students that in addition to spreading the seeds, the mistletoe bird also spreads pollen from plant to plant. Ask students: *What other animals can you think of that help pollinate flowers?* (Examples: bees, butterflies, and other insects; bats; monkeys)

USE GRAPHIC ORGANIZERS If students have difficulty creating a graphic organizer, tell them to draw three circles and label them *Birds*, *Trees*, and *Mistletoe plants*. Then suggest that they connect the circles in some way and add labels to indicate the relationships between these organisms.

USING GRAPHS The data in the bar graph on page 127 show a decline in the number of mistletoe berries produced in a two-year period. Ask students: *What did the scientists learn from the first year's results?* (The mistletoe plants were able to reproduce.) *What did they learn from the second year's results?* (The birds alone were not able to pollinate as many plants as the birds and the scientists did the year before.)

The bar graph below shows the number of mistletoe berries produced during the first two years of their study.

▸ ***The number of birds that visited the mistletoe flowers stayed about the same in both seasons. Why do you think there was such a difference in the number of berries that were produced?***

Scientists pollinated the flowers by hand in the 1994–95 season, so the number of birds that visited the flowers didn't matter.

▸ ***Do you think this experiment supports the scientists' hypothesis about why the number of mistletoe plants have decreased? Why or why not? How could you improve the experiment to make the results more accurate? Explain your answer.***

Accept well-supported answers. The results don't necessarily support the explanation. There could have been other reasons that fewer berries were produced during the second year—a drought, for example. A good way to improve the experiment would be to continue testing for more seasons.

MAKE A PREDICTION Using what you know about mutualistic relationships, what is a possible outcome if the number of birds that feed on mistletoe in the area continues to decline? Explain your answer.

If the number of birds continues to decline, then the number of mistletoe plants in this region would probably decline, too. The trees that the mistletoe grows on might be healthier as a result.

Connections

MATH After students have answered the questions on this page, provide the following data for later seasons in the study. Have students create a bar graph that incorporates these data with the data in the graph on this page.

1996–1997	246
1997–1998	210
1998–1999	150
1999–2000	135
2000–2001	110
2001–2002	95

Assessment

Skill: Predicting

Use the following question to assess each student's progress:

Suppose a disease killed the predators that had been introduced into New Zealand. What might happen to the number of mistletoe berries produced each year? Why do you think so? (The number of birds would increase. More birds would distribute more mistletoe berries. The number of mistletoe plants would increase, which would increase the number of berries produced each year.)

MAKE A PREDICTION Point out that if both the bird population and the mistletoe plant population are declining, more trees might survive. Ask students to predict what would happen if more trees survived as a result of the decline in birds and mistletoe plants. (The animals, plants, and other organisms that benefit from the trees would increase.) Then ask: *What do you think would happen if the scientists fenced off the area?* (There would be fewer predators in the area, so the birds might return. More seeds might be produced, and more mistletoe plants would grow.)

Point of Lesson

Some plants have adaptations that enable them to capture and consume insects.

Focus

- Form and function
- Structure and function in living systems
- Diversity and adaptations of organisms

Skills and Strategies

- Comparing and contrasting
- Making inferences
- Generating ideas
- Creating and using tables

Advance Preparation

Vocabulary

Make sure students understand these terms. Definitions can be found in the glossary at the end of the student book.

- adaptation
- carnivore
- nectar
- nutrient
- predator
- prey
- species
- tissue

Materials

Gather the materials needed for ***Read*** (p. 129), ***Enrichment*** (p. 129), and ***Connections*** (p. 130).

Plant Adaptations

NOT YOUR USUAL CARNIVORES

Venus flytrap ▶ ***(Dionaea muscipula)***

Not enough nutrients in the soil? That's no problem if you're a Venus flytrap.

Most plants are able to get the nutrients they need from the soil. But in some areas, the soil lacks an essential nutrient that plants need in order to survive. Certain plants have evolved an unusual adaptation to obtain the nutrient that is missing from the soil. They catch and digest insects. One carnivorous plant is the Venus flytrap, found mostly in North and South Carolina.

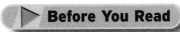

Before You Read

BUGGED Many animals capture insects for food. Fill in the chart below to identify the method each animal uses to capture insects.

ANIMAL	HOW IT CATCHES INSECTS
spider	*spins a sticky web that traps insects*
frog	*quickly sticks out a long, sticky tongue*
bat	*uses sounds (echolocation) to locate insects, then grabs them*

TEACHING PLAN pp. 128–129

INTRODUCING THE LESSON

This lesson describes a different kind of predator-prey relationship—one in which the predator is a plant.

Point out the lesson title, and ask students to explain what the term *carnivore* means. Also ask them to name some carnivores. If students name only mammals such as lions and wolves, encourage them to think of other types of animals—reptiles, fish, amphibians, insects, and spiders.

Students may think that only animals can be carnivores. Explain that a carnivore is *any* organism that eats animals and that such organisms include plants as well as animals.

Draw students' attention to the name "Venus flytrap" in the photo caption and the text on this page. Explain that the plant is also known as "Venus's-flytrap." In both cases, the scientific name is the same.

Before You Read

BUGGED Before students begin filling in the chart, remind them that many insects feed on other insects. Ask them to suggest examples of carnivorous insects. (Examples: praying mantises, ladybugs, crickets) Also ask students to describe how each insect captures its prey, if they are familiar with the method.

Read

Some plants have more in common with carnivorous animals than you might expect.

A Mean, Green Predator

Snap! The two jaws slam shut on the clumsy animal. The long, thin teeth interlock, so that escape is impossible. The jaws press closer together, crushing the creature. Digestive juices flow, slowly breaking down its soft tissues. After the resulting broth has been absorbed...the jaws open and the remains of the prey are dropped.

Too bad for the victim. It shouldn't have been so careless around this hungry predator. And what predator is that? Alligator? Wolf? Snake? Shark? Squat little plant? It's a squat little plant—the Venus flytrap. Of course, they're not real jaws. They only look like jaws. And move like jaws. And capture like jaws. But the jaws are really just a leaf.

interlock: join together—like your fingers when your grip your hands together
digestive juices: chemicals that break down food
broth: a liquid in which meat or other foods are mixed
absorbed: taken in
prey: an organism that is eaten by another organism
predator: an organism that eats another organism
squat: low to the ground

From: Kneidel, Sally. *Skunk Cabbage, Sundew Plants & Strangler Figs: And 18 More Of The Strangest Plants On Earth.* John Wiley & Sons, Inc.

NoteZone

This reading mentions the word "jaws" eight times. Underline the sentence that explains what the "jaws" actually are.

FIND OUT MORE
SCIENCESAURUS
Feeding Relationships 133

Enrichment

Time: will vary
Materials: carnivorous plants in their original soil; clear glass or plastic containers for use as terrariums; reference sources about growing carnivorous plants

Students might like to grow carnivorous plants in the classroom. Several species are generally available from biological supply houses or may be found in nurseries or even the floral department of large supermarkets. You can also find sources on the Internet. Emphasize to students that they should never collect carnivorous plants from the wild.

Encourage students to read about the natural environment of these interesting plants so they can design a suitable environment in the classroom. Many species of carnivorous plants thrive in high humidity and would benefit from being placed in a small terrarium. Almost any clear glass or plastic container could be used so long as it has a cover to hold in moisture. Make sure students punch ventilating holes in the cover.

Read

Time: 10 minutes
Materials: plant fertilizer packaging

Remind students that although plants make their own food, they need nutrients from the soil in order to carry out their life processes. Ask students to examine plant fertilizer packaging and find the names of the nutrients included. One important nutrient needed by plants is nitrogen. This is the first nutrient listed on fertilizer labels. Explain that this nutrient is missing in the wet, acidic soil where carnivorous plants live. Instead, the plants obtain nitrogen from the body tissues of their insect prey.

CHECK UNDERSTANDING

Skill: Comparing and contrasting
Ask students: *What characteristics does the Venus flytrap have in common with animals?* (It captures insects and digests them to obtain nutrients.) *What characteristics does it have in common with other plants?* (It makes its own food.)

More Resources

The following resource is also available from Great Source.

ScienceSaurus

Feeding Relationships 133

Connections

Time: about 90 minutes
Materials: *Little Shop of Horrors* videotape

MUSIC *Little Shop of Horrors* was originally a long-running off-Broadway musical, later made into a movie. The musical is about a tiny carnivorous plant from outer space that demands to be fed in order to maintain its prodigious growth. Although the subject matter is somewhat gory, students will enjoy the story. In fact, the musical is often staged by student groups. You could show this movie to the class after students have designed carnivorous plants in the Take Action activity.

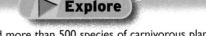

Explore

Scientists have identified more than 500 species of carnivorous plants. Different species have different adaptations for attracting and capturing insects.

MAKE INFERENCES Use the following descriptions and pictures to infer how each plant attracts and traps insects.

Most species of pitcher plants are found in the southeastern United States. The plant's leaves are shaped like a pitcher. The outside of the pitcher is colorful and looks like a flower. The pitcher is lined with small, stiff hairs that point downward. At the bottom of the pitcher are digestive juices.

► ***How do you think a pitcher plant attracts and captures insects?***

Insects are attracted to the colorful, flower-like leaves. When they walk around at the top of the pitcher, they slip down inside it. The downward-pointing hairs keep them from climbing back out.

Pitcher plant
(Sarracenia rubra)

Sundew plants are found all over the world. Their leaves are covered with hundreds of hairs. At the tip of each hair is a drop of sticky fluid that shines like nectar in a flower. This fluid contains digestive juices. When a leaf is touched, it folds up like a fist.

► ***How do you think a sundew attracts and captures insects?***

Insects are attracted to the drops, which look like nectar. When they land on a leaf, they stick to the hairs, and the leaf folds up around them.

Common Sundew
(Drosera rotundifolia)

Teaching Plan pp. 130–131

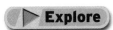

Explore

MAKE INFERENCES After students have examined the photographs and read the descriptions of the three carnivorous plants, they should be able to recognize the adaptations that enable the plants to attract and trap insects.

Ask students: *What plant feature do the leaves of the pitcher plant and common sundew look like?* (flowers) *How does this adaptation benefit the plant?* (Insects are attracted to the flower-like leaves, and the plant can trap them.)

Butterwort plants are found mostly in North America, Asia, and Europe. The plant's leaves lie flat on the ground. The leaves are covered with a shiny, sticky liquid. The leaves curl up slowly when they are touched.

► ***How do you think a butterwort attracts and captures insects?***

Insects are attracted to the shiny liquid that looks like nectar. When they walk on a leaf, they get stuck in the liquid. Then the leaf curls up and traps them.

Butterwort
(Pinguicula moranensis)

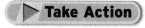

Take Action

CREATE A PLANT Design your own carnivorous plant. Draw and label a diagram to show how the plant attracts and traps insects.

Students' plant designs will vary.

131

Assessment

Skill: Recognizing cause and effect

Use the following questions to assess each student's progress:

Which structures of the carnivorous plants you studied in this lesson are adapted for capturing insects? (the leaves) *Why is it necessary for these plants to trap and digest prey?* (The soil where they grow doesn't contain nitrogen, a nutrient that plants need. The plants get nitrogen from the insects they digest.)

Take Action

CREATE A PLANT Students could work individually or in pairs. Before they begin their diagrams, tell them to make sure that the plant's structures include the following adaptations:

- a way to attract prey
- a way to trap prey
- a way to digest prey

Encourage students to be inventive as they design these three structural adaptations. Tell them not to copy the specific adaptations of the plants presented in the lesson. Have students present their diagrams to the class and explain how the plants' structures enable them to attract, capture, and digest prey.

Point of Lesson

Flowers have features that attract insects.

Focus

- Form and function
- Structure and function in living systems
- Diversity and adaptations of organisms
- Abilities necessary to do scientific inquiry

Skills and Strategies

- Making and using models
- Identifying and controlling variables
- Observing
- Collecting and recording data
- Recognizing cause and effect
- Interpreting data

Advance Preparation

Vocabulary

Make sure students understand these terms. Definitions can be found in the glossary at the end of the student book.

- flower
- nectar
- reproduction

(continued on page 133)

Plant Adaptations

What Attracts Insects to Flowers?

▲ Ladybug beetles *(Coleomegilla maculata)*

Flowering plants and insects depend on each other to survive.

Flowering plants and insects have a mutualistic relationship. Flowers produce nectar that is food for insects. Insects carry pollen from flower to flower, which enables plants to reproduce. Flowers have adaptations that attract insects. These adaptations include the color of the petals, nectar, and honey guides. Honey guides are lines that lead to the flower's center, where the nectar and pollen are located.

Activity

TESTING FLOWERS

Which feature—color, honey guides, or nectar—is most important for attracting insects? Put the question to the test by making model flowers.

What You Need:

- cardboard
- pink and white construction paper
- scissors
- thin black marker
- 8 skewers
- honey (small jar)

What to Do:

1. Make a cardboard pattern for a flower shaped like the one shown here. The flower should be 6–8 cm wide.
2. Trace your pattern on construction paper to make four pink flowers and four white flowers. Cut out the flowers.
3. Number the pink flowers 1–4. Number the white flowers 5–8.
4. Use the black marker to draw honey guides on Flowers 1, 2, 5, and 6.
5. Stick a skewer through the center of each flower.

FIND OUT MORE
SCIENCESAURUS
Plant Life Cycles 108
Sexual Reproduction 114

TEACHING PLAN pp. 132–133

INTRODUCING THE LESSON

In this lesson, students investigate variables that attract insects to flowers. Ask students: *What do you think attracts insects to flowers?* (Examples: smell, color, pattern of coloration, shape)

Some students might think that an insect goes to every flower it can find to obtain food. Explain that insects are selective and specialized eaters. Bees, for example, usually prefer flowers that are blue, purple, or yellow. They are also attracted to flowers with petals that form a landing platform and have a sweet scent. Butterflies tend to favor flowers that are orange, yellow, pink, or blue. They prefer flowers with a wide landing pad but will also visit tubular ones. Moths are active at night and so require flowers that open at night. White flowers with a very strong, sweet scent are easiest for them to locate. Often these nocturnal flowers attract bats as well. Beetles visit dull, reddish-brown flowers that smell spicy or like rotting fruit.

Activity

Time: 40–45 minutes (You could have students do steps 1–5 one day and steps 6–7 another day.)

Materials: cardboard, pink and white construction paper, scissors, thin black marker, 8 skewers, honey (small jar)

Caution: Before students do this activity, find out if any are allergic to bee stings. If so, those students could take part in making the flowers and analyzing the data but not in the direct observations.

- Have students work in groups of four or more, with each student observing no more than two flowers.

Flower	Color	Honey Guides	Honey	Number of Insects
Flower 1	pink	yes	yes	
Flower 2	pink	yes	no	
Flower 3	pink	no	yes	*Answers*
Flower 4	pink	no	no	*will*
Flower 5	white	yes	yes	*vary.*
Flower 6	white	yes	no	
Flower 7	white	no	yes	
Flower 8	white	no	no	

6. Choose a sunny day when flowers are blooming. Go outside and stick the model flowers in the ground. Put them close to each other.
7. Put a drop of honey in the center of Flowers 1, 3, 5, and 7.

► ***Which flower do you think will attract the most insects? Why?***

Answers may vary. Most students will probably choose Flower 1, since it has all three features that attract insects.

► ***Which flower do you think will attract the fewest insects? Why?***

Answers may vary. Most students will probably choose Flower 8, which lacks all three features that attract insects.

8. Observe your model flowers for 15 minutes. Each time an insect lands on a flower, make a tally mark in the last column of the chart. After 15 minutes, count the tally marks in each box and write the number.

► ***Which flower attracted the most insects?*** *probably Flower 1*

► ***Compare the counts for Flowers 2–7. Which feature do you think is most important in attracting insects? What evidence do you have to support your choice?***

Answers will vary. Example: Honey is the most important feature. The flowers with honey attracted many more insects than the flowers without honey.

133

(continued from page 132)

Materials

Gather the materials needed for ***Activity*** (p. 132).

Assessment

Skill: Identifying and controlling variables

Use the following questions to assess each student's progress:

What variables did you test in the activity? (color, presence of honey, presence of honey guides) *Why did you need to make so many flowers to test the variables?* (Each possible combination of variables had to be tested separately.)

- You may want to substitute a sugar-water solution for the honey, as some insects may get stuck in the honey.
- Observations should be made on a warm day because insects are not as active when temperatures are cold.
- Suggest that students wear light colors and not use scented products on the day of the activity.
- Make sure students understand what tally marks are and how to use them. Show them an example on the board for a group of five insects—one vertical line each for insects 1–4, then one horizontal line for insect 5: ~~||||~~.

CHECK UNDERSTANDING

Skill: Identifying and controlling variables

Ask students: *Why was it important to put all the model flowers close to each other?* (The Activity was not testing the effect of location on the insects' behavior. The flowers were put close to each other so differences in location would not affect the results.)

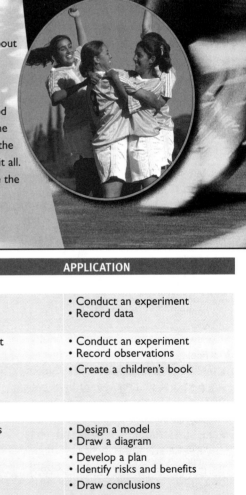

About the Photo

During any activity—whether a strenuous race or deep sleep—all body systems work together to keep the individual alive and healthy. Although the man in this photo must rely on a wheelchair instead of walking or running on his own, with this one exception his body systems function normally. His skeletal and muscular systems enable him to move the wheelchair. His nervous system controls and coordinates his movements and all other bodily functions. His respiratory and circulatory systems supply the oxygen he needs for strenuous activity. His digestive system absorbs the nutrients his cells need. The normal functioning of these systems is more about "ability" than "disability."

About the Charts

A major goal of the *Science Daybooks* is to promote reading, writing, and critical thinking skills in the context of science. The charts below describe the types of reading selections included in this unit and identify the skills and strategies used in each lesson.

UNIT 4 Human Body Systems

Do you know how strong your heart is?

End to end, your blood vessels could circle the globe more than twice! The heart needs to be strapping and tough in order to push blood that far. There are certain things you can do to keep it that way—like paying attention to what you eat, whether you smoke, and how much exercise you get.

Your body is like an all-star team—every part plays a specific role that contributes to the good of the whole. The body is a series of systems, each taking care of a few things in a very efficient way. In this unit, you'll learn about some of the most important systems. One system collects and distributes information, one helps you move around, and another processes the food you eat. Another system helps keep the health of your body in check, and like the coach or captain, your brain oversees it all. Working together, these systems make the body a winner!

134

SELECTION	READING	WRITING	APPLICATION
CHAPTER 13 • COMING TO OUR SENSES			
37. "Surprise! Fat Proves a Taste Sensation" (science news magazine)	• Make a list • Directed reading	• Analyze a graph • Interpret results	• Conduct an experiment • Record data
38. "This Way Up" (nonfiction science book)	• Prior knowledge • Directed reading	• Interpret experiment	• Conduct an experiment • Record observations
39. "Hey, That Tickles! Ouch, Now THAT Hurts!" (medical school Web site)	• Prior knowledge • Directed reading	• Interpret data • Draw conclusions	• Create a children's book
CHAPTER 14 • BODY WORK			
40. "Digesting Food Takes Guts" (NIH Web site)	• Multisensory activity • Directed reading	• Record observations • Draw conclusions	• Design a model • Draw a diagram
41. "Amazing Heart Facts" (TV Web site)	• Draw a picture • Read for details	• Analyze a graph • Draw conclusions	• Develop a plan • Identify risks and benefits
42. "Muscles and Motion" (children's TV)	• Critical thinking	• Hands-on activity	• Draw conclusions

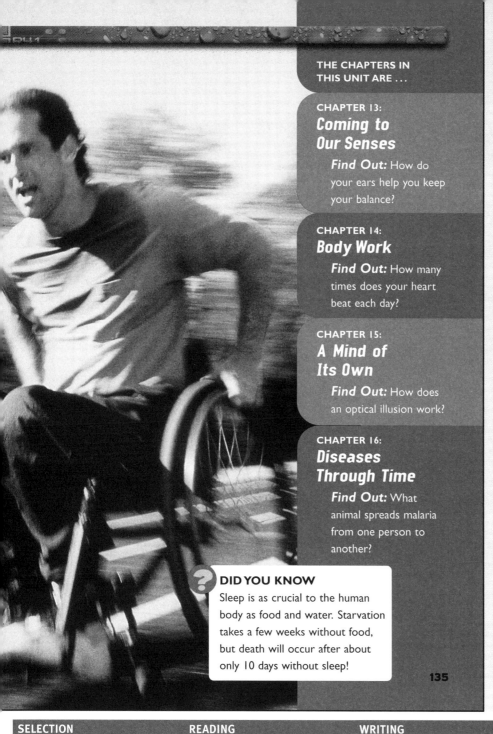

THE CHAPTERS IN THIS UNIT ARE . . .

CHAPTER 13:
Coming to Our Senses
Find Out: How do your ears help you keep your balance?

CHAPTER 14:
Body Work
Find Out: How many times does your heart beat each day?

CHAPTER 15:
A Mind of Its Own
Find Out: How does an optical illusion work?

CHAPTER 16:
Diseases Through Time
Find Out: What animal spreads malaria from one person to another?

DID YOU KNOW
Sleep is as crucial to the human body as food and water. Starvation takes a few weeks without food, but death will occur after about only 10 days without sleep!

135

Answers to *Find Out* Questions

Chapter 13
Fluid in the inner ear sloshes around when you move your head. This movement bends tiny hairs in the inner ear and tells your brain where your head is. (p.140)

Chapter 14
Your heart beats about 100,000 times each day. (p.151)

Chapter 15
The brain learns assumptions and shortcuts to make sense of visual images. An optical illusion uses these assumptions and shortcuts to trick the brain into misinterpreting an image. (p. 163)

Chapter 16
the *Anopheles* mosquito (p. 170)

SCILINKS. THE WORLD'S A CLICK AWAY
www.scilinks.org
Keyword: New Teacher Resources
Code: GSSD02

SELECTION	READING	WRITING	APPLICATION
CHAPTER 15 • A MIND OF ITS OWN			
43. "Don't Be Fooled" (nonfiction science book)	• Critical thinking • Generate questions	• Interpret a diagram • Draw conclusions	
44. Why Do We Sleep? (news article)	• Prior knowledge • Directed reading	• Analyze a graph • Draw conclusions	• Hands-on activity • Report results
45. "Fooling the Brain" (nonfiction science book)	• Interpret a drawing • Critical thinking	• Record observations • Draw conclusions	• Create an optical illusion
CHAPTER 16 • DISEASES THROUGH TIME			
46. "Jonas Edward Salk" (biography)	• Brainstorming • Read for details	• Draw a diagram • Risk analysis • Make predictions	• Conduct an interview • Write a historical account
47. "Epidemic!" (nonfiction science book)	• Read for details • Math calculation	• Interpret a diagram • Critical thinking	
48. "An Ounce of Prevention Keeps the Germs Away" (CDC Web site)	• Prior knowledge • Directed reading	• Critical thinking • Expository writing	• Make a list • Create a poster

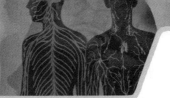

Coming to Our Senses

LESSON 37

Testing Taste Buds

Point of Lesson: ***Scientists are investigating whether humans can taste fat.***

Researcher Richard Mattes is trying to determine whether humans can taste fat. Students analyze Dr. Mattes's experiment, compare his procedure with the results, and consider the views of another scientist who disagrees with Dr. Mattes's conclusions. Students also conduct their own research into the effect of color on the taste of jellybeans.

Materials

Before You Read (p. 136), for each work station:

- brown paper (Kraft) bags
- samples of fatty foods (such as potato chips, French fries, cheese, chocolate chip cookies, butter, and slices of hot dog)
- samples of nonfatty foods (such as slices of apple, carrot, raw potato, and cooked turkey)

Science Scope Activity (pp. 136B and 137), for each group:

- index cards
- resources on human biology

Take Action (p. 139), for each group:

- 5 small paper bags
- 100 jellybeans, 20 each of 5 flavors
- 10 paper cups
- water

Laboratory Safety

Review the following safety guidelines with students before they do the Before You Read and Take Action activities in this lesson.

- Do not taste any substance in the laboratory unless you are instructed to do so.
- If you have an allergy to any food item, do not handle it or eat it.
- Make sure your work area is clean and free of chemical residues and other hazardous substances.
- Wash your hands thoroughly after each activity.

LESSON 38

Balancing Act

Point of Lesson: ***Our inner ears help us maintain balance.***

In this lesson, students consider all the factors that affect their ability to balance and identify games and sports that require good balance. They then perform an activity to discover how the sense of vision affects their own ability to balance.

Materials

Introducing the Lesson (p. 140), for the class:

- 2 or more batons

Read (p. 140), for teacher demonstration:

- glass or clear plastic jar with screw-on lid
- water

Activity (p. 141), for each group:

- firm cushion
- blindfold

Check Understanding (p. 141), for the class:

- picture of a person involved in an activity that requires the sense of balance; the person's eyes, ears, and hands should be visible.

Connections (p. 141), for the class:

- diagram of human head with internal structures

Laboratory Safety

Review the following safety guidelines with students before they do the activities in this lesson:

Introducing the Lesson:

- Do not swing or throw the baton.

Activity:

- Do the activity in a clear area without obstructions.
- One or more student spotters must stand within arm's reach, ready to catch the blindfolded student if he or she stumbles.
- Exercise care when blindfolded or when working around people who are blindfolded.

LESSON 39

How Does It Feel?

Point of Lesson: ***Our sense of touch provides important information about our environment.***

Students read an explanation about the difference between a tickling sensation and pain. They then conduct an activity to explore how their sense of touch varies on different parts of the arm and hand, relating their results to the distance between sensory receptors in parts of the skin. Students conclude by constructing a "touch book" of textures that would be of interest to a young child.

Materials

Activity (p. 144), for each pair:

- metric ruler
- 5 paper clips (standard size)
- tape
- blindfold
- pen

Propose Explanations (p. 144), for the class:

- diagram that shows the areas of the brain's surface devoted to different senses and body parts (See page 144 for possible sources.)

Take Action (p. 145), for the class:

- fabric
- aluminum foil
- sandpaper
- other materials with different textures
- paper
- clips to bind book pages

Laboratory Safety

Review the following safety guidelines with students before they do the Activity in this lesson.

- Use the skin testers carefully. Apply only gentle pressure. Do not use sharp jabs.
- Inform your teacher immediately in case of injury.

Science Scope Activity

A Human Systems Debate

NSTA has chosen a Science Scope *activity related to the content in this chapter. The activity begins here and continues in Lesson 37, page 137.*

Time: ongoing

Materials: see page 136A

Procedure

Students may work on this activity throughout this entire unit (Chapters 13–16).

1. Write each of the following names of body systems on an index card: digestive system, circulatory system, endocrine system, reproductive system, excretory system, respiratory system, and nervous system.
2. Divide the class into seven groups.
3. Turn the cards face down, and let each group pick one card.

(continued on page 137)

Background Information

Lesson 37

Most people are familiar with the four basic tastes—sweet, sour, salty, and bitter. In 1908 a Japanese scientist named Kikunae Ikeda described a fifth taste, umami. This taste—which has been described as meaty, earthy, or brothy—could not be accounted for through any combination of the four other tastes. In 2000, scientists finally discovered umami receptors on the tongue and in the brain, proving that umami is in fact a distinct basic taste.

Lesson 38

The neurovestibular system is made up of the structures in the inner ear and parts of the brain that contribute to balance. Weightlessness or microgravity in space flight can cause balance problems for astronauts, so the National Space Biomedical Research Institute is doing research to find solutions. It is hoped that this research will also help people suffering from neurovestibular diseases on Earth.

Lesson 39

There are two main types of touch receptors: *mechanoreceptors* sense pressure and motion; *thermoreceptors* sense temperature changes. There are several types of mechanoreceptors: one delivers messages about pain, another signals when a limb has moved, and another senses the shape, size, and texture of objects that touch the skin. There are only two types of thermoreceptors, one that senses heat and another that senses cold.

Point of Lesson

Scientists are investigating whether humans can taste fat.

Focus

- Evidence, models, and explanation
- Structure and function in living systems
- Understanding about scientific inquiry
- Nature of science

Skills and Strategies

- Comparing and contrasting
- Interpreting data
- Identifying and controlling variables
- Generating questions
- Creating and using graphs
- Creating and using tables
- Understanding that scientists may disagree about interpretation of the evidence and even arrive at conflicting conclusions

Advance Preparation

Vocabulary

Make sure students understand these terms. Definitions can be found in the glossary at the end of the student book.

- control
- experiment
- fat
- variable

(continued on page 137)

Testing Taste Buds

Thanks to your tongue, you can enjoy many flavors. Is fat one of them?

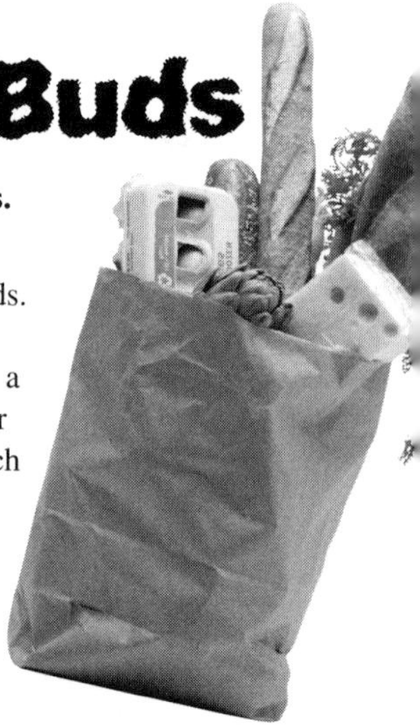

Your tongue is covered with tiny structures called taste buds. Sense cells inside the taste buds detect four basic tastes—sweet, sour, salty, and bitter. The flavors of most foods are a combination of these tastes plus the odors detected by your nose. But what about fat? Many people like fatty foods such as butter, cheese, and fried foods. Does fat have its own taste? To try to find an answer, scientist Richard Mattes did some "tasteful" research.

Before You Read

FOOD FOR THOUGHT Imagine that you are visiting your local supermarket. As you wheel your shopping cart down the aisles, you fill it only with foods that have a high fat content, such as ice cream, butter, and potato chips.

- ***List five other foods that you would include in your cart.***

Answers will vary. Examples: cheddar cheese, whipped cream, mayonnaise, hamburger meat, and bacon

Many people today are concerned about eating a healthy diet. As a result, some food companies have produced "low-fat" or "fat-free" versions of their normally "fat-full" products.

- ***Have you ever tried foods such as fat-free cream cheese or fat-free cookies? If so, describe what they tasted like.***

Answers will vary. Example: I've tried fat-free ice cream. It tasted sweeter and wasn't as creamy as regular ice cream.

TEACHING PLAN pp. 136–137

INTRODUCING THE LESSON

This lesson describes an experiment designed to determine whether our taste buds can distinguish fat. Ask students what they know about our sense of taste. Students may believe that we can sense a wide variety of tastes. Explain that scientists are certain of only four tastes that humans can discern: salty, sweet, sour, and bitter. All the flavors we sense are combinations of these four basic tastes plus the odors of the substances. You could also mention that in recent years, researchers have identified a fifth taste, *umami*, which is present in the flavor enhancer MSG (monosodium glutamate) and in Parmesan cheese.

Ask students to list their most memorable tastes (emphasize the strongest, not necessarily their favorite). Then ask them to categorize these. (For example, ice cream, candy, cakes, pies, and so forth should be grouped together.) Then ask them to describe the common taste sensation for each category. With guidance, these should break down into groupings that the students will perceive as primarily the four tastes listed above: salty, sweet, sour, and bitter.

Before You Read

Time: 10–15 minutes
Materials: brown paper (Kraft) bags; samples of fatty foods (such as potato chips, French fries, cheese, chocolate chip cookies, butter, and slices of hot dog) and nonfatty foods (such as slices of apple, carrot, raw potato, and cooked turkey)

FOOD FOR THOUGHT Students may or may not be aware of which kinds of foods contain high levels of fat. You can use this simple activity to let them identify some fatty foods. Cut up paper bags into squares. Put out the squares

Read

Read about the experiment Dr. Richard Mattes conducted to find out whether fat has its own taste.

SURPRISE! FAT PROVES A TASTE SENSATION

For [many years], scientists...argued that fat has no taste...[because] our mouths lack taste buds...[that are] tuned to fat. That view may be slipping away.... By studying 19 adults, Richard D. Mattes of Purdue University in West Lafayette, Indiana, has shown that the [amount of eaten] fat that travels...into a person's bloodstream depends on whether the person tasted fat to begin with.

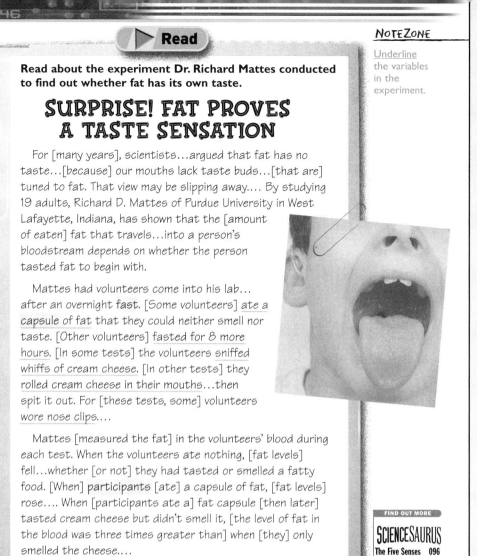

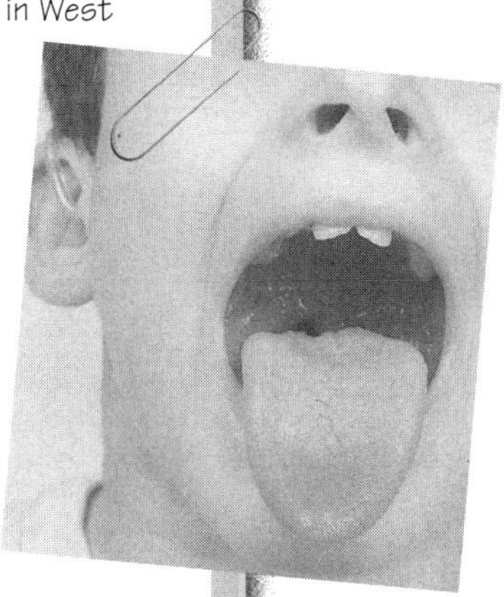

Mattes had volunteers come into his lab... after an overnight fast. [Some volunteers] ate a capsule of fat that they could neither smell nor taste. [Other volunteers] fasted for 8 more hours. [In some tests] the volunteers sniffed whiffs of cream cheese. [In other tests] they rolled cream cheese in their mouths...then spit it out. For [these tests, some] volunteers wore nose clips....

Mattes [measured the fat] in the volunteers' blood during each test. When the volunteers ate nothing, [fat levels] fell...whether [or not] they had tasted or smelled a fatty food. [When] participants [ate] a capsule of fat, [fat levels] rose.... When [participants ate a] fat capsule [then later] tasted cream cheese but didn't smell it, [the level of fat in the blood was three times greater than] when [they] only smelled the cheese....

fast: a period of time without eating any solid or liquid food
capsule: a small pill, usually with a gelatin covering, that contains a substance
participants: people who take part in an activity

From: Raloff, Janet. "Surprise! Fat Proves A Taste Sensation." *Science News.*

NOTEZONE

Underline the variables in the experiment.

FIND OUT MORE
SCIENCESAURUS
The Five Senses 096

SCILINKS. THE WORLD'S A CLICK AWAY
www.scilinks.org
Keyword: The Senses
Code: GSLD18

137

(continued from page 136)

Materials

Gather the materials needed for ***Before You Read*** (p. 136) ***Science Scope Activity*** (p. 136B and p. 137), and ***Take Action*** (p. 139).

Science Scope Activity

(continued from page 136B)

4. Tell students that they will debate which of the seven body systems is the most important. Point out that in real life, no one system is more important than any other. All systems are vital to keep the body alive and healthy.
5. Explain that each group must complete a research paper describing the system and stating their arguments. Tell them to make notes on index cards with information about the other systems to use as reference during the debate.
6. Explain that each group will have 15 minutes for debate—6 minutes to explain why the system is most important, 2 minutes to talk about other systems, 2 minutes for rebuttal of other groups' arguments, and 5 minutes to summarize and restate their arguments. Tell students that after the debate, they will vote on which group presented the best argument.

and the food samples at a work station. (**Caution:** Tell students they must NOT taste the foods, since other students will have handled them.) Have students rub each food on a paper square and let the spot dry. If fat is present, light will show through the spot when the paper is held up to a lamp. Ask volunteers to create a class chart of high-fat, low-fat, and fat-free foods.

Read

Point out that Dr. Mattes did not test the sense of taste directly. He tested the effect of smell and taste on the absorption of fat into the bloodstream. Discuss whether only 19 test subjects was a sufficient sample. Ask: *Do you think wearing nose clips, as the participants in this study did, would affect the volunteers' sense of taste?* (yes) If students are unsure, remind them how things taste when they have a cold and their nose is stuffed up. Ask students to think of possible sources of experimental error. (Examples: Volunteers could have cheated on their fasting; volunteers may have had a poor sense of smell or a stuffy nose; fat that was dissolved in saliva when volunteers tasted cream cheese could have been swallowed even though the cream cheese was spit out.)

CHECK UNDERSTANDING
Skill: Making inferences
Ask: *Why did Dr. Mattes use cream cheese in his experiment?* (Since he was testing fat levels in the bloodstream, he must have chosen cream cheese because it is high in fat.)

More Resources

The following resources are also available from Great Source and NSTA.

SCIENCESAURUS

The Five Senses 096

READER'S HANDBOOK

Elements of Graphics: Bar Graph 549

Reading Tools: Critical Reading Chart 670

MATH ON CALL

Graphs That Compare 291

Single-Bar Graphs 292

Interpreting Data: Correlation Versus Cause and Effect 309

SCILINKS. THE WORLD'S A CLICK AWAY

www.scilinks.org
Keyword: The Senses
Code: GSLD18

Connections

MATH To help students interpret the results of their Take Action research, discuss different ways of displaying statistics. Ask: *What type of bar graph will allow you to compare two different sets of data?* (a double bar graph)

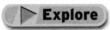

Explore

EXPERIMENT PROCEDURE The chart below summarizes all the tests in Dr. Mattes's experiment.

	TEST 1	TEST 2	TEST 3	TEST 4	TEST 5
Step1	fasted overnight, then came to lab	fasted overnight, then came to lab	fasted overnight, then came to lab	fasted overnight, then came to lab	fasted overnight, then came to lab
Step2	ate fat capsule	ate fat capsule	ate fat capsule	fasted for 8 more hours	fasted for 8 more hours
Step3	no nose clips; rolled cream cheese in mouth for 10 seconds, then spit it out	wore nose clips; rolled cream cheese in mouth for 10 seconds, then spit it out	sniffed whiffs of cream cheese for a couple of hours	no nose clips; rolled cream cheese in mouth for 10 seconds, then spit it out	did not smell or taste cream cheese

ANALYZE A GRAPH This graph shows the results of the experiment.

EXPERIMENT RESULTS

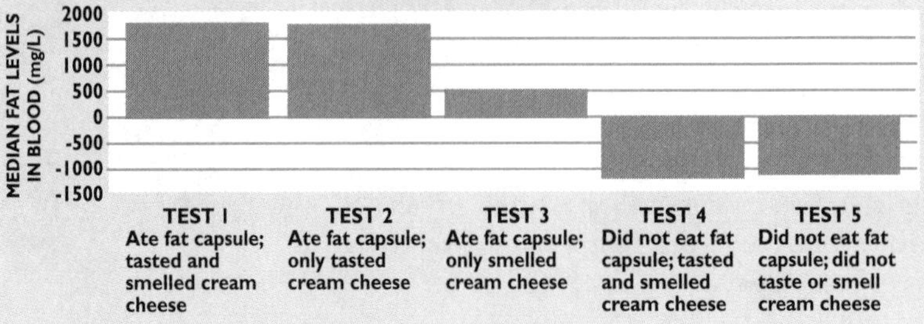

► *In which two tests were fat levels the highest? What variables were the same in both of those tests?*

Tests 1 and 2; eating a fat capsule and tasting the cream cheese

► *Was it necessary to already have fat in the blood to get high fat levels in the tests?*

Yes; volunteers who didn't eat a fat capsule had the lowest fat levels.

► *Which test was the control in the experiment?*

Test 5

138

TEACHING PLAN pp. 138–139

Explore

EXPERIMENT PROCEDURE Ask students to identify the variables in the experiment. (eating a fat capsule, smelling the cream cheese, tasting the cream cheese) Then ask them to consider how Dr. Mattes isolated and controlled each variable. For example, ask: *What was different about the procedures followed in Test 1 and Test 4?* (In Test 1, subjects ate a fat capsule, but in Test 4 they fasted for 8 more hours.)

ANALYZE A GRAPH Ask students to identify the tests in which blood fat levels were highest. (Tests 1 and 2) Ask them to identify the factors those tests had in common. (eating a fat capsule and tasting cream cheese) To answer the second question in this section, students need to look at the graph to determine what happened to blood fat levels when no fat was eaten. (The lowest blood fat levels were produced when no fat capsule was eaten.) If students have difficulty deciding which test was the control, remind them that a control is the part of the experiment in which no variables are tested. Tell them to think about the three variables that were changed from one test group to another, then choose the one that did not test any of those variables.

Propose Explanations

WHAT DO YOU THINK?

- ***Why did Dr. Mattes have the volunteers fast overnight?***

  He wanted to make sure they didn't already have fat in their bloodstream when they started the experiment.

- ***Why did Dr. Mattes have the volunteers wear nose clips in Test 2?***

  Smelling the cream cheese while they tasted it might have changed the fat levels in the bloodstream.

- ***If you were a scientist working with Dr. Mattes, what other questions about the sense of taste would you research?***

  Answers will vary. Examples: Do strong flavors keep you from tasting mild flavors? Are there flavors that lower fat levels in the bloodstream? Would results be the same if you did the experiment using fat-free cream cheese?

- ***Another scientist, Dr. Edmund T. Rolls, doesn't agree with Dr. Mattes's interpretation of the results. He thinks that fat levels in the blood may increase when the tongue senses the texture of fat (how it feels in the mouth), not its taste. What would you do to test Dr. Rolls's hypothesis?***

  Answers will vary. Example: Set up an experiment like Dr. Mattes's, but instead of cream cheese, use a substance that has a fat-like texture but doesn't actually contain fat.

Take Action

DO RESEARCH How much of a jellybean's flavor is due to its appearance? Try this experiment. Write the numbers 1 through 5 on paper bags. Put 20 of one flavor of jellybean in each bag—a different flavor for each bag. Provide 10 cups of water. Ask 10 students to close their eyes, eat a jellybean from each bag, and write down what flavor they think it is. Between jellybeans, the students should take a few sips of water to rinse their mouths. Then have them repeat the experiment with their eyes open. Make a chart of your results. Did not seeing the jellybeans make it harder for the students to identify the flavors accurately?

Results will vary.

139

Assessment

Skill: Identifying and controlling variables

Use the following question to assess each student's progress:

What were the variables in Dr. Mattes's experiment? (eating a fat capsule, smelling the cream cheese, and tasting the cream cheese)

Propose Explanations

WHAT DO YOU THINK? The first two questions in this section require students to make inferences based on the experiment procedures and results. For the third question, students' responses should be based on the reading and test results. Let students share their responses to the last question. Tell them it is not unusual for different scientists to interpret the results of an experiment in different ways and sometimes even draw conflicting conclusions.

Take Action

Time: 30 minutes

Materials: (for each group) 5 small paper bags; 100 jellybeans, 20 each of 5 flavors; 10 paper cups; water

DO RESEARCH **Caution:** Before students begin this activity, find out whether any have allergies, diabetes, or other conditions requiring them to avoid sugary foods.

Students may want to use a simple tally system or a chart to keep track of their results. Tell students to give participants the candy bags in random order. After conducting the test, students should interpret their results to see whether a relationship exists between vision and the perception of taste.

Point of Lesson

Our inner ears help us maintain balance.

Focus

- Evidence, models, and explanation
- Structure and function in living systems
- Abilities necessary to do scientific inquiry

Skills and Strategies

- Collecting and recording data
- Observing
- Comparing and contrasting
- Recognizing cause and effect

Advance Preparation

Materials

Gather the materials needed for ***Introducing the Lesson*** (p. 140), ***Read*** (p. 140), ***Activity*** (p. 141), ***Check Understanding*** (p. 141), and ***Connections*** (p. 141).

More Resources

The following resource is also available from Great Source.

READER'S HANDBOOK

Reading Paragraphs 47

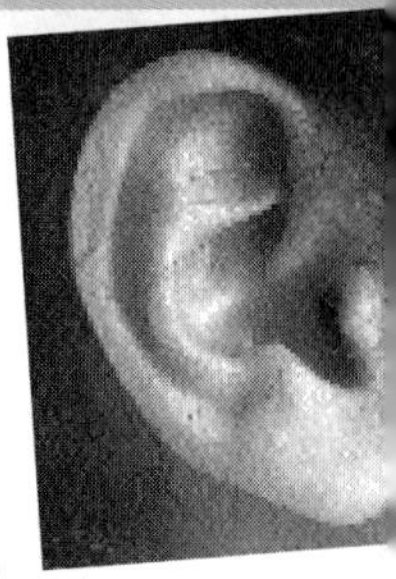

Balancing Act

Your ears not only enable you to hear—they also help you keep your balance.

Learning to ride a bicycle takes skill, practice, and a sense of balance. To keep your balance, your brain has to receive information from many parts of your body. These include motion detectors in your inner ear, pressure detectors in your skin, stretch detectors in your muscles and skin, and visual clues from your eyes.

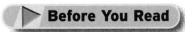

Before You Read

THINK ABOUT IT Most of the time, you take your sense of balance for granted. Whether you're walking down the street or lifting a heavy object, you don't think about how your body keeps from falling over or tipping to one side.

But there are certain times when the human sense of balance seems remarkable. Think about the tight-rope walker at a circus. Imagine a child who has learned to ride a bicycle. Write down some of your favorite sports or other activities that require a strong sense of balance.

Answers will vary. Examples: ice skating, gymnastics, surfing

NOTEZONE

Underline all the things in your ear that help you keep your balance.

Read

How do your ears help you stand up?

This Way Up

Sit up straight—you might learn something! It's as easy as falling off a log. How do you know? The little...hairs [inside your inner ear] tell you. Your ear is not just about hearing. It is also about balance. In your inner ear are three tubes, joined to each other at right angles. They are filled with fluid that sloshes about when you move your head. The [movements] of the fluid bend these hairs and tell your brain exactly where your head is.

right angle: a 90-degree angle, such as that in the corner of a square

sloshes: splashes back and forth inside a container

From: Janulewicz, Mike. *Yikes! Your Body, Up Close.* Simon & Schuster, Inc.

TEACHING PLAN pp. 140–141

INTRODUCING THE LESSON
Time: 10 minutes
Materials: 2 or more batons

This lesson demonstrates that sight plays an important role in maintaining balance. Give each volunteer a baton, and tell them to balance it vertically on the palm of one hand. Ask them to describe what they have to do to keep the baton balanced. Guide students to see that balancing the baton requires sight as well as a sense of balance.

Before You Read

THINK ABOUT IT In a very real sense, balance requires inner ear-hand-eye coordination. Ask students whether any have younger sisters or brothers who are learning to ride a bicycle. Ask them to describe just how difficult it can be. How often does the child lose balance and topple over?

Read

Time: 10 minutes
Materials: glass or clear plastic jar with screw-on lid, water

Use a simple model to demonstrate how the movement of fluid in the inner ear "tells" the brain how the body is oriented in space. Fill a jar half full with water. Screw on the lid very tightly. Hold the jar in front of the class and tip the jar in different directions. Tell students to watch the level of the water in the jar and describe it. (It moves to remain level with the floor.) Ask: *What do you think happens to the fluid in your inner ear when you bend over?* (It moves to remain level.) Explain that the tiny hairs lining the tubes in the inner ear are connected to sensory cells that send signals about the motions to your brain.

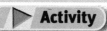

Activity

FOOLING YOUR SENSE OF BALANCE

Find out what happens to the sense of balance when sensory information is not received from the eyes.

What You Need: firm cushion, blindfold (such as a handkerchief)

What to Do:

1. Ask a volunteer to stand on the cushion in stocking feet. Put the blindfold over the volunteer's eyes. *Caution:* Have another student stand near the volunteer to prevent him or her from falling.
2. Have the volunteer hold both arms out to the side and try to stand on one foot. Can the volunteer balance well? Record your observations.
3. Have the volunteer remove the blindfold, step off the cushion, and stand on the floor. Put the blindfold on the volunteer again. Have the volunteer repeat step 2. How was the volunteer's sense of balance affected by wearing the blindfold? Record your observations on the chart.

WHAT DID YOU SEE?

Standing on cushion	Standing on floor
Answers will vary. Example: The student wobbled a lot and had a hard time balancing on one foot.	*Answers will vary. Example: The student still wobbled but could stand on one foot for a longer period of time.*

WHAT DO YOU THINK?

► ***Why do you think it was more difficult for the volunteer to balance on the cushion than on the bare floor?***

The surface of the cushion kept tilting.

► ***Why was it difficult for the volunteer to balance with the blindfold on?***

He/she couldn't use sight to tell whether his/her body was straight or tipped.

▲ **Korean tightrope walker**

141

Connections

Time: 15 minutes
Materials: diagram of human head with internal structures

HEALTH Ask students whether their ears have ever plugged up when they had a bad cold. Show them a diagram of the head's internal structures, and point out the passageway (the Eustachian tube) between the middle ear and the back of the throat. Explain that mucus can "back up" from the nose and throat into this tube, carrying cold viruses into the middle ear. Ask: *What do you think the result would be if the infection spread to the inner ear?* (The infection would prevent the structures in the inner ear from functioning normally.) *Could this affect your sense of balance? Why?* (Yes; the fluid and tiny hairs would not move correctly to tell your brain where your body is.)

Assessment

Skill: Making inferences

Use the following question to assess each student's progress.

What is the connection between our ears and our sense of balance? (Fluid and tiny hairs in our inner ears tell the brain where the body is in space so we can keep our balance.)

Activity

Time: 15 minutes
Materials: firm cushion, blindfold

- Have students work in groups of three or four.
- **Caution:** Remove any obstructions, including desks, from each group's work area.
- Remind students to watch carefully to see what head and body movements the volunteer makes while balancing on one foot. Have them record their observations in the chart.

WHAT DO YOU THINK? Tell students to use their own experience as well as their observations in this activity to answer the questions. Ask: *How do in-line skaters or skateboarders adjust their bodies as they move around obstacles?* Encourage students to speculate about how making exaggerated adjustments would affect someone who was trying to maintain balance. (Adjusting too far in one direction or another would make the person tend to wobble and require more adjustments to keep from falling.)

CHECK UNDERSTANDING
Time: 10 minutes
Materials: picture of a person involved in an activity that requires the sense of balance; the person's eyes, ears, and hands should be visible.

Skill: Communicating
Show students the picture. Ask them to identify each part of the body involved as the person maintains his or her balance.

Point of Lesson

Our sense of touch provides important information about our environment.

Focus

- ▶ Change, constancy, and measurement
- ▶ Structure and function in living systems
- ▶ Abilities necessary to do scientific inquiry

Skills and Strategies

- ▶ Collecting and recording data
- ▶ Interpreting data
- ▶ Making inferences
- ▶ Communicating

Advance Preparation

Vocabulary

Make sure students understand this term. The definition can be found in the glossary at the end of the student book.

- ▶ organ

Materials

Gather the materials needed for ***Activity*** (p. 144), ***Propose Explanations*** (p. 144), and ***Take Action*** (p. 145).

Coming to Our Senses

How Does It Feel?

You have knowledge about the sense of touch right at your fingertips.

What's the largest organ of the human body? The liver? The lungs? You might be surprised to learn that the answer is your skin. Your skin provides your brain with important information about the world around you through your sense of touch.

▶ Before You Read

MAKING SENSE Think about all the different kinds of information you get through your sense of touch. By running your finger over a surface, you can tell if it is rough or smooth, wet or dry. If you accidentally touch the blade of a very sharp knife, the skin on your fingers sends a pain message to your brain.

▶ ***Describe an example of a time when your sense of touch helped you avoid being injured.***

Answers will vary. Example: touching a very hot object and jerking your hand away

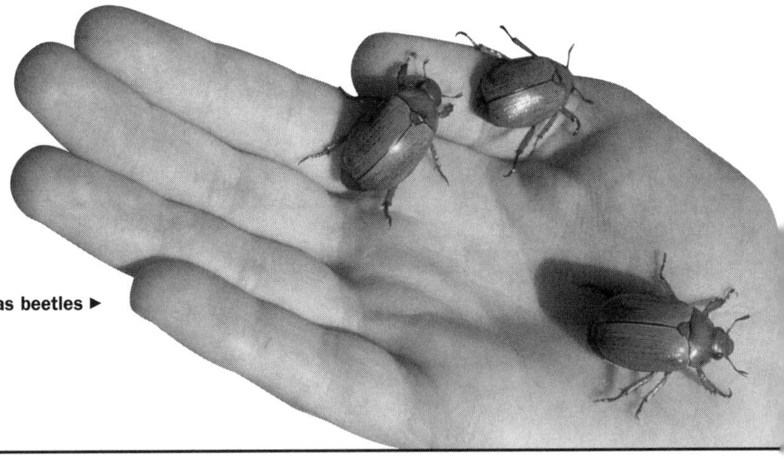

Christmas beetles ▶

TEACHING PLAN pp. 142–143

INTRODUCING THE LESSON

This lesson discusses the types of information we receive through our sense of touch, then gives students an opportunity to test sensitivity on different areas of skin. Ask students to identify the different sensations we can feel with our skin. (texture, temperature, and so forth) Point out that just as the tongue can detect only four basic tastes, the skin can detect only four basic sensations: heat, cold, pressure, and pain.

▶ Before You Read

MAKING SENSE Ask students to name as many adjectives as they can think of to describe all the sensations they feel with their skin. (warm, hard, slimy, cool, smooth, rough, greasy, bumpy, dry, wet, fuzzy, soft, and so forth) Write the list on the board so students can refer back to it for the Take Action activity at the end of the lesson.

If students have difficulty thinking of an example for this section, suggest that they think about sports activities, helping with family meals, or camping experiences. Explain that our sense of touch sometimes acts as an early warning defense system, "telling" the body of a risk of possible injury.

Read

A middle school student wrote to a website and asked how our nerves know the difference between something that hurts and something that tickles. Here's what a scientist had to say.

Hey, That Tickles! Ouch, Now THAT Hurts!

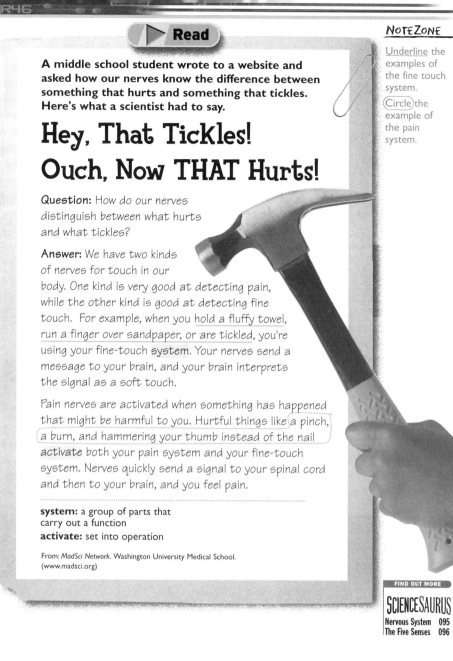

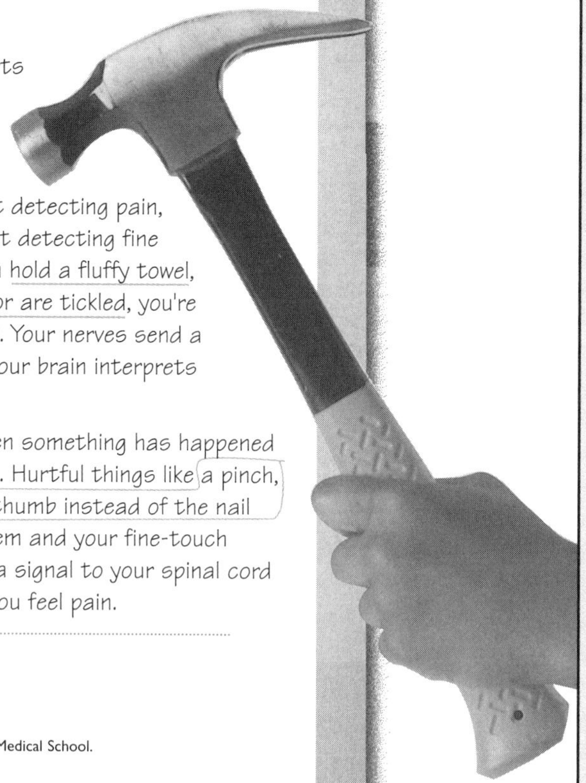

Question: How do our nerves distinguish between what hurts and what tickles?

Answer: We have two kinds of nerves for touch in our body. One kind is very good at detecting pain, while the other kind is good at detecting fine touch. For example, when you hold a fluffy towel, run a finger over sandpaper, or are tickled, you're using your fine-touch system. Your nerves send a message to your brain, and your brain interprets the signal as a soft touch.

Pain nerves are activated when something has happened that might be harmful to you. Hurtful things like a pinch, a burn, and hammering your thumb instead of the nail activate both your pain system and your fine-touch system. Nerves quickly send a signal to your spinal cord and then to your brain, and you feel pain.

system: a group of parts that carry out a function

activate: set into operation

From: *MadSci Network*. Washington University Medical School. (www.madsci.org)

NOTEZONE

Underline the examples of the fine touch system.

Circle the example of the pain system.

FIND OUT MORE

SCIENCESAURUS

Nervous System 095

The Five Senses 096

143

Enrichment

Suggest that students repeat the touch activity on the next page with members of their family. Suggest that they test other areas of the body, such as the face, neck, and back of the hand. Students might also want to investigate whether there is a difference in touch sensitivity between older people and very young children.

Read

Explain that the sensors for pressure are part of the skin's fine-touch system, while the sensors for hot, cold, and pain are part of the skin's pain system. Ask: *How could sensing heat or cold warn you of possible injury?* (Sensing heat would protect you from being burned. Sensing cold would warn you of possible frostbite or hypothermia.)

After students complete the reading, encourage them to make a K-W-L chart to identify what they already know, what they want to know, and what they learned from the reading. One example is shown below.

What I Know	What I Want to Know	What I Learned
Feeling texture is different from feeling pain.	Where in the skin are touch sensors located?	There are only two systems, and both can be activated at the same time.

CHECK UNDERSTANDING

Skill: Making inferences

Tell students to imagine themselves participating in an arm-wrestling match with someone of equal strength. Ask them to describe each touch sensation that their hands would feel. (first, the warmth and texture of the opponent's hand, then the pressure of the grip; perhaps some pain if the grip is strong; possibly moisture if the hands sweat) Ask them to identify the touch system involved in each sensation. (texture, pressure, moisture—soft touch system; warmth, pain—pain system)

More Resources

The following resources are also available from Great Source.

SCIENCESAURUS

Nervous System 095

The Five Senses 096

WRITE SOURCE 2000

Narrative Paragraph 101

Braille Alphabet and Numbers 460

MATH ON CALL

Graphs and Statistics:

Recording Data 268

Data in Tables 285

READER'S HANDBOOK

Elements of Nonfiction:

Cause and Effect 275

Reading Tools: K-W-L Chart 673

Activity

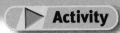

GETTING IN TOUCH WITH TOUCH

You and a partner can test each other's touch systems.

What You Need:

- a partner
- metric ruler
- 5 paper clips (standard size)
- tape
- blindfold
- pen

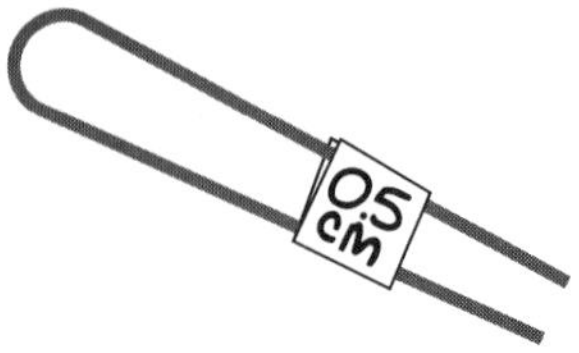

What to Do:

1. Straighten a paper clip to make a skin tester with one point.
2. Bend a second paper clip into a U shape. Use a metric ruler to space the two points 0.5 cm apart. Wrap a small piece of tape around the U to keep the points from moving apart. Use a pen to label this piece of tape "0.5 cm."
3. Repeat step 2 to make and label paper clip U's with points that are 1 cm, 2 cm, and 3 cm apart.
4. Ask your partner to sit and put on a blindfold. Using one of the five paper clip testers, *gently* touch your partner's skin with both points of each tester in the five different places listed in the chart. Ask your partner to tell you how many points he or she feels. Record that number in the box that tells the points you used.
5. Repeat step 4 with each of the other four testers. Record the results.
6. Change places with your partner and repeat steps 4 and 5.

POINTS TOUCHED TO MY PARTNER'S SKIN

TESTING AREAS	One point	Two points			
		0.5 cm apart	1 cm apart	2 cm apart	3 cm apart
Fingertip					
Palm of hand					
Back of hand			*Answers will vary*		
Inside of lower arm					
Outside of lower arm					

144

TEACHING PLAN pp. 144–145

Activity

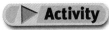

Time: 30 minutes
Materials: metric ruler, 5 paper clips (standard size), tape, blindfold

- **Caution:** Emphasize to students that the touch they apply with the testers should be very gentle, not strong pressure or a sharp jab.
- Ask students what it means if you feel only one point when two points are actually touching the skin. (The tester is touching only one touch receptor. You know the receptors are farther apart.)

Propose Explanations

Time: 10–15 minutes
Materials: diagram that shows the areas of the brain's surface devoted to different senses and body parts; such a diagram can be found at the following Web sites:
www.cogsci.kun.nl/cogw/curs/2000-2001/c0340/sheets/mypenfield.gif
www.mis.atr.co.jp/~mlyons/pub_pdf/Lyons_chi2001.pdf

WHAT DID YOU LEARN? Show students the diagram. They may be surprised to learn what a large proportion of the human brain is devoted to the senses. From this diagram, students should be able to identify the areas of the body most and least sensitive to touch. Encourage students to compare these observations with the results of the Activity on this page. They will find that the diagram supports the idea that the distance between receptors indicates the importance of the sense of touch in different body parts.

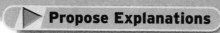

Propose Explanations

WHAT DID YOU LEARN?

▸ *Which skin area felt two points the most often? In other words, which skin area is most sensitive to touch?*

the fingertip

▸ *Which skin area felt two points the least often? In other words, which skin area is least sensitive to touch?*

the outside of the lower arm

▸ *Why did the test include using a paper clip with only one point?*

to compare that feeling with the feeling of two points

▸ *What surprised you about the results of this test?*

Answers will vary. Example: The fingertips are very sensitive to touch, but the arm couldn't tell how many points were touching it.

The distance between sensory receptors on your skin is not the same all over your body. That's what makes the skin in some places more sensitive to touch than the skin in other places.

▸ *Based on your test, where do you think touch receptors are closest together?*

the fingertips

▸ *Where do you think touch receptors are farthest apart?*

outside of the lower arm

▸ *Why do you think touch receptors are closer together in some areas than in others?*

Receptors are closer together in areas that are used for feeling objects and materials.

Take Action

MAKE A "TOUCH BOOK" Create a book that would help a young child explore the sense of touch. Attach objects with different textures to the pages, and add words that invite the child to touch the pages. For example, a page might have a piece of rough sandpaper, a piece of smooth plastic, something sticky, something soft, and so on. (*Caution:* Make sure all the objects are safe for a young child.) Give the book to a young child to enjoy.

145

Assessment

Skill: Inferring

Use the following questions to assess each student's progress.

▸ *How many touch systems are there, and what are their names?* (There are two touch systems: the fine-touch system and the pain system.)

▸ *Are all areas on the body equally sensitive to touch?* (No, some areas are more sensitive than others.)

▸ *What makes some areas more sensitive than other areas?* (Touch receptors are closer together in more sensitive areas.)

Take Action

Time: 45 minutes

Materials: fabric, aluminum foil, sandpaper, and other materials with different textures; paper; clips to bind book pages

MAKE A TOUCH BOOK Suggest that students refer back to the list of touch adjectives that you compiled in Before You Read, page 142. They can use those words and the images and sensations the words conjure up to help them select interesting textures and materials to include in their books. Remind them that young children learn much about the world using all their senses.

Caution: Explain that young children often place objects in their mouths to investigate them. Remind students to be especially careful not to include in the book any sharp objects or small objects that could be detached and swallowed.

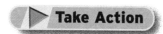

Body Work

LESSON 40

In One End...

Point of Lesson: ***The digestive system breaks down food and absorbs nutrients.***

An exercise in observing what happens as they chew food introduces students to the process of digestion. After reading a brief description of the journey food takes through the digestive system, students construct a simple model of the stomach and mimic its action as it churns food and mixes it with digestive juices. Students compare the model with the real stomach, suggest ways in which the model could be improved, and design their own models of the entire digestive system.

Materials

Before You Read (p. 146), for each student:
- piece of carrot

Enrichment (p. 147), for each group:
- 2 small glass or plastic jars
- a few drops of cooking oil
- $\frac{1}{4}$ teaspoon baking soda
- 2 stirrers
- water

Activity (p. 148), for each group:
- gallon-sized plastic resealable bag
- soft, ripe banana, peeled and sliced
- 3 crushed crackers
- 3 tablespoons of water
- 3 or 4 drops of food coloring (red, blue, or green)

Connections (p. 149), for the class:
- poster or other large illustration of the Food Guide Pyramid

Laboratory Safety

Review the following safety guidelines with students before they do the activities in this lesson.

Before You Read
- Perform this activity in a clean area that is free of chemical residues and other hazardous substances.
- Students with allergies or other conditions requiring them to avoid carrots should not do this activity unless you provide an alternate food.

Enrichment* and *Activity
- Do not taste any substance in the laboratory unless instructed to do so.
- Clean up spills immediately to avoid risk of slips and falls.
- If you have an allergy to any of the materials used in this activity, wear gloves or avoid coming into contact with the materials.
- Wash your hands thoroughly after the activity.

LESSON 41

The Beat Goes On

Point of Lesson: ***The health of the circulatory system is affected by diet and behavior.***

In this lesson, students learn some surprising heart facts, then analyze a graph that shows how rates of death from heart disease increased dramatically during much of the twentieth century. They examine a table listing risk factors for heart disease that can be controlled by the individual. By comparing the diet and activity levels of the typical American today with those of 100 years ago, students are led to conclude that heart health is in their control if they establish good habits in their early years.

Materials

Read (p. 150), for the class:
- several tennis balls

Enrichment (p. 151), for the class:
- science textbooks that include diagrams of the circulatory system
- blue and red pencils

LESSON 42

On the Move

Point of Lesson: ***The human body has three types of muscles: skeletal muscle, cardiac muscle, and smooth muscle.***

In this lesson, students read an article on the three types of muscle in the body. They then explore voluntary movement that occurs while performing a simple task using the arm and identify how muscles functioned to complete the task.

Materials

none

Background Information

Lesson 40

The digestive system is composed of a chain of hollow organs that form a complex tube from the mouth to the anus. The tube is lined with mucosa, or mucous membrane, which contains glands that produce digestive juices in the mouth, stomach, and small intestine. In addition, the liver, gall bladder, and pancreas release digestive juices into the intestine through small tubes. The process of digestion varies depending on the nutrients present in the food. Carbohydrates, fats, and proteins are broken down into smaller molecules to make them usable by the body. Vitamins are absorbed in both the small and large intestines. The large intestine also absorbs water.

Lesson 41

The heart beats at different rates depending on whether the person is at rest or active. As part of the circulatory system, healthy blood vessels constrict when less blood is needed by the body and dilate to enable more blood to flow. Heart disease or heart failure indicates a condition in which the heart is no longer functioning efficiently. The most common cause of heart failure is coronary artery disease, a condition in which the arteries supplying blood to the muscle of the heart become too narrow. This disease often begins early in life. Early prevention through lifestyle management is thought to be the best treatment for the disease.

Lesson 42

The points where muscles attach to bones are located close to the joints, which allows for the greatest range of motion with the least contraction of muscle fibers. In fact, most muscle fibers can contract only about 20 percent of their resting length.

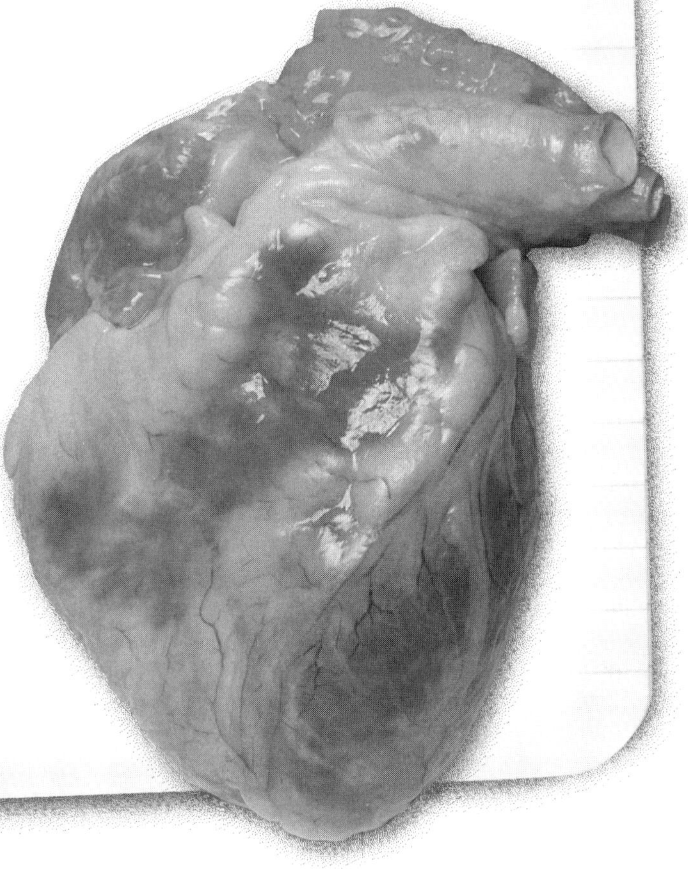

Point of Lesson
The digestive system breaks down food and absorbs nutrients.

Focus
- ► Systems, order, and organization
- ► Structure and function in living systems
- ► Evidence, models, and explanation

Skills and Strategies
- ► Observing
- ► Comparing and contrasting
- ► Making and using models
- ► Drawing conclusions
- ► Making inferences

Advance Preparation

Vocabulary
Make sure students understand these terms. Definitions can be found in the glossary at the end of the student book.

- ► digestion
- ► digestive system
- ► energy
- ► large intestine
- ► liver
- ► nutrient
- ► organ
- ► pancreas
- ► small intestine
- ► stomach

Materials
Gather the materials needed for *Before You Read* (p. 146), *Enrichment* (p. 147), *Activity* (p. 148), and *Connections* (p. 149).

In One End...

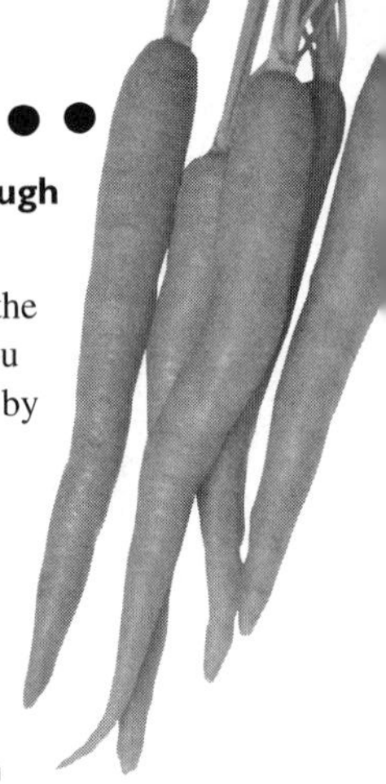

After you finish your lunch, it continues on a journey through your digestive system.

How does your body break down the tasty food you eat to release the energy in it? How does your body separate the parts of the food you need from the parts you don't need? Both functions are performed by the digestive system. The organs that make up this system work together to break down food, absorb the substances you need, and get rid of the waste materials.

► Before You Read

CRUNCHING AND MUNCHING Digestion begins as soon as you put a piece of food in your mouth. Your teeth act like a food processor, chopping up food into smaller pieces. Saliva helps, too, by moistening the food to make it easier to swallow. Saliva contains chemicals called *enzymes* that start to break down food before you even swallow it.

Although you eat every day, you may have never thought about what's going on inside your mouth as you chew. To help you explore the first part of the digestive system, start by chewing a piece of carrot. As you chew, pay close attention to what is happening in your mouth.

► ***How did your tongue help "process" the carrot?***

My tongue moved the carrot around my mouth. This helped mix the carrot pieces with saliva and made sure they were chewed into small pieces.

► ***How did your teeth "process" the carrot?***

My front teeth broke off a piece of carrot that could fit in my mouth. My back teeth ground the carrot into smaller and smaller pieces.

TEACHING PLAN pp. 146–147

INTRODUCING THE LESSON
This lesson explains the roles of the mouth and stomach in the process of digestion. Ask students to describe the path of food through the digestive system, naming the organs in order from the mouth to the large intestine. Ask: *When do you think digestion starts?* Students may think digestion begins when food enters the stomach. Explain that digestion starts in the mouth and that the mouth is part of the digestive system.

► Before You Read

Time: 15 minutes
Materials: pieces of carrot

CRUNCHING AND MUNCHING Slice the carrots into pieces that will be too large for students to put in their mouths so they will have to bite off a piece of carrot with their front teeth. **Caution:** Make sure the carrots have been peeled and thoroughly cleaned. Also determine whether any students are allergic to carrots. If so, have them skip the activity, or provide an alternate hard food for them.

Point out that an enzyme is a protein molecule that helps speed up chemical reactions taking place inside the body. Explain that different enzymes are produced by different glands and organs throughout the digestive system.

Read

Digestion begins in your mouth, but there's a lot more that has to happen to food before your body can use the nutrients in it. After you swallow food, what happens next?

Digesting Food Takes Guts

[When] food...enters the stomach, [it] has three mechanical tasks to do. First, 1 the stomach must store the swallowed food and liquid. This requires the muscle of the upper part of the stomach to relax and accept large volumes of swallowed material. The second job is 2 to mix up the food, liquid, and digestive juice produced by the stomach. The lower part of the stomach mixes these materials by its muscle action. The third task of the stomach is 3 to empty its contents slowly into the small intestine.

As the food is digested in the small intestine and dissolved into the juices from the pancreas, liver, and intestine, the contents of the intestine are mixed and pushed forward to allow further digestion....The digested **nutrients** are absorbed through the [walls of the small intestine]. The waste products...are [pushed] into the [large intestine], where they remain, usually for a day or two, until the **feces** are expelled by a bowel movement.

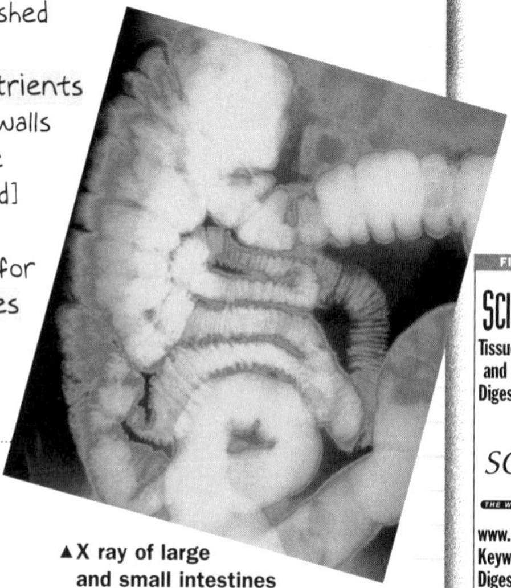

▲X ray of large and small intestines

nutrients: substances in food that the body needs in order to function properly

feces: the waste products of digestion

From: "Your Digestive System and How It Works." *National Digestive Diseases Information Clearinghouse*. National Institutes of Health. (www.niddk.nih.gov/health/digest/pubs/digesyst/newdiges.htm)

NOTEZONE

Number the three mechanical tasks of the stomach.

Circle the names of all the digestive organs mentioned in this reading.

FIND OUT MORE

SCIENCESAURUS

Tissues, Organs, and Systems 082
Digestive System 089

SCILINKS.

THE WORLD'S A CLICK AWAY

www.scilinks.org
Keyword: Digestive System
Code: GSLD19

147

Enrichment

Time: 25 minutes

Materials: 2 small glass or plastic jars, a few drops of cooking oil, $\frac{1}{4}$ teaspoon baking soda, stirrers

The following activity models how bile from the liver helps break up fat particles in the small intestine. Students can work in pairs or small groups. Give them the following instructions:

1. Fill two jars halfway with water.
2. Add a few drops of oil to each jar.
3. Add $\frac{1}{4}$ teaspoon of baking soda to one jar.
4. Stir the contents of both jars.

The oil in the jar with the baking soda will begin to break apart. The oil in the other jar will form a separate layer on top of the water. Ask students to explain what the baking soda and the oil represent. (The baking soda represents bile; the oil represents fat particles in the small intestine.) Also ask students to explain why fat particles must be broken down during digestion. (The particles would be too large to pass through the wall of the small intestine and be absorbed into the bloodstream.)

Read

Point out that the food enters the stomach through a long, narrow tube called the *esophagus*, which connects the mouth to the stomach. After students complete the NoteZone activity, have them use the words they circled to construct a flow chart showing the movement of food through the digestive system. (Note that students will need to place the pancreas and liver to the *side* of the small intestine, since food does not pass through those two organs.)

Finally, point out that any useful substances in the leftover materials, such as water and minerals, are absorbed through the walls of the large intestine and into the bloodstream. The remains are formed into semisolid feces, ready to be eliminated from the body.

CHECK UNDERSTANDING

Skill: Drawing conclusions

Ask: *What is the function of the tongue in digestion?* (It moves food around in the mouth to mix it with saliva and help the teeth break it into small pieces.)

More Resources

The following resources are also available from Great Source and NSTA.

SCIENCESAURUS

Tissues, Organs, and Systems 082
Digestive System 089

READER'S HANDBOOK

Note-taking 646

WRITE SOURCE 2000

Descriptive Paragraph 100

SCILINKS. THE WORLD'S A CLICK AWAY

www.scilinks.org
Keyword: Digestive System
Code: GSLD19

Activity

CREATE A MODEL

Make this model and use it to "digest" some food. Compare the model to what you know about how your own stomach works.

What You Need:

- gallon-sized plastic resealable bag
- soft, ripe banana, peeled and sliced
- 3 crushed crackers
- 3 tablespoons of water
- 3 or 4 drops of food coloring (red, blue, or green)

What to Do:

1. Put the banana, crushed crackers, water, and food coloring into the bag.
2. Flatten the bag to get most of the air out. Then seal the bag tightly.

► ***What do you observe happening inside the bag?***

nothing (The cracker pieces may start to absorb some of the liquid.)

3. Gently mash and squeeze the bag for 15–30 seconds. Examine the contents again.

► ***What do the contents look like now?***

The banana, cracker pieces, water, and food coloring are all mixed together.

INTERPRET YOUR MODEL

► ***In your model, what did your hands represent?***

the muscles in the lower part of the stomach

► ***What did the water and food coloring represent?***

the digestive juices produced by the stomach

148

TEACHING PLAN pp. 148–149

Activity

Time: 15 minutes
Materials: gallon-size plastic resealable bag; soft, ripe banana, peeled and sliced; 3 crushed crackers; 3 tablespoons of water; 3 or 4 drops of food coloring (red, blue, or green)

- Have students work in groups of two to four.
- Caution students not to mash and squeeze the bag roughly, as the contents may rupture the bag.

INTERPRET YOUR MODEL Point out that the physical breakdown of food in both the mouth and the stomach is known as mechanical digestion. Remind students that in addition to mechanical digestion in the stomach, digestive juices called enzymes are also at work to speed up the process of digestion that takes place there.

Propose Explanations

DRAW CONCLUSIONS

- *How do the churning motions of the stomach muscles help with digestion?*

  The motions mix the digestive juices with the pieces of food so the juices can break the food down even more.

- *If food were not broken into smaller pieces in the mouth, what do you think would happen in the stomach?*

  The pieces would be too large. The stomach wouldn't be able to function properly, and the food would be passed along as chunks. Many of the nutrients would be lost.

- *How could you improve this model so that it more accurately shows all three mechanical tasks of the stomach?*

  Answers will vary. Example: Add a tube for the partially mashed food to enter through and a way for the churned food to slowly leave the stomach, as if it were entering the small intestine.

- *In the small intestine, the partly digested food is mixed with digestive juices from the liver and pancreas. What structures do you think produce this mixing action?*

  There must be muscles in the small intestine like the muscles in the stomach.

Take Action

IT SLICES, IT DICES, IT DIGESTS On a separate sheet of paper, design your own model that performs all the functions of the digestive system you've learned about. Make sure your model includes each part of the digestive system. Draw a diagram of your model. Add arrows to your diagram to show the passage of food through the model. Label the diagram to tell what each part of the model does.

Students' models will vary.

149

Connections

Time: 10 minutes

Materials: poster or other large illustration of the Food Guide Pyramid

HEALTH Display the Food Guide Pyramid. Explain that it shows the recommended daily servings for six major food groups. Ask students what they think the purpose of the Pyramid is. (It helps people plan a balanced diet.) Tell students to keep a record of their meals for three days to see how their diets compare with the recommendations given in the Pyramid.

Assessment

Skill: Sequencing

Use the following question to assess each student's progress:

What happens at each stage of digestion? (In the mouth, the teeth break food down into smaller pieces, and enzymes in saliva start digesting the pieces. The stomach mixes the food with more enzymes that further digest it. In the small intestine, the tiny particles of food are dissolved in enzymes from the liver, pancreas, and small intestine, and nutrients are absorbed through the walls of the small intestine. The large intestine holds the waste materials until they are expelled as feces.)

Propose Explanations

DRAW CONCLUSIONS Ask students: *What happens to digested food while it is in the small intestine?* (Nutrients in the food pass through the walls of the small intestine and are absorbed into the bloodstream.) *What happens to the leftover materials that cannot be digested?* (They pass along to the large intestine.) You may want to mention that besides holding waste materials, the large intestine absorbs much of the water still left in the materials.

Have students share their ideas for improving their models. If feasible, let them make the changes and report their results.

Take Action

IT SLICES, IT DICES, IT DIGESTS You might want to let students work in pairs or small groups to design the model and draw the diagram. Allow time for students to share their diagrams and explain what the different parts of the model are and how each one works.

Point of Lesson
The health of the circulatory system is affected by diet and behavior.

Focus
- Systems, order, and organization
- Structure and function in living systems
- Personal health

Skills and Strategies
- Creating and using graphs
- Interpreting data
- Making inferences
- Generating ideas

Advance Preparation

Vocabulary
Make sure students understand these terms. Definitions can be found in the glossary at the end of the student book.

- behavior
- blood
- cell
- heart
- lungs
- organ

Materials
Gather the materials needed for ***Read*** (p. 150) and ***Enrichment*** (p. 151).

Body Work

The Beat Goes On

That thump-THUMP, thump-THUMP in your chest is the sound of your heart sending blood throughout your body.

Most of the time, you probably take your heart for granted. You don't think about the number of times that this powerful organ beats each day, sending oxygen-rich blood throughout your body. Since every cell in your body needs oxygen, your heart has a very important role.

Before You Read

BY HEART Draw the heart in this picture of a person's chest. Show what you think is the heart's shape and size and its location in the chest.

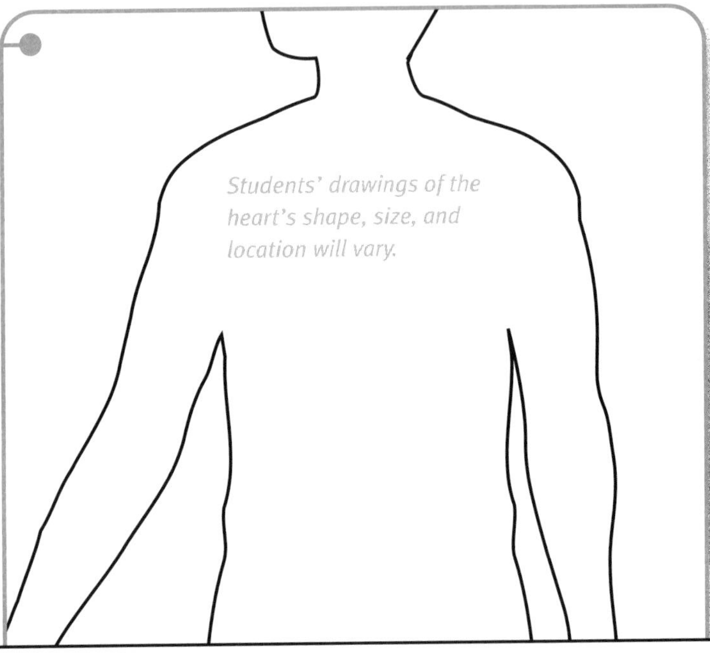

Students' drawings of the heart's shape, size, and location will vary.

Teaching Plan pp. 150–151

INTRODUCING THE LESSON
This lesson focuses on the heart and describes the risk factors that contribute to heart disease. Students also develop a plan to improve their health habits and help prevent heart disease.

Students may not realize that they should start taking care of their heart now. Point out that even though heart disease usually affects adults, healthy habits and lifestyle choices they start now can affect the health of their hearts later in life.

Before You Read
BY HEART Allow students to correct their drawings if necessary after they complete the reading on the next page. Tell students that even when they are resting, their heart muscle is working harder than the leg muscles of a person sprinting.

Ask students how much blood they think is in the body. Tell them that the body has about 5.6 liters (6 quarts) of blood, which travels throughout the body about three times every minute. In a single day, their blood travels a distance equivalent to going from coast to coast four times.

Read
Time: 20 minutes
Materials: tennis balls

Explain to students that the thump-THUMP sounds of the heart are caused by the closing of the valves between the heart's chambers. Show students how to take their pulse by placing two fingers below the jawbone on the side of the neck or on the inner wrist. Have them count the beats for 15 seconds and then multiply by 4 to get the number of heartbeats per minute. Have students use their own heartbeat rate to calculate the number of times their

Read

You know your heart pumps blood, but there's a lot more to this incredible organ.

AMAZING HEART FACTS

- In one day, your blood travels a total of 19,000 km (12,000 miles)—that's four times the distance across the U.S. from coast to coast.
- Your heart beats about 100,000 times in one day and about 35 million times in a year....
- Put your hand on your heart. Did you place your hand on the left side of your chest? Many people do, but the heart is actually located almost in the center of the chest, between the lungs. It's tipped slightly so that a part of it sticks out and taps against the left side of the chest, which is what makes it seem as though it is located there.
- If you're a kid, your heart is about the same size as your fist, and if you're an adult, it's about the same size as two fists.
- Give a tennis ball a good, hard squeeze. You're using about the same amount of force your heart uses to pump blood out to the body....

From: "Amazing Heart Facts." *Nova Online*. WGBH. (www.pbs.org/wgbh/nova/heart/heartfacts.html)

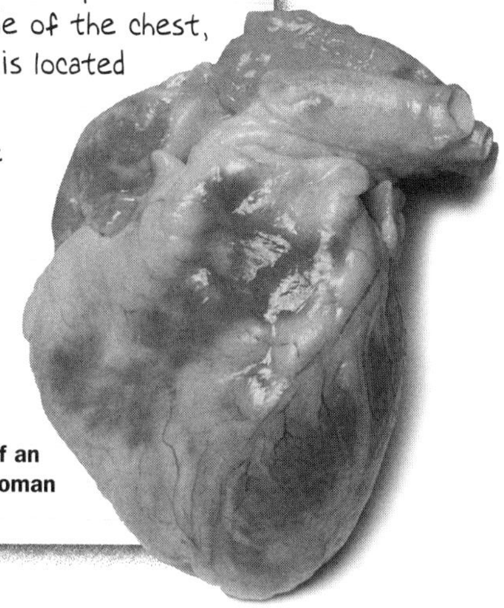

► **Heart of an adult woman**

NOTEZONE

About how many times does your heart beat during one science class?

To calculate the answer: 100,000 beats per day ÷ 24 hours = about 4,200 beats/hour × science class's percentage of 1 hour

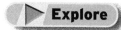

Explore

UNHEALTHY HEARTS Hundreds of thousands of Americans lose their lives each year to heart attacks, strokes, and other heart-related diseases. But back in 1900, only about 25,000 people in the U.S. died of heart disease. That's about 33 deaths per 100,000 people. Compare that with about 266 deaths per 100,000 people in 1999. What caused this dramatic increase in heart-related deaths? One reason may be that people in 1999 were living longer than people did in 1900, so they were more likely to experience heart disease, which occurs more frequently with age. Scientists are investigating other causes as well.

FIND OUT MORE
SCIENCESAURUS
Circulatory System 093

Enrichment

Time: 25 minutes

Materials: science textbooks that include diagrams of the circulatory system; blue and red pencils

Invite students to consult science textbooks to find out more about the anatomy of the heart—its four chambers and the vessels that carry blood to and from the heart. Have students create a flowchart or draw and label a diagram that shows the path of blood through the heart.

Point out to students that scientific illustrations usually use red to represent blood carrying oxygen from the lungs to the heart and then to the rest of the body. Blue is used to represent low-oxygen blood returning to the heart from the body and then to the lungs. Encourage students to use these colors in their diagrams.

hearts beat in one day. (student's rate per minute × 60 min/hr × 24 hrs) Have students compare that result with the 100,000 figure given in the reading. Provide tennis balls so students can try the last item in the reading.

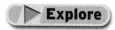

Explore

UNHEALTHY HEARTS Ask: *How much did the rate of heart-related deaths increase per 100,000 persons from 1900 to 1999?* (233 deaths per 100,000) Tell students that the average life expectancy in 1900 in the U.S. was 46.3 years for males and 48.3 for females. Explain that the leading causes of death in 1900 were pneumonia and tuberculosis.

Then point out the sentence in the paragraph that suggests one reason for the increased rate of heart disease since 1900, and ask: *What other reasons might account for the increase?* (Students may suggest that people smoke more, do not eat healthy diets, and do not get as much exercise.)

CHECK UNDERSTANDING

Skill: Concept mapping

Have students draw a concept map showing facts about the heart's function, size, location in the chest, and beating rate. (Concept maps may include the following: sends oxygen-rich blood throughout the body; about the size of one or two fists; located in the center of the chest with part tipped to the left side, beats about 100,000 times in one day.)

More Resources

The following resources are also available from Great Source.

SCIENCESAURUS	
Circulatory System	093
READER'S HANDBOOK	
Elements of Graphics: Line Graph	554
MATH ON CALL	
Single-Line Graphs	298
Trends	310
WRITE SOURCE 2000	
Expository Paragraph	102

Connections

MATH Remind students that line graphs show change over time. The label on the horizontal (x) axis identifies the period of time that the graph represents. The label on the vertical (y) axis identifies the type of data being graphed. The graph's title identifies the relationship between the data and the time period. Ask students to find examples of line graphs in newspapers and magazines. Have them identify the time period and the type of data represented by each graph.

ANALYZE A GRAPH Use the graph to answer the following questions.

U.S. Deaths from Heart Disease 1900–1999

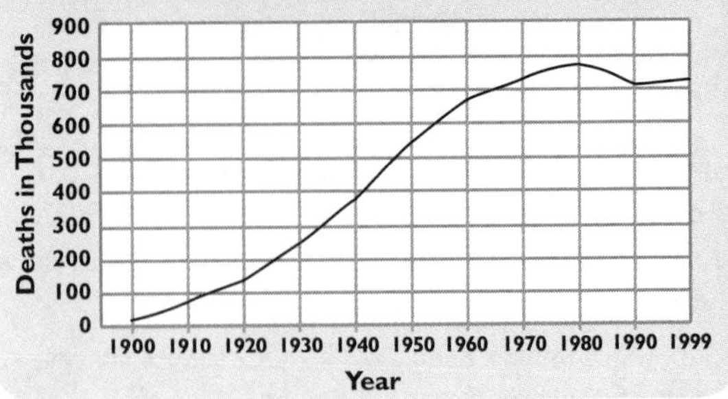

► *About how many deaths from heart disease occurred in each of the following years?*

1920: *about 150,000* deaths

1950: *about 550,000* deaths

1999: *about 725,000* deaths

► *When were heart-related deaths most common?*

during the late 1970s and early 1980s

► *Since 1980, what has happened to the number of deaths from heart disease?*

The number of deaths decreased slightly from 1980 until 1990, then started to rise again, but very slowly.

EXAMINE THE RISK FACTORS Not everyone has the same risk of developing heart disease. According to doctors, people who are likely to develop heart disease share a number of risk factors—conditions and behaviors that may lead to the disease. People cannot control some risk factors, such as their age, but there are other factors that people can control.

RISK FACTORS THAT CAN BE CONTROLLED
SMOKING Smoking increases the risk of heart disease.
HIGH CHOLESTEROL People with high amounts of fatty cholesterol in their blood are more than twice as likely to develop heart disease. Fatty cholesterol is found in high-fat foods such as ice cream, butter, and fried foods.
HIGH BLOOD PRESSURE One in four American adults has high blood pressure. Eating salty foods, drinking alcohol, smoking, not getting enough exercise, and being overweight can all contribute to high blood pressure.
LACK OF EXERCISE Lack of exercise contributes to more than 25,000 deaths from heart disease a year.
OBESITY People who are extremely overweight are three times more likely to develop heart disease.

TEACHING PLAN pp. 152–153

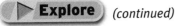

Explore *(continued)*

ANALYZE A GRAPH Call attention to the graph's vertical (y) axis, and point out that the numbers indicate the number of deaths in thousands—that is, each number on the axis must be multiplied by 1,000 to find the number of deaths. Point out that the total population of the United States has increased since 1900, so it follows that the total number of deaths from heart disease also would have increased. Emphasize that it is the *rate* of heart disease—the number of deaths *per thousand* people—that is most important.

Ask: *Why do you think the number of heart-related deaths decreased from 1980 to 1990?* (Students may mention healthier lifestyles, better medical treatment, and new medicines.)

EXAMINE THE RISK FACTORS Discuss the risk factors one at a time. Tell students that cholesterol is a fatty-like substance that is found in animal fats, meats, and dairy products. There are two types of cholesterol—HDL ("good") cholesterol and LDL ("bad") cholesterol. LDL cholesterol is "bad" because it clogs blood vessels that lead to and from the heart.

For each risk factor listed, ask students to suggest ways that people can reduce their risk of heart disease. For example, to help keep LDL cholesterol low, they can eat a diet that is low in fatty foods and high in fruits and vegetables. People should also exercise regularly and avoid smoking and alcoholic beverages. Students can find out more about risk factors for heart disease at the following Web sites:
www.americanheart.org
www.cardiologytulsa.com/factors.htm

Propose Explanations

PUTTING IT TOGETHER Think about how the daily activities and habits of Americans have changed over the last 100 years.

- ***In 1900, there was no such thing as "convenience foods." Most people had to cook their own food or buy it from someone else who cooked it. How is this different from the situation today?***

  People today eat more processed foods and fatty foods from fast-food restaurants.

- ***How has this diet change affected the number of people who develop heart disease?***

  Fatty foods can cause people to be overweight and have higher cholesterol levels in their blood. These factors increase the risk of heart disease.

- ***Think about the kinds of work that most Americans did in the early 1900s and the kinds of work Americans do now. Do Americans today get more or less daily exercise than they did then? What are some inventions that have contributed to this change?***

  In general, people in the U.S. today are less physically active than they were 100 years ago. The less active lifestyle is partly due to inventions such as tractors, TVs, personal computers, cars, elevators, and the like.

- ***Look back at the list of risk factors that can be controlled. In order for the number of annual heart-related deaths in the U.S. to decrease, how would Americans need to change their lifestyles?***

  More Americans would have to stop smoking, eat a healthier low-fat diet, and exercise regularly.

Take Action

DEVELOP A PLAN Most types of heart disease take years to develop. The health habits you develop as a teenager could affect your risk of developing heart disease when you're older. On a separate sheet of paper, create a healthy menu and exercise plan for one week. Explain how each of the foods and behaviors in your plan could affect your risk factors for heart disease. Find out about other benefits of these health habits.

Students' plans will vary.

153

Assessment

Skill: Predicting

Use the following task to assess each student's progress:

Have students list risk factors that contribute to heart disease. (smoking, high cholesterol, high blood pressure, lack of exercise, obesity) Then have them suggest ways that people can reduce their risk of heart disease. (Avoid smoking, alcohol use, salty foods, and fatty foods; exercise regularly; maintain a healthy weight.)

Propose Explanations

PUTTING IT TOGETHER Ask students how many of them eat at fast-food chains. Stress that many fast foods and other convenience foods have a high fat content. Point out that healthy foods are actually more available now in the United States than they were in the past, when fresh fruits and vegetables were available only seasonally. Also mention that although people 100 years ago had diets relatively high in fat, their more active lifestyles helped offset the potential risks.

Take Action

DEVELOP A PLAN Allow students time to share their plans and ideas. Also spend time discussing the other health benefits their plans would provide. Ask students if they think implementing their plans would be difficult, and if so, to explain why. Let the class brainstorm some strategies for overcoming difficulties.

Point of Lesson

The human body has three types of muscles: skeletal muscle, cardiac muscle, and smooth muscle.

Focus

- Systems, order, and organization
- Structure and function in living systems

Skills and Strategies

- Observing
- Recognizing cause and effect
- Organizing information
- Making inferences

Advance Preparation

Vocabulary

Make sure students understand these terms. Definitions can be found in the glossary at the end of the student book.

- cell
- digestive system
- heart
- joint
- tissue

Body Work

On the Move

Jumping, kicking, and even breathing would be impossible without your mighty muscles.

Sometimes in a movie, the good guy will tell the bad guy, "Don't move a muscle." In real life, it's impossible for a living person to stop all muscle activity. Just standing still takes constant muscle activity. Also, many muscles in your body are constantly in motion, such as those in your digestive system and your heart. Other muscles you can control.

NOTEZONE

Which kind of muscles are used when you do jumping jacks?

skeletal muscles

Read

There are three types of muscles in your body.

Muscles and Motion

Muscles are the motors of the human body, allowing us to walk, pumping our blood, making us breathe and pushing our food through the digestive system. In order to do these different types of jobs, muscles come in three forms. Cardiac muscle is found only in the heart, smooth muscle lines our blood vessels and digestive system, and skeletal muscle makes us move.

...[Skeletal] muscle is...made up of thousands of individual cells, each wrapped in connective tissue. These elongated cells, referred to as fibers, are arranged in bundles. Thin threadlike structures called myofibrils run through each fiber, and when a muscle contracts, these myofibrils pull past each other, shortening the cells.

Skeletal muscles create motion by pulling on tough cords of connective tissue called tendons. These tendons in turn pull on the bone, which creates motion. Since muscles can only contract, each joint must have two opposing sets of muscles to give the full range of motion.

▼ Cardiac muscle tissue

FIND OUT MORE SCIENCESAURUS Muscular System 087

cardiac: having to do with the heart
vessels: thin tubes in the body that carry blood
skeletal: attached to or formed by the skeleton
elongated: long and thin
contracts: tightens and shortens

From: "Muscles and Bones; Einstein; Stars Chat; Raptor Center." *Newton's Apple*. KTCA. (www.pbs.org/ktca/newtons/newtonsclassics/classic11.html)

UNIT 4: HUMAN BODY SYSTEMS 154

TEACHING PLAN pp. 154–155

INTRODUCING THE LESSON

This lesson describes the three types of muscle tissue and demonstrates that skeletal muscles function in pairs. Ask students to describe how muscles work when you move a part of your body—bend your knee, for example. Many students may realize that such movements require pairs of muscles acting in opposition to each other. Some students, however, may think that skeletal muscles work individually. Tell students that in this lesson they will learn about muscles working in pairs.

Read

Ask students which of the three types of muscles can be controlled voluntarily—that is, which type can we *choose* to move? (skeletal muscles) Point out that skeletal muscles are responsible for the movement of our arms, legs, head, and other body parts. Ask students to give some examples of voluntary movements. (walking, running, throwing a ball, waving your arms, and so forth)

Explore

GOING UP, GOING DOWN Hold a heavy book in one hand, and put your other hand around your upper arm. Lift the book up toward your shoulder very slowly. What do you feel in your upper arm? Now slowly lower the book. What do you feel in your upper arm?

When I raise and lower the book slowly, I can feel the muscles in my upper arm tighten and bulge.

► ***Which type of muscle did you use?*** *skeletal*

Propose Explanations

THINK ABOUT IT The muscle at the front of your upper arm is called the biceps. The muscle at the back of your upper arm is called the triceps.

► ***Explain what your biceps and triceps did as you raised and lowered the book. How could you tell what the muscles were doing? (Hint: Remember what you learned in the reading about skeletal muscles working in pairs.)***

When I raised the book, my biceps shortened to pull my lower arm toward my shoulder. I could feel the bulge as it tightened. When I lowered the book, my triceps shortened to pull my lower arm down.

► ***As you lowered the book, did the biceps relax completely? Why do you think that happened?***

No, the muscle stayed tightened. If it had relaxed completely, my lower arm would have dropped down quickly and I might have dropped the book.

More Resources

The following resources are also available from Great Source.

SCIENCESAURUS

Muscular System 087

WRITE SOURCE 2000

Expository Paragraph 102

Assessment

Skill: Classifying

Use the following question to assess each student's progress:

What are the three types of muscles in the human body, and where are they found? (Cardiac muscle is found only in the heart, smooth muscle lines the blood vessels and digestive system, and skeletal muscles are attached to bones.)

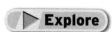

Explore

GOING UP, GOING DOWN Explain that the strength of a muscle's contraction depends on the number of muscle fibers that contract all at once. It takes more muscle fibers to swing a baseball bat than it does to lift a book. Each muscle fiber contracts either completely or not at all.

Propose Explanations

THINK ABOUT IT Point out that muscle pairs are responsible for movements in other parts of the body, such as the legs, shoulders, wrists, neck, and feet. Even the face has pairs of muscles that enable a person to smile or frown. Ask students to describe other muscle pairs in the body and the action that results from the contraction of each muscle in the pair.

CHECK UNDERSTANDING

Skill: Making inferences

Ask: *Would it require pairs of muscles to kick a soccer ball?* (Yes; pairs of muscles flex and extend the ankle, knee, and hip.)

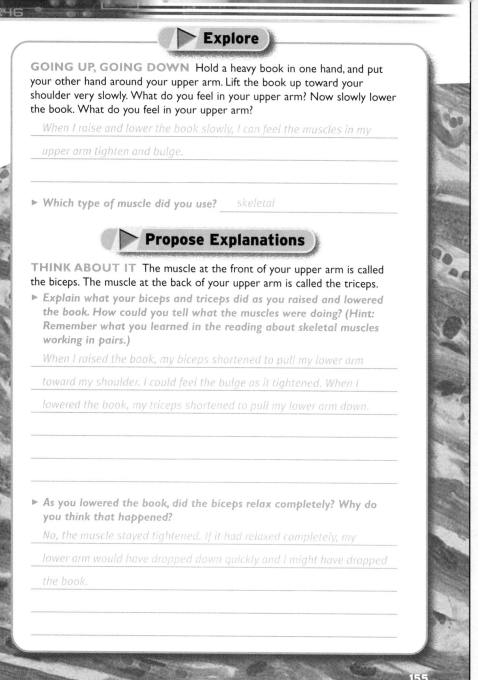

A Mind of Its Own

LESSON 43

Brain Scan

Point of Lesson: ***Different parts of the brain do different things.***

After reading a brief description of the brain, students observe diagrams showing which areas of the brain are active during different tasks involving spoken and written language. They then consider how brain injury due to a stroke might affect a person's ability to process language in different ways.

Materials

none

LESSON 44

Sleep On It

Point of Lesson: ***Sleep may play an important role in learning.***

Students read about an experiment in which scientists tested the effect of sleep on learning. They find out that not all scientists agree on the role or function of sleep. Students learn about the stages of sleep, interpret a graph showing how sleep changes over the course of a seven-hour period, and apply their knowledge of learning and sleep cycles to a real-life situation. They then test whether their own ability to learn is improved when they have a chance to "sleep on" new information.

Materials

Science Scope Activity (p. 159 and p. 163), for the class working in groups and at stations:

- bowl of cooked oatmeal
- raw cauliflower
- unshelled walnut
- computer floppy disk
- orange
- instruction manual
- model of human brain
- models or specimens of animal brains: fish, sheep, cow, pig, cat, rabbit
- labels
- latex gloves and safety goggles if using brain specimens
- balloons
- foam-plastic packing material
- bubble wrap
- yarn
- pipe cleaners
- flour
- water
- newspaper

Laboratory Safety

Review these safety guidelines with students before they do the Science Scope Activity in this lesson and the next.

- Do not taste any substance in the laboratory.
- Do not handle biological specimens with bare hands. Wear gloves and safety goggles.
- Handle biological specimens with care. Some specimens may contain germs or may have been prepared with chemicals that are hazardous to humans.
- Wash your hands thoroughly after the activity.

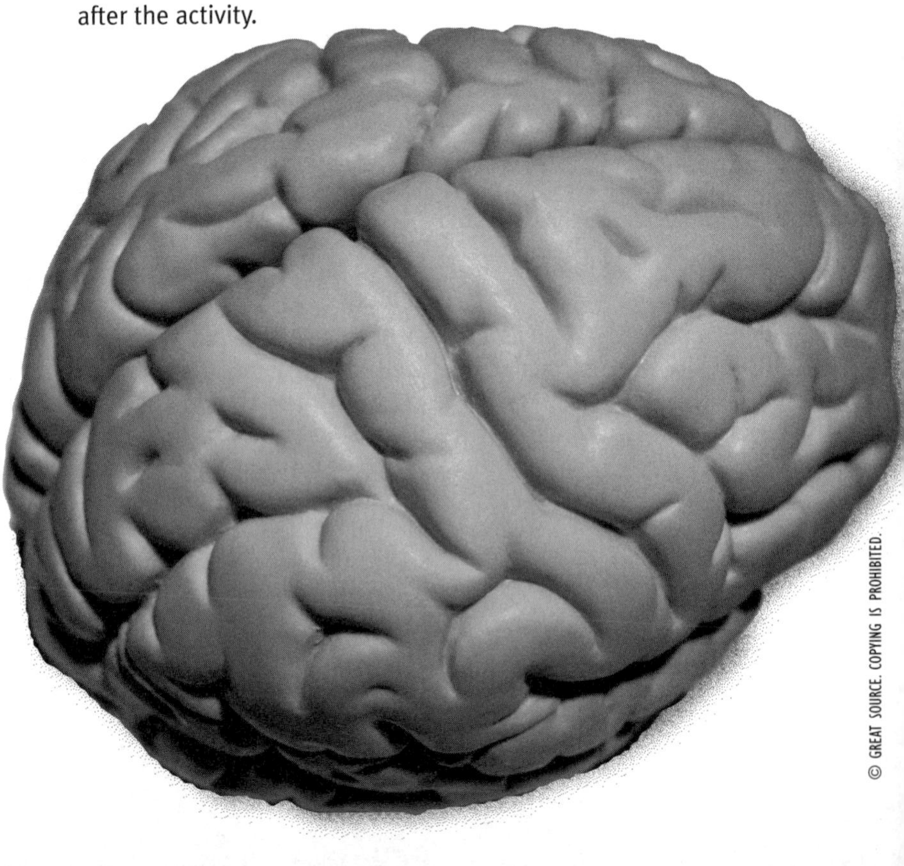

LESSON 45

Seeing Things

Point of Lesson: ***The brain interprets what the eye sees.***

Optical illusions occur when the brain misinterprets visual information. This lesson explains these events as being caused by faulty assumptions. Students then have the opportunity to identify the assumptions in optical illusions and create their own illusion that exploits an assumption to "trick the eye."

Materials

Science Scope Activity *continued* (p. 163): See list for Lesson 44.

Explore (p. 164), for each student:

- ruler
- protractor
- compass

Laboratory Safety

See guidelines for Lesson 44.

Science Scope Activity

Brain Exploration

NSTA has chosen a Science Scope *activity related to the content in this chapter. You'll find the activity in Lesson 44, page 159, and Lesson 45, page 163.*

How to make papier mâché (for step 4, page 163): Mix one part flour with about 2 parts water until it is the consistency of thick glue. If necessary, add more water or flour. Mix the paste well to remove all lumps. Brush the paste onto strips of newspaper and apply them to an inflated balloon or other base. Let dry for a few days.

Disposal Note: Dispose of biological specimens according to the supplier's guidelines and your school's regulations.

(continued on page 159)

Background Information

Lesson 44

Although rapid eye movement (REM) sleep occurs furthest into the sleep cycle, it is not the deepest stage of sleep. Stages 3 and 4 of slow-wave sleep, which include the longest-wavelength brain waves (delta waves), are the deepest. It is more difficult to wake a sleeper during these stages than any other.

REM sleep is sometimes called "paradoxical sleep" because of its seemingly contradictory effects. The brain is most active during REM sleep, and heart rate and respiration are greater than during the slow-wave stages. However, the major voluntary muscle groups of the body are paralyzed. Scientists have long assumed that this is a safety mechanism to prevent the sleeper from acting out dreams.

Both sleep walking (somnambulism) and night terrors (experienced by some young children) occur during Stage 4 slow-wave sleep. For this reason, sleep walking and night terrors are more common earlier in the night, when slow-wave sleep is dominant, while nightmares tend to occur later in the sleep period, when REM periods are longest.

Point of Lesson

Different parts of the brain do different things.

Focus

- Systems, order, and organization
- Regulation and behavior
- Structure and function in living systems

Skills and Strategies

- Interpreting scientific illustrations
- Making inferences
- Recognizing cause and effect

Advance Preparation

Vocabulary

Make sure students understand these terms. Definitions can be found in the glossary at the end of the student book.

- brain
- organ

More Resources

The following resources are also available from Great Source and NSTA.

SCIENCESAURUS

Nervous System 095

(continued on page 157)

A Mind of Its Own

Brain Scan

The human brain is an amazing organ. It's even beginning to figure itself out!

Your brain runs the show. It creates what you think, what you feel, and what you do. One of the ways your brain does this is by using different areas for different things. But these different areas are constantly communicating with each other.

Read

Here is one description of the brain.

DON'T BE FOOLED

The brain is the body's control center. It is involved with what we do and what we think as well as what we feel and remember. We also use our brains to learn. [Generally,] the left-hand side of our brain controls the right side of the body, and the right-hand side of our brain controls the left side of the body.

It has been found that each side of our brain is responsible for different skills. The right side holds our artistic talent and imagination, and the left side is more responsible for practical abilities and logical thinking.

practical: having to do with ordinary activities

logical: having to do with reasoning

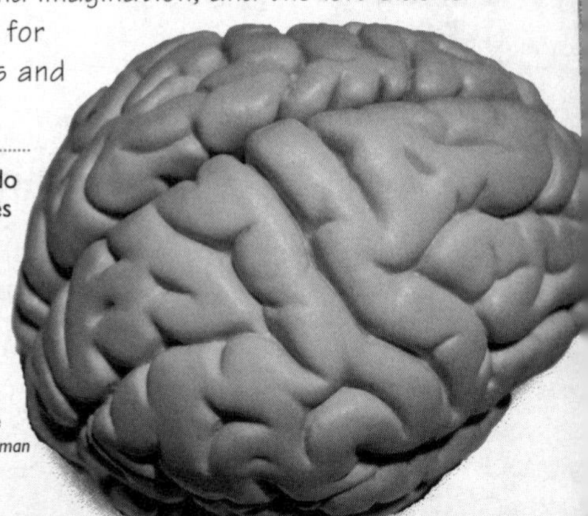

From: Barnes, Kate, and Steve Weston. *How it Works: The Human Body.* Barnes & Noble Books

NOTEZONE

What other questions do you have after reading this?

FIND OUT MORE

SCIENCESAURUS
Nervous System 095

SCILINKS. THE WORLD'S A CLICK AWAY
www.scilinks.org
Keyword: Human Brain
Code: GSLD20

UNIT 4: HUMAN BODY SYSTEMS

TEACHING PLAN pp. 156–157

INTRODUCING THE LESSON

This lesson focuses on the brain and the various functions that are controlled by different areas.

Ask students to suggest examples of the brain at work. Have them try to classify each example as an artistic and creative thinking process or an example of more practical and logical thinking.

Students may think that brain functions occur randomly in the brain. Explain that different processes occur in different brain areas. For example, the cerebellum is responsible for coordination of movement, while the hypothalamus regulates body temperature.

Read

Explain that the reading's description of all brain activity as left side or right side is an oversimplification of the complex activities the brain performs. Also tell students that many of the brain's higher functions, such as reasoning and remembering, are so complex that scientists have only an elementary understanding of the processes. Ask students how they think scientists discovered which areas of the brain control which functions. If they do not know, explain that during brain surgery, doctors can stimulate specific areas and observe the person's reaction. In addition, when a specific area of the brain is damaged, doctors can determine if a specific function is lost either temporarily or permanently.

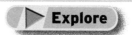

Explore

THINKING ABOUT THINKING A brain scan is a picture of the brain. One kind of brain scan shows the areas we are using lit up. Scientists use brain scans to show which areas of the brain are active during an activity. For example, the diagrams below show which areas of your brain are active when you use language.

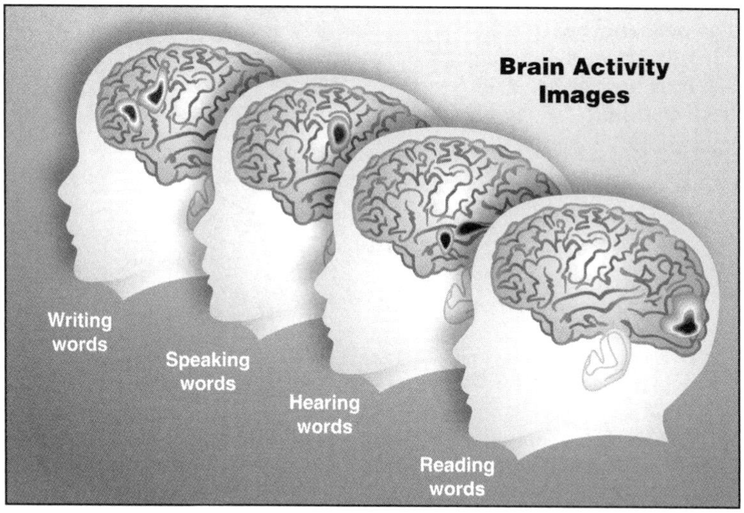

► *Study the diagrams. Is your entire brain active when you use language?*

No, only some areas are active.

► *During a stroke, some areas of the brain can be injured. What problems could a person have after a stroke if the areas shown in the diagrams were injured?*

The person might not be able to speak at all or might have difficulty talking or understanding speech.

157

(continued from page 156)

READER'S HANDBOOK

Comparison-Contrast Order 62
Cause-Effect Order 111
Elements of Graphics: Diagram 552

SCILINKS THE WORLD'S A CLICK AWAY

www.scilinks.org
Keyword: Human Brain
Code: GSLD20

Assessment

Skill: Generating ideas

Use the following task to assess each student's progress:

Draw students' attention to the sentences just below the lesson title and ask: *What do you think the sentence means when it says that the human brain is beginning to figure itself out?* (Humans are using their brains to try to discover how the brain works.)

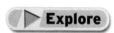

Explore

THINKING ABOUT THINKING Discuss the four types of language use identified in the diagram. Ask: *Why do you think different uses of language are controlled by different areas of the brain?* (Students should realize that each use involves a different combination of skills, sense organs, and muscles.)

To help students answer the second question, explain that a stroke is a sudden stoppage in the blood supply to the brain, damaging or killing nerves. The stoppage might occur when a blood vessel ruptures or is blocked. The part of the brain where the stoppage occurred may no longer function normally.

You may want to tell students that there are different types of brain scans. An electroencephalogram (EEG) records electrical impulses throughout the brain. A computer axial tomography (CAT) scan observes cross-sections of the brain and can locate tumors and blockages of blood vessels. A positive emission tomography (PET) scan reads isotopes injected into the brain. Magnetic resonance imaging (MRI) uses powerful magnetic fields to provide detailed pictures of the brain. Ultrasonic scans use sound waves to reveal brain structure.

CHECK UNDERSTANDING

Skill: Comparing and contrasting

Have students determine which side of the brain would be most active in each of the following activities:

- solving a math problem (left)
- writing a poem (right)
- playing a musical instrument (left)
- putting together a picture puzzle (left)
- reading a map (left)
- painting a picture (right)

Point of Lesson
Sleep may play an important role in learning.

Focus
- Systems, order, and organization
- Science as a human endeavor
- Understanding about scientific inquiry
- Personal health
- Structure and function in living systems

Skills and Strategies
- Sequencing
- Drawing conclusions
- Recognizing cause and effect
- Creating and using graphs
- Comparing and contrasting

Advance Preparation

Vocabulary
Make sure students understand these terms. Definitions can be found in the glossary at the end of the student book.

- experiment
- frequency
- horizontal axis
- variable
- vertical axis

Materials
Gather the materials needed for *Science Scope Activity* (p. 159 and p. 163).

SLEEP ON IT

You've probably heard that it's important to get a good night's sleep. There may now be scientific evidence to back that up.

It's 11 P.M. and you have a big math test tomorrow morning. You've been studying for several hours and feel tired. But you'd like to go over a few more problems to make sure you understand how to solve them. Should you study some more or go to bed?

Before You Read

SEQUENCE Think about the last time you had to study for a big test. What did you do the night before to prepare for it? Did you study continuously for a long time or in several short sessions? Did you study until the wee hours of the morning, or did you get up early the next morning to study? Describe what you did to prepare for the test.

Answers will vary.

TEACHING PLAN pp. 158–159

INTRODUCING THE LESSON
In this lesson, students learn about studies that analyze how sleep affects learning. Ask students to describe the different stages of sleep they go through during the night. Some students may mention being aware of dreaming, but many may not know that they sleep differently at different times throughout the night. Explain that sleep involves alternating periods of dreaming and periods of deep sleep without dreaming.

Also point out that sleep is essential for normal brain functioning. Someone who is deprived of sleep for several days cannot think clearly, has impaired hearing and eyesight, and may hallucinate.

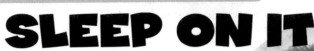

Before You Read

SEQUENCE Students will undoubtedly describe a wide variety of experiences with studying and the amount of sleep needed for effective learning. Stress that learning is a complex process that is greatly affected by a variety of factors in addition to the amount and timing of sleep in conjunction with studying. Ask students to identify some of these factors. (Examples: the nature of the material being studied, distractions during studying, physical comfort)

Read

Why do we sleep? No one really knows for sure. Some experiments, such as the one described below, suggest that sleep is important for learning.

Why Do We Sleep?

Procedure

Human subjects were trained to identify letters that appeared for a blink of an eye on a computer screen. Then, half of the subjects were sent home to sleep, while the other half were deprived of sleep for the entire night.... Two days later...the scientists checked [the subjects'] ability to read the flashing letters. None of the [subjects] were tired and yet the people who went to sleep right after the training performed much better than the ones who went to sleep a day later. This suggests that the night sleep immediately after the activity was [very important] for gaining the most from the training session....

Results

Conclusion

The fact that during...childhood and adolescence, people sleep much more than during their adulthood, also supports the view that sleeping plays a role in learning. Yet, some scientists claim that this evidence is still weak, and more importantly, that other experiments yield [opposite] results. Therefore, they argue, declaring that the mystery of sleep is resolved, and that the main function of sleep is to [help] learning, would be premature. Only future research can decide this debate.

subjects: the people who are studied in an experiment
deprived of: kept from
adolescence: the teenage years
premature: too early

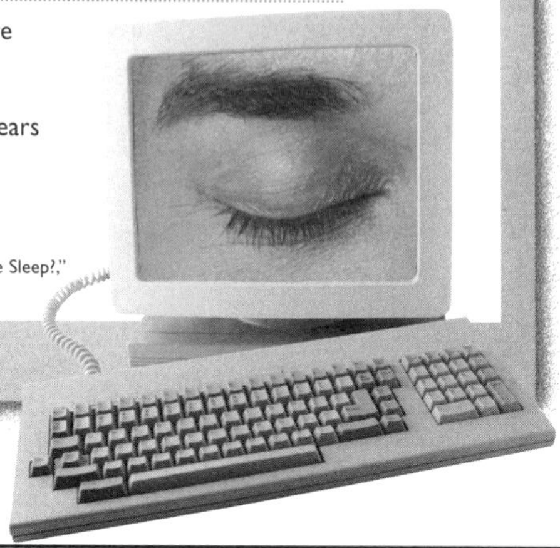

From: "The Teenage Brain: Why Do We Sleep?," *The Secret Life of the Brain*

NOTE ZONE

Circle and label the procedure, results, and conclusion in the experiment.

What variable was different between the two groups in the experiment?
sleep or no sleep

FIND OUT MORE
SCIENCESAURUS
Nervous System 095

159

Science Scope Activity

Brain Exploration

Time: 40–45 minutes each for step 1, steps 2 and 3 together, and step 4
Materials: *Step 1 only*: bowl of cooked oatmeal; raw cauliflower; unshelled walnut; computer floppy disk; orange; instruction manual. *Steps 1 and 2*: model of human brain. *Step 2 only*: models or specimens of animal brains (fish, sheep, cow, pig, cat, rabbit); labels; latex gloves and safety goggles if using brain specimens. *Step 4*: balloons; foam-plastic packing material; bubble wrap; yarn; pipe cleaners; flour; water; newspaper

Procedure

Divide the class into groups of four.

1. Give each group one of the items listed above for step 1 only. Tell students to compare their item with the model of the human brain and create a Venn diagram showing the comparison. (Example: In left circle: *human brain:* gray; soft; moist; large; deep wrinkles. In right circle: *walnut:* brown; hard; dry; small. In overlap area: ridges; two hemispheres; bumps)

(continued on page 163)

Read

The NoteZone task will help students identify the steps in the experiment, but interpreting the results depends on noting the relationship between learning the new task and the timing of the sleep period. Have students suggest reasons why keeping half the participants from sleeping the night after studying would affect their performance two days later. (Students should realize there is a direct connection between sleep and learning.) Also have students consider what was required by the participants in order to identify the letters. (concentration, visual memory) Have students compare the study's results with their own experiences when lack of sleep affected their learning and performance.

CHECK UNDERSTANDING
Skill: Evaluating source material
Ask students: *Did this scientific study prove once and for all that sleep affects learning? What makes you think so?* (No; the reading says that some scientists think more research is necessary.)

More Resources

The following resources are also available from Great Source.

SCIENCESAURUS

Nervous System	095

MATH ON CALL

Displaying Data in Tables and Graphs: Histogram	295

READER'S HANDBOOK

Drawing Conclusions	41
Reading Science	100
Elements of Textbooks: Graphs	159

Connections

WRITING After students have completed the lesson, they will be more aware of their sleep patterns. Suggest that they keep a sleep journal over a period of several days, chronicling the time they went to bed and the time they got up, how long it took to fall asleep, and the number of hours they slept. Students could also keep a record of dreams they experienced and estimate how long the dreaming periods lasted. Encourage students to review the sleep journal and look for any patterns.

Explore

SLEEP STAGES A person's brain activity during sleep can be measured by a process called electroencephalography (EEG). Special sensors are attached to the skin on the person's skull. The sensors measure electrical activity in different parts of the brain. This shows which parts of the brain are active.

EEG tests show that people go through two main types of sleep during the night—slow wave sleep (SWS) and rapid eye movement (REM) sleep. Slow wave sleep can be divided into four separate stages according to the strength and frequency of the electrical activity in the brain. But none of the four stages is as active as rapid eye movement sleep. REM sleep is when we dream.

Sleep Stage	Characteristics of Stage
Slow wave sleep (SWS) (Stages 1–4)	Slow EEG activity
Rapid eye movement (REM) sleep	Very active EEG activity; dreaming

Look at the following graph. It shows the different stages of sleep that a person goes through in a typical night. The graph's vertical axis shows which stage of sleep the person is in. The horizontal axis shows how long the person has been sleeping. Use the graph to answer the questions below.

Sequence of Sleep Stages

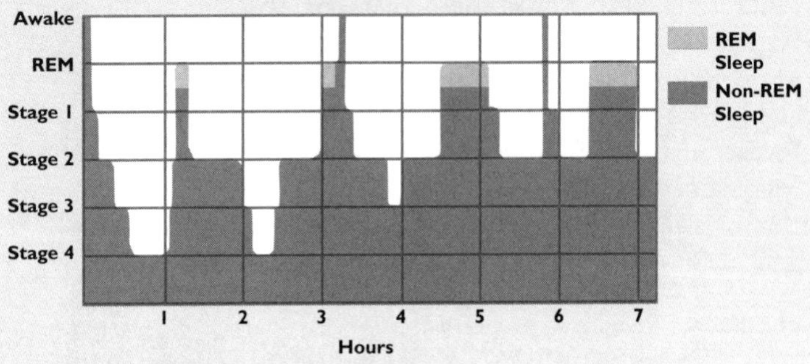

▸ ***What happens to the length of each REM stage as the night goes on?***

Each REM stage gets longer.

▸ ***What pattern do you notice in the graph?***

The stages are repeated again and again.

160

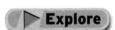

TEACHING PLAN pp. 160–161

Explore

SLEEP STAGES Help students understand the graph by first having them trace a finger from left to right along the tops of the shaded bars. Explain that the bars represent the stages of sleep that are labeled on the graph's vertical axis. The width of the bar at each stage indicates the amount of time spent in that stage, labeled on the horizontal axis. Then help students interpret the graph by asking questions such as: *How many times did the person dream?* (four) and *What happened just after the third hour was up?* (The person had a dream, woke up, and then fell back asleep.)

Propose Explanations

THINK ABOUT IT Experiments suggest that during REM sleep, your brain reviews, sorts, and organizes the information that it has been exposed to during the day. Some of the information is stored and some is discarded.

► ***Your friend says she'll do well on a test because she slept for three hours after studying late into the night. Based on the information in the graph and in the reading, how would you respond to your friend?***

You need to go through REM sleep in order to learn information. REM sleep happens in cycles. A person must sleep 7–8 hours to experience a few hours of REM sleep. She would probably better remember what she studied if she had spent more time in the REM stage of sleep.

► ***Why do scientists think that sleep, especially REM sleep, is important for learning?***

During sleep, the brain enters the REM stage several times. Evidence suggests that during REM sleep, the brain organizes and stores information it has come across. Without sleep, the brain could not sort and store information, so it would forget a lot of it.

Take Action

SLEEP AND LEARN Test how sleep affects your memory. In the morning, study list A for 10 minutes. Then don't look at the list for the rest of the day. After eight hours have passed, write down all the words you can remember.

At night, right before going to bed, study list B for 10 minutes. Be sure to get about eight hours of sleep. Then in the morning, without looking at the list, write down as many words as you can remember.

► ***How did sleep affect your ability to remember a list of words? Were you able to remember more words from list B? Write your results below. Share them with the class.***

List A	List B
horseshoe	quantity
category	medicine
sphinx	funnel
civilian	target
opinion	latitude
animate	scavenger
utility	ornament
segment	graceful
independent	stadium
magnify	journalist

Answers will vary. Students may find that sleeping after studying helped them remember more words. However, students with particularly good visual memory may note no difference.

Assessment

Skill: Making inferences

Use the following question to assess each student's progress:

What is the value of REM sleep? (During REM sleep, the brain reviews, sorts, and organizes information.)

Propose Explanations

THINK ABOUT IT Ask students: *Why do you think your brain sorts and organizes information during REM sleep?* (It has to determine which information is important and should be remembered and which information is not important and can be forgotten.) Also ask students to suggest examples of information that should be stored and information that should be discarded. Help students understand that throughout their waking hours, the brain is exposed to many sights, sounds, and other things that would be useless to remember.

Take Action

SLEEP AND LEARN Let students share their results. Have students suggest other factors that would influence their learning, such as other schoolwork, interrupted sleep, or personal issues that may be bothering them. Students might want to create other learning tasks to perform in conjunction with sleep and test themselves or their classmates.

Point of Lesson

The brain interprets what the eye sees.

Focus

- Evidence, models, and explanation
- Structure and function in living systems

Skills and Strategies

- Observing
- Making inferences
- Creating and using tables
- Generating ideas
- Interpreting scientific illustrations

Advance Preparation

Vocabulary

Make sure students understand these terms. Definitions can be found in the glossary at the end of the student book.

- brain
- organ

Materials

Gather the materials needed for *Explore* (p. 164).

Seeing Things

Your brain wouldn't play tricks on you, would it?

The brain may be a remarkable organ, but even *it* can be fooled. How does your brain get confused? One way is when it sees something different from what's really there. This is called an optical illusion.

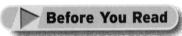

Before You Read

DON'T BE FOOLED! Look at this drawing.

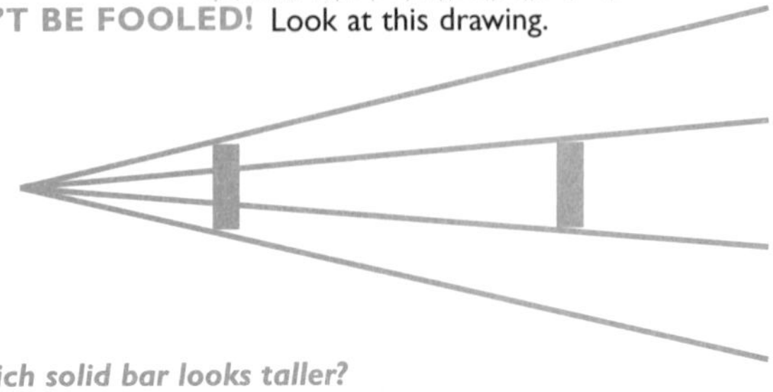

- ***Which solid bar looks taller?***

  the bar on the left

- ***Now measure the heights of the two bars. Are they actually different, or is this an illusion?***

  It's an illusion. The bars are the same height.

- ***Why do you think the left bar looks taller?***

  The slanted lines get closer together near the left bar. Usually, parallel lines are used to compare the heights of two things. Your brain expects that to be the case here. Since four lines touch the left bar and two lines touch the right, if the lines were parallel, that would mean the left bar was taller. Your brain interprets it in this way.

TEACHING PLAN pp. 162–163

INTRODUCING THE LESSON

In this lesson, students learn that the brain can be fooled by some of the information it receives.

Ask students to describe any optical illusions they have seen. (Examples: objects hidden in a drawing; the illusion of water on the road ahead on a hot day; a magician's tricks)

Make sure students can tell the difference between an *illusion* and an *allusion*. Something viewed or seen is an *illusion*. Something that is hinted at but not said directly is an *allusion*.

Before You Read

DON'T BE FOOLED! Introduce the idea that the brain takes in new information, compares the information with what it already knows, then interprets the new information in a way that makes sense.

The optical illusion on this page makes the vertical bars appear to be different sizes. Have students use a ruler to prove to themselves that the bars are actually the same size.

Accept all reasonable answers to the last question. However, if students have difficulty, ask them if they think the left bar would still look bigger if there were no slanted lines in the drawing. Remind them that they are seeing correctly, but the brain misinterprets the visual information.

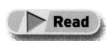

Read

How can your brain be fooled? Here's how.

Fooling the Brain

Optical illusions...are supposed to trick the eye. But...[it's] the brain that is tricked. In early life,...we learn many assumptions and shortcuts to help understand what we see. For instance, if the brain is presented with a regular pattern that has a piece blocked out, it "assumes" the pattern continues into the blank portion, since in daily life this is usually the case. Many optical illusions play on these assumptions by presenting images that do not normally occur in real life. Others exploit the brain's attempts always to make sense of the messages it gets from the eyes.

assumption: belief about what's true based on what's been true before
exploit: make use of or take advantage of

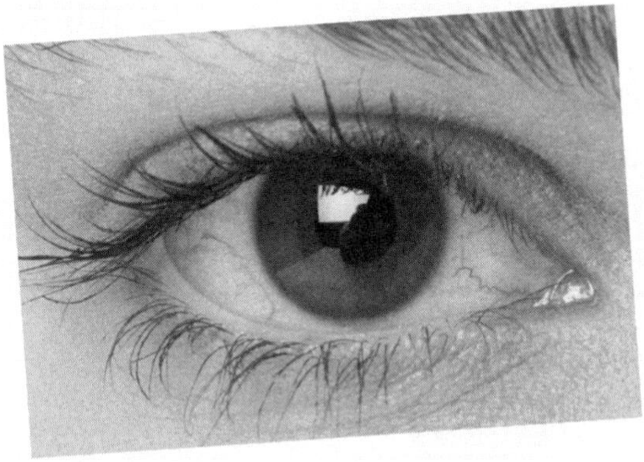

From: Whitfield, Philip, ed. *The Human Body Explained: A Guide to Understanding the Incredible Living Machine.* Henry Holt Co.

NOTEZONE

Why does the reading say that optical illusions trick the brain, not the eye?

The eye simply senses light and colors and sends signals to the brain. It's the brain that interprets the signals.

FIND OUT MORE

SCIENCESAURUS

Nervous System 095
The Five Senses 096

Science Scope Activity

(continued from page 159)

2. Set up stations with one specimen or model of a brain at each station. Number each specimen, but do not include its name. Have each group visit each station and write down their observations comparing the cerebrum, cerebellum, and brain-stem of different brains. (**Caution:** If actual specimens are used, have students wear latex gloves and safety goggles.)
3. On the board, list the animals whose brain models or specimens students observed. Each group should try to match each brain to the appropriate animal on the list. Explain to students that the size of the cerebellum depends on the size of the animal and the complexity of its movements. The cerebrum became progressively larger relative to other brain parts and more wrinkled over the course of evolution. Have students describe and defend their choices in a class discussion.
4. As a follow-up, ask students to create a replica of the human brain by using the craft materials you supply. (Instructions for making papier mâché are on page 156B.) Have them label the three main parts of the brain and identify the functions that each part controls.

Read

Use the following example to illustrate the assumptions and shortcuts the brain learns early in life. When we see a row of telephone poles stretching into the distance, even though the poles *seem* to be getting smaller, we know they are the same size. Compare this "making sense of things" with the optical illusion on page 162. The slanted lines in the drawing lead the brain to think that the bar on the left is larger.

CHECK UNDERSTANDING
Skill: Drawing Conclusions
Ask students: *Why is it the brain that is tricked by an optical illusion, not the eye?* (The eye is just collecting information, a visual image that it sends to the brain. It is the brain that interprets the image. The brain is tricked because it assumes things it has previously learned, even if they do not match the information it has received.)

More Resources

The following resources are also available from Great Source.

SCIENCESAURUS

Nervous System 095
The Five Senses 096

READER'S HANDBOOK

Reading Science:
Connect 113
Do an Activity 116
Visualizing and Thinking Aloud 664

Connections

ART Have students explore optical illusions in art. The drawings of M.C. Escher, for example, feature impossible geometric solids similar to illusion B on this page and other "trick-the-brain" illustrations. Other artists whose works incorporate optical illusions are Kenneth Noland and Bridget Louise Riley. Invite students to find examples of these artists' work to share with the class. Encourage them to figure out and explain what it is about each illustration that tricks the brain.

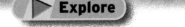

Explore

SEEING ISN'T BELIEVING Look at these optical illusions.

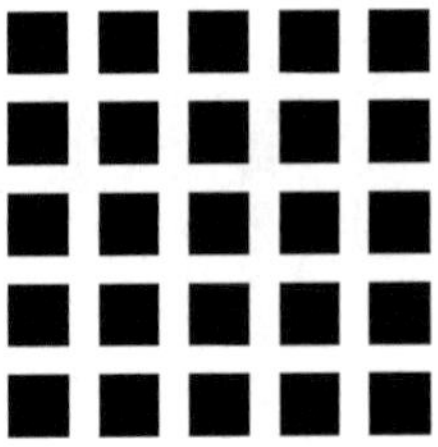

A

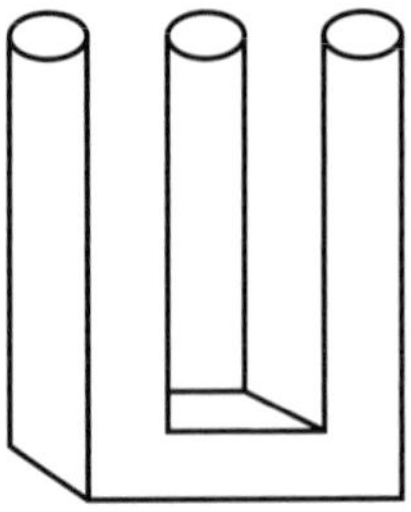

B

C

► ***Describe what you see at first in each illusion. Then describe what you know is true after examining the illusion carefully.***

Illusion	What I see at first	Figure it out	What I know is true
A	*black squares, white lines, and grey spots where the white lines cross*	Look at the point where the white lines cross. Then, cover up the squares around it.	*There are no grey spots.*
B	*3-pronged, 3-dimensional object that then switches to a U-shaped, 3-dimensional object*	Trace your finger along the lines to see the entire shape.	*The object could not actually exist.*
C	*thin lines spiralling in towards the center dot*	Trace your finger along the thin lines. What shape are they?	*The thin lines form circles, not a spiral.*

TEACHING PLAN pp. 164–165

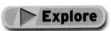

Explore

Time: 20 minutes
Materials: ruler, protractor, compass

SEEING ISN'T BELIEVING Call on volunteers in turn to explain what they saw when they first looked at the optical illusions and what they realized when they examined the illusions carefully. For most people, each illusion will seem perfectly reasonable at first, followed by a realization that something is "wrong" about the drawing, such as gray spots in A or the columns in B not being realistically solid. Ask students to explain why they think their brain was fooled by these illusions.

Students may want to redraw illusions B and C to undo their effects. Connecting the columns correctly in B and drawing a spiral in C will show students how the illusion works. Students can use a ruler, protractor, and compass to verify shapes and lines.

Take Action

BE A BRAIN TEASER Choose one of the optical illusions on page 164. Think about the assumption your brain makes that causes you to see the illusion. Then use that assumption to create your own optical illusion. For example, in the Before You Read illusion, the brain assumes that the bars are two different sizes. The slanted lines that hit the bars at different places trick the brain into thinking the bars are different sizes.

▶ ***Make a drawing of your optical illusion.***

Illusions will vary. Example: Which of the top lines appears longer?

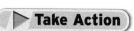

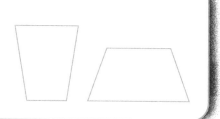

▶ ***Describe the illusion you are trying to create.***

Answers will vary. Example: The top line of the right shape appears longer than the top line of the left shape, but they are actually the same size. The different slanted lines of the two shapes fool your brain into thinking that the top lines are different sizes.

▶ ***Show your drawing to your classmates and find out what they see. Was your illusion successful? Why or why not?***

Answers will vary.

165

Assessment

Skill: Making predictions

Use the following task to assess each student's progress:

Explain why your brain is fooled by the optical illusions on page 164. (**Illusion A:** The brain "assumes" that the dark areas continue into the white space between the squares. **Illusion B:** The brain interprets the three columns and the table-like shape at the bottom as solid objects connected in a realistic way. **Illusion C:** The brain is tricked because the center of all the circles except the smallest one are actually off center and the background shapes hide the spaces between the circles.)

Take Action

BE A BRAIN TEASER Have students label their drawings to identify which illusion's assumption they used. If students create illusions that do not work, have them explain what they were attempting to do and then analyze why the drawings did not create an illusion. By altering their first attempt, their later drawings may be more successful.

Diseases Through Time

LESSON 46

Conquering Polio

Point of Lesson: ***Vaccines help the body's immune system fight the viruses that cause polio.***

This lesson describes the fear that families lived in before the polio vaccine became available. Students are introduced to how vaccines work, then read an account of Jonas Salk's development and testing of the killed-virus polio vaccine in the 1950s. Students express their understanding of how the immune system works by drawing a diagram. They interview a person who was a child during the time when polio epidemics were a threat and then when vaccines first became available.

Materials

Enrichment (p. 167), for the class:

- research sources about infectious diseases

Connections (p. 169), for the class:

- video documentary of the life of Franklin Delano Roosevelt (such as the biography *FDR* from the *Presidents Collection* of the PBS series *The American Experience*)

LESSON 47

The Buzz on Malaria

Point of Lesson: ***Malaria is an infectious disease that continues to plague the world today.***

Students learn about the spread of malaria and why attempts to eliminate it by eradicating the *Anopheles* mosquito were ultimately unsuccessful. They consider the chain of events that spread malaria-causing protozoa and interpret a diagram showing how the disease is spread.

Materials

Read (p. 170), for class demonstration:

- stopwatch or clock with second hand

LESSON 48

Help Yourself Stay Healthy

Point of Lesson: ***Infectious diseases can be prevented.***

Students read the steps for helping to prevent the spread of infectious diseases, as recommended by the Centers for Disease Control and Prevention. They consider ways to prevent the spread of infectious diseases at home and at school, then apply their knowledge of rules for safe food handling to the planning of an imaginary picnic with friends.

Materials

Enrichment (p. 173), for the class:

- hand lotion
- glitter
- bucket or trash can
- paper towels
- cold water
- warm water
- soap

Take Action (p. 175), for each group:

- poster paper
- colored markers

Laboratory Safety

Review the following safety guidelines with students before they do the Enrichment activity in this lesson.

- Handle glitter carefully. Do not rub your eyes when you have glitter on your hands. Do not inhale glitter.
- If your skin is sensitive or you have allergies to some skin products, do not do this activity.
- Wipe up spills immediately to avoid risk of slips and falls.
- Wash your hands thoroughly after the activity.

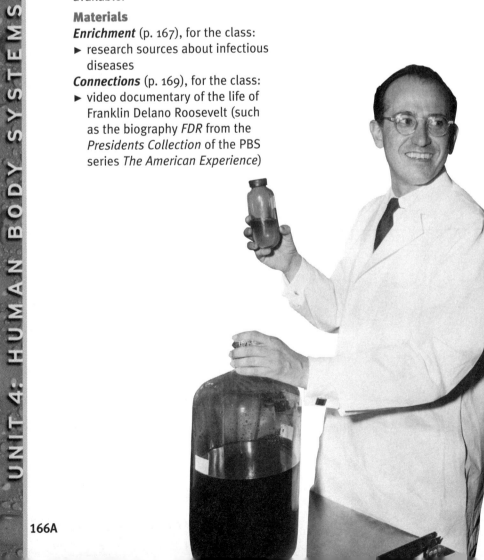

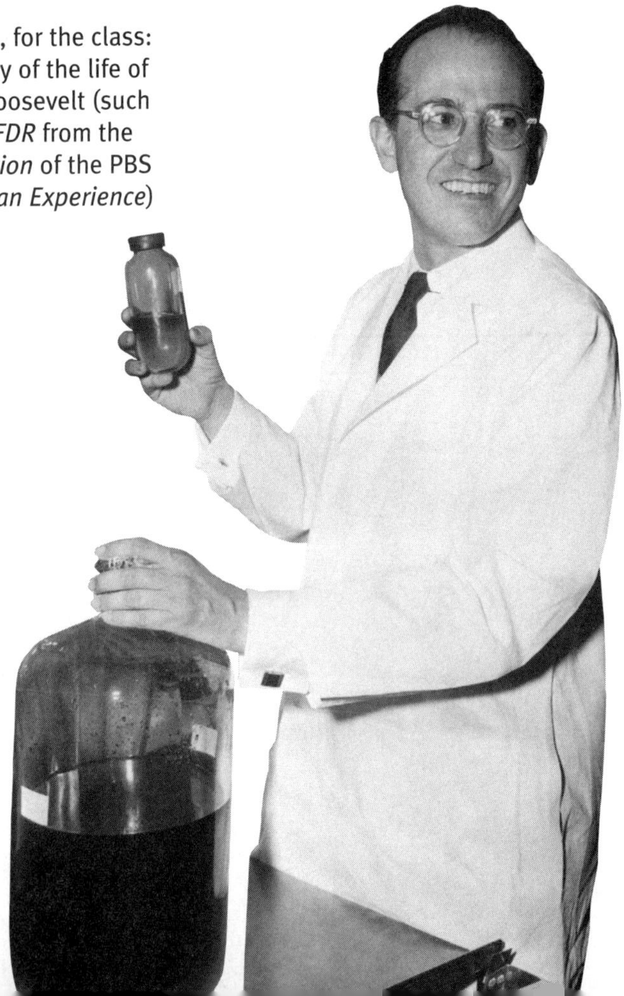

Background Information

Lesson 46

Polio is an infectious disease caused by the poliomyelitis virus. A polio infection generally starts with flulike symptoms and diarrhea. These symptoms may progress to muscle pain and stiffness, including pain in the back, neck, and limbs. In severe cases, the virus destroys motor cells in the spinal cord; this causes paralysis that can vary from temporary weakness to complete permanent paralysis. This paralysis may affect the use of limbs or the ability to breathe, swallow, or speak. Sometimes, muscles that recover from weakness are later affected again and may become weak or paralyzed. According to the Centers for Disease Control and Prevention, polio cases worldwide dropped from about 350,000 in 1988 to fewer than 1,000 in 2001.

Lesson 47

Although malaria is often considered a "tropical" disease, it was a serious public health problem in Europe and North America until after World War II, when pesticides were used to kill the mosquitoes that carry the disease. (In the 1940s, malaria was a problem in 36 states.) The Office of Malaria Control in War Areas was established in 1942 to rid the United States of malaria; this agency later became the Centers for Disease Control and Prevention (CDC).

Lesson 48

According to the CDC, proper handwashing is the single most effective method of preventing the spread of infectious disease. In October 2002, the CDC launched a program to improve hand hygiene in hospitals and health care facilities. The CDC estimates that almost 2 million patients contract an infectious disease in the hospital each year in the United States. Increasing the rate and effectiveness of handwashing by health care providers will help prevent the spread of infection from one patient to another.

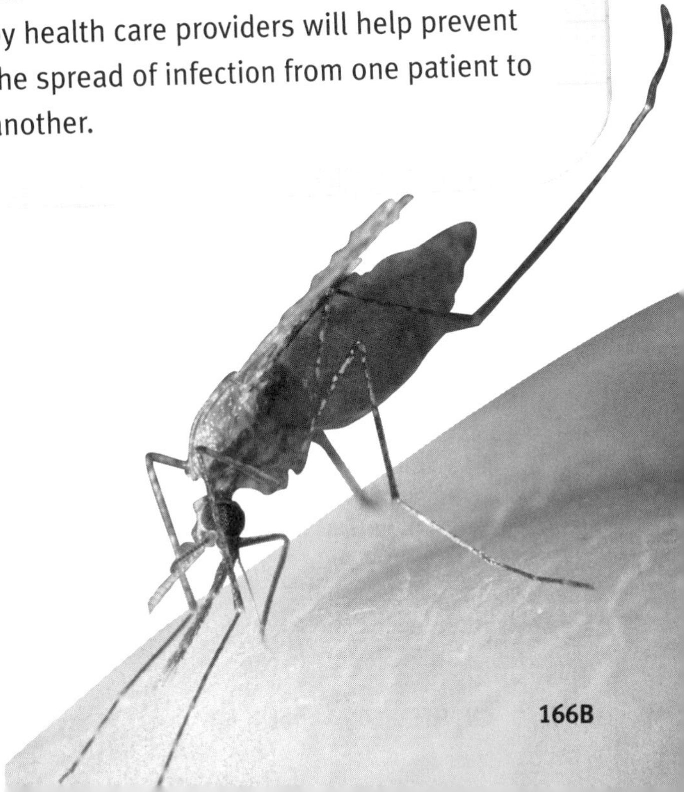

Point of Lesson

Vaccines help the body's immune system fight the viruses that cause polio.

Focus

- Evidence, models, and explanation
- Science as a human endeavor
- Risks and benefits
- History of science
- Personal health
- Science and technology in society
- Understanding about scientific inquiry

Skills and Strategies

- Making inferences
- Creating and using graphs
- Making and using models
- Sequencing
- Predicting
- Communicating

Advance Preparation

Vocabulary

Make sure students understand these terms. Definitions can be found in the glossary at the end of the student book.

- bacteria
- bar graph
- immune system

(continued on page 167)

Conquering Polio

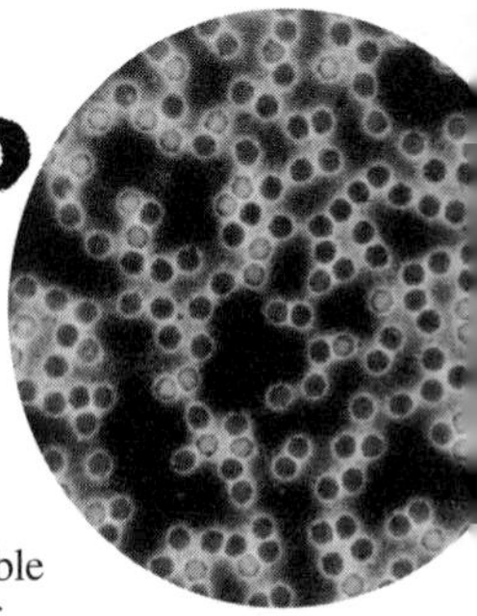

▲Polio virus

Until the mid-1900s, summer was a scary time. Parents were afraid that their children would get polio from public places like swimming pools and drinking fountains, and become handicapped or die.

Polio is a serious disease that attacks the nerves that control muscles. It is especially dangerous if it affects the muscles that enable a person to breathe or swallow. In the 1940s and '50s, thousands of children in the United States died each year from polio. Scientists worked hard to find a way to prevent the disease. Dr. Jonas Salk made the first polio vaccine from killed viruses. Dr. Albert Sabin made a vaccine from weakened live viruses. Thanks to these scientists, polio is no longer a major threat in this country.

Before You Read

UNDER ATTACK When any disease-causing bacteria or virus enters your bloodstream, your body responds. Your immune system produces special proteins called antibodies—a different one for each type of germ. The antibodies attack the germs to try to prevent them from infecting the body's cells. The antibodies stay in the body for a period of time, even after the germs are gone. If the same kind of germ enters again, the antibodies are already there to attack the germ instantly. If a germ is very strong and attacks quickly, the body may not be able to respond in time to prevent a serious infection.

Vaccines made from viruses also cause the body to produce antibodies. But because the viruses are weakened or killed, they do not cause the actual disease.

THINK ABOUT IT

- *Why do you think injecting the body with a vaccine would help the body protect itself if it were to get the virus in the future?*

The antibodies that were produced with the vaccine would be ready to attack the virus if it entered the body.

TEACHING PLAN pp. 166–167

INTRODUCING THE LESSON
This lesson describes how vaccines work with the immune system to produce antibodies and develop immunity. Ask students to describe how they think vaccines help prevent the spread of disease. Students may think that because some diseases have been almost eliminated in the United States, they are not a problem anymore. Explain that many of these diseases still exist in other parts of the world. Also, vaccines are not 100 percent effective, so some vaccinated people are still susceptible to the disease.

Before You Read

UNDER ATTACK In addition to the polio vaccine, you may want to discuss other vaccines, such as the first vaccine, which was developed for smallpox in 1798 by Edward Jenner. Explain that vaccines have been developed for diseases caused by bacteria as well as those caused by viruses, and point out that vaccines are still being developed. Lead students to understand that we do not yet have vaccines for all known diseases because scientists and medical researchers are still discovering the causes of some illnesses. In addition, new diseases continue to emerge, and some disease-causing bacteria and viruses change rapidly.

THINK ABOUT IT Make sure students understand that the antibodies produced by the body in response to a vaccine are specific to the germs that cause the disease and that the antibodies remain in the body. With some diseases, booster shots are needed to maintain immunity.

Read

Dr. Jonas Salk wanted to make a vaccine against polio by using killed polio viruses.

JONAS EDWARD SALK

Salk...had developed a killed-virus vaccine.... Salk found that...the dead virus vaccine could cause the body to make...antibodies against polio. He had tested his vaccine on animals and had enough faith in it to inject it into himself, his family, and some friends.... In 1952 Salk conducted small but successful trials.... In all instances the antibody levels against the virus were [much higher]....

The [large-scale] field trial was started on April 26, 1954. Because parents were anxious for their children to have protection against polio...over 650,000 children in forty-four states received...injections of Salk vaccine.

The result, screamed in headlines all over the world: The vaccine was safe and it worked! [O]verall, it was between 80 and 90 percent effective against...polio.

Over the next several years there was a [big] decline in the number of polio cases.... [I]n 1952 a severe epidemic had caused 58,000 new cases of polio, [but] the number of cases reported in 1962 had dropped to just over 900. Polio was on its way out.

instances: reported cases
field trial: a test of a new product on the general public
epidemic: an outbreak of a disease that affects many people

From: Curtis, Robert H., M.D. *Medicine: Great Lives.* Charles Scribner's Sons Reference, a unit of Macmillan Library Reference USA.

NOTEZONE

Make a bar graph to compare the number of new polio cases in 1952 and 1962.

Students' graphs should show 58,000 cases in 1952 and just over 900 cases in 1962.

FIND OUT MORE

SCIENCESAURUS
Immune System 098

SCILINKS.
THE WORLD'S A CLICK AWAY
www.scilinks.org
Keyword: Vaccines
Code: GSLD21

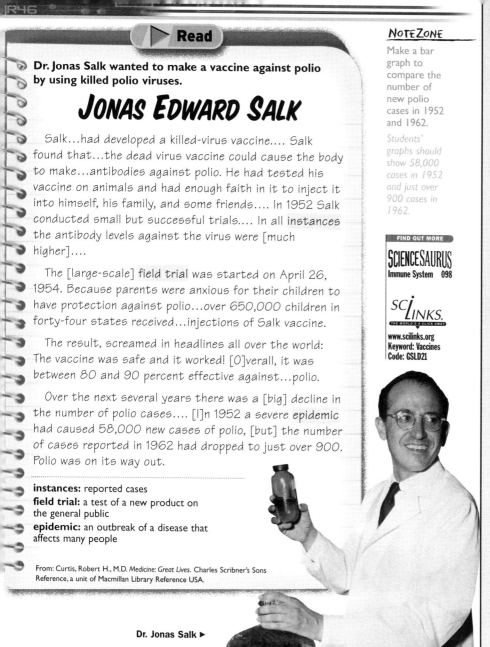

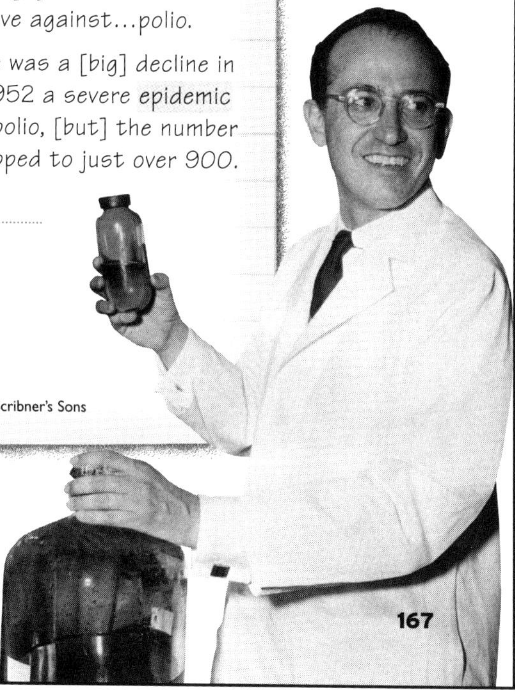

Dr. Jonas Salk ►

167

(continued from page 166)

Materials

Gather the materials needed for ***Enrichment*** (below) and ***Connections*** (p. 169).

Enrichment

Time: 40 minutes
Materials: research sources about infectious diseases

Remind students that early disease treatments may have been crude, but they represented the best medical knowledge of the time. For example, early Greeks made medical diagnoses based on what they called "the four humors"—blood, phlegm, black bile, and yellow bile. They believed that an imbalance among the humors would lead to disease. Point out that many of today's treatments may look strange to future generations.

Divide the class into seven groups. Assign each group one of the following diseases: smallpox, impetigo, yellow fever, typhus, diphtheria, scarlet fever, and influenza. Have students use library resources and the Internet to research the diseases and learn more about ancient and modern medical treatments. When students have completed their research, have each group prepare and present a brief report on ancient and modern methods of treating the disease.

Read

Encourage students to underline phrases or sentences that describe the scientific methods Jonas Salk used in developing and introducing the polio vaccine. After students have read the selection, lead a class discussion about the methods Salk used. Ask: *How do you think Salk could tell whether the vaccine worked on animals?* (Salk tested their blood for polio antibodies; if more antibodies were present after the vaccine than before, the vaccine was effective.)

When students have completed the NoteZone task, ask: *What does the bar graph represent?* (It shows that there were many more cases of polio in 1952 than in 1962.) Discuss whether the graph contains enough information to prove that the polio vaccine was effective. Lead students to understand that you would need more information. For example, it would be more accurate if you compared the number of polio cases per year before the vaccine was introduced and the number of polio cases per year after it was introduced.

CHECK UNDERSTANDING
Skill: Sequencing
Ask students to write a set of instructions describing how to develop a vaccine, based on the steps Jonas Salk followed in creating the polio vaccine. (Students' instructions should include the following steps: identify the virus, make a killed-virus vaccine, test the vaccine on animals, test the vaccine on a few people, and then test the vaccine in a large-scale field trial.)

More Resources

The following resources are also available from Great Source and NSTA.

SCIENCESAURUS
Immune System 098

READER'S HANDBOOK
Visualizing and Thinking Aloud 664

MATH ON CALL
Graphs and Statistics:
Graphs That Compare 291
Single-Bar Graphs 292

WRITE SOURCE 2000
Thinking Through an Argument 121
Interviewing Tips 170

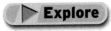

SCILINKS. THE WORLD'S A CLICK AWAY

www.scilinks.org
Keyword: Vaccines
Code: GSLD21

Explore

DRAW A DIAGRAM Show what happens in the body as a result of vaccination. First, draw the body's response to the vaccine. Include the vaccine and the antibodies. Then draw what happens later when the person is infected by the live virus. Include the virus and the antibodies. Label your drawings.

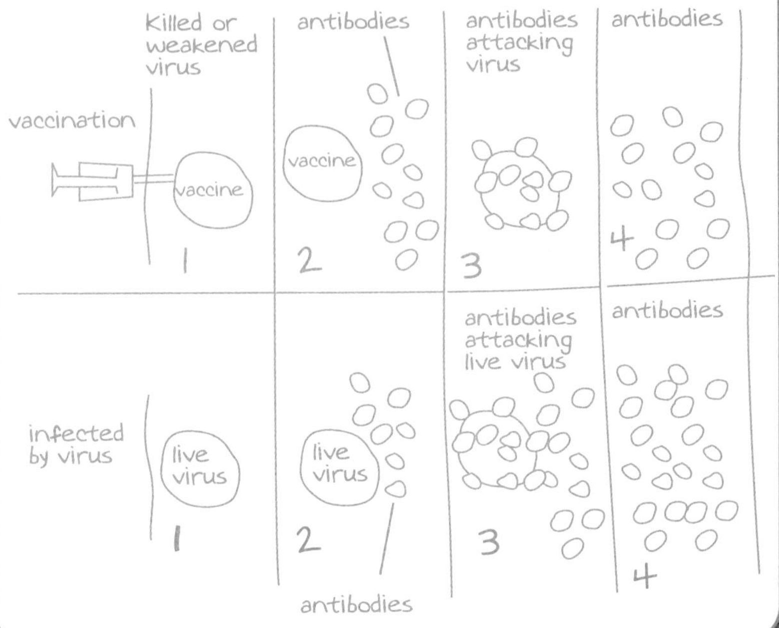

► ***Dr. Salk tested his polio vaccine on his family and friends. Do you think it was right to do that? Explain your answer.***

Answers will vary, but students should understand that testing the vaccine on people carried a risk of unknown side effects not seen in animals.

TEACHING PLAN pp. 168–169

Explore

DRAW A DIAGRAM After students answer the question on this page, discuss the risks involved in developing vaccines or medicines for humans. Students may have questions about Salk's qualifications to do this work; for example, students may be interested to know that Jonas Salk graduated from medical school in 1938 and that he had already helped develop a vaccine for influenza, which was used by the United States armed forces during World War II. This may help students decide whether they think it was right to test the vaccine on humans. Also point out that federal law now requires that tests on humans be approved by the U.S. Food and Drug Administration.

Propose Explanations

MAKE A PREDICTION If students have difficulty answering the question, have them draw a third diagram showing what would happen if the live virus infected a person who had not been immunized. Students may realize that the person's body would probably make antibodies in response to the live virus, just as it does to the killed or weakened virus in the vaccine. Point out that in many cases, these antibodies would be able to ward off the disease, although the infected person might still be able to spread the disease to others. However, according to Access Excellence at the National Museum of Health, 10 percent of nonvaccinated people infected with the polio virus would not be able to make enough antibodies to fight the virus; 1 percent of nonvaccinated infected people would become paralyzed.

Propose Explanations

MAKE A PREDICTION

▸ *How would the body's response to a disease-causing virus be different without a vaccination?*

No antibodies would be present yet to kill off the virus, so the virus could cause serious illness or even death.

Take Action

LIVING HISTORY Interview a family member or friend who was a child in the 1940s or 1950s. Ask the person to describe his or her memories of polio epidemics and of polio vaccinations. Take notes during the interview. Then write a brief account of the person's experiences.

Students' accounts will vary.

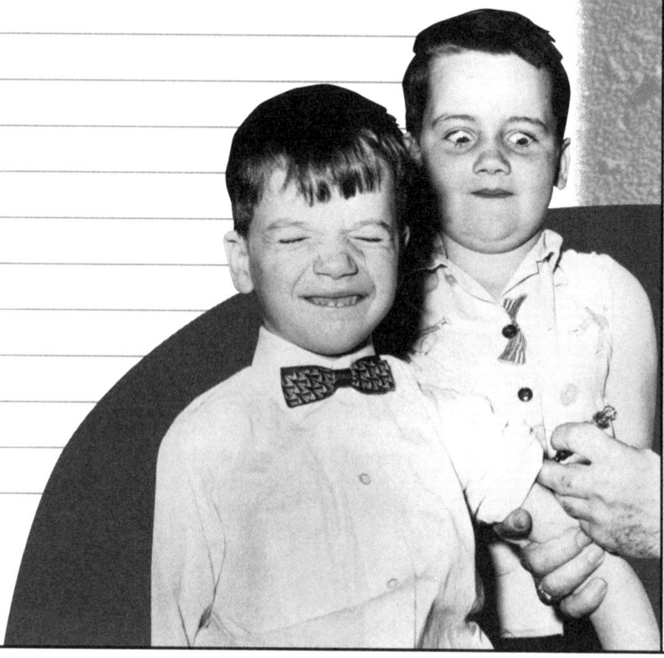

Connections

Time: will vary

Materials: video documentary of the life of Franklin Delano Roosevelt (such as the biography *FDR* from the *Presidents Collection* of the PBS series *The American Experience*)

SOCIAL STUDIES One of the most famous polio victims was President Franklin Delano Roosevelt, who was infected with the virus in 1921. Let students view the video to learn how polio affected Roosevelt's life. Have students present their findings to the class in the form of a class discussion or short presentations.

Assessment

Skill: Drawing conclusions

Use the following question to assess each student's progress:

If your body has antibodies for one type of disease, are you protected from all diseases? Why or why not? (No; each type of antibody is specific to one disease. To be protected against other diseases, you would need to have antibodies specific to those diseases.)

Take Action

LIVING HISTORY Help students identify people who would make good interview subjects. Explain that someone who was born in 1940 would have been 60 in the year 2000. Ask students if they have relatives or family friends who are in their 60s, 70s, or even older. As a class, brainstorm a list of questions for students to ask in their interviews. Decide how many questions each interview should cover, and have students choose the best questions from the list. Point out that if they all ask the same questions, they will be able to compare their results. Students may want to include one or two questions that address their particular interests as well.

After students have conducted their interviews, discuss the results. Ask: *Were there any similarities in the responses? Did anyone interview someone who was not affected by polio epidemics?*

Point of Lesson

Malaria is an infectious disease that continues to plague the world today.

Focus

- Systems, order, and organization
- Personal health
- Populations, resources, and environments

Skills and Strategies

- Interpreting scientific illustrations
- Making inferences
- Recognizing cause and effect

Advance Preparation

Vocabulary

Make sure students understand these terms. Definitions can be found in the glossary at the end of the student book.

- epidemic
- infectious
- joint
- life cycle
- organism
- protists
- red blood cells
- reproduce
- species

Materials

Gather the materials needed for *Read* (p. 170).

Diseases Through Time

THE BUZZ ON MALARIA

The word *malaria* means "bad air." People used to think that this disease was caused by breathing the air in swamps.

Malaria is an infectious disease spread by the *Anopheles* mosquito. In the mid-1900s, poisons were used to kill these mosquitoes, and malaria was nearly wiped out. Then the *Anopheles* species began to change as it became resistant to the poisons. In time, the poisons no longer worked. The number of malaria cases increased. If malaria is treated immediately, it can be cured. But the medicines are expensive and many people cannot afford them.

NoteZone

About how many children died of malaria during the time it took you to read this?

To calculate the answer, the student should divide the time it took to read the excerpt by 30 seconds.

Read

Time how long it takes you to read the following paragraphs.

Epidemic!

[M]alaria is...caused by one of several protozoan species of the genus *Plasmodium*. *Plasmodium* is spread to humans by the bite of the female *Anopheles* mosquito, which breeds in slow-moving, clear water.

The symptoms of malaria are fever and shaking chills, headache, and joint pain. During part of its life cycle, *Plasmodium* invades the red blood cells, using them as a place to reproduce and destroying the cells in the process. The result is severe anemia, and, often, fatal damage to the brain and other vital organs.

An estimated 300 million people are infected with malaria, and between 1 and 1.5 million die every year. Most of the victims are children, who die...before they are able to develop immunity. According to [the World Health Organization], a child dies of malaria every thirty seconds.

protozoan: a single-celled organism in the Protist kingdom
symptoms: signs of a disease
anemia: a condition of weakness caused by defective or not enough red blood cells
fatal: deadly
vital organs: body parts you need to survive
immunity: protection against a disease

From: DeSalle, Rob. *Epidemic!: The World of Infectious Disease*. The New Press

FIND OUT MORE

SCIENCESAURUS

Circulatory System	093
Immune System	098
Protist Kingdom	156

UNIT 4: HUMAN BODY SYSTEMS

170

TEACHING PLAN pp. 170–171

INTRODUCING THE LESSON

This lesson introduces malaria as an example of an infectious disease. Ask students to talk about the relationship between humans and mosquitoes. Common misconceptions include the ideas that malaria is not a serious illness for otherwise healthy people and that malaria is incurable. Explain that malaria can be quite serious even for healthy people, but it can be completely cured if appropriate treatment is begun early enough. However, malaria prevention is the best strategy for remaining healthy.

Read

Time: 15 minutes
Materials: stopwatch or clock with second hand

After students have read the introduction, talk about what it means for mosquitoes to become resistant to the poisons that had been used to kill them. Explain that individual mosquitoes do not develop resistance to a poison. Rather, the mosquito population as a whole becomes more resistant until the poison is useless. This happens because some of the mosquitoes are naturally resistant to the poison and do not die. When these mosquitoes reproduce, their offspring are also resistant to the poison. Because mosquitoes reproduce so quickly, soon all the mosquitoes in an area will be resistant to the poison, while all the mosquitoes that were susceptible to the poison will have been killed.

To complete the NoteZone task as a class activity, ask for three volunteers—one to read the selection aloud, another to time the reader, and a third to calculate the number of children who died during the reading.

Explore

FOLLOWING THE CHAIN

Plasmodium has a complex life cycle. It reproduces inside *Anopheles* mosquitoes. It is passed from one person to another by these mosquitoes. A mosquito bites a person who has malaria and sucks up the person's blood, which has the *Plasmodium* in it. When the same mosquito bites another person, some of the *Plasmodium* passes into that person's blood. That person may then become infected with malaria.

As long as *Anopheles* mosquitoes exist, malaria will continue to be passed along in an unbroken chain. The diagram shows the connection between people, *Anopheles*, and *Plasmodium*.

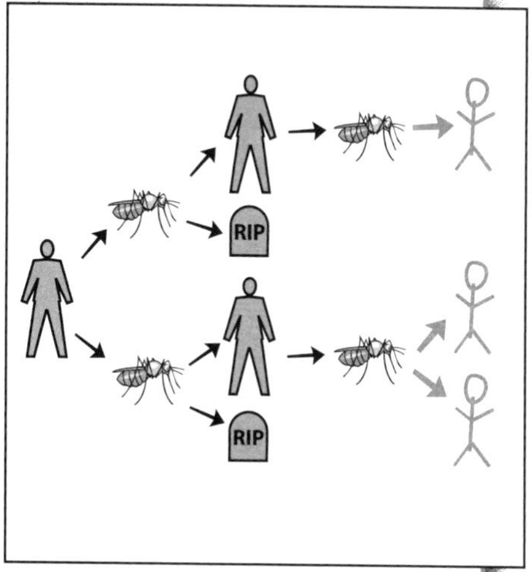

INTERPRETING THE DIAGRAM

- ***What does each tombstone represent?***

  one person who died from malaria

- ***According to the diagram, can malaria pass directly from one person to another person? Explain.***

  No; the Plasmodium has to be carried from one person to another by a mosquito.

- ***Which organism involved in the spread of malaria cannot be seen in the diagram? Why not?***

  Plasmodium; it is inside the mosquito and is too small to be seen without a microscope.

- ***Some people don't get malaria even if they're bitten by an infected Anopheles mosquito. Change the diagram above to include those people.***

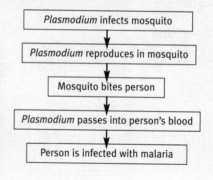

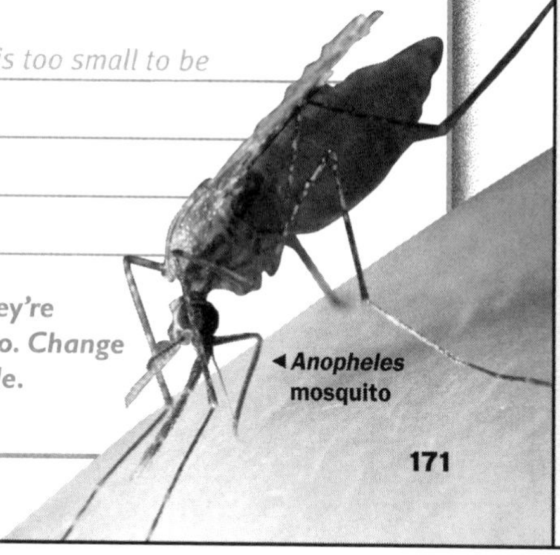

◄ ***Anopheles* mosquito**

171

More Resources

The following resources are also available from Great Source.

SCIENCESAURUS

Circulatory System 093
Immune System 098
Protist Kingdom 156

READER'S HANDBOOK

Elements of Graphics: Diagram 552
Cause-Effect Organizer 644

MATH ON CALL

Mental Division 173
Interpreting Quotients and Remainders 182

Assessment

Skill: Concept mapping

Use the following task to assess each student's progress:

Have students create a flowchart to show the sequence of events leading to a person being infected with malaria. A sample flowchart is shown below.

Plasmodium infects mosquito
↓
Plasmodium reproduces in mosquito
↓
Mosquito bites person
↓
Plasmodium passes into person's blood
↓
Person is infected with malaria

Explore

FOLLOWING THE CHAIN Have students match the description in the text to the diagram as they read. For example, they could number each stage of the diagram and then use the number to identify the text that describes what happens at that stage.

INTERPRETING THE DIAGRAM When students have changed their diagrams, have a volunteer share the answer with the class. Encourage students to develop explanations of why some people would not develop malaria when they are bitten by infected mosquitoes. (Possible explanation: Some people must have antibodies or other defenses that kill the *Plasmodium*.)

Students may wonder whether there is a vaccine that would allow people to avoid catching malaria. Explain that scientists are working on a vaccine, but the complexity of *Plasmodium* makes developing a vaccine very difficult.

CHECK UNDERSTANDING

Skill: Generating questions

Tell students to imagine that they are doctors who treat malaria patients. Have students suggest questions to ask and tests to perform to help them determine whether a patient has malaria. (Students' questions and tests should be designed to identify the symptoms described in this lesson—fever, shaking chills, headache, joint pain, and anemia.)

Point of Lesson
Infectious diseases can be prevented.

Focus
- Systems, order, and organization
- Personal health
- Science and technology in society
- Regulation and behavior

Skills and Strategies
- Recognizing cause and effect
- Generating ideas
- Communicating

Advance Preparation

Vocabulary
Make sure students understand these terms. Definitions can be found in the glossary at the end of the student book.

- bacteria
- fungi
- infectious
- microscopic

Materials
Gather the materials needed for *Enrichment* (p. 173) and *Take Action* (p. 175).

HELP YOURSELF STAY HEALTHY

Children and adults get sick all the time. Here are some ways to help yourself stay healthy.

Infectious diseases are caused by many kinds of microscopic germs such as viruses, bacteria, and fungi. These germs can be passed from one person to another by coughing or sneezing, or when saliva or mucus gets on the infected person's hands and the person touches objects that are then touched by uninfected people. Germs cause illnesses that range from the common cold to more serious and sometimes deadly diseases such as polio, the flu, and pneumonia. The Centers for Disease Control and Prevention, a government agency, works to help reduce the spread of infectious diseases.

Before You Read

THINK ABOUT IT What things do you do to keep from getting an infectious disease such as a cold?

Possible answers: washing hands before eating and after going to the bathroom; covering your mouth when you cough and sneeze; cleaning up in the kitchen; eating foods that are washed and well cooked; getting vaccinations

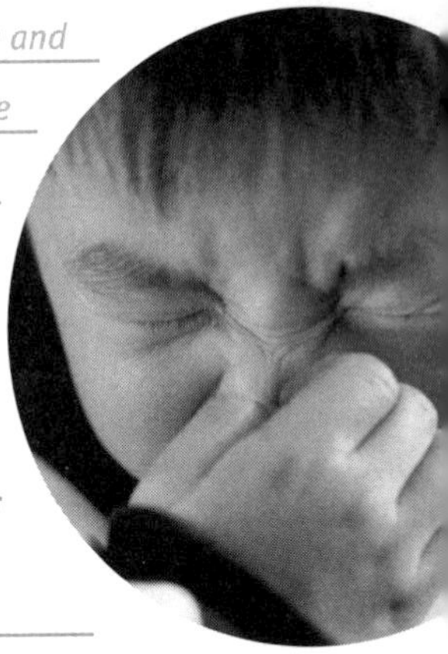

- ***Think about the last time you had a cold, the flu, or another infectious disease. Do you know how you came into contact with the germs? Do you think you passed the germs on to someone else? What could you have done to better protect yourself from getting sick?***

Answers will vary.

TEACHING PLAN pp. 172–173

INTRODUCING THE LESSON
This lesson presents simple ways to avoid catching an infectious disease. Ask students to tell you what they know about preventing disease and staying healthy. Students may think that antibiotics or other medicines only need to be taken until the person is feeling better. Explain that medicine should be taken as prescribed because it is possible to start feeling better when there are still dangerous levels of germs in the body. If a person stops taking the medicine too soon, some germs may not be killed and could cause more illness. Also, the germs may become resistant to the medicine used to treat the disease.

Before You Read

THINK ABOUT IT In addition to the diseases listed in the text, encourage students to talk about infectious diseases they are aware of, especially if they live in an area that has recently experienced a disease outbreak. Students may also be interested in diseases that have been featured in the news or in movies, such as West Nile Virus, Ebola, hantavirus, or meningitis.

Read

NoteZone

Which of these steps do you usually follow?

The Centers for Disease Control and Prevention suggests seven steps for helping to prevent infectious diseases.

An Ounce of Prevention Keeps the Germs Away

1. **Wash your hands often.** The proper way to wash your hands is to wet them first, apply soap, then rub and scrub them vigorously for 10 to 15 seconds. Rinse and dry.
2. **Get immunized.** Getting immunizations is easy, inexpensive, and saves lives.
3. **Routinely clean and disinfect surfaces.** Cleaning with soap, water, and scrubbing removes dirt and most germs. Disinfecting with a bleach solution or another disinfectant kills additional germs.

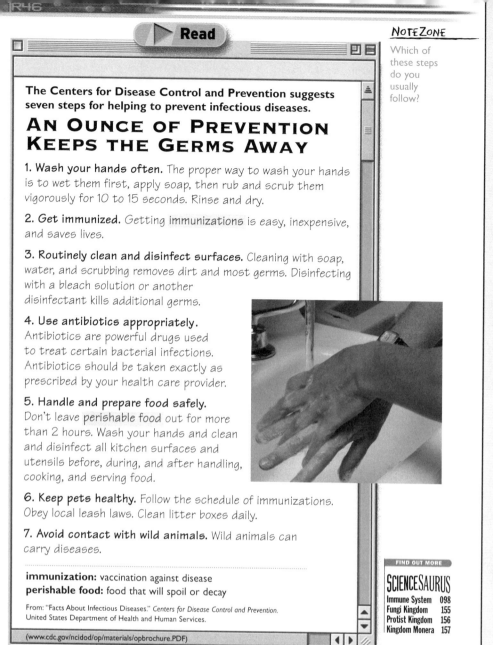

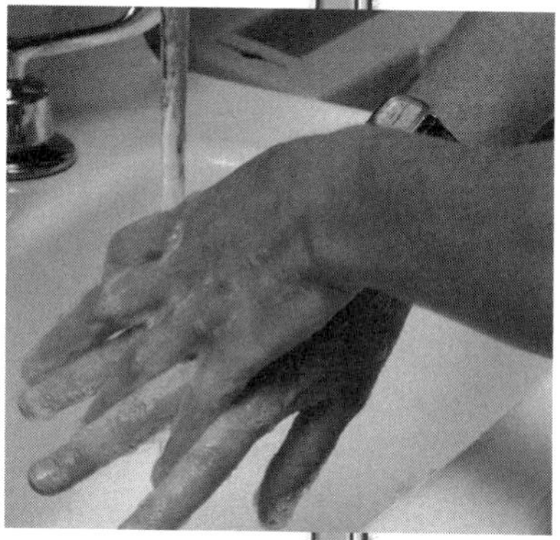

4. **Use antibiotics appropriately.** Antibiotics are powerful drugs used to treat certain bacterial infections. Antibiotics should be taken exactly as prescribed by your health care provider.
5. **Handle and prepare food safely.** Don't leave perishable food out for more than 2 hours. Wash your hands and clean and disinfect all kitchen surfaces and utensils before, during, and after handling, cooking, and serving food.
6. **Keep pets healthy.** Follow the schedule of immunizations. Obey local leash laws. Clean litter boxes daily.
7. **Avoid contact with wild animals.** Wild animals can carry diseases.

immunization: vaccination against disease
perishable food: food that will spoil or decay

From: "Facts About Infectious Diseases." *Centers for Disease Control and Prevention.* United States Department of Health and Human Services.

(www.cdc.gov/ncidod/op/materials/opbrochure.PDF)

FIND OUT MORE
SCIENCESAURUS
Immune System 098
Fungi Kingdom 155
Protist Kingdom 156
Kingdom Monera 157

Enrichment

Time: 30 minutes
Materials: hand lotion, glitter, bucket or trash can, paper towels, cold water, warm water, soap

Tell students that this activity will use glitter to represent germs and show why handwashing is so important.

Caution: Tell students not to rub their eyes when their hands are covered with glitter. At the end of the activity, make sure all students wash their hands thoroughly to remove all the glitter.

Have students apply a small amount of hand lotion to their hands. Then have students hold their hands over a bucket or trash can while you sprinkle glitter onto their hands. Divide the class into four groups. The first group should try to remove the glitter using a dry paper towel, the second group should use cold water, the third group cold water and soap, and the fourth group warm water and soap. Have students compare their results and explain why it is important to use warm water and soap to wash their hands. Have students evaluate the model and explain how the glitter used in this activity is similar to germs. (Like germs, the glitter can be spread between people and objects, and it is difficult to remove without warm water and soap.)

Read

As students read the steps, encourage them to come up with examples for the general terms used. For example, ask students to list some examples of antibiotics as they read step 4 and some examples of perishable foods as they read step 5.

You may want to introduce the concept of public health at this point or later in the lesson. To do this, point out that the measures described here not only help the person doing them stay healthy, they also prevent disease from spreading to other people. Discuss why it is so important for people to work together to prevent the spread of disease. Ask students what systems are in place in our society to make sure people follow these guidelines. (Students may mention health codes that affect doctors' and dentists' offices, supermarkets, restaurants, swimming pools, and the school cafeteria.)

CHECK UNDERSTANDING
Skill: Communicating
Ask students to describe three ways diseases are spread and what steps help prevent spreading each one. (*Spread of disease:* dirty hands, unclean food preparation areas, misuse of antibiotics, failure to wash hands before and after preparing food, unhealthy pets, contact with wild animals; *Prevention:* washing hands, disinfecting surfaces, taking medicines as prescribed, handling and preparing food safely, keeping pets healthy, avoiding contact with wild animals)

More Resources

The following resources are also available from Great Source.

ScienceSaurus

Immune System	098
Fungi Kingdom	155
Protist Kingdom	156
Kingdom Monera	157

Reader's Handbook

The Reading Process: Connect	35

Write Source 2000

Brainstorming for Ideas	10

Connections

MATH According to the Centers for Disease Control and Prevention, food poisoning is suspected as the cause in 76 million illnesses, 325,000 hospitalizations, and 5,200 deaths in the United States every year. Tell students that the population of the United States is approximately 285 million people. Have them calculate the percentage of people in the U.S. who suffer from a food-borne illness each year. For an additional challenge, have them calculate the percentage who are hospitalized for their illness and the percentage who die from food-borne illness.

(continued on page 175)

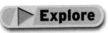

Explore

KEEP IT CLEAN Many infectious bacteria live in raw or undercooked foods, so keeping the kitchen clean is very important. You should wash your hands before and after preparing food. You should even wash them during preparation—for example, after cutting meat and before making a salad. Counters and other surfaces should be cleaned and disinfected regularly. Paper towels are good to use for this because they can be thrown away. Cloth towels should be washed with detergent in very hot water.

Meat, poultry, seafood, and eggs are especially likely to carry infectious bacteria. These foods should be kept in separate containers so they won't contaminate other foods. Eggs should never be eaten raw or partially cooked. All poultry and meat should be cooked until the juices run clear. Cold foods should be kept cold, and hot foods should be kept hot.

USE WHAT YOU KNOW Suppose you are planning a picnic with your friends. At your picnic you plan to grill hamburgers. You want to have them with all the fixings—buns, ketchup, relish, lettuce, onion, tomato, and cheese. You also plan to take canned drinks and fresh fruit for dessert.

► ***What steps should you take to make sure that your meal is as safe as possible from germs?***

Possible steps: Keep the meat in a cooler until it is cooked; cook the meat until the juices run clear; use wet wipes to wash hands before, during, and after handling food; wash the fruit and vegetables and keep them and the cheese in a cooler separate from the meat; use paper plates and napkins and plastic utensils that can be thrown away

Teaching Plan pp. 174–175

Explore

KEEP IT CLEAN As students read this section, ask them to think about how these rules apply in restaurants and food stores as well as how they apply at home. Point out that restaurants are required by law to follow most of these requirements. Ask: *How are these laws enforced?* (Health inspectors do inspections.) *Do you think it is safer to eat in a restaurant or in a private home?* (Examples: Restaurants are safer because they are regulated by law. Home-cooked food is safer because it is prepared by someone you know who has a personal interest in maintaining food safety.) Suggest that students look for caution signs addressed to employees the next time they visit a restroom in a restaurant or grocery store.

USE WHAT YOU KNOW Students' answers should reflect an understanding of the need to keep hot foods hot and cold foods cold as well as providing a solution to the problem of washing hands, utensils, and work areas when eating a meal outdoors.

Take Action

MAKE OBSERVATIONS You and your classmates can help prevent the spread of infectious diseases in your school. Look around the school. Watch the activities that go on. Pay attention to what you and your classmates do. Do you see ways to use the seven steps to prevent infectious diseases? List them below.

Possible answers: Keep pet cages clean; wash hands before eating; wash hands after using the bathroom; don't bring perishable foods for lunch; don't come to school when you are sick.

MAKE A POSTER Design a poster to remind other students to do their part to keep your school healthy. Use the ideas in the list you made above. Draw cartoons to make your messages fun to read. Sketch your poster design in the space below.

Poster designs will vary.

175

(continued from page 174)

If necessary, remind students how to calculate the percentages. (Divide each smaller number by 285,000,000. Show students how to reduce the numbers first—for example, 325 ÷ 285,000. *Calculations:* illness about 27%; hospitalizations about 0.11%; deaths about 0.002%)

Assessment

Skill: Using space/time relationships

Use the following task to assess each student's progress:

Tell students to imagine that they have taken a one-day babysitting job. During the day, they will perform the following activities: change a diaper four times, prepare food two times, read seven picture books, play catch, and use the bathroom three times. List these activities on the board, an overhead transparency, or a handout. Have students identify when they should wash their hands to prevent spreading disease. (before and after preparing food, after changing diapers, after using the bathroom) Ask them how many times they would wash their hands that day. (at least 11 times)

Take Action

MAKE OBSERVATIONS This activity can be performed as a classroom brainstorming activity. Alternatively, you may want to lead students on a tour of the school, stopping in different areas to brainstorm ways to use the seven steps in each part of the building. Students' ideas should be based on the steps in the reading on page 173 and the methods described in Keep It Clean on page 174.

MAKE A POSTER
Time: 40–45 minutes
Materials: poster paper, colored markers

Once students have sketched their poster designs, have them work in small groups to create posters to hang in the classroom and elsewhere in the school. Encourage students who have similar ideas to work together, incorporating ideas from each student's design.

About the Photo

Once found only in grasslands and open country of the southwestern United States and Mexico, the coyote *(Canis latrans)* now occupies a variety of habitats from Panama to Alaska. One reason coyotes are so successful in many different habitats is that their diet is extremely diverse. In addition to the types of foods described in the student reading on page 189, coyotes scavenge on carrion and occasionally prey on domestic animals. However, many attacks attributed to coyotes are actually the work of feral dogs.

Efforts to exterminate coyotes by poisoning and hunting, particularly in sheep-ranching areas, have met with limited success due to the coyote's wariness and its ability to retreat to and thrive in less hospitable areas.

About the Charts

A major goal of the *Science Daybooks* is to promote reading, writing, and critical thinking skills in the context of science. The charts below describe the types of reading selections included in this unit and identify the skills and strategies used in each lesson.

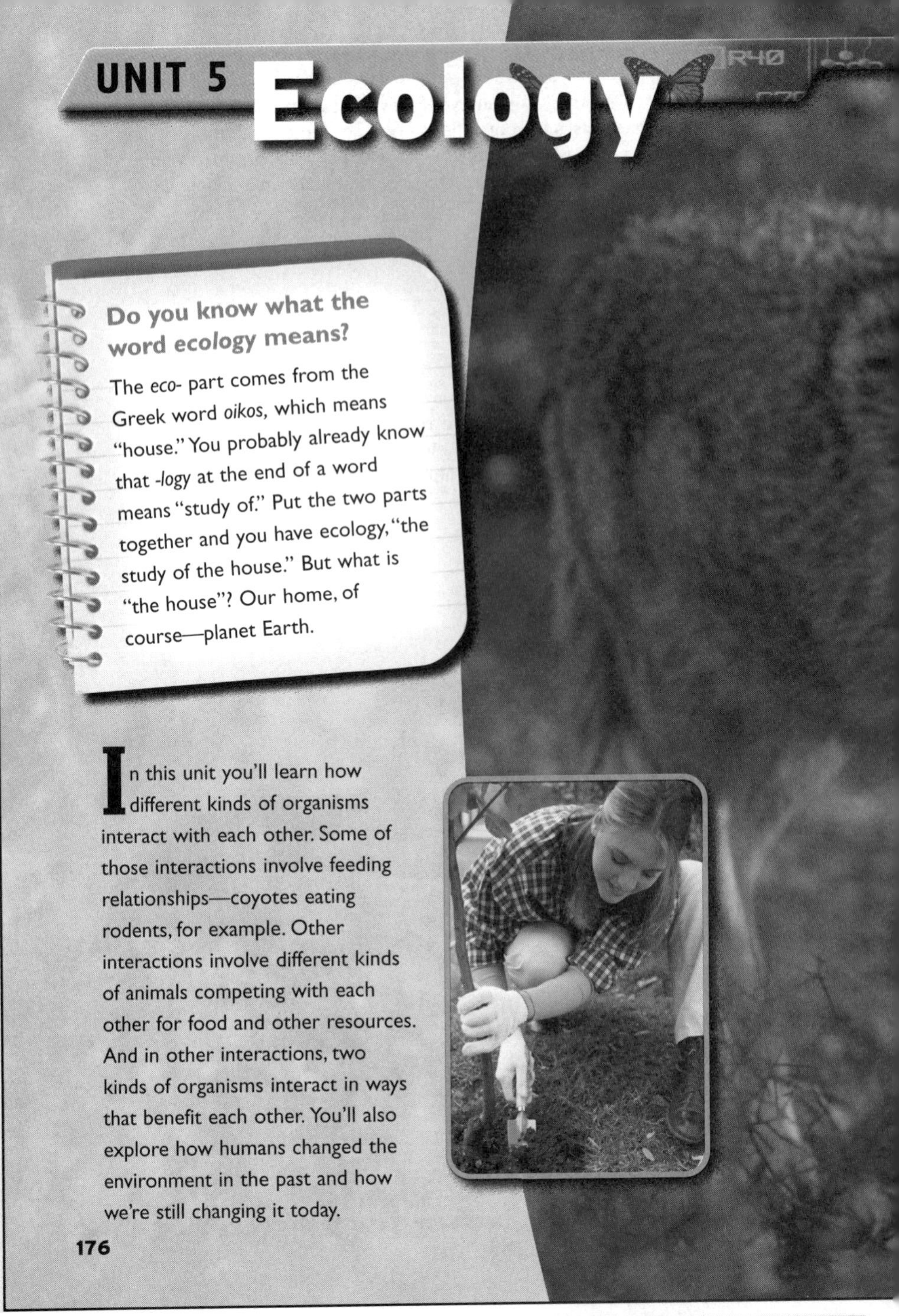

UNIT 5 Ecology

Do you know what the word ecology means?

The *eco-* part comes from the Greek word *oikos*, which means "house." You probably already know that *-logy* at the end of a word means "study of." Put the two parts together and you have ecology, "the study of the house." But what is "the house"? Our home, of course—planet Earth.

In this unit you'll learn how different kinds of organisms interact with each other. Some of those interactions involve feeding relationships—coyotes eating rodents, for example. Other interactions involve different kinds of animals competing with each other for food and other resources. And in other interactions, two kinds of organisms interact in ways that benefit each other. You'll also explore how humans changed the environment in the past and how we're still changing it today.

176

SELECTION	READING	WRITING	APPLICATION
CHAPTER 17 • POPULATIONS, COMMUNITIES, AND ECOSYSTEMS			
49. "The Unwanted Amphibian" (nonprofit organization article)	• Brainstorming • Directed reading	• Gather information from a map • Make inferences	• Write a letter
50. "Cane Toad Venom" (museum fact sheet)	• Use prior knowledge • Directed reading	• Interpret a diagram	• Do a research project
51. "Disaster or Disruption?" (university Web site)	• Formulate a question	• Cause and effect	
CHAPTER 18 • UNDER THE GRASSLAND SKY			
52. "The View from Bald Hill" (eyewitness account)	• Create a concept map • Directed reading	• Write a hypothesis • Analyze data	• Do a research project
53. "The View from Bald Hill" (eyewitness account)	• Directed reading	• Analyze data • Draw conclusions	• Hold a debate
54.	• Create a concept map	• Make a list • Risks and benefits	• Create an environmental checklist

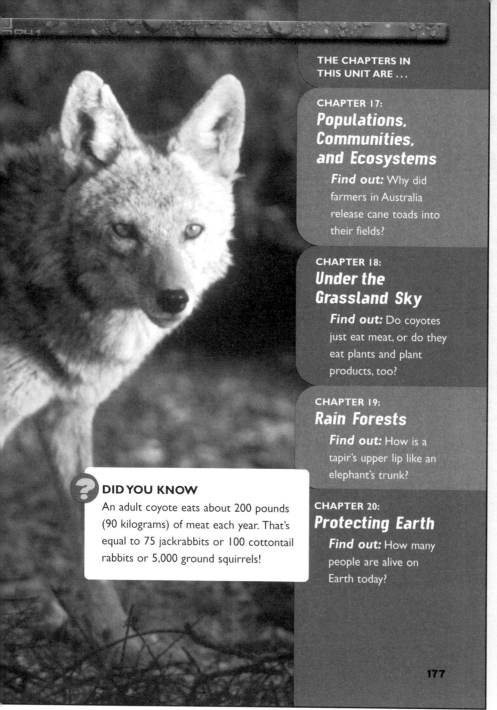

THE CHAPTERS IN THIS UNIT ARE . . .

CHAPTER 17:
Populations, Communities, and Ecosystems

Find out: Why did farmers in Australia release cane toads into their fields?

CHAPTER 18:
Under the Grassland Sky

Find out: Do coyotes just eat meat, or do they eat plants and plant products, too?

CHAPTER 19:
Rain Forests

Find out: How is a tapir's upper lip like an elephant's trunk?

CHAPTER 20:
Protecting Earth

Find out: How many people are alive on Earth today?

DID YOU KNOW

An adult coyote eats about 200 pounds (90 kilograms) of meat each year. That's equal to 75 jackrabbits or 100 cottontail rabbits or 5,000 ground squirrels!

177

Answers to *Find Out* Questions

CHAPTER 17
They hoped the cane toads would eat the cane beetles that fed on sugar cane plants and damaged their crops. (p. 178)

CHAPTER 18
Coyotes eat a wide range of foods, not only meat but plants and plant products as well. (p. 189)

CHAPTER 19
The tapir's upper lip curves down like an abbreviated elephant trunk. (p. 199)

CHAPTER 20
about 5.5 billion people (graph, p. 213)

SCILINKS
THE WORLD'S A CLICK AWAY

www.scilinks.org
Keyword: Mentoring
Code: GSSD06

SELECTION	READING	WRITING	APPLICATION
CHAPTER 19 • RAIN FOREST			
55. "A Rain Forest Resident" (science newsletter)	• Use reference materials • Directed reading	• Make inferences • Draw conclusions	• Complete an adaptations chart
56. "How Tapirs Spread Seeds" (science newsletter)	• Read with a purpose • Connect to prior knowledge	• Use information from a graph • Make predictions	• Write a research proposal for funding
57.	• Review a satellite photo	• Risk analysis	• Research a question about the rainforest
CHAPTER 20 • PROTECTING EARTH			
58. "Easter's End" (magazine article)	• Brainstorming • Read with a purpose	• Compare and contrast • Complete a chart	• Create a Venn diagram
59. "Human Impacts" (NSTA online course)	• Read with a purpose	• Complete a line graph	• Make predictions
60. "Living Treasure" (children's science book)	• Formulate an opinion • Read for details	• Hands-on activity • Analyze observations	• Write a research report

Populations, Communities, and Ecosystems

LESSON 49

The Cane Toad Invasion

Point of Lesson: ***Cane toad populations in Australia have grown at an alarming rate.***

In this lesson, students "meet" the cane toad, an amphibian that has become a case study in the dangers of introducing non-native species to an ecosystem. Students read an article describing adaptations that have made the cane toad so successful in Australia since its introduction in 1935. They then interpret a map showing the cane toad's natural range and its introduced range. By reviewing data in the article and map, students conclude why the cane toad population has increased at the expense of native Australian frog populations. They also predict whether cane toads would be a threat in a temperate climate.

Materials

Take Action (p. 181), for the class:
- world map (optional)

LESSON 50

Poison Toads

Point of Lesson: ***A cane toad population interacts with other populations in its community.***

Students consider the effect of a new population—cane toads—on the existing animal populations within an ecological community. After reviewing the concept of community, students read a passage describing how one of the cane toad's adaptations, poisonous venom, can adversely affect other species that live alongside a cane toad population. Students then explain why people would want to reduce the population of cane toads wherever possible. Finally, students research another invasive species and describe the trouble its introduction has caused in its adopted communities.

Materials

Enrichment (p. 183), for each student:
- colored pencils or markers
- drawing paper

Take Action (p. 185), for the class:
- research sources about invasive species

LESSON 51

Bad Neighbors

Point of Lesson: ***Cane toad populations affect their entire ecosystem.***

Students read the first-hand account of a landowner who graphically describes her observations of a cane toad invasion and its aftermath. Based on the landowner's observations, students identify which nonliving factor cane toads most affect in their environment. They then list factors that may have limited the success of huge populations of cane toads and that contributed to the survival of some native species despite a cane toad infestation.

Materials

none

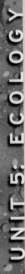

Background Information

Cane Toads

A research group called Commonwealth Scientific & Industrial Research Organization (CSIRO) has been studying the effects of the cane toads since the 1990s in an effort to discover a method of controlling the cane toad population without causing harm to vulnerable native species. Researchers at CSIRO investigated natural controls on the native cane toad population in Venezuela, and they discovered viruses called *ranaviruses* that are deadly to cane toads. However, laboratory experiments showed that while these viruses killed cane toads, they also killed some native Australian frog species.

The CSIRO researchers then began a study of the cane toad genetic code, looking for a gene that controls the toads' development from tadpole to adult. To be useful in reducing the toad population, this gene would have to be unique to cane toads, not shared with native Australian frogs. If this gene could be identified and manipulated, the cane toad tadpoles would not be able to grow into adults. If they can isolate the gene, CSIRO researchers plan to develop a ranavirus that infects cane toad tadpoles and replaces the gene for normal development with a modified version of the gene. The weakened ranavirus would act as a carrier to infect the cane toads with the modified gene. Other amphibians and fish would not be harmed by infection with the gene-carrying ranavirus. Researchers expect that it will be at least ten years before this plan can be put into effect. In the meantime, Australians are watching the continued spread of cane toads and waiting to see what the long-term effects will be.

Point of Lesson

Cane toad populations in Australia have grown at an alarming rate.

Focus

- Systems, order, and organization
- Reproduction and heredity
- Populations and ecosystems
- Diversity and adaptations of organisms
- Populations, resources, and environments

Skills and Strategies

- Interpreting scientific illustrations
- Making inferences
- Communicating
- Recognizing cause and effect

Advance Preparation

Vocabulary

Make sure students understand these terms. Definitions can be found in the glossary at the end of the student book.

- amphibian
- environment
- fungi
- lungs
- organism
- species

Materials

Gather the materials needed for ***Take Action*** (p. 181).

The Cane Toad Invasion

Populations of cane toads are flourishing in parts of Australia, and no one knows how to stop them!

Cane toads are normally found only in parts of South, Central, and North America. But in 1935 farmers in Gordonvale, Australia, sent for some of the toads, hoping they would eat the cane beetles that fed on sugar cane plants and damaged the crops. As it turned out, the toads were too big and clumsy to leap up and reach the beetles on the tall sugar cane stalks. The toads were good at something, though—making more toads.

Before You Read

IDENTIFY POPULATIONS A population is a group of organisms of the same species that live in the same area. The cane toads released into the sugar fields of Gordonvale, Australia, formed one population. Soon the cane toad population grew and expanded into different areas to form new populations.

► ***Name some populations you can identify in the area where you live. Explain why these groups are populations. Remember—plants, fungi, and microorganisms form populations, too.***

Answers will vary. Examples: populations of deer in the neighborhood, mice in an attic, and mold on a piece of fruit. The groups are populations because each consists of organisms of the same species living in the same place.

Teaching Plan pp. 178–179

INTRODUCING THE LESSON

This lesson presents cane toads as an example of a population and describes the traits that make cane toads so successful. Ask: *What do you think the word* population *means in science?* Let students offer their ideas without correcting them.

Ask: *What might happen if a new species were introduced into an environment?* Students may think that a single species does not have much of an impact on its environment. Guide students to understand that even when the environment is healthy for the newly introduced plant or animal, the species may be harmful to the other species already living in that environment. If you know of an example of a non-native species having an adverse effect on an ecosystem in your area—gypsy moths, kudzu, Africanized honey bees, or fire ants, for example—describe it to the class.

Before You Read

IDENTIFY POPULATIONS Make sure students understand that all members of a population are the same species. To emphasize this, have students read their responses aloud, and ask the class to comment on their accuracy.

Read

When 102 cane toads were let loose in Gordonvale, Australia, the toad population began to grow at an alarming rate.

The Unwanted Amphibian

After arriving in Australia, the toads were on their own and they proved to be very hardy survivors. It didn't take long to find out how well the toads would do in their new home. There are many reasons why cane toads became a pest so quickly.

- They breed like flies, as the saying goes. Each pair can lay more than 30,000 eggs every few weeks during summer!
- Their young develop faster than many Australian frogs so they eat up much of the food before frogs can get to it.
- Toads seem to be resistant to some herbicides and poor quality water which would normally make frogs ill and die.
- Almost all stages of a toad's life are poisonous so they have no natural predators to keep their numbers in check.
- Toads not only eat the food normally available to Australian frogs, they also eat small frogs [and] other wildlife such as baby snakes.

hardy: capable of surviving in harsh conditions
breed: reproduce, make more of one's own kind
resistant: unaffected by
herbicides: chemicals used to kill unwanted plants
predators: organisms that hunt other organisms for food

From: "The Unwanted Amphibian." *Frog Decline Reversal Project.* Frog Decline Reversal Project, Inc. (www.fdrproject.org/pages/TDprogress.htm)

NOTEZONE

Circle the items in the list that describe how the toads interact with other living things in their environment.

Underline the items that describe how the toads interact with nonliving things in their environment.

FIND OUT MORE

SCIENCESAURUS

Reproduction 113
Populations 130
Relationships Between Populations 132

Enrichment

Remind students that cane toads were originally brought to Australia to help control the cane beetles that were damaging the sugar cane crop. Tell students to imagine that it is 1935 and they are living in Australia. Divide the class into two groups. Assign one group to represent the farmers who want to bring cane toads to Australia and the other group to represent concerned citizens who oppose the introduction of the cane toads. Remind students that before cane toads were released, no one knew what their impact would be. Lead a class debate of the issue, first giving students time to develop their arguments. After the debate, hold a class discussion to develop a list of questions that should be addressed before introducing a new species into an established ecosystem.

Read

As students read the list of cane toad characteristics, encourage them to predict one effect of each characteristic on the environment. For example, for the first item on the list, students could note that a population of 102 cane toads could potentially increase to over one million cane toads in only a few weeks.

Have students share their responses to the NoteZone tasks. Make sure they are able to differentiate between living (biotic) and nonliving (abiotic) factors.

Remind students that populations of different species that live in the same area may compete for the same resources; in other words, resources in an ecosystem are limited. Ask students to describe the role of predators in an ecosystem and to predict what would happen to a population that has no natural predators.

CHECK UNDERSTANDING

Skill: Drawing conclusions

Ask: *Why were cane toads introduced in Australia?* (Farmers brought them in to eat the cane beetles that were damaging the sugar cane crops.) *What happened when the toads had been living in Australia for a while?* (They became pests. They multiplied rapidly and ate food that native frogs normally ate. They also ate small frogs and snakes.)

More Resources

The following resources are also available from Great Source.

SCIENCESAURUS
Reproduction 113
Populations 130
Relationships Between Populations 132

READER'S HANDBOOK
Elements of Graphics: Map 555

WRITE SOURCE 2000
Writing in the Workplace 237
Writing Business Letters 241

Connections

SOCIAL STUDIES Cane toads are not the only species to travel from North, Central, and South America to other parts of the world. List on the board the following plants and animals that are native to the Americas but have been introduced to other parts of the world: turkeys, muskrats, cacti, corn, tomatoes, squash, sunflowers, tobacco, beans, chili peppers, vanilla, and chocolate. Encourage students to discuss the impact that these species may have had on the native populations in their new environments.

(continued on page 181)

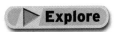

Explore

WHERE DO CANE TOADS LIVE? Cane toads are native to parts of South, Central, and North America. Populations have also increased in places where the toads have been introduced by people, including Hawaii, Australia, the Philippines, Florida, and Puerto Rico. The following map shows the locations of cane toad populations.

LOCATIONS OF CANE TOAD POPULATIONS

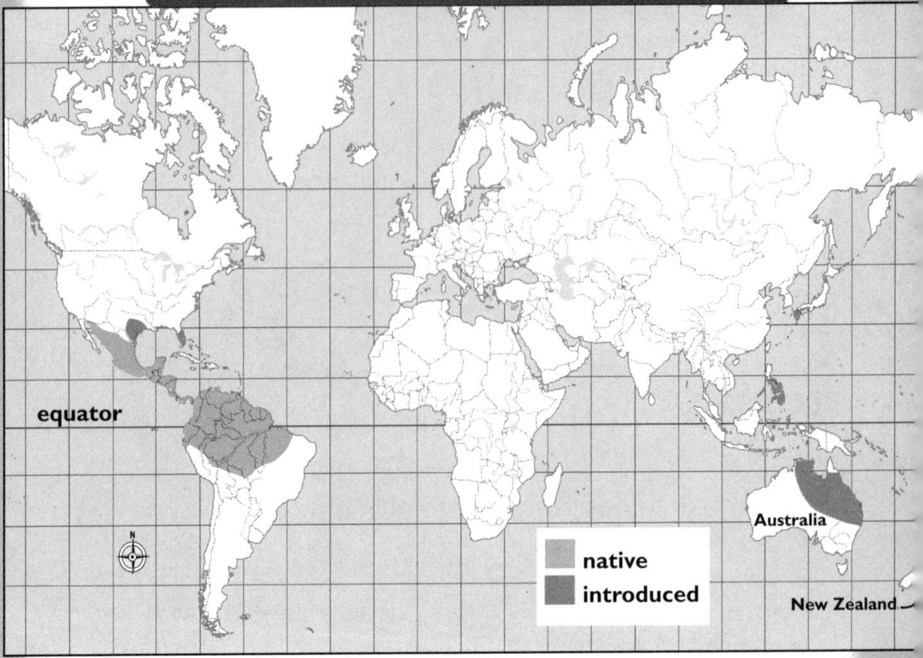

▶ ***What do all the cane toad locations have in common?***

All of them are near the equator.

▶ ***Look at the map. What can you infer about the best climate for cane toads?***

Cane toads cannot survive in cold climates or climates with cold seasons.

TEACHING PLAN pp. 180–181

Explore

WHERE DO CANE TOADS LIVE? Review basic map reading skills with students, including climate change associated with latitude. Have students identify where they live on the map, and then have them describe general trends in climate as you travel north and south of that location. Students may not understand how climate patterns in the northern and southern hemispheres mirror each other, so you should repeat the exercise for a location in the other hemisphere.

As a follow-up to the questions on this page, ask students to identify places on the map where the cane toads could probably survive, even though they do not live there now. (regions of Africa and Asia that are near the equator)

Propose Explanations

THE POPULATION EXPLOSION Students' responses should indicate an understanding of the role one population can play in a complex ecosystem. If students have difficulty answering the first question, encourage them to develop a model (such as a series of side-by-side sketches) to help them compare cane toad development with frog development.

To help students with the second question, have them suggest a series of cause-and-effect statements to identify the impact of the toads' diet on the other organisms in the environment. Students may realize that the ability to eat a wide variety of food enables cane toads to compete successfully with many other species for food and minimizes the competition for food within the cane toad population itself.

Propose Explanations

THE POPULATION EXPLOSION Scientists studying cane toads have found that cane toad tadpoles hatch very quickly, most of the time within three days. The tadpoles also develop lungs and legs early, and so are able to leave the water and live on land sooner than most frogs' tadpoles.

► ***How do these traits make the cane toad population very successful?***

The small toads could begin feeding on land prey sooner and so outcompete the frogs for food. Also, if the toads develop faster, they will become adults faster and so reproduce sooner. This would increase their population growth.

► ***Native frogs in Australia eat only certain types of food. But a cane toad will eat anything that moves past it and fits in its mouth. How could the cane toad's diet contribute to its success?***

Cane toads don't need to look for special food types. Spending less time looking for food means more time is available for meeting other needs, such as finding mates.

Take Action

WRITE A LETTER You are working as an ecologist in Kakadu National Park in northern Australia. Cane toads have just begun to appear there. The toads migrated north from Queensland. One day, you receive a letter from another ecologist who works in a park in the southern part of New Zealand's South Island. She is worried that the cane toads will one day arrive on the South Island in boat cargo and travel to her park. Review the map and questions on the previous page. Write a letter to her on a separate piece of paper. Include information about cane toads, what risks they pose for your park, where they normally live, and the likelihood of cane toads invading her park.

Letters should reflect the fact that the southern part of South Island is probably too cold for cane toads.

(continued from page 180)

Students may be aware that some food plants native to the Americas are commonly grown and used in other cultures, such as tomatoes in Italy and chili peppers in Asia and India.

Assessment

Skill: Recognizing cause and effect

Use the following questions to assess each student's progress:

What features of the environment made the cane toads so successful in Australia? (Answers may vary but should include the climate and plentiful food sources.) *What characteristics of cane toads created problems in their new environment?* (Answers should include their rapid breeding and development, their resistance to herbicides and other toxins, the lack of natural predators, and the fact that they eat a wide range of food, including food normally eaten by native frogs.)

Take Action

Time: 30 minutes
Materials: world map (optional)

WRITE A LETTER Have students review the information in the lesson and make notes about how the cane toads might be affecting the other species in Kakadu National Park. Remind students to locate New Zealand's South Island on the map on page 180 and to use what they know about climate and latitude to determine whether the toads would be a threat to the park in the southern part of the island. You may need to display a large world map so students can see the South Island's location relative to Antarctica.

Interested students may want to research how cane toads interact with other species in their native environments and include this information in their letters. Explain that some invasive species live in balance in their native environments but cause major problems when they are introduced to new environments.

Point of Lesson

A cane toad population interacts with other populations in its community.

Focus

- Systems, order, and organization
- Reproduction and heredity
- Populations and ecosystems
- Diversity and adaptations of organisms
- Understanding about scientific inquiry

Skills and Strategies

- Comparing and contrasting
- Interpreting scientific illustrations
- Making inferences
- Recognizing cause and effect
- Communicating

Advance Preparation

Vocabulary

Make sure students understand these terms. Definitions can be found in the glossary at the end of the student book.

- life cycle
- organism
- population
- predator
- species

Materials

Gather the materials needed for *Enrichment* (p. 183) and *Take Action* (p. 185).

Poison Toads

If you're big and slow, how can you escape hungry predators?

By most accounts, cane toads are big, slow, and ugly. They can grow up to 24 cm in length and weigh over 1 kg. Their rough, dry skin is covered with bumps that look like warts. But size and looks are not enough to scare away hungry predators that want to eat them. Cane toads have a special defense that protects them from many attackers in their communities.

Before You Read

DESCRIBE A COMMUNITY Different populations living together in the same area form a community. A cane toad population lives among populations of native frogs, snakes, water rats, ibis, crows, and other organisms.

A common way populations of organisms in a community interact is by eating each other. For example, a mosquito population serves as food for the cane toad population. At the same time, the cane toad population serves as food for the population of Keelback snakes, which aren't affected by the toads' toxin. Snakes are eaten by foxes, dogs, and other animals.

- ***Think about the community in which you live. Describe three animals' defenses that help them survive in your community.***

Answers will vary. Examples: Porcupines have sharp quills; houseflies have large, protruding eyes to see approaching danger; skunks spray attackers.

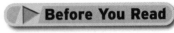

TEACHING PLAN pp. 182–183

INTRODUCING THE LESSON
This lesson discusses interactions between the cane toad population and other populations in the community, particularly the effect of cane toad venom on other animals. Ask students: *What are some ways that populations in an area interact with each other?*

Students may not realize that populations can be affected indirectly. For example, if a new predator is introduced into a community, the prey populations would decrease. As a result, populations of plants or animals eaten by those prey populations would increase, which in turn would affect other populations.

Before You Read

DESCRIBE A COMMUNITY Have students use the feeding relationships described in this section to draw a food web showing how cane toads fit into their community. Remind students to draw the arrows *from* the animal *being* eaten *to* the animal *doing* the eating.

Before students write their answers, have them brainstorm a list of populations found in their community. Prompt them to describe relationships between populations, including how different animals use their natural defenses to survive.

Read

Cane toads have an unusual—and deadly—way of defending themselves.

Cane Toad Venom

One of the most important factors in the success of the cane toad is that they are highly poisonous to eat, at every stage of their life cycle.

All frogs and toads may have enlarged chemical-secreting glands at particular points on their bodies, or small glands spread over the whole skin. The chemicals they produce...may be highly toxic. The cane toad is one such amphibian. A cane toad's reaction to a threat is to turn [so that] the venom glands face [the attacker]. Cane toad venom is also found all over their skin. Animals [that pick up] a cane toad [in their mouth] and [receive] a dose of venom may die within fifteen minutes.

The glands on the cane toads' shoulders are also capable of oozing venom or even squirting it over a distance of up to 2 m if the toad is particularly roughly treated.

...[Cane toads'] diet includes small lizards, frogs, mice and even younger cane toads. They have also been known to steal food from dog and cat bowls.

secreting: releasing
glands: organs that release chemicals used in other parts of the body
toxic: poisonous, deadly
amphibian: an animal that starts life in water and uses gills to breathe but lives on land, or both on land and in water, and uses lungs to breathe as an adult
venom: a poisonous substance released by an animal
dose: a specific quantity

From: "Cane Toads—Bufo Marinus." *Australian Museum Fact Sheets.* Australian Museum. (www.amonline.net.au/factsheets/canetoad.htm)

NoteZone

Circle the ways a cane toad protects itself against other populations in its community.

FIND OUT MORE

SCIENCESAURUS

Animal Life Cycles 106
Researching Information 420

Enrichment

Time: 25 minutes
Materials: colored pencils or markers, drawing paper

Suggest that students draw a series of diagrams or pictures illustrating the cane toad's reaction to a threat as described in the reading. Encourage students to be creative. Some students may want to create a comic strip with a story line showing the adventures of a venomous cane toad. Others may want to create a series of scientific illustrations.

Read

When students have completed the NoteZone task, call on volunteers to identify the defenses they circled in the reading. Ask students to identify behaviors that help the cane toad survive, such as eating a varied diet or stealing dog food, and behaviors that protect it against other populations, such as turning and squirting venom.

Explain that although cane toad venom can kill or injure predators that try to eat the toad, the threat to humans is not as severe. The venom can irritate the skin, cause temporary blindness if it gets in the eyes, and cause an increase in heart rate.

You may want to tell students that scientists are studying cane toad venom to see if it may be useful in medicines. Scientists have found that the venom contains substances that are similar to ones that doctors use to treat heart problems.

CHECK UNDERSTANDING
Skill: Drawing conclusions
Ask: *Do you think cane toads are the only toads that produce venom? Why or why not?* (No; the reading states that all frogs and toads may have glands that secrete toxic chemicals.)

More Resources

The following resources are also available from Great Source.

SCIENCESAURUS

Animal Life Cycles 106
Researching Information 420

READER'S HANDBOOK

Elements of Nonfiction:
Cause and Effect 275
Elements of Graphics: Diagram 552

Connections

LANGUAGE ARTS Frogs and toads have figured prominently in the folklore of many cultures. Have students research images of frogs and toads in folklore and literature and compare those descriptions to scientific descriptions. One good source of information is the Exploratorium Web site: www.exploratorium.edu/frogs/folklore/index.html.

Explore

INTERACTIONS WITHIN A COMMUNITY The diagram at right shows the life cycle of the cane toad.

Adult cane toads with their developed venom glands are highly poisonous. But cane toads at other stages of their life cycle—including eggs, tadpoles, and young toads—are also poisonous.

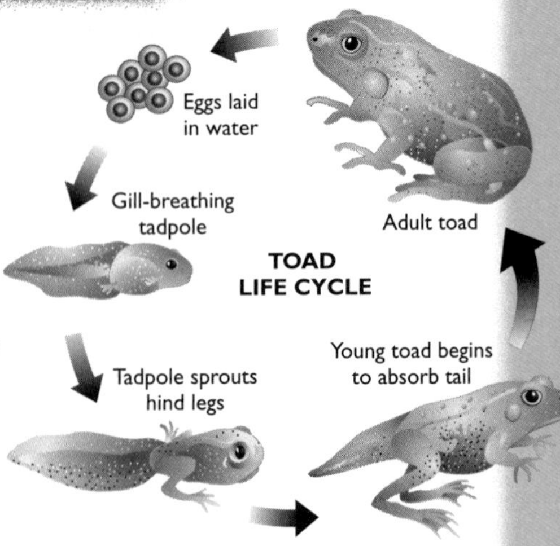

► ***Which other population might be affected by poisonous toad eggs in a pond? (Hint: What other animal shares the pond?) How would it be affected? What change might it produce?***

Fish in the water might eat the eggs and die, reducing the fish population.

► ***How might another population in the community such as egrets be affected by this change?***

Egrets that fed on the fish might have less to eat. A population of water insects normally eaten by fish may grow out of control.

► ***Which other populations in the cane toad community might be affected directly or indirectly by the toad? Base your answer on the feeding relationships that exist within a community of animals.***

Animals that fed on any stage of the cane toad life cycle would probably die. Animals whose prey were killed by the cane toads would also be affected.

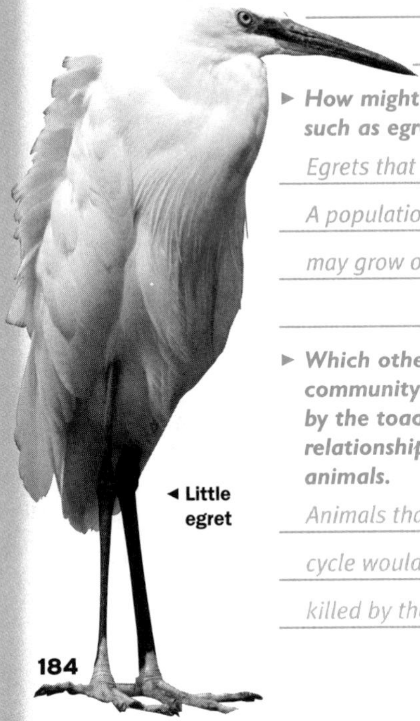

◄ Little egret

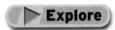

184

TEACHING PLAN pp. 184–185

Explore

INTERACTIONS WITHIN A COMMUNITY Tell students that as they review the Toad Life Cycle diagram, they should think about what role the cane toad plays in the community at each stage of its life cycle. For example, ask students how a pond full of poisonous tadpoles would affect the other populations in and around the pond. (The tadpoles would consume the food supply and would kill any other animals that ate them.) Students should realize that the cane toad interacts with other populations and with nonliving things at every stage of its life cycle. To answer the last question on this page, students might find it helpful to refer to the food webs they drew in Before You Read, page 182.

Propose Explanations

THINK ABOUT IT Remind students that the Keelback snake is not affected by the cane toad's venom. Ask them to predict how the cane toad population and the Keelback snake population might interact. (The snake population might increase as the cane toads became a plentiful food supply. The snakes might be able to reduce the number of toads in the community.)

Discuss the possibility of finding natural methods to control the cane toad population, such as introducing a

Propose Explanations

THINK ABOUT IT Based on what you know about cane toad venom and the diet of cane toads, what impact do you think invading cane toads have on native populations of animals living in the area?

The cane toads' venom would kill animals that try to prey on them. The toads would probably outcompete other populations for food. With their varied diet, the toads would prey on animals that might have had few predators previously.

► ***Why do you think people are trying to reduce cane toad populations and keep them from spreading into new communities?***

People worry that native species will be killed off by the toads.

► ***How could you find out whether invading cane toads were affecting other populations in the community? Describe the kind of data you would gather and the period of time over which you would gather it.***

Student proposals should include looking at changes in the population of other animals in the community. They should also suggest looking at these results over generations, not just for one season.

Take Action

RESEARCH AN INVADING SPECIES The cane toad is not the only animal that has been introduced to a new area to solve a problem, only to end up causing new problems in the community.

► ***What other animal populations have been introduced to new areas? Research one of the following introduced species, or choose another. Why was the species introduced? Was it introduced on purpose or by accident? How did the species affect the native populations in the community?***

- American bullfrog *(Rana catesbeiana)*
- House sparrow *(Passer domesticus)*
- Gypsy moth *(Lymantria dispar)*
- Zebra mussel *(Dreissena polymorpha)*
- Muskrat *(Ondatra zibethicus)*
- Starling *(Sturnus vulgaris)*

185

Assessment

Skill: Communicating

Use the following questions to assess each student's progress:

How do cane toads poison animals that may try to eat or attack them? (Animals that eat the toad at any stage in its life cycle will probably die from eating the poison. Adult cane toads can also squirt venom or make it ooze from the glands on their shoulders.) *How long does it take for the poison to work?* (Animals that eat cane toads or even just pick them up with their mouths can die within 15 minutes.)

species that preys on cane toads. Ask students to consider the advantages and disadvantages of such a solution. (Natural controls might be less harmful to the environment than using poisons, but introducing another new species to the ecosystem may have harmful effects on native populations.)

Before students respond to the third question on page 185, encourage them to use scientific methods as they generate ideas for collecting data. They may propose finding a similar community that the cane toads have not yet invaded to use as a control.

Take Action

Time: will vary

Materials: research sources about invasive species

RESEARCH AN INVADING SPECIES You may want to suggest other species to research, including purple loosestrife *(Lythrum salicaria)*, coqui *(Eleutherodactylus coqui)*, and the golden apple snail *(Pomacea canaliculata)*. Point out that some non-native species were imported intentionally, but others arrived accidentally as "stowaways" or "piggyback" species, hidden in plant soil, water in the holds of ships, or imported grain.

As students research the impact of each species on its new environment, they should also research methods that have been used to control the invading species. In a class discussion, have students explain whether any of the invading species have been controlled successfully.

Point of Lesson

Cane toad populations affect their entire ecosystem.

Focus

- Systems, order, and organization
- Populations and ecosystems
- Regulation and behavior
- Evolution and equilibrium

Skills and Strategies

- Recognizing cause and effect
- Generating questions
- Making inferences

Advance Preparation

Vocabulary

Make sure students understand these terms. Definitions can be found in the glossary at the end of the student book.

- ecosystem
- predator
- population
- species

More Resources

The following resources are also available from Great Source and NSTA.

ScienceSaurus

Animal Behavior 110
Ecosystems 129
Relationships Between Populations 132

(continued on page 187)

Bad Neighbors

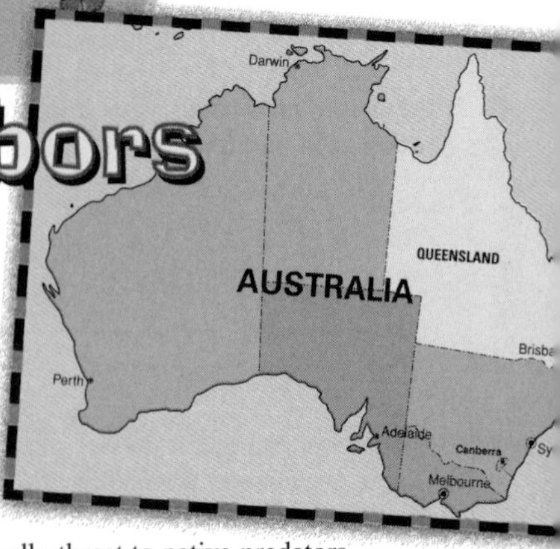

Cane toads are everywhere! But are they a disaster or just a disruption?

Until cane toads were introduced in 1935, Australia didn't have any native toad species. The toads' impact on the ecosystems to which they spread was immediate and severe. The hungry toads wiped out food supplies, leaving many native frog species without anything to eat. They also posed a deadly threat to native predators that tried to eat them. But what are the long-term effects of a toad invasion?

Read

How severe is the cane toad threat? A land manager in Queensland, Australia, shares her observations.

Disaster or Disruption?

Chris Holt was invaded [by cane toads] twice.... A decade ago she and husband Malcolm owned Balbarini station...where they were attacked en masse. "They came by the road, not in the creeks as we had been told they would," she recalled. "It was just disgusting. The road was like a moving carpet at night. It was as if they sent in big shock troops because some of the ones at the front were as big as bread and butter plates. They were huge." Ms. Holt remembers the initial effects were devastating. "We found lots of dead freshwater crocodiles in the shallow water holes in the river. We found dead goannas and had no snakes at all that year."

She said the tree frogs nearly disappeared, but by the end of the dry [season] the toads had no more food and the Holts found themselves surrounded by dead cane toads.... The Holt family...watched as native species managed to survive. "The native animals seem to learn

FIND OUT MORE

ScienceSaurus

Animal Behavior 110
Ecosystems 129
Relationships Between Populations 132

SciLinks. THE WORLD'S A CLICK AWAY

www.scilinks.org
Keyword: Populations, Communities, and Ecosystems
Code: GSLD22

UNIT 5: ECOLOGY

186

TEACHING PLAN pp. 186–187

INTRODUCING THE LESSON

This lesson explores the long-term effects of the cane toad invasion in one locale in Australia. Ask students to predict the long-term effects of cane toads on the ecosystems they have invaded. Students may think that the initial devastation caused by the cane toads will continue until the toads have completely destroyed the ecosystems. Explain that many ecosystems will eventually reach a new state of balance, even though the initial effects appear to be devastating.

Read

Before students read the excerpt, have them compare the map on this page with the map on page 180. Point out that cane toads have spread throughout Queensland, the setting of this reading. As students read, encourage them to circle any sections that confirm their predictions about the cane toads' long-term effects on the ecosystems and to underline any sections that surprise them and change their ideas.

When students have completed the NoteZone task, use their questions as the basis for a class discussion. Read each question aloud, and let students offer their ideas. Remind them to look for answers in the chapter's readings and to make sure their answers are supported by the text. For any questions that remain unanswered, ask volunteers to research the answers and present their findings to the class.

quite quickly that you can't eat them," explains Ms. Holt. "In our experience [the cane toads] had no long-term effect on the wildlife whatsoever."

Many of those living in the Gulf region report how quickly predatory birds learned to adjust to the poison sacs the cane toads carry on their backs. "The crows and kites have learned to live with them," says [Louise] Martin. "They pick the cane toads up and turn them over and pick their guts out."

en masse: in a large group

shock troops: soldiers specially trained to lead an attack

initial: first

goannas: Australian monitor lizards

predatory: hunting and eating other organisms

kites: birds that eat small animals, including toads

From: Schulz, Dennis. "The Cane Toad Dialogues: Disaster or Disruption?" *Tropical Savannas Cooperative Research Centre*. Northern Territory University. (savanna.ntu.edu.au/publications/savanna_links16/toad.html)

NOTEZONE

Write a question to ask your teacher about this reading.

Propose Explanations

THE END OF THE EXPLOSION Which nonliving part of the cane toad's ecosystem is most changed by a cane toad population? How do you think this might in turn affect other populations in the ecosystem?

Water. The toads' eggs and tadpoles poison the water source they're in. The poisoned water kills other species that are born or live in the water or drink it.

▶ ***Why do you think the cane toad population at Balbarini station increased so rapidly at first?***

The toads were able to outcompete other populations for food, and they avoided predation by being toxic to eat.

▶ ***What factors do you think might contribute to the decline of a cane toad population after several months or years?***

Once the food supplies diminish, there is less to eat, so cane toads starve. Also, predators learn to avoid the cane toads' toxic parts.

187

(continued from page 186)

SCILINKS. THE WORLD'S A CLICK AWAY

www.scilinks.org
Keyword: Populations, Communities, and Ecosystems
Code: GSLD22

Assessment

Skill: Solving problems

Use the following questions to assess each student's progress:

In this reading, Chris Holt says that she thinks the cane toads had no long-term effect on the environment. How could scientists determine whether the cane toads did have a long-term effect on an ecosystem? What information would they need in order to reach a scientific conclusion? (They would need data about the ecosystem before the cane toads' arrival—what other populations live in the ecosystem, the sizes of those populations, each species' needs, water quality analysis, and so forth. They would then need to collect the same data after the arrival of the cane toads, taking several measurements over time. By comparing and analyzing the two sets of data, scientists could determine what long-term effect the toads had on the ecosystem.)

Propose Explanations

THE END OF THE EXPLOSION Students should understand that the ecosystem will continue to change over time as the cane toads' food supply diminishes and predators learn to avoid the toxins. However, some of the initial changes caused by the cane toads may prove to be permanent. For example, as their food supply diminishes, the cane toads may still outcompete the native frogs and prevent them from surviving in the community.

CHECK UNDERSTANDING

Skill: Identifying cause and effect

Ask students to make a table with three columns. In the first column, have them list as many effects of the introduction of cane toads into Australia as they can. In the second column, have them identify whether each effect is direct or indirect. In the third column, have them identify whether the effect is short-term or long-term.

Students' tables should indicate an understanding of the complexity of the ecosystem as well as the ability of the organisms within the ecosystem to adapt to the cane toads' arrival. One example is shown below.

Cane Toads' Effects	Direct or Indirect	Short-Term or Long-Term
Birds die from cane toad poison.	Direct	Short-term (Birds learned not to eat the toads.)

Under the Grassland Sky

LESSON 52

Eat or Be Eaten

Point of Lesson: ***Coyotes and rodents illustrate predator-prey feeding relationships in a desert ecosystem.***

This lesson introduces students to feeding relationships in an ecosystem through the work of two wildlife biologists, Carl and Jane Bock. Students read an excerpt describing coyotes and their prey from the Bock's book, *The View from Bald Hill.* Then students analyze data from an experiment on the effect of large predators on prey populations. Students draw conclusions from the results of the experiment, identify variables that might affect the outcome of the experiment, and research another predator to determine its role in its own ecosystem.

Materials

Enrichment (p. 189), for the class:
- index cards
- field guides and other research sources

LESSON 53

A Place of Their Own

Point of Lesson: ***Different species can survive in the same ecosystem by occupying different habitats.***

Students explore the concepts of habitat and niche in this lesson. A description of sparrow species studied by the Bocks is followed by a data table listing the habitat of each of the 12 species. After discovering that some habitats support more than one sparrow species, students are introduced to the concept of niche: within a given habitat, each species uses slightly different resources. Students apply their new knowledge of sparrow habitats in a debate over the development of an imaginary piece of land.

Materials

Science Scope Activity (p. 188B and p. 193), for each group:
- 11" × 17" sheet of paper
- scissors

LESSON 54

The Fragile Land

Point of Lesson: ***Humans often make changes that affect ecosystems.***

In this lesson, students consider the impact that humans have on ecosystems in their own area. After constructing a food web of plants and animals in a local ecosystem, students identify ways in which human-built structures may have affected the ecosystem. The lesson concludes with students creating a checklist of environmental questions for developers to help ensure that building plans consider the needs of plant and animal species on a building site.

Materials

none

Science Scope Activity

A New Way of Looking at the World

NSTA has chosen a Science Scope *activity related to the content in this chapter. The activity starts here and continues in Lesson 53, page 193.*

Time: 45 minutes for each Part

Materials: see page 188A

Procedure

Part 1: Constructing the game

Tell students that they will make and play a game called Ecoregion IQ.

1. Draw a large 3 by 3 grid on the board. Across the top of the grid, list three category headings: *Plants and Animals; Climate;* and *Geographic Features*. Tell students that this grid will serve as the game's score board and that teams will compete to win boxes on the grid.
2. Divide the class into teams of three students each, and give each team scissors and a sheet of 11" × 17" paper. Tell students to use the paper to make two smaller versions of the grid. These will serve as their team's game board.
3. Assign each team a map and region from the following Web site: www.nationalgeographic.com/wildworld

Instruct students through the remaining steps as follows:

4. Use the Web site to find information about your team's region that fits each of the three categories on the grid.

(continued on page 193)

Background Information

The Research Ranch

In the mid-sixteenth century, Francisco Vasquez de Coronado introduced domestic cattle, sheep, and horses to the American Southwest. Since their introduction, these grazers have changed the grasslands in many ways. In 1968, the Appleton-Whittell Research Ranch in Arizona banned grazing on over 8,000 acres of semi-desert grasslands, oak savannah, and oak woodlands. In this refuge, fences are removed and natural grasses are replaced in an effort to restore the land to its natural state. The land serves as an experimental control that allows researchers to compare the effects of different types of land use.

Point of Lesson

Coyotes and rodents illustrate predator-prey feeding relationships in a desert ecosystem.

Focus

- Systems, order, and organization
- Populations and ecosystems
- Abilities necessary to do scientific inquiry

Skills and Strategies

- Developing hypotheses
- Interpreting data
- Drawing conclusions
- Creating and using graphs
- Identifying and controlling variables
- Predicting

Advance Preparation

Vocabulary

Make sure students understand these terms. Definitions can be found in the glossary at the end of the student book.

- data
- desert
- ecosystem
- experiment
- feces
- food web
- grassland
- organism
- photosynthesis
- predator
- prediction
- prey

(continued on page 189)

Eat or Be Eaten

In the desert grasslands of southern Arizona, life-and-death struggles happen every day.

Carl and Jane Bock are scientists who have studied the Sonoita grasslands for more than 20 years. They were interested in learning about the trials that living things face in this dry, southeastern Arizona area. One of their areas of study was predator-prey relationships, especially among coyotes and rodents such as rats and mice. First, the Bocks learned all they could about coyotes, in both legend and science. They observed coyotes and rodents in the wild. Then they conducted experiments to learn more about how predators and their prey interact.

Before You Read

THINK ABOUT IT Every ecosystem is a study in survival. Animals must constantly look for food and avoid being food for something else. Plants (producers) make food by photosynthesis. Plant-eaters (herbivores) eat plants. Meat-eaters (carnivores) eat herbivores. Carnivores are also called predators, and the animals they eat are their prey.

Any series of eating relationships is called a food chain. Grass → mouse → snake → hawk is an example of a food chain. The arrows point from the organism being eaten to the organism doing the eating. In nature, many food chains usually overlap to create a food web.

Think of the wild organisms in your area. Who eats what? What would happen to the prey if its predators were removed?

Answers will vary. Example: Hawks eat squirrels; squirrels eat nuts. If the hawks were removed, the number of squirrels would increase.

DRAW A FOOD CHAIN Show the feeding relationships between some wild organisms that live in your area. Label the producers, herbivores, and carnivores. Then label the predators and prey.

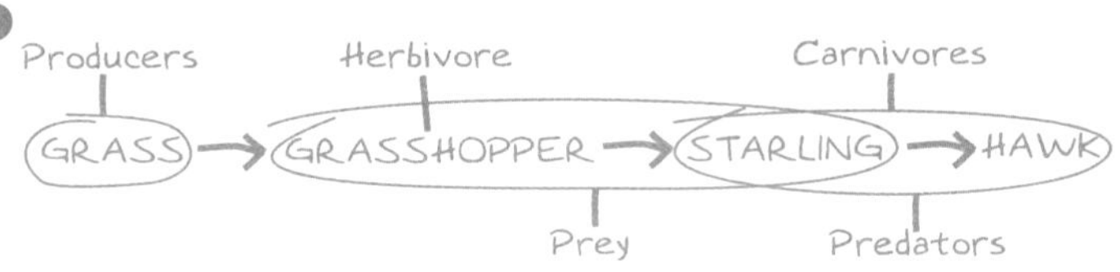

Teaching Plan pp. 188–189

INTRODUCING THE LESSON

This lesson introduces feeding relationships, food chains, and the interconnectedness of organisms within an ecosystem.

Ask students to define the terms *predator* and *prey* in their own words. Then have them identify specific examples of each.

Some students may think that coyotes are nothing but a nuisance or even dangerous. They may have read news reports about coyotes attacking household pets or even young children. Emphasize that such attacks are very rare. Also explain that coyotes play an important role in their ecosystem. After students have completed this lesson, discuss how their thoughts about coyotes may have changed.

Before You Read

THINK ABOUT IT Before students answer the question, have them name a variety of wild plants and animals in their area. Let students share their answers to the questions.

DRAW A FOOD CHAIN Ask students if they can think of a simple food chain such as the one annotated on the student page above.

Read

Here is what the Bocks observed about how coyotes and rodents interact.

The View from Bald Hill

Few animals provoke such strong and varied opinions as coyotes. They are "ruthless" if they kill livestock and they are "useful" if they kill mice and jackrabbits that otherwise might "overrun the range."

Coyotes, of course, are neither ruthless or useful. They just are, and at the Research Ranch they were welcomed as part of the natural scene. We found dens...where coyotes raised their pups, some surprisingly close to roads and houses. Coyotes hunt the mesas and washes at dawn and at dusk, mostly alone but sometimes in pairs. They watched us as intently as we watched them and usually did not run unless we got too close.

When we examined coyote scat, we found the digested remains of desert cottontails, black-tailed jackrabbits, rock squirrels, pocket mice, woodrats, harvest mice, cotton rats, white-tailed deer, mule deer, pronghorn, peccaries, cattle, grasshoppers, beetles, moths, spiders, sparrows, lizards, grass, acorns, juniper seeds, cactus fruits, and mesquite beans.

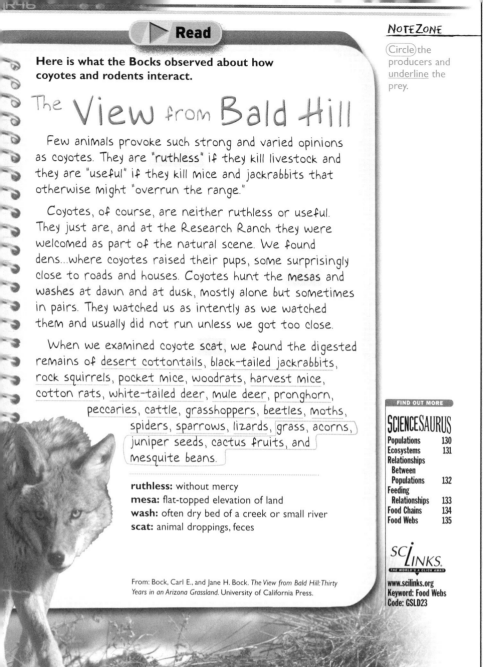

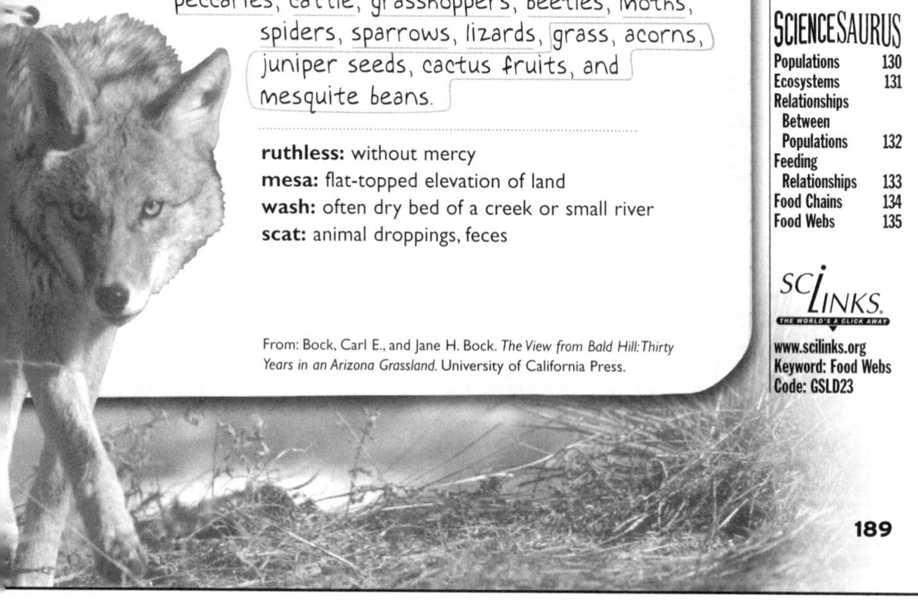

ruthless: without mercy
mesa: flat-topped elevation of land
wash: often dry bed of a creek or small river
scat: animal droppings, feces

From: Bock, Carl E., and Jane H. Bock. *The View from Bald Hill: Thirty Years in an Arizona Grassland.* University of California Press.

NOTEZONE

Circle the producers and underline the prey.

FIND OUT MORE

SCIENCESAURUS

Populations 130
Ecosystems 131
Relationships Between Populations 132
Feeding Relationships 133
Food Chains 134
Food Webs 135

SCILINKS. THE WORLD'S A CLICK AWAY

www.scilinks.org
Keyword: Food Webs
Code: GSLD23

189

(continued from page 188)

Materials

Gather the materials needed for ***Enrichment*** (below).

Enrichment

Time: 40 minutes

Materials: index cards; field guides and other research resources.

Let students do the following activity in groups of two or three. Beforehand, develop a list of ecosystems that are markedly different from the desert ecosystem described in this lesson. Write the name of each ecosystem on an index card.

Give each group an index card. Have the students in each group use the Internet and the resources you have provided to research the organisms that inhabit their assigned ecosystem. Tell students to list the names of various organisms and, for each one, find out what plants or animals the organism eats and what animals eat that organism.

Using this basic information, students should then identify at least three food chains for their ecosystem. Once the food chains are identified, students can look for "overlaps" and weave the different chains together into a food web. Let each group share its findings in a poster or bulletin board display.

Read

Encourage students to highlight any unfamiliar words or terms they find in the passage and to highlight in another color any sections that change their ideas about coyotes.

You may want to introduce the concept of food webs at this point or later in the lesson. To do this, first have students make possible desert food chains from the types of plants and animals in the selection. (They may have to look up some of the less familiar examples.) Then explain that food webs are combinations of food chains. Ask them to create food webs with producers, predators, prey, and decomposers from the desert ecosystem.

CHECK UNDERSTANDING

Skill: Organizing information

Diagram a simple food chain on the board—for example, grass → rabbit → wolf. Ask students to identify first the producer, herbivore, and carnivore in the chain and then the predator and prey. Next, have students identify organisms that could be added to form other food chains, such as clover → rabbit → wolf and clover → mouse → hawk. Finally, ask them to draw a food web that includes all the chains.

More Resources

The following resources are also available from Great Source and NSTA.

ScienceSaurus

Ecosystems 129
Populations 130
Relationships Between Populations 132
Feeding Relationships 133
Food Chains 134
Food Webs 135

Math on Call

Graphs That Compare 291
Single-Bar Graphs 292

Reader's Handbook

Elements of Graphics: Bar Graph 549

SciLinks
THE WORLD'S A CLICK AWAY

www.scilinks.org
Keyword: Food Webs
Code: GSLD23

Explore

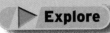

FORM A HYPOTHESIS The Bocks counted and recorded the number of rodents in an area of the Research Ranch for three years. Then they asked, "What would happen to the number of rodents if coyotes were eliminated from one area of the Research Ranch?" After asking the question, they formed a hypothesis—a prediction that can be tested.

► ***Form your own hypothesis to answer the question. Use an "if / then" sentence: IF something happens, THEN something else will happen.***

If coyotes were removed from one area of the ranch, then the number of rodents in that area would increase.

The Bocks hypothesized that if they eliminated coyotes and other predators from one area, then the number of prey animals in that area would increase. The Bocks carried out experiments to test their hypothesis. In one such experiment in 1989, they counted and recorded the number of rodents trapped in two areas of the Research Ranch. One area was open to predators. The other area was fenced off so that large predators could not eat any of the rodents, but the rodents could enter and exit the fenced-off area.

The Bocks set out thousands of traps during the year. Each trap set out overnight was called one "trap-night." They recorded the number of rodents that were trapped, then calculated the average number caught per 100 trap-nights. The following graph shows their results.

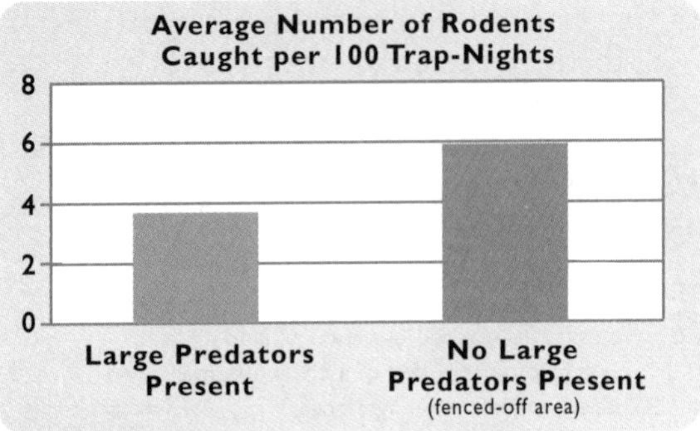

ANALYZE THE DATA

► ***Examine the results shown on the graph. Do the data support your hypothesis? Explain your answer using the data.***

Yes, the data support my hypothesis. The graph shows that the number of rodents caught in the fenced area was greater than the number caught in the unfenced area.

190

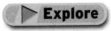

Teaching Plan pp. 190–191

Explore

FORM A HYPOTHESIS Students should be able to hypothesize that the removal of the coyotes would result in an increase in their prey.

ANALYZE THE DATA The graph shows a larger rodent population in the area where the coyotes were excluded. The data support the Bocks' hypothesis that reducing the predator population would increase the prey population. Extend this concept by having students refer back to their food webs (if they created them). Ask: *What effect might an overpopulation of rodents have on the rest of the ecosystem?* (The rodents might over-forage, depleting the food supply for other small animals. Some of them would die for lack of food. In turn, animals that rely on them for food would starve.)

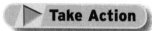

Propose Explanations

WHAT DO YOU THINK? Based on the Bocks' results, what conclusion could they draw about coyotes and rodents in the Research Ranch ecosystem?

Example: Eliminating coyotes from an area leads to an increase in the number of rodents in that area.

► *What could be the reasons for the difference in the number of rodents in the fenced and unfenced areas? Try to think of as many reasons as you can.*

The fence kept out large predators such as coyotes that feed on rodents.

IDENTIFY VARIABLES

► *What factors other than predators would affect how many rodents are in the area? (Hint: What do rodents need to survive?)*

Other factors include the amount of food and suitable nesting sites available for the rodents.

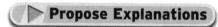

Take Action

DO RESEARCH Form groups in your class and choose an animal from the list below. Then do research to find out if any local or state agencies have plans to eliminate or control that animal. Based on what you've read about coyotes and rodents, describe the effect that killing the animal you chose would have on the ecosystem in which it lives.

Raccoons	Rats	Crows	Skunks	Foxes
Deer	Opossums	Pigeons	Woodchucks	Mice
Alligators	Snakes	Buzzards	Squirrels	

Answers will vary. Eliminating or controlling the animal would decrease the sizes of the populations of animals that eat it and would increase the sizes of the populations of animals it eats.

191

Connections

MATH Review with students the difference between a line graph and a bar graph. Ask: *What sort of data are bar graphs appropriate for?* (Bar graphs are used to compare different quantities side-by-side.) *What sort of data are line graphs appropriate for?* (Line graphs are generally used to show how values change over time.)

Assessment

Skill: Making predictions

Use the following task to assess each student's progress:

Ask students to predict what the impact might be if a new animal were introduced to the ecosystem. For example, ask: *If domestic goats were to graze on the grasslands, eating the same plants as the rodents, what might the short-term impact be? The long-term impact?* (Students might predict that if the goats ate a lot of the plants, then the number of plants would decrease. That could mean that populations of rodents that depend on those plants would decrease in the short run. In the long run, the number of coyotes and other predators that depend on the rodents for food would also decrease.)

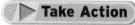

Propose Explanations

WHAT DO YOU THINK? Emphasize to students that their conclusions must be based on evidence from the Bocks' study. Accept other reasonable conclusions, such as *Predator populations help control prey populations.* If necessary, remind students not to draw conclusions that are overly broad.

IDENTIFY VARIABLES If students have difficulty thinking of factors, briefly discuss their ideas about what the rodents need in order to survive and maintain healthy populations.

Take Action

DO RESEARCH Help students research population management plans that local or state agencies might have for pests or predators in your area. (Help students as needed to find contact information for these agencies.) For instance, are the animal populations controlled by hunting seasons, sterilization, or trapping? Is there a difference between the steps taken to deal with backyard pests (such as skunks, raccoons, deer, and crows) and the steps taken to deal with potentially dangerous carnivores?

Lead students to understand that the elimination of any one population in an ecosystem can have a significant effect on other populations in that ecosystem.

Point of Lesson

Different species can survive in the same ecosystem by occupying different habitats.

Focus

- Systems, order, and organization
- Populations and ecosystems
- Diversity and adaptations of organisms
- Nature of science
- Abilities necessary to do scientific inquiry

Skills and Strategies

- Communicating
- Making inferences
- Predicting
- Interpreting data
- Drawing conclusions

Advance Preparation

Vocabulary

Make sure students understand these terms. Definitions can be found in the glossary at the end of the student book.

- community
- competition
- data
- ecosystem
- environment
- grassland
- habitat
- organism
- population
- predator
- species

(continued on page 193)

A Place of Their Own

In any ecosystem, many different organisms interact with each other. With limited resources, how do they all survive?

Every ecosystem has resources such as food sources and water. Only a certain amount of those resources is available. The Bocks asked a scientific question: How do so many things live together in an area with limited resources? In the area of the Research Ranch, the Bocks observed a number of species of sparrows and similar birds. Then they collected data that told them about the relationships between the birds and the factors in their environment, including food and nesting sites.

NOTEZONE

Underline the two possible reasons that the different bird species live in different habitats.

Read

Here are more of the Bocks' observations.

The View from Bald Hill

Sparrows are among the dullest of birds. Nearly all are brown and gray, and they spend most of their lives on the ground, quietly searching for seeds and insects while avoiding being eaten themselves. They are distinctive only when they sing to proclaim their territories and attract mates. Yet, sparrows have much to tell us about the ecology of grassland communities of which they are a part.

A dozen species of ground-dwelling and seed-eating songbirds winter regularly on the Research Ranch. Six of them are migratory and come only in winter, five are residents year round, and one is sometimes there in both winter and summer. The twelve species divide up the habitats in generally predictable ways, regardless of their numbers from one year to the next. Avian ecologists have arrived at two different explanations for the patterns they found. First, it may be the result of competition for the limited seed supply they all share.

FIND OUT MORE

SCIENCESAURUS

Factors That Affect Populations 131
Relationships Between Populations 132

TEACHING PLAN pp. 192–193

INTRODUCING THE LESSON

This lesson addresses how species live together in an ecosystem that has limited resources. Ask students to identify resources that animals need in order to survive. Have students consider what might happen when animals living in one area need the same resources.

Students may think that animals of the same general type, such as birds or insects, directly compete with each other for resources. Ask: *Do different kinds of birds build their nests in the same area? Do they eat the same food?* Explain to students that different types of birds do not always have the same requirements for survival. They may live within the same area but inhabit different places within that area. Some of them may compete for the same food, but some may eat different things.

Read

Point out that the Bocks are faced with a scientific question—how can many different species live in an area with limited resources—and two possible explanations, stated in the reading. The Bocks tested whether these explanations are supported by observable data.

Ask students to suggest two possible food chains that include sparrows—one chain with the sparrows as herbivores and the other chain with sparrows as carnivores. (herbivores: seeds → sparrows → hawks; carnivores: grass → insects → sparrows → hawks)

Perhaps each species forages most efficiently and successfully in a particular habitat and aggressively keeps other species away. A second possibility is that the birds are choosing those habitats where they are best able to avoid being eaten by predators.

distinctive: noticeably different
proclaim: declare publicly
winter: spend the winter in a place
migratory: living in different places at different times of the year
avian: relating to birds
forage: search for food

From: Bock, Carl E., and Jane H. Bock. *The View from Bald Hill: Thirty Years in an Arizona Grassland.* University of California Press.

White-crowned sparrow

Explore

ANALYZE DATA The Bocks predicted that different species of birds live in different habitats within the grassland ecosystem. To test their prediction, the Bocks set up observation stations in many different kinds of habitats on the Research Ranch. Then they observed and recorded the species of birds that appeared in each habitat. Study the table below. It shows where sparrows and other small seed-eating birds live within the ecosystem of the Research Ranch.

Species	Major Habitat
White-crowned sparrow	Heavy brush along drainages
Rufous-crowned sparrow	Shrubby ravines and tall grasslands
Canyon towee	Woodlands and shrublands
Chipping sparrow	Oak woodland
Vesper sparrow	Shrubby grasslands
Savannah sparrow	Shrubby grasslands
Cassin's sparrow	Shrubby grasslands
Eastern meadowlark	Grasslands with variable cover
Grasshopper sparrow	Open grasslands, heavy grass cover
Baird's sparrow	Open grasslands, heavy grass cover
Horned lark	Open grasslands with bare ground
Chestnut collared longspur	Open grasslands with bare ground

brush: low vegetation
drainage: area of land that drains surface water
ravine: narrow, steep valley

(continued from page 192)

Materials

Gather the materials needed for ***Science Scope Activity*** (p. 188B and p. 193).

Science Scope Activity

(continued from page 188B)

5. Use the research you and your team found to write nine questions—three for each category—that increase in difficulty.
6. Cut nine paper squares that are the size of the boxes on the game board. On one side of the square, write the question and category. On the other side, write the answer.
7. Then, in each category, arrange the questions on the game board from easiest to most difficult. On the "question" side, add the point value (100 for easiest answer, and so on).

Part 2: Playing the game

8. The first team, Team 1, picks a category. Another team reads the 100-point question from their game board. The first team uses research materials to find the answer.
9. If Team 1 answers correctly, write 1 in the appropriate square on the large score board. Team 1 continues until they miss.
10. Teams play until all squares are won. The team with the most points wins.

Explore

ANALYZE DATA Tell students to read the data in the table. Then ask: *What do you notice about the number of bird species in each habitat?* (Some habitats are occupied by one species, while other habitats are occupied by two or three different species.) *Why do you think it's possible for different species of birds to live in the same habitat?* (Sample answer: They do not require the same resources.)

CHECK UNDERSTANDING
Skill: Communicating
Ask: *What initial observations about birds prompted the Bocks to study the sparrows and their habitats?* (They observed a number of sparrows and similar birds living in the same ecosystem.) *What prediction did the Bocks make about the bird species?* (The Bocks predicted that different species live in different habitats within the ecosystem.)

More Resources

The following resources are also available from Great Source.

ScienceSaurus

Factors That Affect Populations 131
Relationships Between Populations 132

Reader's Handbook

Drawing Conclusions 41
Argument or Persuasive Writing 274

Connections

SOCIAL STUDIES Explain that the term *niche* also applies to the business world. Certain businesses provide a product to a specific group of people within the general population. For example, a small grocery store that sells only organic produce can compete with large supermarkets that do not offer many of these products. Ask students: *What other examples of niche markets do you know?* (Example: a store that sells handmade candies) *How are a niche market and a niche in a habitat alike?* (They both involve specialization that avoids direct competition.) *How are they different?* (Niche markets are focused on business profits; niches in habitats enable living organisms to survive.)

DRAW CONCLUSIONS Based on their observations, the Bocks concluded that the 12 species of birds can all survive in the ecosystem because they live in different habitats. Explain how the data in the table on page 193 support and do not support the Bocks' conclusion.

The data support the conclusion because there are up to eight different habitats that sparrows live in. The data do not support the conclusion because more than one kind of sparrow live in some of the habitats.

Propose Explanations

FILLING A NICHE Each species fills its own niche—or territory—within a habitat. For a bird, its niche provides what it needs: the food it requires, an escape from predators, and a place to nest. Some bird species have different requirements, but others compete for the same things. If two species need the same resources, the more aggressive species will usually force the weaker one out.

► ***How could different niches make it possible for the vesper sparrow and Cassin's sparrow to live in the same habitat?***

They may have different needs for food, nesting, or escaping predators, so they could share the same habitat.

The Bocks performed another experiment. They put piles of branches around the Research Ranch where there weren't any before and observed what happened. They found that grasshopper sparrows and horned larks left the area while some chipping sparrows arrived. Vesper sparrows became the most common bird species in the area.

► ***Refer to the table again. Why did the chipping sparrows and vesper sparrows arrive?***

The branches provided them with the habitat they usually live in.

► ***Given what you learned about niches, what is a possible reason the grasshopper sparrows and horned larks left?***

The chipping sparrows and vesper sparrows probably competed with them for food and forced them out.

194

Teaching Plan pp. 194–195

Explore (continued)

DRAW CONCLUSIONS Ask students to suggest reasons why different species of birds could possibly be able to live in the same habitat within an ecosystem. (Different species could live in the same habitat if they do not compete for the same food and other resources.)

Propose Explanations

FILLING A NICHE Explain to students that the time of day when a species is active also determines how it occupies a niche. Many animals, such as several species of desert rodents, are nocturnal (active only at night). They would not necessarily compete with animals in the same habitat that are not nocturnal.

MAKE PREDICTIONS Remind students that each species is adapted to survive in a certain habitat. If the habitat changes, that species will move out of the area, and other species may move in.

MAKE PREDICTIONS What if all the trees in the study area were cut down? Based on the data in the table, predict what would happen to the populations of canyon towees and chipping sparrows.

They would leave because their habitat was removed.

Take Action

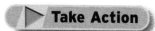

HAVE A DEBATE A construction company wants to build a mall on some land outside your town. Right now, the land is filled with weeds and shrubs. The mall would have more than 60 stores that will bring more business into your town. It will also provide hundreds of jobs for local residents. Use the spaces below to write your arguments for and against building the mall.

Class Debate Side 1: Argue in favor of building the mall.

Sample answer: The mall is good for business and will create badly needed jobs. Besides, the land is just wasteland, and new, decorative shrubs will be planted around the building.

Class Debate Side 2: Argue against building the mall.

Sample answer: What seems like a wasteland to some people is an important habitat for certain plants and animals. A change in the plants and animals in an ecosystem could have unexpected results.

▲ Chipping sparrow

195

Assessment

Skill: Predicting

Use the following questions to assess each student's progress:

Have students refer to the table on page 193. Ask: *What might happen to the birds in the Bocks' study area if unusually hot, dry weather killed all the grasses? Which species would survive in the area? Which would not be able to survive?* (The white-crowned sparrow, canyon towee, and chipping sparrow would survive; the remaining species would not.)

Take Action

HAVE A DEBATE Assign a moderator for the debate whose job it is to ensure that equal time is allowed for both sides. Remind students that they should be respectful of each other's opinions. They also should allow each other to speak without interruption, listen carefully to each other's arguments, and take notes for a counter-argument.

You may want to assign specific roles to students. For example:

- a single parent who needs a job
- a landowner who needs the money from the sale of the land to the mall developer
- a member of the town's Environmental Commission who knows what animals and plants are living there
- a nearby dairy farmer who worries that his cows would be affected by the noise and pollution caused by the increase in traffic

Point of Lesson

Humans often make changes that affect ecosystems.

Focus

- Systems, order, and organization
- Populations and ecosystems
- Populations, resources, and environments

Skills and Strategies

- Making inferences
- Recognizing cause and effect
- Organizing information
- Generating ideas

Advance Preparation

Vocabulary

Make sure students understand these terms. Definitions can be found in the glossary at the end of the student book.

- ecosystem
- environment
- food web
- organism
- species

Under the Grassland Sky

The Fragile Land

A healthy ecosystem supports a diversity of life. Even suburbs, cities, and towns have ecosystems that can be disturbed. What about the one where you live?

Human beings share an environment with many other organisms. Unlike the animals studied by the Bocks, our food and shelter often come from far-away places. Even so, we have a big impact on our surrounding ecosystems.

Explore

DIAGRAM YOUR ECOSYSTEM Think about where you live. Like the Sonoita grasslands, your suburb, city, or town is filled with living things that are all trying to survive.

- *Construct a food web of the plants and animals where you live. Also include food sources that arrive from outside the ecosystem. Draw an arrow from each organism to every other organism that eats it.*

Sample food web for a prairie ecosystem

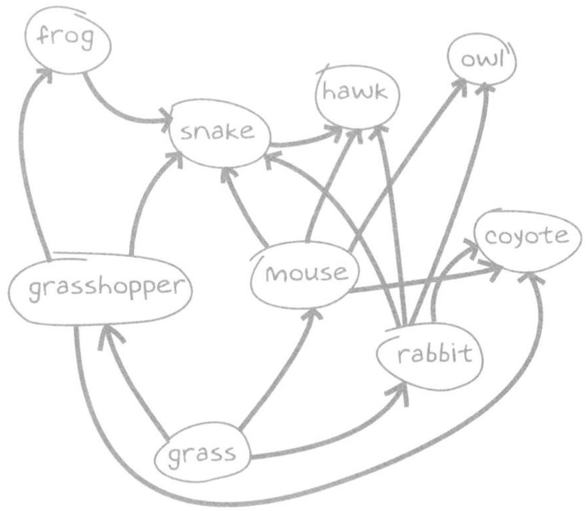

FIND OUT MORE
SCIENCESAURUS
Ecosystems 131
Factors That Affect Populations 131
Relationships Between Populations 132
Feeding Relationships 133
Food Webs 135

TEACHING PLAN pp. 196–197

INTRODUCING THE LESSON

In this lesson, students consider ways that humans affect their ecosystem. Ask students to describe the ecosystem they live in and identify resources in it.

Students may think that ecosystems exist only in undeveloped areas. Ask students if they think a big city has an ecosystem. What do they know about a city's ecosystem? (It contains plants, trees, birds, mammals, insects, and many other organisms as well as non-living factors such as water, air, and sunlight.)

Explore

DIAGRAM YOUR ECOSYSTEM Remind students that each arrow in a food web points from an organism that is being eaten to an organism that is eating it.

Food sources from outside the ecosystem might include bird food in a bird feeder, human food purchased in a supermarket, a pet cat that is allowed to roam free, and the like.

Propose Explanations

CHANGES MADE BY HUMANS Humans often make changes that affect the ecosystem. We build structures like roads, houses, dams, and bridges to make our environment more livable for ourselves. But these changes may make the environment a less friendly place for other organisms.

► *List several structures in your ecosystem that were made by people.*

Answers will vary. Example: a shopping mall

► *How do you think these structures might threaten some animals and plants in your area? How might these structures be useful to animals and plants?*

Example: The mall would threaten animals and plants by destroying their natural habitats, but the buildings could provide nesting sites for birds and the landscaping could offer new habitats.

Take Action

MAKE ROOM FOR ALL Your town needs new housing for 100 families. As a member of the Environmental Planning Commission, you want to make sure the building plan disrupts the ecosystem as little as possible.

Create a checklist for developers to fill out in order to get permission to build. Think of the types of organisms in your environment and the nonliving factors they depend on for survival. What recommendations would you make to protect plant and animal species and the environment they depend on for food and shelter?

Answers will vary. Sample checklist:

- ☐ *Doesn't cut down too many trees*
- ☐ *No endangered animals live on the site*
- ☐ *Leaves undeveloped open space between house lots*
- ☐ *Doesn't release waste or chemicals into the soil or groundwater*
- ☐ *Existing ponds, streams, and marshes are not destoyed or damaged*

197

More Resources

The following resources are also available from Great Source.

ScienceSaurus

Ecosystems 129
Factors That Affect Populations 131
Relationships Between Populations 132
Feeding Relationships 133
Food Webs 135

Reader's Handbook

Elements of Nonfiction: Cause and Effect 275
Elements of Graphics: Diagram 552

Assessment

Skill: Predicting

Use the following question to assess each student's progress:

Suppose a developer wanted to clear a wooded area to build a 50-unit housing development. How would this affect the ecosystem? (Many organisms that depend on the woods for survival would die out or would have to move to another area. Organisms that are adapted to survive in a wooded environment would move in.)

Propose Explanations

CHANGES MADE BY HUMANS Point out to students that human-made structures can also include power lines, fences, drainage pipes, cultivated land such as crop fields or gardens—anything that alters the natural environment. Remind students that not all structures are harmful to animals and plants but can sometimes offer them unique habitats. For example, red-tailed hawks whose natural habitat is high rocky cliffs have found an urban habitat in tall city buildings. This habitat also provides them with pigeons, squirrels, and rats for prey.

Take Action

MAKE ROOM FOR ALL Guide students by explaining that one way to organize their thoughts before they make the checklist is to think about cause-and-effect relationships. Suggest that they create a list of the organisms and the nonliving factors that might be found in the proposed development site. When they create the checklist, they should think about how organisms and factors might be disrupted by the development.

CHECK UNDERSTANDING

Skill: Recognizing cause and effect

Ask students to think of an environment in their area that has been altered by people but is no longer being used—for example, an abandoned building in a city neighborhood, an area that was excavated when a bridge was built but is no longer needed, or an unused animal enclosure on an old farm. Ask: *What could people do to convert the area into a more "environmentally friendly" place?* (Accept all reasonable answers.)

Rain Forest

LESSON 55

Let It Rain

Point of Lesson: ***The tapir's structural adaptations enable it to survive in its tropical rain forest ecosystem.***

This lesson introduces students to the lowland tapir, an endangered mammal that lives in the tropical rain forests of South America. Students read about the physical adaptations of this unusual animal, then evaluate how each adaptation helps it survive in its environment.

Materials

Before You Read (p. 198), for each pair:

- meter stick or metric tape measure
- adding machine tape

Read (p. 199), for the class:

- world map or globe

Science Scope Activity (p. 198B, p. 199, and p. 203), for each group:

- half-gallon juice carton
- scissors
- small paper cup
- 1-gallon plastic storage bag with twist tie
- soil
- sand
- 8–10 marigold or other flower seeds
- 4–6 bean or pea seeds
- about $\frac{1}{4}$ cup quick-growing grass seed
- water
- craft stick
- newspaper
- tape
- small index card
- Model Biome Log Sheet (copymaster pp. 230–231)

Laboratory Safety

Review the following safety guidelines with students before they do the Science Scope Activity in this lesson.

- Do not taste any substance in the laboratory.
- Handle seeds carefully so you do not inhale them.
- Keep your hands away from your face when handling soil and sand.
- Handle plants with care.
- Wash your hands thoroughly after the activity.

LESSON 56

The Seeds of Biodiversity

Point of Lesson: ***Tapirs serve an important role in maintaining the biodiversity of the tropical rain forest.***

In this lesson, students find out how tapirs' eating habits help disperse plants throughout the area of tropical rainforest where they live. Students predict how the survival of one kind of plant would be affected if tapirs were to disappear from the habitat. Students interpret a graph showing population changes for a species of tapir in Panama, then write a proposal for funding their own imaginary field research on another tropical rain forest animal.

Materials

Science Scope Activity *continued* (p. 203): See list for Lesson 55.

Laboratory Safety

See guidelines for Lesson 55.

LESSON 57

Going, Going...Gone?

Point of Lesson: ***If the deforestation of tropical rain forests is not slowed, one of Earth's most valuable ecosystems will be destroyed.***

In this lesson, students examine the issues surrounding rain forest use and conservation. They observe a satellite photo showing patterns of rain forest destruction, evaluate how various human activities affect the rain forest, and research a rain forest topic that interests them.

Materials

Introducing the Lesson (p. 206), for the class:

- United States map

Science Scope Activity

Model of a Biome

NSTA has chosen a Science Scope *activity related to the content in this chapter. The activity begins here and continues in Lesson 55, page 199, and Lesson 56, page 203.*

Time: 40–45 minutes for initial setup; 5 min/day for two weeks for follow-up observations

Materials: see page 198A

As an ongoing project throughout this chapter, students can create a model of a biome. Have students work in pairs or small groups.

At the end of the observation period, provide time for students to present their biomes to the class. Let students who created the same type of biome work together to prepare and give their presentations. Have students discuss similarities and differences between the different types of biomes.

(continued on pages 199 and 203)

Background Information

Lessons 55 and 56

There are four species in the genus *Tapirus* (tapirs). One species lives in Southeast Asia; the other three species live in Central and South America. All four species have similar feeding habits.

Lesson 57

Although tropical rain forests cover only about 7 percent of Earth's land surface, it is estimated that they contain more than half of Earth's plant and animal species. According to a group at NASA working on setting priorities for biodiversity conservation, an estimated average of 100 species will become extinct every day for the next 40 years unless effective and targeted conservation measures are implemented.

Many conservationist groups believe that efforts should be focused on rain forests because they are home to so many species, many of which have not yet been identified or studied by scientists. Over 25 percent of all drugs and 70 percent of plants with anti-cancer properties are derived from the rain forest. Medical researchers fear that the loss of tropical rain forest species could deprive us of powerful new medicines.

Point of Lesson

The tapir's structural adaptations enable it to survive in its tropical rain forest ecosystem.

Focus

- Systems, order, and organization
- Structure and function in living systems
- Populations and ecosystems
- Diversity and adaptations of organisms

Skills and Strategies

- Measuring
- Comparing and contrasting
- Making inferences
- Creating and using tables

Advance Preparation

Vocabulary

Make sure students understand these terms. Definitions can be found in the glossary at the end of the student book.

- adaptation
- behavior
- environment
- endangered species
- fossil
- habitat
- mammal
- order
- predator
- reproduce

(continued on page 199)

Let It Rain

The tapir may look unusual, but it is well adapted to survive in the Amazon rain forest.

Tropical rain forests are very wet and very warm. Average yearly rainfall is 200–450 cm, and the average temperature is about 25°C all year long. These warm, wet conditions provide a lush environment for thousands of unique plant and animal species.

Before You Read

TAKING MEASUREMENTS See how much rain actually falls in a tropical rain forest each year. Measure the rainfall on a long strip of adding machine tape. Use a meter stick or a metric tape measure to measure 200 cm and 450 cm from one end of the strip. Mark and label each measurement.

Next, use a world almanac or the Internet to find the average rainfall each year in your area. (It may be called average precipitation.) Write that information below. Then measure and mark your area's rainfall on the strip.

Average yearly rainfall in my area: ______________________

► ***How does the yearly rainfall in your area compare with the yearly rainfall in a tropical rain forest?***

Except for students who live in a rain forest environment, such as Hilo, Hawaii, or the Pacific Northwest, the rainfall in their area will be much less.

UNIT 5: ECOLOGY

Teaching Plan pp. 198–199

INTRODUCING THE LESSON

This lesson explains how an animal's adaptations help it survive in its particular habitat. Ask students what they know about the rain forest and the animals that live there. Ask if they have ever seen a tapir in a zoo or a nature film and if so, have them describe the animal. (The correct pronunciation is TAY-per.)

Before You Read

Time: 20 minutes
Materials: meter stick or metric tape measure, adding machine tape

TAKING MEASUREMENTS To help students compare their own area to the Amazon rain forest, convert the metric measurements given in the text to their English equivalents:
average temperature: 25°C = 77°F
average rainfall: 200–450 cm = $6\frac{1}{2}$–15ft

When students have marked the levels of rainfall on the adding machine tape, you may want to supervise two responsible students as they use a stepladder to tape the strip to a high wall, such as in a gym or cafeteria.

To save time, you may want to provide students with the average yearly rainfall in your local area or have them do the research as homework rather than as a classroom activity. As an extension, provide or have students look up average annual precipitation for U.S. cities with various climates—for example, Las Vegas as an example of a desert climate and New Orleans as a warm and humid climate.

Read

The tapir is one of the more unusual mammals found in a tropical rain forest.

A Rain Forest Resident

The lowland tapir [is] found in [tropical rain] forests from northern Colombia to northern Argentina....

Tapirs are the only [living] native American members of *Perissodactyla*, the ancient order to which horses and rhinoceroses belong. Like their relatives, they are far from dainty, averaging six feet (195 cm) long and three feet (85 cm) high and weighing about 440 pounds (200 kg). At one end of their hefty, rotund bodies are short, stumpy tails. At the other [end are] elongated upper lips that curve down like abbreviated elephant trunks. They use this flexible proboscis as a dining tool, sniffing out and sweeping tasty vegetation and fruits into their mouths.

They are an endangered species because their forest habitats are rapidly being logged and developed, they reproduce slowly,...and they are hugely popular game animals....

dainty: delicate
hefty: big and heavy
rotund: round, plump
stumpy: short and thick
elongated: having more length than width
abbreviated: shortened
proboscis: a long, flexible snout
game animals: wild animals that are hunted for sport or food

From: Medici, Patricia, and J. Pablo Juliá. "Scientists Trap, Tag, And Track Tapirs To Design A Survival Strategy." *Eco-Exchange*. Rainforest Alliance. (ra.org/programs/cmc/newsletter/nov01-2.html)

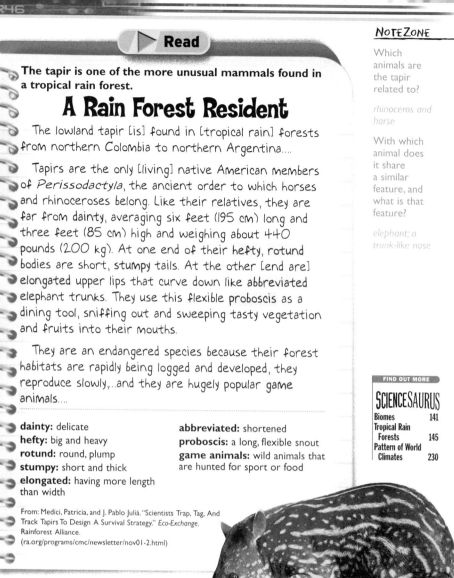

Baby tapir ►

NoteZone

Which animals are the tapir related to?

rhinoceros and horse

With which animal does it share a similar feature, and what is that feature?

elephant; a trunk-like nose

FIND OUT MORE

SCIENCESAURUS

Biomes	141
Tropical Rain Forests	145
Pattern of World Climates	230

(continued from page 198)

Materials

Gather the materials needed for ***Before You Read*** (p. 198), ***Read*** (p. 199), and ***Science Scope Activity*** (p. 198B, p. 199, and p. 203).

Science Scope Activity

(continued from page 198B)

Procedure

Give each pair of students a copy of the Model Biome Log Sheet and the following instructions:

1. Choose one of the following biomes: desert, grassland, deciduous forest, or rain forest.
2. Carefully cut one complete side from the juice carton.
3. Cover your work area with newspaper. Lay the carton on the newspaper with its open side facing up.
4. Fill the carton about 6 cm deep with soil. For a desert biome, use a mixture of one-third regular soil and two-thirds sand. For the other biomes, use just the regular soil.
5. Use the craft stick to gently push seeds about 1 cm deep into the soil, with 8–10 flower seeds at one end of the carton, 4–6 vegetable seeds in the middle, and grass seed at the other end.
6. Add water to soak the soil.

(continued on page 203)

Read

Time: 15 minutes
Materials: world map or globe

To introduce the reading, have students locate the range of the lowland tapir from northern Colombia to northern Argentina on a map or globe.

As students read about the tapir, have them rephrase the description using the words in the definitions listed below the reading. Discuss whether the rephrased description creates the same visual image and is as interesting as the original description. Point out that replacing difficult words with more familiar words can help you understand the meaning of the new words.

CHECK UNDERSTANDING

Skill: Organizing information

Have students describe the rain forest environment based on the information on these two pages. (The rain forest gets a lot of rain, and the temperature is high all year long. Thousands of unique plants and animals live in the lush environment.)

More Resources

The following resources are also available from Great Source.

SCIENCESAURUS

Biomes	141
Tropical Rain Forests	145
Pattern of World Climates	230

READER'S HANDBOOK

Reading Know-how: Making Inferences	40
Reading Science: During Reading	108
Reader's Almanac: Inference Chart	672

Connections

MATH Possibly as part of the Before You Read task, have students research temperature and precipitation data for your area and the Brazilian rain forest over a five-year period. Using these data, students can make a double-bar graph comparing the two areas' precipitation and a double-line graph comparing temperatures. Ask students to explain why a bar graph is appropriate for the precipitation data and a line graph for the temperature data. (Bar graphs are used to show the same kind of data at different times. Line graphs are used to show changes over time.)

Explore

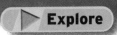

THINK ABOUT IT Adaptations are physical or behavioral features that help a species survive and reproduce in its environment. For example, adaptations might help a species gather food, escape from predators, catch prey, locate and attract others of its species, or survive harsh conditions such as extreme heat or cold.

Based on fossil evidence, scientists have concluded that the tapir's physical features and behavior haven't changed much over the last 20 million years.

► ***What does this tell you about the tapir's habitat long ago?***

Its habitat was probably similar to the tropical rain forests where it lives today and probably has not changed much during that time.

Like its ancient ancestors, the tapir today is a large, heavy animal with a long snout, powerful jaws, excellent swimming skills, and a vegetarian diet. Because of its heavy, round body, you might think that the tapir is easily caught by predators. Actually, when a tapir is threatened, it can escape quickly by running into thick, low brush. If it is near a body of water, it can escape by swimming away.

MAKE INFERENCES Look at the chart on the next page. The left column identifies many of the tapir's adaptations. Using what you've read so far and what you know about other animals, fill in the right side of the chart. Explain how each adaptation might help tapirs survive. The first answer is done for you.

Adult tapir ▲

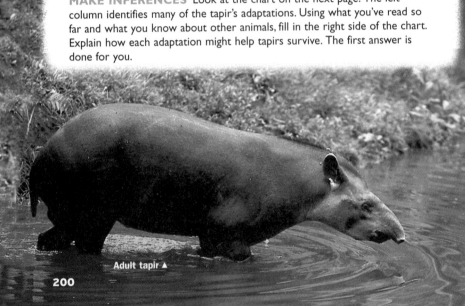

TEACHING PLAN pp. 200–201

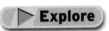

Explore

THINK ABOUT IT To introduce the concept of adaptations, lead a discussion about the adaptations of wild animals that live in your area. For example, if students live in a cold climate, discuss the structural adaptations and behaviors that help local animals survive the winter. In a desert climate, talk about the adaptations that help animals survive in an arid environment with extreme temperatures.

Point out that although the tapir's adaptations have enabled it to survive for 20 million years, all four species of tapir are now endangered. Ask students to suggest factors that might be causing or contributing to the species' decline. (Based on their prior learning, students will probably be able to suggest factors such as hunting, heavy predation by nonnative species that have been introduced into the area, and habitat destruction caused by logging, farming, and ranching.)

MAKE INFERENCES Remind students that their inferences should be based on the text but that not all the information they need will be in the text. To get started, ask students to brainstorm the kinds of situations that tapirs are likely to face in the rain forest. Prompt students to think about how the tapir's adaptations help it find food, escape predators, and move around the forest.

Adaptations of the Tapir	How These Adaptations Help the Tapir Survive in the Rain Forest
long, flexible snout that can pull and move objects	helps push food into its mouth
thick, hard, tough skin	*protects it against the bites of insects or predators; protects it against being injured when it moves through thorny plants or sharp branches*
powerful jaws	*help defend it against predators; help it chew tough or hard foods*
large size; great strength; powerful legs	*help it fight or run away from predators*
strong swimmer; can even walk along the bottom of streams and rivers	*helps it escape predators or move to a new food source*
Baby tapirs have striped and spotted coats.	*makes the babies blend into their surroundings and hide from predators*

Take Action

AMAZON ADAPTATIONS Research another animal that lives in the tropical rain forests of South America. Identify some of the animal's adaptations. Explain how each adaptation helps it survive. Present your findings in a chart similar to the tapir chart on this page.

Animal choices and charts will vary.

201

Assessment

Skill: Recognizing cause and effect

Use the following question to assess each student's progress:

What adaptations do tapirs have that help them survive in the rain forest? (Students could name any of the adaptations included in the chart on this page.)

Take Action

AMAZON ADAPTATIONS You might want to provide a list of animals for students to choose from, including those listed at right. To make research more efficient, students who choose the same animal could work together in pairs or small groups. When students have completed their charts, have them compare their findings to determine whether there are any similarities between different animals. Point out that unrelated species living in the same environment may have evolved similar adaptations. (This process, called *convergent evolution*, is described in more detail in Chapter 7, Lesson 21.)

- red piranha (*Serrasalmus nattereri*)
- spectacled caiman (*Caiman crocodilus*)
- red howler monkey (*Aloutta seniculs*)
- anaconda (*Eunectes murinus*)
- jaguar (*Panthera onca*)
- basilisk (*Basiliscus plumifrons*)
- Amazon river dolphin (*Inia geoffrensis*)
- sloth (*Choloepus didactylus*)
- three-toed sloth (*Bradypus variegates*)
- kinkajou (*Potos flavus*)
- yellow and black poison arrow frog (*Dendrobates leucomelas*)
- red-eyed tree frog (*Agalychnis calidryas*)
- toucan (*Ramphastos toco*)
- bush dog (*Speothos venaticus*)
- giant otter (*Pteronura brasiliensis*)

UNIT 5 Ecology

CHAPTER 19 / LESSON 56

Point of Lesson

Tapirs serve an important role in maintaining the biodiversity of the tropical rain forest.

Focus

- Systems, order, and organization
- Structure and function in living systems
- Populations and ecosystems
- Diversity and adaptations of organisms

Skills and Strategies

- Generating ideas
- Predicting
- Creating and using graphs
- Making inferences
- Communicating

Advance Preparation

Vocabulary

Make sure students understand these terms. Definitions can be found in the glossary at the end of the student book.

- behavior
- environment
- energy
- extinct
- habitat
- mammal
- organism
- population
- predator
- seed
- species
- wildlife preserve

Rain Forest

The Seeds of Biodiversity

As tapirs eat their way through the rain forest, they help preserve it.

Patricia Medici and Juan Pablo Juliá are South American scientists who study the lowland tapir. Together, they work on Project Tapir, a research project to learn about the behavior of this strange-looking creature. Their goal is to figure out how to save the endangered tapir from extinction. They also study how to protect the wide variety, or diversity, of species that live in the rain forest.

Project Tapir began in 1996 in Morro do Diabo State Park near São Paulo, Brazil. Medici estimates that there are about 400 tapirs in this wildlife preserve. She and Juliá have trapped, collared, and tracked 18 tapirs during the past five years. Through their studies, they have learned a great deal about the tapirs' habits and movements.

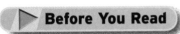

Before You Read

SPECIES INTERACT Select a wild animal that lives in your area. Describe some of the ways that this animal interacts with other organisms and with nonliving things in its natural environment. How could you find out more about your animal's behavior?

Answers will vary. Example: A pelican interacts with fish by eating them. It interacts with humans by avoiding them. It flies from place to place and perches on piers and the prows of boats in the harbor. It also floats on the water. I could find out more about this bird's behavior by watching it or by researching it on the Internet or in books.

Teaching Plan pp. 202–203

INTRODUCING THE LESSON

This lesson discusses the tapir's niche in the rain forest ecosystem, from distributing the seeds of fruits and other plants to providing food for predators.

Lead a class discussion about biodiversity. If students are unfamiliar with the term, have them break it into parts to figure out its meaning. (*bio*—life; *diversity*—variety) Ask students how maintaining biodiversity in the rain forest could be important for humans.

Students may think that because rain forests cover only a small percentage of Earth's surface, they must contain only a small number of plant and animal species. Explain that the lush environment in rain forests makes them home to about half the world's plant and animal species.

Before You Read

SPECIES INTERACT As a class, brainstorm a list of wild animals that live in your area and a list of nonliving factors in the environment. Ask students: *What are some ways that wild animals interact with their environment?* (Examples: finding food, escaping predators, finding places to sleep and raise young) Encourage students to use their answers to this question to guide them as they complete the activity.

Read

Tapirs cannot digest the seeds in the fruit they eat. This is good news for the rain forest!

How Tapirs Spread Seeds

Tapirs are extremely important to the health and **biodiversity** of tropical forests, because they are among the best **agents** of seed **dispersal**. Like [many] other mammals that are **herbivores**, they lack the **enzymes** that can digest plant **cellulose**, so their stomachs have separate **chambers** where microorganisms live and digest the vegetation. Since this isn't a very efficient system, they must [eat] large quantities of plants and fruits for sufficient energy....

[Then, the tapir expels large] amounts of droppings, which are loaded with seeds and other undigested material. Seeds dropped by roaming tapirs grow into the same plants and trees that provide future tapirs—and of course, many other animals—with future meals and shelter. "Morro do Diabo would be a very different forest if we didn't have tapirs," [biologist Patricia] Medici acknowledges.

biodiversity: the variety of species in an environment
agents: causes
dispersal: scattering
herbivores: animals that eat only plants
enzymes: chemicals in the digestive system that help break down food
cellulose: tough fibers found in plants
chambers: sections

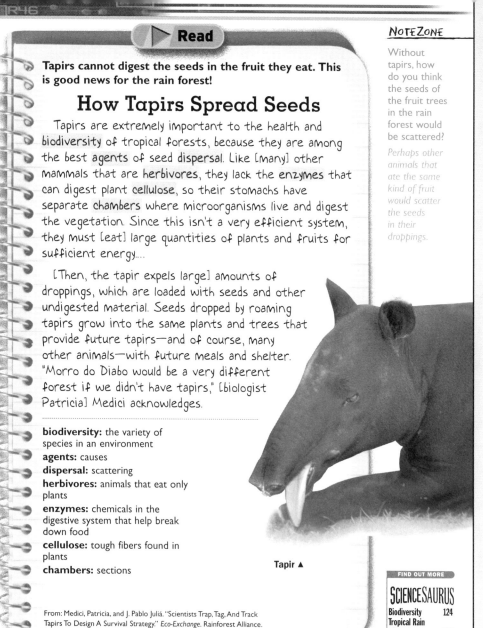

Tapir ▲

From: Medici, Patricia, and J. Pablo Juliá. "Scientists Trap, Tag, And Track Tapirs To Design A Survival Strategy." *Eco-Exchange*. Rainforest Alliance. (ra.org/programs/cmc/newsletter/nov01-2.html)

NOTEZONE

Without tapirs, how do you think the seeds of the fruit trees in the rain forest would be scattered?

Perhaps other animals that ate the same kind of fruit would scatter the seeds in their droppings.

FIND OUT MORE

SCIENCESAURUS

Biodiversity 124
Tropical Rain Forests 145

Science Scope Activity

(continued from page 199)

7. Put the biome in the plastic bag and tie the bag tightly closed.
8. Write your name and the biome type on an index card and tape it to the bag.
9. Put your biome in one of these locations:
   - desert biome—in direct sunlight
   - grassland or deciduous forest biome—in filtered sunlight, moderate temperature
   - rain forest biome—in a hot area such as near a radiator or heat vent.
10. Fill out the top of your Model Biome Log Sheet and check it to see how much water and light your biome requires. Visit your biome every day to remove it from the bag and adjust the water and light levels if needed.
11. Spend five minutes each day examining your biome and entering your observations on the Log Sheet.
12. When plant sprouts appear, remove the biome from its plastic bag. If you have a rain forest biome, keep it in the bag for three more days after sprouts appear.
13. Continue making and recording observations for two more weeks.
14. At the end of the two-week period, answer the questions at the end of the Log Sheet and give it to your teacher.

Read

Before students read the passage, briefly review the process of digestion. Make sure students understand that indigestible materials such as seeds and tough cellulose fibers pass through the tapir's system intact.

Draw students' attention to the map on the previous page. Point out that Morro do Diabo State Park is a wildlife preserve consisting of 86,450 acres (35,000 hectares) of protected lowland Atlantic rain forest. Explain that a wildlife preserve is a place where wild plants and animals are protected by the national government. Ask students why they think it is important to designate areas of rain forest as wildlife preserves. (Students may know that many rain forest species are endangered; setting aside an area of rain forest as a wildlife preserve helps protect the species from becoming extinct.)

CHECK UNDERSTANDING

Skill: Organizing information

Ask students: *Is it better for the rain forest if the tapirs eat more fruits or less? Why?* (Better; if they eat more fruits, they will drop more seeds, which will enable more new plants to grow.)

More Resources

The following resources are also available from Great Source.

ScienceSaurus

Biodiversity 124
Tropical Rain Forests 145

Math on Call

Graphs That Show Change Over Time 297
Single-Line Graphs 298
Correlation Versus Cause and Effect 309

Reader's Handbook

Reading Know-how: Finding the Main Idea 54
Elements of Nonfiction: Cause and Effect 275
Elements of Graphics: Line Graph 554

Connections

SOCIAL STUDIES Tropical rain forests are the source of many products used throughout the world. Have students brainstorm (or research) a list of rain forest products. (Examples: nuts, coffee, coconuts, bananas, woods such as teak and mahogany, and plants used in body care products and medicines)

Explore

TAPIR TRACKS To learn about the tapir, Juliá and Medici tracked its paths through the forest. From careful observation, they learned some surprising information about this species' habits. Medici likes to describe the tapirs as "landscape detectives" because their movements show conservationists exactly which parts of the rain forest need protection.

Palm fruits are one of the tapir's favorite foods. It must eat large quantities of these plants to survive. Palm fruits are also a popular food for humans in the area. But the trunk of the palm tree is hard and slippery, making it difficult to climb. So, to get the fruit, the people chop down the trees. In contrast, when the tapirs eat the fruit that falls from the trees, they help spread the palm fruit's seeds. Some of the seeds will eventually grow into new trees.

▸ ***If the tapir became extinct, what do you think would happen to the palm trees? Why?***

The number of palm trees would probably decrease because tapirs would no longer scatter their seeds.

▸ ***Tapirs are hunted and eaten by jaguars, crocodiles, and people. How would these predators be affected if the tapir became extinct?***

The tapir's predators would have to hunt and eat other animals.

Propose Explanations

POPULATION DENSITY Other scientists have tracked the tapir population on Barro Colorado Island in Panama. The graph on the next page shows the density of the tapir population from 1920 to 1990. "Density" means the average number of tapirs per square kilometer of forest.

▸ ***When did the tapir species come closest to extinction in this area? Explain why.***

In the late 1930s; the tapirs were being hunted by humans.

204

Teaching Plan pp. 204–205

Explore

TAPIR TRACKS As students read and answer the questions, encourage them to identify ways in which tapirs and humans interact. (Humans study tapirs; both humans and tapirs eat palm fruits; humans hunt and eat tapirs.) Ask students to predict what would happen to tapirs if humans harvested all the palm fruits. (Tapirs would have to find another food supply.) Ask what would happen to the palm trees in this situation. (Their numbers would diminish because all the trees eventually would be cut down and tapirs would not be able to redistribute the seeds.)

Encourage students to draw a food web showing the relationships described on this page and then draw another diagram showing what the food web would look like if tapirs became extinct. (Students' diagrams should show that the extinction of tapirs would affect all other organisms in the web.)

Propose Explanations

POPULATION DENSITY Tell students that Barro Colorado is widely used for rain forest research. The island has an area of 15 km^2 (6 sq mi) and has been a protected rain forest since 1923. Ask students to explain why the island is a good site for wildlife research. (Students may realize that the island is a small, isolated ecosystem, which makes it easier for researchers to keep track of the animals in the area.)

Point out that the numbers on the graph's vertical axis identify the number of tapirs *per square kilometer.* Ask

▶ ***When did the tapir's numbers increase, and why?***

From the mid-1930s to the mid-1970s; humans brought more tapirs back into the area. From the 1960s to the 1980s; humans provided additional food for the tapirs.

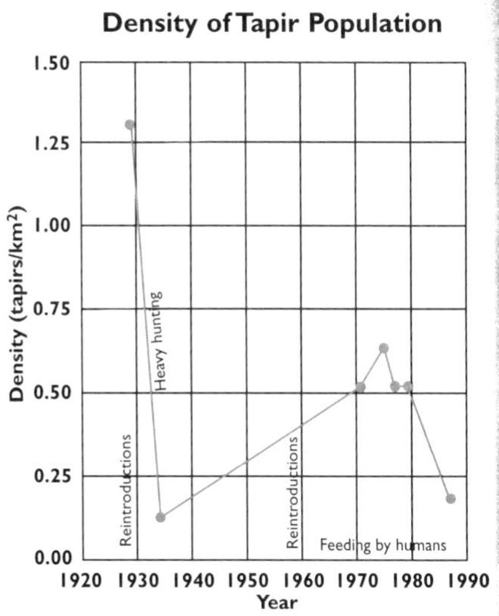

▶ ***The tapir's numbers decreased sharply again after 1975, even though people were feeding them. What might have caused this decline? (Hint: Review the reading on page 199.)***

Answers will vary. Examples: Many of the tapir's forest habitats might have been destroyed by human activities. The tapirs might have become dependent on people for food and couldn't find food on their own anymore. A deadly disease might have struck the tapirs in 1975.

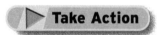

Take Action

FUNDING THE RAIN FOREST Imagine you are a scientist researching an animal that lives in the rain forest. Choose the rain forest animal you would like to study. Then write a proposal to the National Science Foundation (NSF) requesting funding to carry out your research. Include the following in your proposal:

- a description of the animal
- why you want to study it
- what makes it an important research subject
- how it lives in its habitat (what it eats, how it moves around, how it escapes predators)
- why you need funding to carry out your research

Students' proposals will vary.

Assessment

Skill: Making inferences

Use the following questions to assess each student's progress:

▶ *Why are scientists concerned about declining numbers of tapirs in the rain forest?* (Tapirs serve an important function in the rain forest; if tapirs did not spread seeds, some plants might not be able to reproduce and would die out.)

▶ Allow students to use the graph on this page to answer the following question: *What roles have humans played in helping or hurting the tapir population on Barro Colorado Island?* (Humans reintroduced tapirs to the island in 1930. During the 1930s, humans hunted tapirs heavily. Humans reintroduced tapirs again in 1960 and fed them from that time until the late 1980s.)

students to calculate the total number of tapirs on the island for each data point on the graph, given the island's area of 15 km^2. (1930—19 or 20; 1933—1 or 2; 1970—7 or 8; 1975—9 or 10; 1978 to 1980—7 or 8; 1988—2 or 3)

Students may think the graph shows that being fed by humans caused the tapir's numbers to decrease. Remind students that the graph shows a correlation between these two events but not necessarily a cause-and-effect relationship. Ask students to suggest questions for further research into the causes of the tapir population's declining numbers.

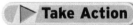

Take Action

FUNDING THE RAIN FOREST Encourage students to write their proposals for the animals they researched in Take Action on page 201. Students could create brochures to accompany their proposals, using text and images to support their requests for funding.

In a class discussion before students write their proposals, have them discuss what they think makes an animal a good candidate for research. When students complete their proposals, let each pair or group identify their animal and explain why it is an important research subject. Challenge the class to decide which animals would be the best candidates and which research projects should receive funding.

Point of Lesson

If the deforestation of tropical rain forests is not slowed, one of Earth's most valuable ecosystems will be destroyed.

Focus

- Systems, order, and organization
- Populations, resources, and environments
- Risks and benefits
- Science and technology in society

Skills and Strategies

- Interpreting scientific illustrations
- Making inferences
- Comparing and contrasting
- Organizing information
- Generating ideas

Advance Preparation

Vocabulary

Make sure students understand these terms. Definitions can be found in the glossary at the end of the student book.

- ecosystem
- satellite
- species

Materials

Gather the materials needed for *Introducing the Lesson* (p. 206).

Going, Going...Gone?

Earth's most complex ecosystems—tropical rain forests—are rapidly being destroyed by human activity.

During the 1990s, more than 15 million hectares (almost 58,000 square miles) of tropical rain forest were lost every year. At that rate, all of Earth's tropical rain forests could be gone in only 75 to 100 years.

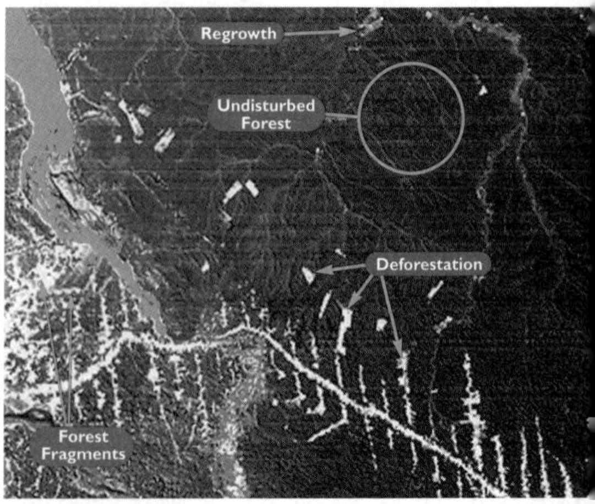

▲Satellite image of rain forest in Brazil

Explore

PICTURES FROM SPACE How do scientists know how much rain forest has been destroyed? The National Aeronautics and Space Administration (NASA) has been studying rain forest destruction for many years. NASA uses satellites orbiting Earth to take pictures of rain forests around the world. By analyzing these images, scientists can tell how much of a rain forest has been cleared and how much remains.

- ***Examine the satellite image above. Areas of rain forest that have been cleared are shown in white. What do you think the straight white lines represent?***

roads that have been built through the rain forest

WHY DO PEOPLE CLEAR RAIN FORESTS? Three types of human activities are responsible for most rain forest destruction—farming, cattle ranching, and logging. Here are some questions you might want to investigate.

- ***Most rain forest land is cleared using a method called* slash and burn*. What is slash and burn? How does it damage the land? When can it actually be good for the land?***

UNIT 5: ECOLOGY 206

TEACHING PLAN pp. 206–207

INTRODUCING THE LESSON
Time: 20 minutes
Materials: United States map

This lesson outlines the issues surrounding the deforestation and conservation of rain forests. To help students understand the rate of deforestation stated in the text, point out that the state of Georgia has an area of 15,257,705 hectares (58,910 square miles), which is slightly larger than the area of rain forest lost each year during the 1990s. Have students locate Georgia on a U.S. map.

Explore

PICTURES FROM SPACE If students have difficulty answering the question, have them compare the satellite image to a road map.

WHY DO PEOPLE CLEAR RAIN FORESTS? Encourage students to suggest ways to find more information on each of the four issues listed in this section, including keywords to use in an Internet search.

WHAT ARE SOME OTHER CHOICES? Invite someone who is involved in ecotourism, sustainable harvesting, or shade agriculture in the rain forest to visit your classroom. Have students prepare a list of questions before the visit.

- *What is subsistence farming? Why do so many local people need to clear land to raise crops? How do subsistence farmers help take care of the land?*
- *Loggers use selective cutting to obtain valuable wood such as mahogany and teak. What is selective cutting? How does it help preserve a rain forest? How does it damage the forest?*
- *Who buys the meat from cattle that were raised on ranches cleared from tropical rain forests?*

WHAT ARE SOME OTHER CHOICES? Conservationists, government officials, and local people are working together. They are trying to find ways to preserve rain forests and still meet people's needs. You might want to investigate these questions.

- *What is ecotourism? How does it help preserve rain forests? In what ways can it damage a rain forest? How does it benefit a nation's economy? How does it benefit local people?*
- *What does sustainable harvesting mean? How does it help preserve rain forests? How do local people benefit? What types of resources are harvested?*
- *What is shade agriculture? Which types of plants can be grown using this farming method?*

FIND OUT MORE
SCILINKS. THE WORLD'S A CLICK AWAY
www.scilinks.org
Keyword: Rainforest
Code: GSLD24

Take Action

FINDING ANSWERS Decide on a rain forest topic that interests you. Choose one or more of the questions posed in this lesson, or think of your own questions. Use the library or Internet resources to find the answers to the questions.

Cleared rain forest ▸

More Resources

The following resources are also available from Great Source and NSTA.

READER'S HANDBOOK

Reading a Website 514–526

SCILINKS. THE WORLD'S A CLICK AWAY

www.scilinks.org
Keyword: Rainforest
Code: GSLD24

Assessment

Skill: Recognizing cause and effect

Use the following task to assess each student's progress:

Ask students to identify three ways that humans use the rain forest and describe the benefits and drawbacks of each use. (Answers will vary, but students should recognize that most human uses of the rain forest have both benefits and drawbacks.)

Take Action

FINDING ANSWERS Students could work individually, in pairs, or in small groups. Encourage groups to divide the research tasks and then work together to compile their findings into a report or short presentation. Help students select keywords to use in an Internet search. Also suggest the Web sites listed at right. When students have completed their research, provide class time for them to present their findings.

Tropical Rain Forest Information Center
www.bsrsi.msu.edu/trfic

Rainforest Action Network
www.ran.org/info_center

Rainforest Alliance
www.ra.org

CHECK UNDERSTANDING

Skill: Recognizing cause and effect

Ask: *What human activities are responsible for most rain forest destruction?* (farming, cattle ranching, and logging) *If the current rate of rain forest destruction continues, how long will it be before all tropical rain forests are gone?* (75–100 years)

Protecting Earth

LESSON 58

The Lesson of Easter Island

Point of Lesson: ***The earliest civilization on Easter Island destroyed the island's natural resources.***

In this lesson, students ponder the historical disaster that destroyed the natural ecology of Easter Island. Through an excerpt from a magazine article, students are introduced to the remote, mysterious island and its enigmatic giant statues. They then compare changes that Easter Islanders made with similar changes that have been made in their own communities. Students are encouraged to explain why Easter Islanders did not have the same options that their own communities have for dealing with the effects of habitat destruction.

Materials

Enrichment (p. 209), for each group:
- brick
- 8–10 wooden dowels about 5" (13 cm) long
- shims and other small pieces of wood
- heavy string
- scissors
- spring scale
- trowel

Propose Explanations (p. 210), for the class:
- world map

Take Action (p. 211), for the class:
- research sources about Easter Island

Laboratory Safety

Review the following safety guidelines with students before they do the Enrichment activity in this lesson:
- Handle the brick and trowel carefully. Do not drop them on anyone.
- Do not use the spring scale to lift the brick off the ground. You would break the spring scale.
- Wash your hands thoroughly after the activity.

LESSON 59

People Make a Difference

Point of Lesson: ***Human population growth has a direct impact on aquatic ecosystems.***

Students investigate how human needs and human population growth correlate with damage to aquatic ecosystems. They interpret a graph showing changes in the size of the human population over the past 2,000 years and relate increasing population to possible increases in loss of aquatic ecosystems.

Materials

none

LESSON 60

Be an Eco-Hero

Point of Lesson: ***Biodiversity can be found in even a small plot of land.***

Biodiversity is the focus of this lesson. Students first consider that many organisms are small and may escape notice. They then read a book excerpt about the incredible number of species living on Earth. An activity takes students outdoors to explore biodiversity close to home through a survey of species in a nearby plot of land.

Materials

Enrichment (p. 215), for the class:
- science or ecology textbooks
- field guides for various ecosystems

Activity (p. 216), for each group:
- meter stick or metric tape measure
- 12 sticks about 10–15 cm long
- string, 25 m
- notebook
- pencil
- large sheet of plain white paper
- trowel or large spoon
- index cards
- magnifier
- field guides

Connections (p. 216), for the class:
- world map

Take Action (p. 217), for the class:
- research sources about biodiversity

Laboratory Safety

Review the following safety guidelines with students before they do the Activity in this lesson.
- Do this activity in an authorized area with other people. Do not work alone.
- Prepare for working outdoors by dressing appropriately for the conditions.
- Observe safety precautions around traffic and other hazards.
- If you have an allergy to any insects or plants, take precautions to avoid them.
- Exercise care when working with living things. Do not handle unidentified plants or animals.
- Wash your hands thoroughly after the activity.

Background Information

Lesson 58

By studying pollen from core samples taken from swamps and ponds, scientists have determined that Easter Island was once home to a lush subtropical forest and at least 25 species of nesting birds. However, according to pollen records, deforestation on Easter Island was in an advanced stage by the year A.D. 800; core samples from this time contain charcoal from wood fires but very little tree pollen. By the 1400s, most of the trees and every species of land bird on the island had become extinct.

Lesson 59

According to the United Nations, Earth's human population is estimated to grow from around 6 billion to approximately 9.3 billion by the year 2050, with all of the population growth occurring in developing countries. Today's 49 least-developed countries are projected to almost triple in population, from 668 million to 1.86 billion people. While population growth causes problems for aquatic ecosystems around the world, the poorest countries currently face the most challenges from pollution and water degradation. Rates of consumption increase as the population increases, but they also increase within a population as incomes grow. These factors pose a serious threat to aquatic ecosystems worldwide.

Lesson 60

At this point, no one is sure how many different species live on Earth. At the same time, the International Union for the Conservation of Nature and Natural Resources estimates that the rate of extinction is much higher than would be expected through natural processes. Over the past 400 years, 611 extinctions have been documented. This is thought to be less than the actual number of extinctions because a large number of living species have not yet been identified and therefore their extinctions may have passed unnoticed.

Point of Lesson
The earliest civilization on Easter Island destroyed the island's natural resources.

Focus
- Change, constancy, and measurement
- Populations, resources, and environments

Skills and Strategies
- Generating ideas
- Creating and using tables
- Making inferences
- Comparing and contrasting
- Recognizing cause and effect
- Concept mapping

Advance Preparation

Vocabulary
Make sure students understand these terms. Definitions can be found in the glossary at the end of the student book.
- continent
- environment
- population

Materials
Gather the materials needed for ***Enrichment*** (p. 209), ***Propose Explanations*** (p. 210), and ***Take Action*** (p. 211).

Protecting Earth

The Lesson of Easter Island

Hundreds of giant stone statues are scattered across Easter Island. They are the remains of a society that once thrived on the island.

Easter Island is a tiny island in the Pacific Ocean, known best for its many ancient stone statues. The island is very isolated. It is more than 2,000 miles (3,200 km) from the nearest continent, South America, and 1,400 miles (2,240 km) from the nearest island where people live. The first people on Easter Island probably arrived around 400 A.D. At that time, the island was covered by lush subtropical forests. Eventually, as many as 20,000 people lived there.

Today there are no trees over 10 feet (3 m) tall on the island, and it is home to only about 2,000 people. Researchers who studied Easter Island discovered that the ancient society used up the island's resources. They wiped out the forests and drove plants and animals to extinction. Evidence shows this happened in just a few hundred years. The loss of resources led to the destruction of the island society.

Before You Read

GENERATE IDEAS The stone statues on Easter Island are as tall as 66 feet (20 m) and weigh up to 270 tons (245 metric tons). The islanders carved the statues in one place and then moved them to other places. Yet, the people didn't have the heavy equipment we have today—only trees, shrubs, vines, and their own muscle power. They did not even have horses or other large animals!

- ***How might the islanders have moved the statues?***

Answers will vary. Example: They might have used tree trunks as rollers. They could have put the statues on rollers and pulled them with ropes made from vines.

Teaching Plan pp. 208–209

INTRODUCING THE LESSON

This lesson examines a dramatic example of humans causing drastic and permanent changes in an environment with limited resources. Ask students to tell you what they know about how humans change their environment. Students may think that only technologically advanced societies can permanently alter an environment. Remind students that some of the changes to the Amazon rain forest are being made by indigenous peoples. Tell them about the dodo and the moa, two bird species that were hunted to extinction by the Maori people after they arrived in New Zealand roughly 1,000 years ago.

No one knows exactly when the first settlers arrived on Easter Island or where they came from. Archaeological and linguistic evidence indicates that it was sometime between A.D. 400 and A.D. 700. Their precise origins remain a mystery.

Before You Read

GENERATE IDEAS Ask students what they think their area was like before European settlers arrived and how it has changed since then. Also ask them to imagine what their area would be like if it were isolated and they could not have any contact with the "outside world." How would people obtain food, building materials, and other supplies? What would people have to do to make sure they did not pollute or run out of the resources they need?

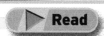

Read

It took only a few hundred years for the people of Easter Island to destroy the island's environment.

Easter's End

[Easter Island's] growing population was cutting the forest more rapidly than the forest was regenerating. The people used the land for gardens and the wood for fuel, canoes, and houses—and...for lugging statues. As the forest disappeared, the islanders ran out of timber and rope to transport and [set up] their statues. Life became more uncomfortable—springs and streams dried up, and wood was no longer available for fires.

People also found it harder to fill their stomachs, as land birds, large sea snails, and many seabirds disappeared. Because timber for building seagoing canoes vanished, fish catches declined and porpoises disappeared from the table. Crop yields also declined, since deforestation allowed the soil to be eroded by rain and wind [and] dried by the sun....

By around 1700, the population began to crash toward between one-quarter and one-tenth of its former number.... Rival clans started to [push over] each other's statues, breaking the heads off....

As we...imagine the decline of Easter's civilization, we ask ourselves, "Why didn't they...realize what they were doing and stop before it was too late?"

▲Statues on Easter Island

regenerating: growing again
lugging: dragging
timber: wood
crop yields: fruit and vegetable harvests
deforestation: destruction of the forest
eroded: washed or blown away
rival: competing

From: Diamond, Jared. "Easter's End." *Discover*

NOTEZONE

Circle the reasons why the population began to crash.

FIND OUT MORE

SCIENCESAURUS

Ecosystems 129
Populations 130
Factors That Affect Populations 131

Enrichment

Time: 35–45 minutes

Materials: (for each group) brick; 8–10 wooden dowels about 5" (13 cm) long; shims and other small pieces of wood; heavy string; scissors; spring scale; trowel

Note: This activity is best done on a flat, even soil surface outdoors so students can dig a shallow hole and tip the base of the "statue" into it when they stand the statue upright.

Divide the class into small groups. Tell students to imagine that they are Easter Islanders who want to move a huge stone statue (represented by the brick) from the place where it was carved to where it will be set up. They must start with the brick lying flat on the ground, pull it with the spring scale for 3 meters, then raise it so it is standing upright. They can use any of the materials you have provided, but they must pull the brick with a force of no more than 5 newtons. When all groups have solved the problem, let each group demonstrate its technique to the class.

Read

Have students recall their answers to the Before You Read question. Ask: *What equipment would the Easter Islanders have needed in order to transport their statues?* (wheels or rollers, ropes) *What materials could they have used to make these things?* (logs, vines) *Where would they get those materials?* (the forests on the island) *How do you think the methods they used to move the statues would have contributed to the destruction of Easter Island's ecosystem?* (As the islanders cut down more and more trees, the forests grew smaller and smaller until they disappeared. Without trees to shade the soil and hold it in place with their roots, the soil dried out and then was eroded by rain and wind. Land birds that lived in the forests no longer supplied food, and canoes could no longer be built.)

CHECK UNDERSTANDING

Skill: Communicating

Have students draw a pair of illustrations or diagrams showing the environment on Easter Island when the population thrived and then after the population crashed. (Students should include as many different resources and products as possible—such as trees, crops, and canoes—and clearly show the changes that took place.)

More Resources

The following resources are also available from Great Source.

SCIENCESAURUS

Ecosystems	129
Populations	130
Factors That Affect Populations	131

READER'S HANDBOOK

Elements of Textbooks: Maps	163
Reading a Magazine Article	234

Connections

LANGUAGE ARTS Tell students to imagine that they are Easter Islanders living at the time when changes to the environment are just starting to be noticed. Have them write a journal entry describing what they see happening around them, what they think might be causing it, and what, if anything, they think should be done about it.

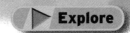

Explore

COMPARE EASTER ISLAND AND YOUR COMMUNITY Easter Island serves as a model of what can happen when humans destroy their environment. Think of places in your community where the natural environment has been changed due to human use such as building roads, dams, and other structures. To compare Easter Island with your community, fill in the chart below. In the first column, identify something humans did that changed the environment on Easter Island. In the second column, identify something humans have done that changed the environment in your community. In the next three columns, compare the types of change in the two places. One example is done for you.

Environmental change on Easter Island	Environmental change in my community	Change: same or different?	Reason for change	Effect of environmental change
Cut down trees	Cut down trees	same	Easter Island: to get fuel My community: to build a skating rink	Easter Island: Eventually there were no trees left. My community: There's no shade to keep the area cool.

► ***Do you think the Easter Island example can help us predict what could happen in other places on Earth? Why or why not?***

Answers will vary. Examples: Yes; what happened on Easter Island shows what could happen if we destroy forests. No; other places aren't isolated like Easter Island is.

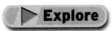

TEACHING PLAN pp. 210–211

Explore

COMPARE EASTER ISLAND AND YOUR COMMUNITY Before students begin filling in the chart, ask the class to identify environmental changes that have taken place in their community. Encourage them to include favorable changes—for example, a reforestation project or restocking a pond with native fish.

When students have completed the chart, let them share their responses by reading them aloud. Have students identify each change as positive or negative and explain the reasons for their choices.

Propose Explanations

Time: 15 minutes
Materials: world map

USE WHAT YOU KNOW Have students look back at the map on page 208. To help them grasp the enormous distance between Easter Island and other land masses, display a world map and have them locate various North American cities—New York, Atlanta, Detroit, Houston, Los Angeles, and Washington, D.C. Then list on the board the following distances and travel times between different cities. (Travel times are based on an average speed of 80 km, 50 mi per hour.)

Atlanta–Washington, D.C.
1,083 km (677 mi)
14 hours by car
1 hour 40 minutes by plane

Detroit–Houston
2,100 km (1,312 mi)
26 hours by car
2 hours 30 minutes by plane

New York–Los Angeles
4,520 km (2,825 mi)
57 hours by car
5 hours 30 minutes by plane

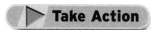

Propose Explanations

USE WHAT YOU KNOW

► ***Why didn't the people of Easter Island trade with other people to get the things they needed? (Hint: Look at the map on page 208.)***

The island was too far from other places where people lived.

► ***Why didn't the people of Easter Island move to another place?***

They didn't have any more wood to build canoes.

► ***What do you think the people of Easter Island could have done to avoid destroying their environment?***

Answers will vary. Examples: They could have built fewer statues. They could have cut only some trees and left others standing. They could have replanted trees after they cut some.

Take Action

COMPARE AND CONTRAST Do research to learn more about Easter Island. Then fill in the Venn diagram below to compare Easter Island before and after deforestation. On the left side, describe Easter Island before deforestation. On the right side, describe Easter Island after deforestation. In the center, list the ways that the island stayed the same.

Answers may vary. Examples are given.

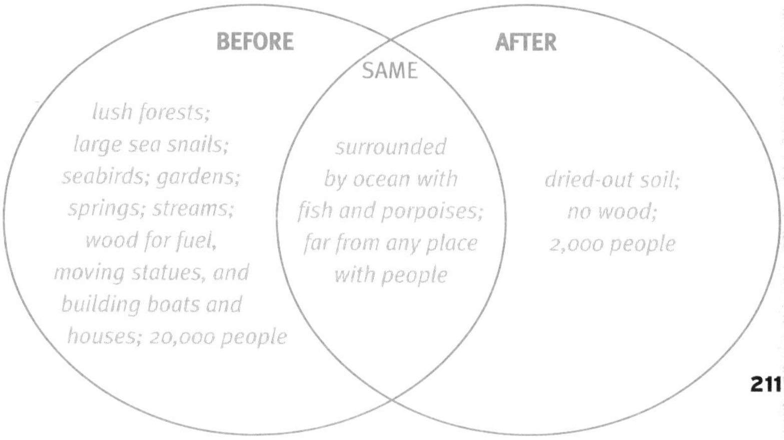

211

Assessment

Skill: Recognizing cause and effect

Use the following questions to assess each student's progress:

► *Why did the Easter Islanders cut down so many trees?* (to burn for fuel, to build houses and canoes, and to transport their large statues)

► *Why were they eventually unable to catch fish and porpoises?* (They could not build canoes.) *Why not?* (They had cut down all the trees.)

► *Why were they eventually unable to grow enough food?* (The soil had eroded.) *Why had that happened?* (They had cut down all the trees.)

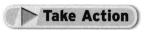

Take Action

Time: will vary
Materials: research sources about Easter Island

COMPARE AND CONTRAST Make sure students understand that "before deforestation" does not mean before the first settlers arrived on Easter Island. Serious damage to the environment did not begin until hundreds of years after their first arrival.

Have students use library resources and the Internet to research the natural history of Easter Island. **Caution:** Archaeological evidence indicates that as the supply of large food animals dwindled, Easter Islanders may have turned to cannibalism to supplement their diets. You may want to screen the library resources and Web sites to make sure students do not encounter this topic.

Point of Lesson

Human population growth has a direct impact on aquatic ecosystems.

Focus

- Change, constancy, and measurement
- Populations, resources, and environments
- Science and technology in society

Skills and Strategies

- Recognizing cause and effect
- Creating and using graphs
- Comparing and contrasting
- Predicting

Advance Preparation

Vocabulary

Make sure students understand these terms. Definitions can be found in the glossary at the end of the student book.

- ecosystem
- population

People Make a Difference

People have the power to destroy ecosystems or preserve them.

Swamps, marshes, and other aquatic ecosystems may seem like unimportant places, but they help prevent floods and are home to a great diversity of life. They are also some of the most easily damaged ecosystems on Earth.

NOTEZONE

Underline the ways that humans damage or destroy aquatic ecosystems.

Read

Our need for electric power, factories, and roads has a large impact on aquatic ecosystems.

Human Impacts

How do humans affect aquatic ecosystems?

Probably, people don't really say, "Let's go out and destroy an aquatic ecosystem just for fun." Instead they say, "I want to do such-and-such and, if an aquatic ecosystem is harmed in the process, well, that's the price of progress. Life is full of compromises."

We plan change and construction to [adjust to] population growth, industry, and demand for electric power. All too often that construction involves draining swamps to "reclaim" dry land, building protective levees, [and] keeping shipping channels dredged.... [It also often involves] building dams for hydroelectric power, building canals, laying water pipes, and carrying out other projects. These activities are carried out by local...agencies...and/or federal units, such as the U.S. Army Corps of Engineers. The projects serve to build communities, redirect water for farms, [and] prevent floods.... [The] projects provide water supplies, support transportation, and [serve] other functions related to the "progress" of humans.

aquatic: relating to water
compromise: giving in partway in order to settle differences
reclaim: return something to an earlier condition for use
levee: a raised area alongside a river to keep it from overflowing
shipping channel: the deeper part of a river or harbor
dredged: deepened a waterway by removing mud from the bottom
hydroelectric power: electricity that is generated by using the energy of moving water

From: Reynolds, Karen. "Human Impacts 101." *JASON Academy.* National Science Teacher's Association. (www.nsta.org/361/)

FIND OUT MORE

SCIENCESAURUS

Freshwater Ecosystems 148
Saltwater Ecosystems 149
Renewable Energy Resources 328
Habitat Loss 341

TEACHING PLAN pp. 212–213

INTRODUCING THE LESSON

In this lesson, students consider the impact of human population growth on aquatic ecosystems. Ask students to identify and describe different aquatic ecosystems, both freshwater and saltwater.

Students may not realize the importance of swamps, marshes, and estuaries. Explain that swamps and marshes absorb huge quantities of water during floods when rivers overflow their banks. Along with estuaries, they also collect decaying organic material. This material provides food for bacteria and other microorganisms, thus forming the base of many different food chains. In addition, the young of many species of crabs, shrimp, and fish migrate from larger bodies of water to swamps, marshes, and estuaries in order to feed on the plentiful organic material. The animals return to the larger bodies of water as they reach adulthood.

Read

Have students brainstorm other examples of human populations affecting aquatic ecosystems. For example, soil runoff clogs waterways. Pesticides, toxic wastes, and other pollutants poison the water. Motorboats and other mechanized watercraft foul the water and injure or kill aquatic organisms.

Explore

USING A GRAPH Why are human activities damaging aquatic ecosystems so much more now than in the past? One major reason is that the world's human population is so much larger today than in the past. This graph shows the growth of Earth's human population during the past 2,000 years.

▸ ***About how large was the world's human population in each of the following years?***

750 A.D. *about 300 million*

1500 A.D. *about 600 million*

2000 A.D. *about 5.5 billion*

▸ ***During the past 250 years, what happened to the rate of world population growth?***

The rate increased rapidly.

WORLD POPULATION GROWTH

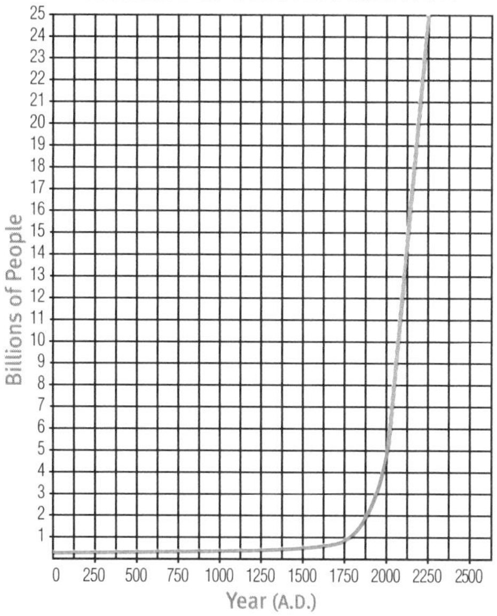

▸ ***Extend the line on the graph to the year 2250. If this growth rate continues, how large will the world's human population be in 2250? How will the size of the population in 2250 compare with the size of today's population?***

About 25 billion; it will be more than four times the size of today's population.

▸ ***As the world human population grows, what is likely to happen to aquatic ecosystems? Why?***

They are more likely to be destroyed. People will probably build more dams, buildings, power plants, roads, and other structures in places where there are now aquatic ecosystems.

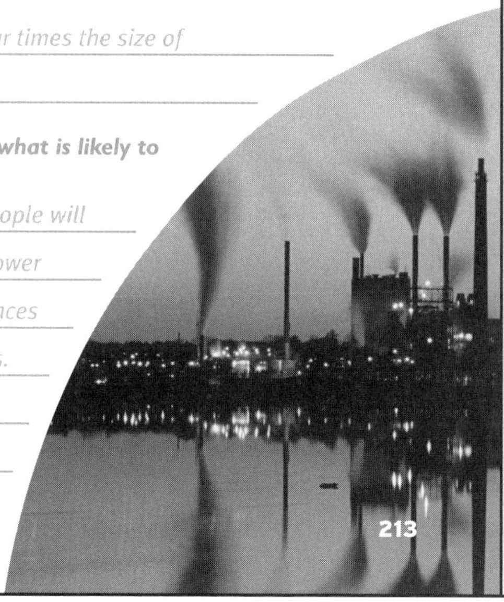

213

More Resources

The following resources are also available from Great Source.

ScienceSaurus

Freshwater Ecosystems	148
Saltwater Ecosystems	149
Renewable Energy Resources	328
Habitat Loss	341

Reader's Handbook

Focus on Persuasive Writing	247
Elements of Graphics: Line Graph	554

Math On Call

Making Graphs	287
Graphs That Show Change Over Time	297
Single-Line Graphs	298

Assessment

Skill: Communicating

Use the following task to assess each student's progress:

Describe three different ways in which aquatic ecosystems are changed by human populations. (Examples: Swamps are drained; channels are dredged; water is polluted by industrial wastes; dams and canals are built; water is diverted for irrigation or to prevent flooding.)

Explore

USING A GRAPH Make sure students understand how to read a line graph. Review what the abbreviation A.D. means.

The graph shows a tremendous increase in the rate of population growth starting in the late 1700s. Ask students to suggest possible factors that led to this increase. (Advances in medicine reduced the mortality rate and lengthened the human lifespan. Advances in agriculture reduced illness and death from malnutrition. The Industrial Revolution made lower-cost products such as warm clothing and canned food available to more people.)

Ask: *Imagine that two more families move into your home. What would change? Would you use more electricity? Hot water? Food? How would you manage your resources?* Help students relate the imaginary increase in the population of their homes to the actual increase in the population of Earth.

CHECK UNDERSTANDING

Skill: Comparing and contrasting

Have students pick a specific aquatic ecosystem—either an actual example or a fictional one. Ask: *What was the ecosystem like 100 years ago? How has it changed? Which of those changes, if any, have been caused by humans?* (Many changes—including pollution, habitat destruction, population decreases due to hunting—are caused by humans. Other changes, such as the succession of a pond to a swamp and then to a meadow, occur naturally.)

Point of Lesson

Biodiversity can be found in even a small plot of land.

Focus

- Systems, order, and organization
- Populations and ecosystems
- Diversity and adaptation of organisms
- Abilities necessary to do scientific inquiry

Skills and Strategies

- Observing
- Collecting and recording data
- Interpreting data
- Recognizing cause and effect

Advance Preparation

Vocabulary

Make sure students understand these terms. Definitions can be found in the glossary at the end of the student book.

- climate
- organism
- population
- species

Materials

Gather the materials needed for *Enrichment* (p. 215), *Activity* (p. 216), *Connections* (p. 216), and *Take Action* (p. 217).

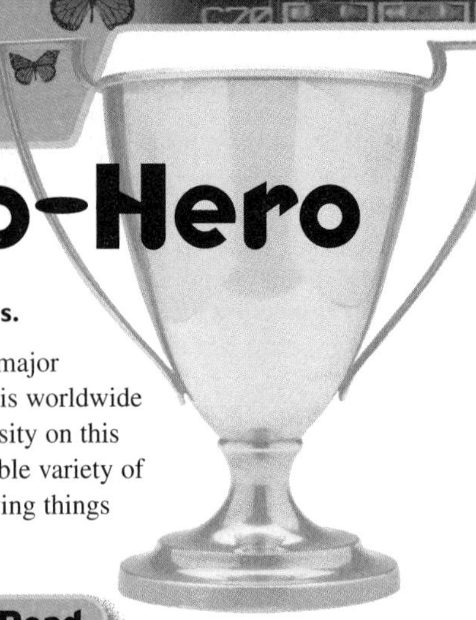

Be an Eco-Hero

Humans don't live on this planet alone. We are just one among millions of species.

Some scientists suggest that humans face three major threats to survival. One is nuclear war. Another is worldwide climate change. The third is the loss of biodiversity on this planet. The word *biodiversity* means the incredible variety of organisms on Earth. There are more kinds of living things than you know!

Before You Read

THINK ABOUT IT Many people try to save large animals such as pandas and elephants. However, most organisms are much smaller and less noticeable. Many people don't know about them or think about them. But species are disappearing from Earth at a rapid rate.

▸ ***If you had to choose between saving pandas and saving a species of small worms, which would you choose? Why?***

Accept all reasonable answers.

Examples: I'd choose the worms because they might have an important role in an ecosystem. I'd choose pandas because they are rare animals.

TEACHING PLAN pp. 214–215

INTRODUCING THE LESSON

This lesson addresses biodiversity—the variety of organisms living in a given area. Ask students to guess how many known species exist in the world. (Do not supply the correct answer. Students will find it in the reading.)

Students may not think of insects, protists, algae, bacteria, molds, and the like when they consider the number of species on Earth. If so, ask leading questions such as: *What organisms do you think you would find in soil?* and *What about organisms you can not see without a microscope?*

Before You Read

THINK ABOUT IT Explain that the number of species is shrinking rapidly. According to the International Union for the Conservation of Nature and Natural Resources, species are going extinct at a rate 1,000 to 10,000 times greater than the rate that would be expected without human interference.

In addition to the panda and the worm, you might want to talk about other species, including those that are annoying or harmful to people. Would students try to save the mosquito from extinction? What about the virus that causes smallpox? This can lead to a discussion of how people decide the importance of other species and how students think importance ought to be judged.

Read

Terry Erwin is a scientist from the Smithsonian Institution in Washington, D.C. Erwin found that in Panama, an incredible diversity of organisms live in a population of 19 trees of the same species.

Living Treasure

Scientists are dazzled and puzzled by the diversity of life on Earth. No one knows how many different kinds of plants, animals, and other organisms there are. But we do know that the organisms identified so far are only a small fraction of all living things....

And biologists have a name for...Earth's incredible variety of life: biodiversity....

Since [the 1700s], more than 1.5 million...species have been discovered and named.

On...[19] trees alone, [Terry Erwin] found more than 12,000 different kinds of beetles. He estimated that one out of seven species lived on that kind of tree and no other....

Until the 1980s, biologists estimated that 3 to 5 million species live on Earth. However, since large numbers of tropical insects and other organisms may live on just one kind of tree, or in one small area of tropical forest, the biodiversity of Earth may be much greater. Terry Erwin has estimated that...Earth may be home to 30 million species of insects alone.

biodiversity: the variety of living organisms in a given area

From: Pringle, Laurence. *Living Treasure: Saving Earth's Threatened Biodiversity.* HarperCollins Children's Books.

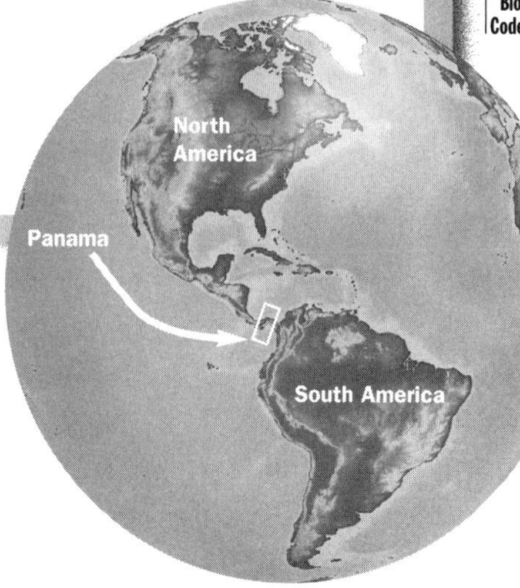

NOTEZONE

How many species have been discovered and named?
1.5 million

How many insect species does Terry Erwin estimate live on Earth?
30 million

About how many beetle species did Erwin estimate live only on those 19 trees?
about 1,700 (12,000÷7)

FIND OUT MORE

SCIENCESAURUS
Biodiversity 124

SCI LINKS
THE WORLD'S A CLICK AWAY
www.scilinks.org
Keyword: Maintaining Biodiversity
Code: GSLD25

Enrichment

Time: 40 minutes

Materials: science or ecology textbooks, field guides for various ecosystems

Divide the class into small groups, and assign each group a different ecosystem—desert, tundra, tropical rain forest, tidal pool, taiga, savannah, deciduous forest, and so on. Each group should do research to find the level of biodiversity normally found in that ecosystem. Encourage students to present their findings in posters or brief oral reports.

Read

Ask: *What would happen to the 12,000 species of beetles if the species of tree they live on became extinct?* (The 1,700 species that live on only that type of tree would most likely become extinct.) Have students recall their answers to the Before You Read question. Ask them whether they would try to save each and every one of those 1,700 species of beetles and to explain their choice.

Because so many familiar species live in many different areas, students may have trouble grasping the idea that a species could live on only one type of tree. Ask them to brainstorm reasons why a beetle species would live on one type of tree and not on any other type. (The beetle species must be adapted to the specific conditions the tree species provides for food, shelter, protection against predators, and the like.)

CHECK UNDERSTANDING

Skill: Making inferences

Why do you think scientists before the 1980s underestimated the number of species living on Earth? (They didn't realize how many different species live in the tropical rain forest.)

More Resources

The following resources are also available from Great Source and NSTA.

SCIENCESAURUS

Change and Diversity of Life 124

WRITE SOURCE 2000

Writing Persuasive Essays 115

SCILINKS. THE WORLD'S A CLICK AWAY

www.scilinks.org
Keyword: Maintaining Biodiversity
Code: GSLD25

Connections

Time: 10–15 minutes
Materials: world map

SOCIAL STUDIES Tell students that warmer, wetter climates, especially those near the equator, tend to have a very high level of biodiversity, and cold climates tend to have a fairly low level of biodiversity. Write the following list on the board: Albania, Greenland, Guyana, Mexico. Have students use a world map to find the location of each country, then rank them according to their probable level of biodiversity, from greatest to least. (Guyana, Mexico, Albania, Greenland)

Activity

BIODIVERSITY IN YOUR WORLD

You do not need to go to a tropical forest to discover biodiversity. All you have to do is look carefully around you.

What You Need:

- meterstick or metric tape measure
- 12 sticks about 10–15 cm long
- string, 25 m
- notebook
- pencil
- large sheet of plain white paper
- trowel or large spoon
- index cards
- hand lens

What to Do:

1. Choose an area that appears to have more than one kind of plant in it. Measure a square that is 3 meters long on each side. Put sticks into the ground to mark the corners. Use string to show the sides.
2. Use the string and the other sticks to divide the square into 9 smaller squares that are 1 meter on each side.
3. In your notebook, make a map of your study plot. Include important features such as large rocks or water.
4. Examine your plot for any living things. Look everywhere—under rocks and logs, on tree trunks and branches, and on plant stems and leaves. Remember that the trees and other plants are living things, too! Use the hand lens to find very small organisms.
5. Dig up some soil and spread it out on the large sheet of paper. Include some decaying leaves, too. Use the hand lens to look for small organisms.
6. On index cards, sketch each kind of organism you found. Number each card. Record the number on your map to show where the organism was found.
7. Include signs of animals such as nests, animal tracks, feathers, cocoons, droppings, and spider webs. Draw each one on an index card. Letter each card, and record the letters on your map.

What Did You Find?

► ***How many different kinds of organisms or signs of organisms did you find?***

Numbers will vary.

► ***Do you think you found every kind of organism living in that plot?***

probably not

216

TEACHING PLAN pp. 216–217

Activity

Time: 40–45 minutes
Materials: meter stick or metric tape measure; large sheet of plain white paper; index cards; 12 sticks about 10–15 cm long; string, 25 m; magnifier; trowel or large spoon; notebook; field guides

Students should do this activity in groups of three or four. To provide more time for investigating the plots, you could have students do steps 1–3 on one day and the remaining steps on a second day.

Wooded areas and natural fields will yield a predictably high number of organisms, but students will probably be surprised at the number of organisms they can find in areas such as the edge of a playground or a parking lot. On the other hand, well-tended lawns and athletic fields tend to be monocultures. If you are in an urban setting, vacant lots are usually home to a surprising number of organisms.

Supply field guides for students to identify the organisms they found. Suggest that they include on the index card each organism's common name and scientific name, if available, but do not expect them to identify organisms more specifically than order or perhaps genus. Also encourage students to expand their observations and notes to include any data they think might be relevant, such as temperature and other weather conditions.

ANALYZE YOUR OBSERVATIONS You may need to help students identify factors that limit biodiversity, such as the possible use of herbicides or pesticides, heavy pedestrian traffic at times of day other than the time of the study, or standing water after a rain.

► *What are some things you did or didn't do that might have kept you from finding some organisms?*

Answers will vary. Examples: I didn't have enough time. I could have looked more carefully. I couldn't see extremely small organisms. I couldn't climb the trees. I only looked during the day. I only looked in one season.

ANALYZE YOUR OBSERVATIONS

► *Examine your map and index cards. How were the organisms spaced around your plot?*

Answers will depend on the area examined.

► *Compare different parts of your plot. Where did you find the most biodiversity? Where did you find the least biodiversity?*

Answers will depend on the area examined.

► *What characteristics of your plot might have limited its biodiversity?*

Answers will vary. Examples: A sidewalk was on one side. Weed killers and insecticides may have been used.

Take Action

Compare the results of your study with what others found in their plots. How are the findings similar? How are they different? Research the importance of biodiversity. How might the biodiversity you found benefit the wildlife in the area? What can you do to help maintain the biodiversity in your community? Write a report to share with the class.

Students' reports will vary.

217

Assessment

Skill: Making inferences

Use the following task to assess each student's progress:

On the board, list the number of species found by each group. Then have students calculate the average number of species found by all groups. Ask: *Do you think this number is an accurate count of the different species in the area we studied?* If students think the count is accurate, ask them to explain why. If they think it is not, ask them to identify specific factors that might have affected their result. (Students may feel that the count is essentially accurate. They may feel that certain factors—for example, one area with a particularly low biodiversity level, such as a paved area—may be skewing the average. Or they may feel that other factors—for example, a recent rain or snowstorm—may be affecting the results of all the surveys.)

Take Action

Time: will vary
Materials: research sources about biodiversity

After students have completed their analyses, have them share their information with the class. Compile data for the class as a whole. In general, what factors affected biodiversity levels? Help students identify the areas with the highest and the lowest levels of biodiversity. Ask them to predict which unexamined areas nearby would be likely to have the most and the least biodiversity.

Glossary of Scientific Terms

A

adaptation: structure, behavior, or other trait in an organism that helps it to survive in its environment

adaptive radiation: an evolutionary pattern in which related species become dissimilar, or less alike

adolescence: the teenage years

amphibian: animal that lives both on land and in water; Amphibians begin life in water with gills, but have lungs and breathe air as adults

antibody: protein made by the body that fights against a certain disease-causing substance

atom: smallest particle into which an element can be divided and still have the properties of that element

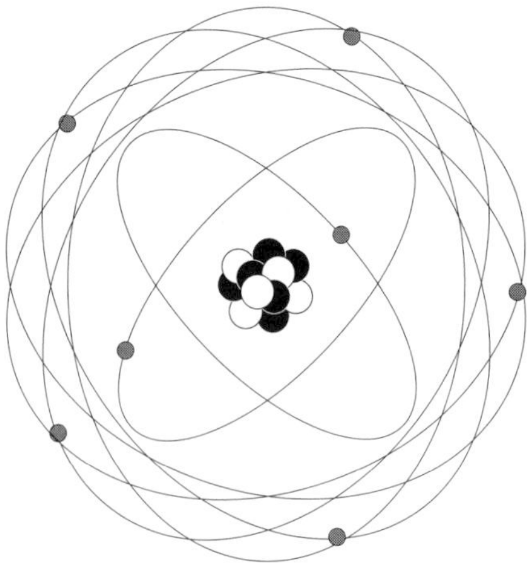

B

bacteria: one-celled organism that lacks a true nucleus

bar graph: graph that uses bars of different lengths to compare data

behavior: an activity or action that generally helps an organism survive in its environment

biodiversity: the variety of organisms in a specific environment or on Earth as a whole

biology: study of living things

blood: a tissue made up of cells and pieces of cells carried in a liquid; transported throughout the body by the circulatory system

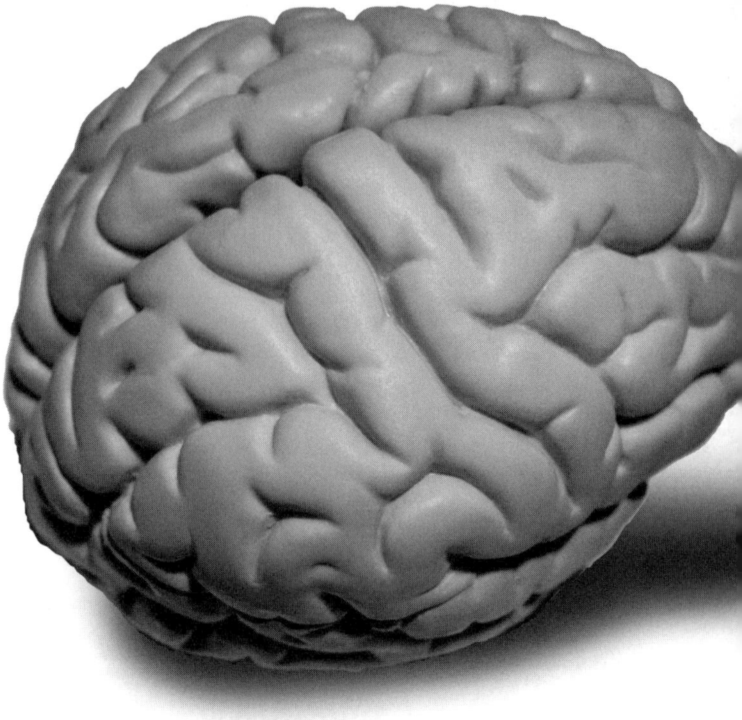

brain: organ that is the control center for actions, thoughts, and emotions

C

carbohydrate: molecule made up of carbon, hydrogen, and oxygen, which is the product of photosynthesis; sugars and starches are examples

cardiac muscle: heart muscle; it is involuntary (not consciously controlled) and keeps the heart beating

carnivore: an animal that feeds on other animals, such as a wolf

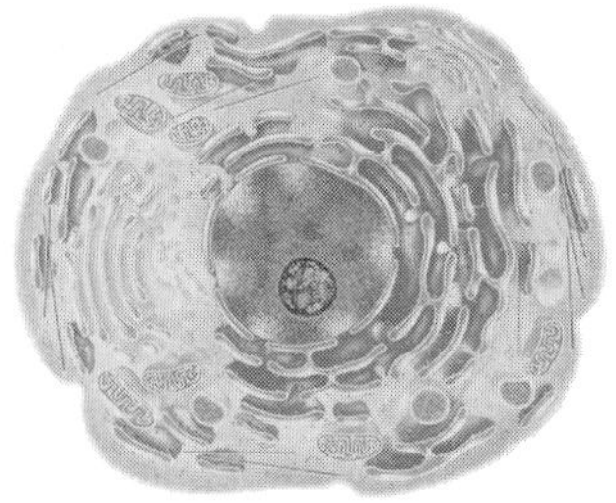

cell: basic unit of structure and function in living things

cell division: process by which cells divide to form new cells

cell membrane: structure that surrounds the cytoplasm of the cell

cellular respiration: process in cells by which oxygen is chemically combined with food molecules and energy is released

chemical equation: a way of writing changes in the arrangement of atoms during a chemical reaction, using chemical symbols

chemical reaction: change that takes place when two or more substances (reactants) interact to form new substances (products)

chlorophyll: green pigment in plants that captures the energy of sunlight for use in photosynthesis

chloroplast: a structure in a plant cell that contains chlorophyll; Sugar molecules are made in chloroplasts through the process of photosynthesis.

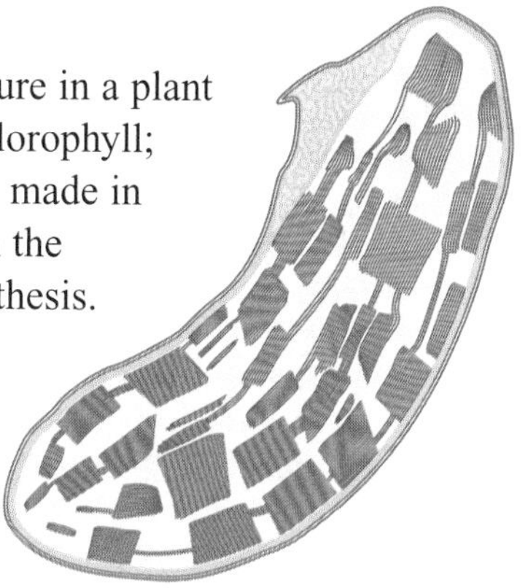

chromosome: the structure located in the nucleus of a cell, made of DNA, that contains the genetic information needed to carry out cell functions and make new cells

circulatory system: organ system that transports needed substances throughout the body and carries away wastes

class: division of organism classification below phylum and above order, as in the class *Insecta* (insects)

classify: to organize into groups based on similar characteristics

climate: the general pattern of weather over a long period of time

commensalism: relationship between species in which one species is helped and the other is unaffected

community: all of the populations sharing a specific area or region; for example, all the organisms in a lake

competition: in an ecosystem, occurs when more than one individual or population tries to make use of the same limited resource

conservation: the wise use and protection of natural resources

conservationist: person who protects endangered species and their habitats

continent: any of Earth's seven large land masses

control: factor in an experiment that is kept the same

convergent evolution: an evolutionary pattern in which unrelated species become more similar in order to survive in similar environmental conditions

culturing: growing living cells or tiny organisms in a protected environment with nutrients

cytoplasm: gel-like fluid that takes up most of the space inside a cell

D

data: collected information; the results of an experiment or other investigation

deforestation: destruction of the forest

desert: dry climate that receives an average of less than 25 cm of rainfall per year

dichotomous key: a system used for identifying plants, animals, rocks, or minerals, that is made up of a series of paired descriptions to choose between

digestion: process of breaking down food into a form the body can use

digestive system: organ system that breaks down food into substances the body can use and absorbs these substances

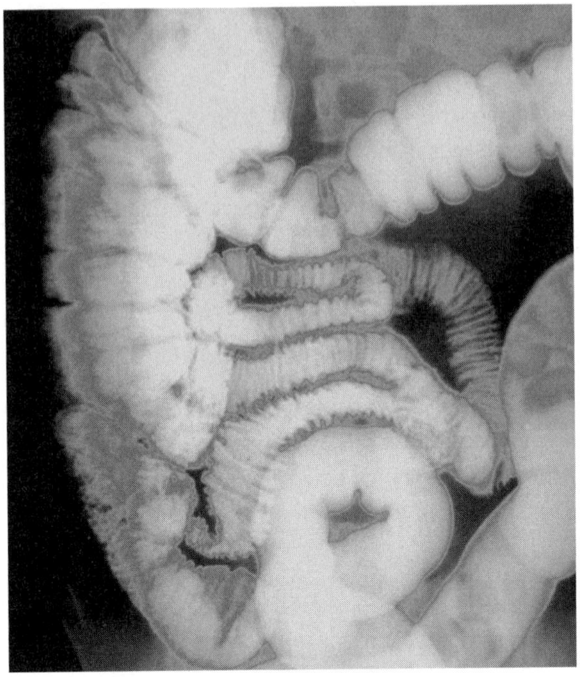

DNA: deoxyribonucleic acid; the material found in a cell's nucleus that determines the genetic traits of the organism

domain: the broadest category in the system used to classify every known organism on Earth

dominant: in a pair of genes, the form that, if present, determines the trait

E

echolocation: a system of using bounced sounds to determine the location of objects

ecology: study of interactions of organisms with each other and their environment

ecosystem: all the living populations in an area along with the nonliving parts of that environment

egg: female sex cell; also an object that contains an animal developing from a fertilized sex cell (such as a bird egg or insect egg)

electric current: the amount of electric charge that moves past a certain point each second; measured in amperes (A)

electricity: general term for interaction of electric charges

endangered species: a species that is in danger of extinction

endocrine system: system of organs that controls body activities through chemical messengers (hormones)

endoplasmic reticulum: structure in a cell that is involved in making proteins and transporting materials

energy: ability to do work

entomology: the science of studying insects

environment: surroundings and conditions in which an organism lives

enzyme: a protein in the body that helps control a chemical reaction, such as digestion

epidemic: an outbreak of a disease that affects many people

epithelial stem cells: cells from an adult's skin that can specialize into different kinds of cells

evolution: theory, based on scientific evidence, that describes how species change over many generations

experiment: series of steps that, under controlled conditions, produces data that test a hypothesis or prediction

extinct: condition in which there are no more living members of a species

F

family: division of organism classification below order and above genus, as in *Felidae* (cats)

fat: kind of organic compound that makes up part of a cell membrane, stores excess food energy for an organism, helps insulate an organism, and has many other roles

feces: solid waste eliminated by the body

fertilization: union of a sperm cell with an egg cell

fetus: a developing mammal from the time its major organs are formed until birth; in humans, this is from 8 weeks to about 40 weeks

food chain: in an ecosystem, path of food energy from the sun to a producer to a series of consumers

food web: in an ecosystem, arrangement of several overlapping food chains

force: a push or a pull

fossil: remains, impressions, tracks, or other evidence of ancient organisms

free-fall: a falling motion that is affected only by gravity, not by a parachute or other object

frequency: number of wave vibrations (oscillations) produced in one second, measured in hertz (Hz)

fungi: single or many-celled organisms that have cells walls, do not have chlorophyll, take food from the environment, and reproduce by budding or by spores

G

gene: segment of DNA, found on a chromosome, that determines the inheritance of a particular trait

generation: one set of offspring

genome: all the genes that an organism has

genus: division of organism classification below family and above species, as in *Felis* (the genus that includes house cats); *See also scientific name*

gills: organs that absorb oxygen in water

glands: specialized organs that make substances (hormones) that control and regulate body processes

glucose: simple sugar made by plants through the process of photosynthesis

Golgi apparatus: cell structure that helps package and distribute products within the cell

grassland: large land region in which the main types of plants are grasses

gravity: force of attraction between any two objects

H

habitat: the place in an ecosystem where an organism lives

heart: organ in the circulatory system that pumps blood throughout the body

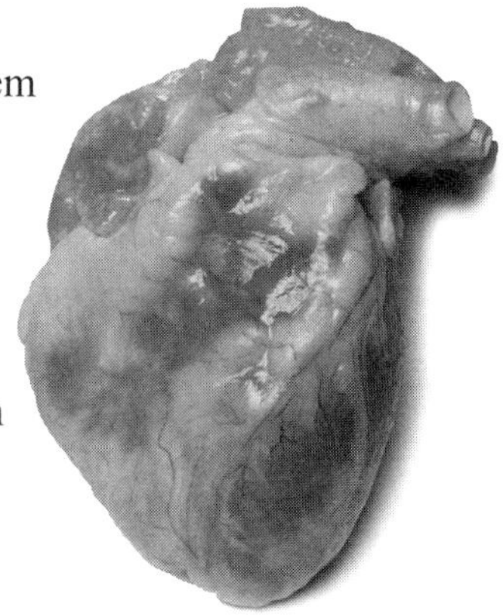

herbicide: chemical used to kill unwanted plants

herbivore: animal that feeds only on plants, such as a deer

horizontal axis: a horizontal line marked with a scale that is used to place data points on a graph; sometimes called the x-axis

hormone: a chemical released by a gland; controls a specific body function

hydroelectric power: electricity that is generated by using the energy of moving water

hyperthyroidism: a condition in which the thyroid gland produces too much of its hormone

hypothesis: an idea that can be tested by experiment or observation

I

immune system: system that protects the body against disease

infectious: capable of spreading disease

inference: an explanation that is based on available evidence but is not a direct observation

intestines: See *large intestine, small intestine*

ion: atom or molecule that has an overall electric charge due to loss or gain of electrons

J

joint: place where two or more bones meet

K

kingdom: largest grouping in organism classification, as in the animal kingdom

L

large intestine: part of the digestive system where water is absorbed from solid waste

life cycle: all stages in the life of an organism

liver: organ in the digestive system that produces bile and enzymes, breaks down toxins and wastes, and has many other functions

lungs: pair of organs in the respiratory system, where carbon dioxide and oxygen are exchanged

M

mammal: animal that has fur or hair, usually gives birth to live young, and can nurse its young with milk

mass: amount of matter in something; measured in grams (g)

metabolism: cellular processes of making, storing, and transporting chemicals; also, the sum of all these processes in an organism

microscopic: object or organism too small to be seen without a microscope

migration: seasonal movement of animals from one place to another

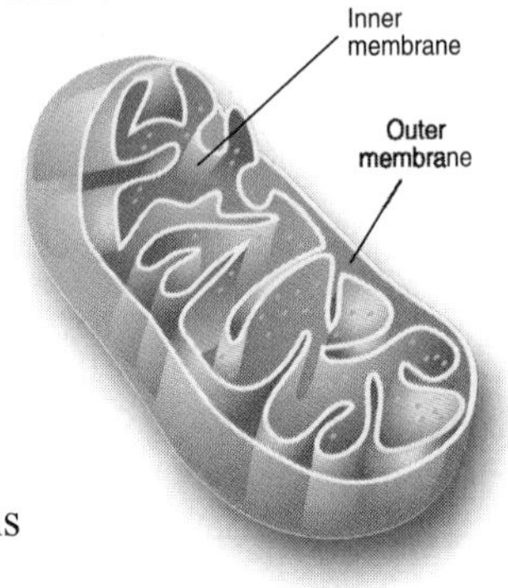

mitochondria: structures in the cell that transform the energy in food into a form cells can use to carry out their activities

model: simplified version of some part of the natural world that helps explain how it functions

molecule: smallest particle of a substance that still has the properties of that substance

mutation: a random change in a gene

mutualism: relationship between two species in which both species benefit

N

natural selection: process by which organisms change over time as those with traits best suited to an environment pass their traits to the next generation

nectar: sweet liquid found in some flowers

niche: role that a species plays in a living community or ecosystem

nucleus: structure near the center of a cell that contains the cell's DNA

nutrient: substance that an organism needs in order to survive and grow

O

order: division of organism classification below class and above family, as in the order *Carnivora* (mammals that feed on other animals)

organ: in an organism, structure made of two or more different tissues that has a specialized function; for example, the lungs

organelles: structures in the cytoplasm of a cell that carry out cell activities

organism: a living thing

organ system: group of organs that work together to do a specific job for an organism, such as the digestive system

osmosis: diffusion of water across a membrane, such as a cell membrane

ovary: female sex organ in which egg cells are produced

P

pancreas: organ of the digestive system and endocrine system; makes enzymes that help in the breakdown of carbohydrates and that help regulate blood sugar levels

parasitism: relationship between species in which one species (parasite) benefits and the other (host) is harmed but not usually killed

photosynthesis: chemical process by which plants use light energy to make glucose from water and carbon dioxide

phylum: first division of organism classification below kingdom, as in the phylum *Arthropoda*

pollen: particles that carry male genetic material, from seed plants

pollination: the transfer of pollen from the male part of a plant (stamen) to the female part (pistil)

population: all the members of a species living in a particular area at a particular time

predator: animal, such as a lion, that kills and eats other animals (prey)

prediction: a guess about what will happen under certain conditions, based on observation and research

prey: organism that is killed and eaten by another organism (predator)

producer: organism that makes its own food, such as a plant or a photosynthetic alga

proteins: organic compounds that make up living things and are essential for life

protists: one-celled or simple many-celled organisms, such as amoebas and algae

R

recessive: in a pair of genes, the form that is masked if a dominant form is present

red blood cell: cell that carries oxygen through the body

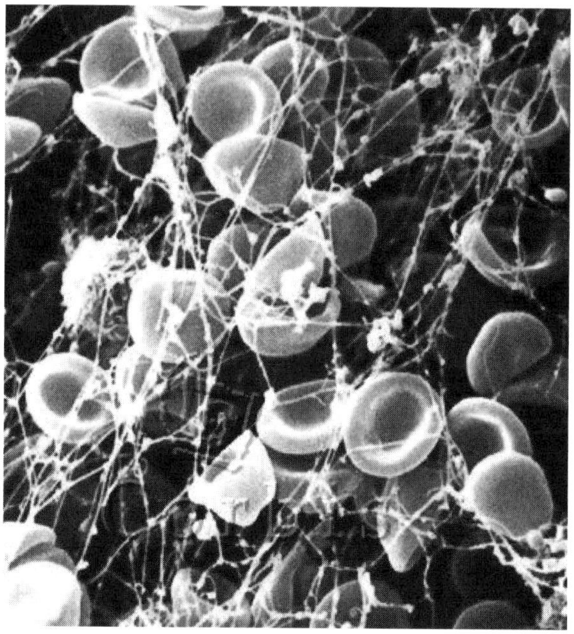

reflex: an animal's automatic response to a stimulus, such as jerking away from a hot surface

reproduce: to make more individuals of the same species from a parent organism or organisms

respiration: See *cellular respiration*

ribosome: structure in a cell where proteins are put together

S

satellite: object that revolves around a larger object in space; The moon is a natural satellite of Earth; the Hubble Space Telescope is an artificial satellite.

scientific name: the genus and species name of an organism; for example, *Aplodontia rufa*, mountain beaver

seed: structure able to sprout and develop into a plant; made of a plant embryo and its food supply

sense organs: organs that gather information about the surrounding environment, including the eyes, ears, nose, mouth, and skin

skeletal muscle: muscle that moves parts of the body and is under conscious control of the organism

small intestine: organ in the digestive system that completes digestion and absorbs nutrients

smooth muscle: muscle, found in many organs, that is not under conscious control of the organism

sound: energy that travels through matter as mechanical waves and can be heard by the ear

species: group of organisms that can mate and produce offspring that in turn can produce more offspring; also, most specific division of organism classification, below genus; *See also scientific name*

sperm: male sex cell, produced in the testes

spinal cord: bundle of nerves that goes from the brain stem down the center of the backbone

stomach: organ in the digestive system where food is stored and partially digested before it enters the small intestine

stomata: tiny openings in plant leaves that take in carbon dioxide and release oxygen

symbiosis: a close relationship between two species

T

tendon: connective tissue that attaches skeletal muscle to bone

thyroid gland: gland that functions in making hormones that control chemical processes in the body

tissue: in plants and animals, a group of cells that work together to do a specific job

trait: an inherited characteristic of an organism

tumor: a growth of cells that is not normal

V

variable: in experiments, a condition that is changed in order to find out the effect of that change

venom: a poisonous substance released by an animal

vertical axis: a vertical line marked with a scale that is used to place data points on a graph; sometimes called the y-axis

W

watt (W): unit of power, equal to one joule per second (1 J/s)

wildlife preserve: special area set aside as a habitat for wild animals and plants; also called wildlife sanctuary

Z

zoology: the science of studying, observing, and classifying animals

Teacher Assessment Rubric

Name ______________________ Assignment ______________ Date __________

	Gold 4	Silver 3	Bronze 2	Copper 1
Comprehension ____ %	Specific facts and relationships are identified and well-defined.	Most facts and relationships are defined.	Some facts are identified but relationships are missing.	No facts or relationships are stated.
Application and Analysis ____ %	A strong plan is developed and executed correctly.	A plan is developed and implemented with some scientific errors.	Some organized ideas toward a weak plan.	Random statements with little relation to the question. No plan present.
Science Content ____ %	Appropriate, complete, and correct scientific facts, ideas, and representations.	Appropriate and correct but incomplete scientific facts, ideas, and representations.	Some inappropriate, incomplete, and/or incorrect ideas, leading to further errors.	Lacking understanding of scientific facts or ideas.
Communication ____ %	Strong and succinct communication of results.	Strong communication of results. Justification for outcome may be weak.	Communication of results is present, but lacks any justification.	No results are communicated. No justification is to be found. A correct answer may have appeared.
Aesthetics ____ %	Exceptional. Attractive. Encourages attention. All requirements exceeded.	Neat and orderly. Requirements met.	Messy and disorganized. Some requirements missing.	Illegible and random information. Most or all requirements missing.

Name ______________________________ Date ______________

Grasshead Data Collection Sheet

Location of grasshead (check one): full sunlight ☐ dim light ☐

Day	Color	Height (cm)	Other Observations
1			
2			
3			
4			
5			
6			
7			
8			
9			
10			
11			
12			
13			
14			

Name ______________________________ Date ______________

Patterns of Inheritance

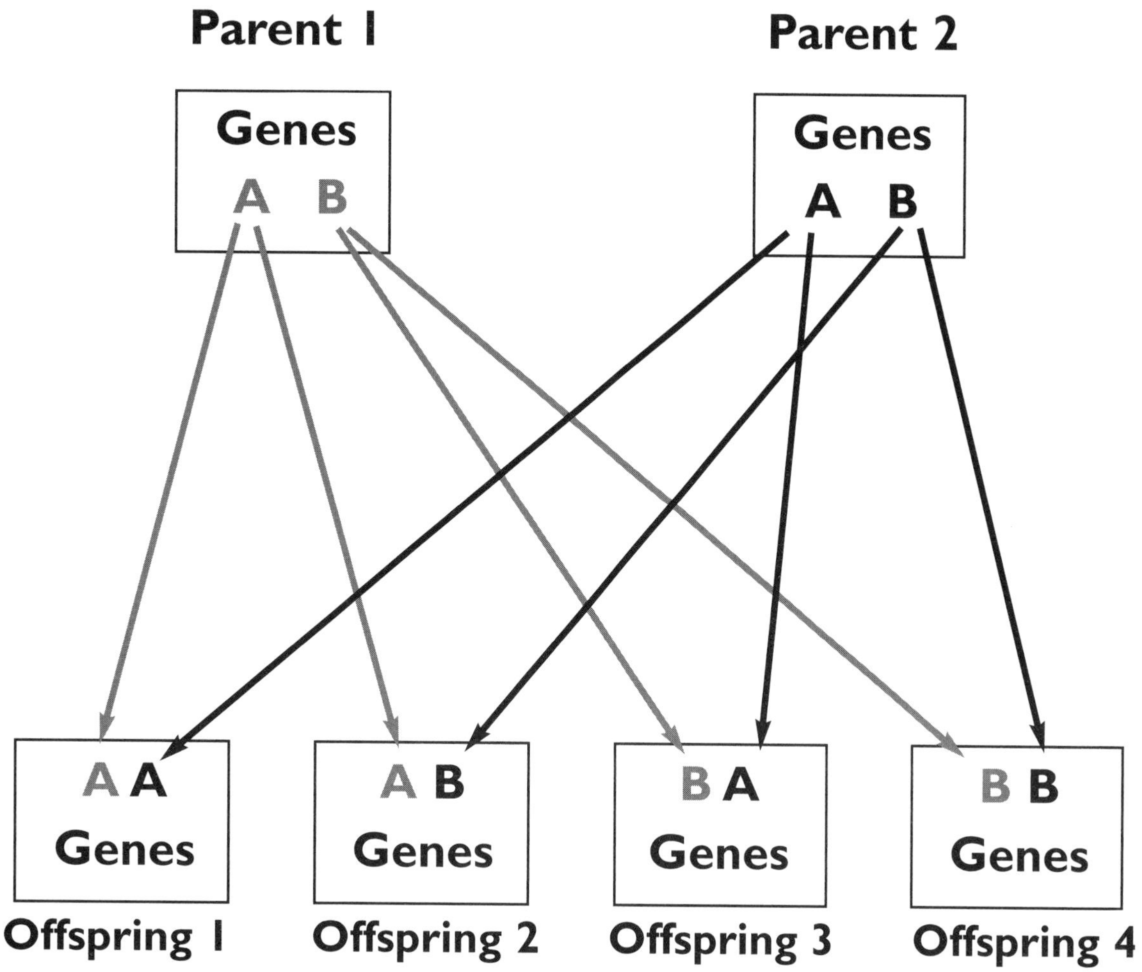

Name ______________________________ Date ______________

Insect Structure

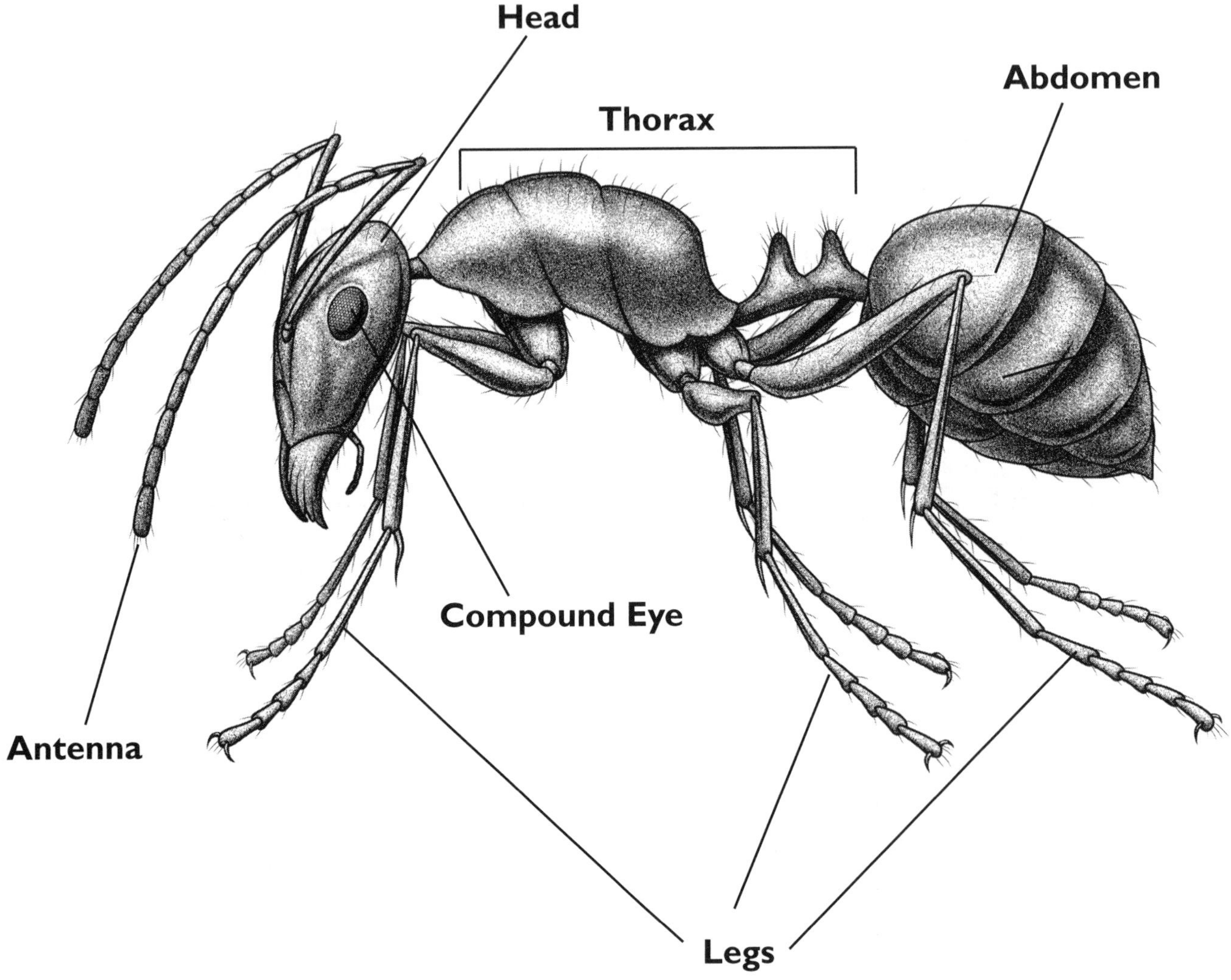

Name ______________________________ Date ______________

Bacteria Samples Data Collection Sheet

Day	Observations
1	
2	
3	
4	
5	
6	
7	
8	

Name ______________________________ Date ________________

Model Biome Log Sheet

Biome ______________________________

Guidelines for maintaining each biome

Desert: direct sunlight (at least 6 hours each day); small amount of water; soil surface should be dry

Rain forest: filtered sunlight; keep soil damp; high temperature

Deciduous forest: filtered sunlight (2 hours each day); moderate amount of water when soil surface is dry; moderate temperature

Grassland: filtered sunlight (about 6 hours each day); moderate amount of water whenever soil surface is dry; moderate temperature

Record your observations in the chart on page 231.

Analysis

Explain why the plants in your biome grew differently from the plants in other students' biomes.

____

____

____

____

____

____

____

____

What were the variables?

____

____

____

____

Name ______________________________ Date ________________

Model Biome Log Sheet

Day	Daily observations
1	
2	
3	
4	
5	
6	
7	
8	
9	
10	
11	
12	
13	
14	
15	
16	
17	
18	
19	
20	

Index

A

Abdomen, 111
Abilities necessary to do scientific inquiry, 90–91, 132–133, 142–145
Abilities of technological design, 44–47
Acoustical image, 115
Adaptation. *See* Diversity and adaptations of organisms.
Adaptive radiation. *See* Natural selection.
Adolescence, 159, 218
Aerial, 111
Airflow, 111
Amphibian, 178–181, 218
Analyzing, 25, 56, 63, 65, 71, 138, 216
See also Comparing and contrasting.
Anemia, 170
Anthropomorphism, 113
Antibiotics, 173
Antibody, 98, 102, 166–168, 218
Atom, 10, 40, 42, 218

B

Bacteria, 10, 218
and disease, 98–101, 172–175
helpful, 102–103
on money, 94–97
resistance to antibiotics, 96–97
Balance, 140–141
Behavior, 114, 218
adaptation, 114–117, 124–127, 200–201
animal, 114–117, 118–121, 122–123, 202–205
dynamics, 122
human, 150–153
insect, 104–107, 108–109
plant, 124–127, 128–131, 132–133
social groups, 121
and survival, 182–185, 199–200, 202–205, 214–217
Bigg, Michael, 122
Biodiversity, 202–203, 214–217, 218
Biology, 85, 114, 121, 122, 123, 218
Biome, 199, 203
Blood, 150–151, 218
Bock, Carl and Jane, 188–191, 192–195
Brain, 41, 43, 156–157, 158–161, 162–165, 218
Breed, 179
Burbank, Luther, 58

C

Carbohydrate, 14, 218
Cardiac muscle, 150–151, 154–155, 218
Carnivores, 82–84, 112, 128–131, 188, 189, 218
Cell(s)
animal, 14, 17, 18, 20, 150, 154
cancerous, 38–39
division, 18, 30–33, 34–37, 218
epithelial stem, 45–47, 220
eukaryotic, 14, 20
membrane, 10–13, 14, 15, 20, 40, 42, 218
nerve, 40–43
plant, 18, 20, 24–25, 28
specialization, 35
structure, 10–13, 14–17, 18–19, 218
survival needs, 14–17, 31, 35, 150
See also Nucleus.
Cellular respiration, 20, 22–23, 28, 218
See also Chemical equation.
Change and diversity of life, 208–211, 212–213
Change, constancy, and measurement, 12–13, 198, 210
Chemical equation, 29, 218
cellular respiration, 20, 22, 28–29
photosynthesis, 24, 25, 28–29
Chemical reaction, 20, 24, 25, 218
Chlorophyll, 24, 218
Chloroplast, 24–25, 28–29, 218
Cholesterol, 152
Chromosome, 18, 25, 30–33, 52–53, 219
Circulatory system. *See* Human body systems.
Classification, 219
class, 82, 85, 87, 105, 219
domain, 82, 83, 219
family, 82, 85, 87, 88, 220
genus, 82, 87, 221
kingdom, 82, 85, 221
order, 82, 83, 84, 85, 87, 198, 199, 222
phylum, 82, 85, 87, 223
reclassification, 90–91
scientific name, 110, 223
species, 82, 86, 87, 89–90, 224
sub-species, 82, 83
Classifying, 14, 15, 48, 49, 82–85, 86–89, 74, 81, 82, 219
Climate, 180, 214, 219
Collecting and recording data/information, 10, 24, 26–27, 30, 32–33, 34–37, 62–63, 69, 76, 78–79, 81, 132–133, 139, 140–141, 142, 144, 148, 214, 216–217
Community, 182–185, 186–187, 188–191, 192–195, 219
Communicating, 14, 17, 18, 19, 20, 30, 31, 33, 52, 53, 76, 79, 107, 110, 113, 115, 118, 121, 141, 142, 145, 173, 178, 181, 182, 185, 192, 193, 195, 202, 205, 209, 213, 214
Comparing and contrasting, 10, 11, 12, 14, 15, 24, 25, 28, 28, 29, 30, 34, 36, 37, 38, 39, 43, 44, 52–53, 54, 68, 70, 72–75, 80, 82, 84, 86, 87, 90–91, 94, 102, 104, 105, 108, 114, 115, 117, 122, 128, 129, 136, 138, 140, 141, 146, 148, 157, 158, 161, 182, 184, 198, 201, 206, 208, 210–211, 212, 213
Connections
Art, 164
Geography, 88
Health, 96, 141, 148
Language Arts, 42, 57, 74, 84, 116–117, 184, 210
Math, 36, 42, 46, 78, 100, 127, 138, 152, 174, 190–191, 200
Music, 16, 130
Physical Education, 120
Social Studies, 12, 26–27, 57, 60, 112, 169, 180, 194, 204, 216
Technology, 106
Writing, 160
Conservation, 77, 207, 219
Continent, 98, 208, 219
Control, 24, 136, 219
Convergent evolution, 80–81, 219
Creative thinking
brainstorming, 15, 35, 69, 77, 153, 175, 204, 212, 215
using analogies, 53
using imagination, 10, 13, 25, 32, 36, 87, 97, 119, 131, 143, 165, 175, 210
Culturing, 45, 219
Cytoplasm, 10, 14, 219

D

Data
analyzing, 65, 120, 132–133, 139, 152, 159–161, 190, 193, 217
interpreting, 10, 12–13, 24, 26–27, 54, 56, 77, 95, 124, 126–127, 136, 139, 142, 144–145, 150, 152, 188, 190–191, 192, 208
Deforestation, 206–207, 208–211, 219
Designing an experiment to test a hypothesis, 129, 136, 139, 158, 161
Developing hypotheses, 24, 26, 27, 35, 95, 188, 190, 205, 221
Dichotomous key, 90–91
Digestion, 219
plant, 129–131
See also Human body systems.
Diseases
bubonic plague, 98–101
infectious, 172–175
malaria, 170–171
polio, 166–169
Diversity and adaptation of organisms, 54–57, 58–61, 72–75, 76–79, 80–81, 82–85, 86–89, 90–91, 94–97, 98–101, 102–103, 104–107, 108–109, 110–113, 124–127, 128–131, 132–133, 128, 130–131, 178–181, 182–185, 192–195, 198–202, 202–205, 214–217, 218
DNA (deoxyribonucleic acid), 219
cloning, 18–19

determining classification, 82, 85, 86, 88–89
genes and chromosomes, 25, 31, 33, 51, 52–53, 68
in viruses, 94
Drawing conclusions, 13, 17, 20, 22, 24, 27, 33, 44, 46, 48, 49, 55, 59, 64, 66–67, 86, 88, 94, 97, 103, 110, 111, 113, 121, 123, 146, 147, 149, 155, 158, 169, 179, 188, 191, 192, 194

E

Echolocation, 114–117, 119, 219
Ecology, 176, 219
Ecosystem, 178–181, 192–194, 196–197, 220
Egg, 12–13, 14, 18, 30, 34, 35, 220
Electricity, 40–43, 84–85, 220
Electrons, 42
Embryo
plant, 58
Endangered species, 198–201, 220
Ender, Peter T., 95
Energy, 15, 17, 20–22, 24–25, 28, 48, 49, 108–109, 146, 202, 220
Entomology, 82–83, 84–85, 220
Environment. *See* Populations, resources, and environments.
Enzymes, 146–149, 203, 220
Esophagus, 147
Epidemic, 167, 170, 220
Erwin, Terry, 215
Evaluating source material, 20, 21, 110, 113
Evidence, models, and explanation, 9B, 10, 11, 13, 22–23, 24–27, 34–37, 60, 71, 101, 121, 136–139, 146–149, 162–165, 166–169, 191, 197, 204–205, 210
Evolution and equilibrium, 72–75, 76–79, 80–81, 186–187, 220
Experiment, 24, 94, 95–96, 102–103, 124, 126–127, 129, 144–145, 173, 188, 190–191, 220
Exponential growth, 34–37, 100
Extinction, 82–85, 202–205, 214–217, 220

F

Fat, 10, 11, 136–139, 147, 220
Feces, 147–149, 188–189, 220
Fertilization, 18–19, 34, 35, 220
cross, 56
Fetus, 46–47, 220
Flora, 95
Flower, 132, 133
Food chain, 188, 192, 220
Food web, 75, 182, 188–189, 196, 204, 220
Force, 46–47, 220
Ford, John, 114
Form and function, 14–17, 40–43, 72–75, 108–109, 128–131
Fossil, 82–83, 198, 200, 220
Free-fall, 44–46, 220
Frequency, 158, 160, 220
Fungi, 172–175, 178, 221

G

Gene(s), 31, 221
and adaptation, 72–75, 76–79
and heredity, 18–19, 52–53, 68, 221
plant, 54–57
Generation, 54–57, 221
Generating ideas, 20, 52, 53, 54, 58, 60, 68, 72, 94, 101, 108–109, 128, 131, 146, 153, 157, 162, 165, 196, 197, 202, 208
Generating questions, 15, 39, 45, 52, 77, 102, 119, 136, 156, 171, 186, 193, 205, 206
Genome, 52–53, 221
Genus. *See* Classification.
Germs. *See* Bacteria.
Gills, 184, 221
Glands, 48–49, 183–184, 221
Glucose, 22, 24, 25, 28, 29, 221
Grassland, 188, 192–193, 221
Gravity, 104, 221
center of, 106–107

H

Habitat, 72–75, 77, 192, 193–194, 198, 202–205, 221
Heart, 150–153, 221
Herbicide, 179, 221
Herbivore, 188, 189, 203, 221
History of science, 8, 16, 18–19, 54–57, 166–169
Hooke, Robert, 8, 16
Horizontal axis, 152, 158, 160, 221
Hormone, 48–49, 221
Host, 95
Human body systems, 134, 221
circulatory, 135B, 150–153, 219
digestive, 83, 135B, 136–139, 146–149, 219
endocrine, 48–49, 135B, 220
immune, 38–39, 94–95, 135B, 166, 170–171, 173, 221
nervous, 156–157, 158–161, 135B
reproductive, 135B
sense organs, 115, 136, 136–139, 140–141, 142–145, 223
skeletal and muscular, 135B, 154–155, 223
Hydroelectric power, 212, 221
Hyperthyroidism, 48–49, 221

I

Identifying and controlling variables, 24, 26–27, 132–133, 136–139, 188–191
Incubation, 95
Infectious, 95, 98–101, 172–175, 221
Interpreting scientific illustrations
interpreting a cladogram, 88–89
interpreting a diagram, 14, 17, 31, 40, 42, 43, 44, 46, 56, 57, 64, 66, 110, 112, 114, 116, 141, 144, 156–157, 182, 184
interpreting a dichotomous key, 90–91
interpreting a graph, 34, 138, 152, 156, 158, 160, 190–191, 200, 202, 204, 212, 213
interpreting a map or globe, 76, 83, 88, 98–99, 180, 186, 199, 217
interpreting optical illusions, 162–165
interpreting illustrations, 155, 162–165, 206
Intestines, 102, 146–149, 221
Ion, 42–43, 221

J

Joint, 154–155, 170, 221
Julía, Juan Pablo, 202–205

K

Kelly, Dr. Dave, 126

L

Large intestine, 146–149, 222
Lattice, 45
Library/internet research, 11, 12, 23, 29, 33, 39, 61, 67, 81, 83, 102, 103, 105, 114, 152, 184, 189, 193, 198, 207, 211
Life cycle, 170–171, 182–185, 222
Liver, 146–149, 222
Lungs, 150–153, 178, 181, 222
Lymph nodes, 100

M

Making and using models, 9B, 10, 11, 21, 25, 30, 32, 34, 36–37, 53, 76, 78–79, 98, 100, 104–107, 132–133, 140, 148–149, 188
Making inferences, 10, 14, 18, 20, 40, 43, 44, 47, 67, 68, 72, 75, 82, 85, 87, 94, 97, 98, 101, 104, 105, 108–109, 110, 112, 114, 116–117, 118, 119, 121, 122, 123, 128, 130, 137, 139, 141, 142, 143, 145, 146, 150, 154–154, 156–157, 162, 165, 178, 180, 182, 186, 187, 192, 196, 197, 198, 200, 202, 205, 206, 208, 217
Making scientific illustrations
concept mapping, 20, 124, 126, 151, 171, 208, 211
creating a bar graph, 124, 126–127, 167, 218

creating a dichotomous key, 91
creating a graph, 35, 136, 139, 150, 152, 200, 212, 213
creating a table, 48, 49, 58, 82, 84, 86–87, 110, 128, 136, 138, 144, 162, 164, 187, 198, 200, 208, 210
drawing a diagram, 13, 29, 35, 41, 71, 100, 107, 109, 131, 151, 168, 171, 183, 196, 204, 209
making a chart, 81, 101, 118, 139, 201, 210
making a flowchart, 147, 151
making a poster, 175
making a sketch, 30, 54, 123, 150, 155, 175, 183
making a timeline, 53
Venn diagram, 29, 37, 159, 211
Mammal, 114, 115, 117, 122, 198, 199, 202, 203, 222
Mass, 104, 106–107, 222
Mattes, Richard, 136–139
Medici, Patricia, 202–205
Mendel, Gregor, 54–57, 60
Metabolism, 48, 222
Microscopic, 172, 222
Migration, 110–113, 222
benefits, 110, 112
Mitochondria, 15, 16, 17, 20–23, 24, 28, 32, 222
Mitosis. *See* Cell division.
Molecule, 10, 11, 14, 22, 28, 40, 52, 53, 68, 222
Mutation, 38–39, 222

N

National Aeronautics and Space Administration, 44
Natural selection, 76–79, 222
adaptive radiation, 80–81, 218
convergent evolution, 80–81
Nature of science, 24–27, 82–85, 86–89, 90–91, 114–117, 118–121, 126–129, 192–195, 214–217, 222
Nectar, 124, 126, 128, 130, 132, 222
Niche, 194–195, 222
Nucleus
of cell, 16, 17, 222
division of, 30–33
and DNA, 18–19, 222
Nutrient, 222
broth, 95, 129
cell, 10, 12, 14, 15, 16, 20, 24

O

Observing, 10, 12, 13, 24, 26–27, 48–49, 54, 55, 64, 91, 114, 117, 118, 120, 122–123, 132–133, 140–141, 146, 148–149, 150, 154–155, 162, 164, 214, 216
Organ, 40, 142, 170, 222
Organelles
endoplasmic reticulum, 16, 17, 220
golgi apparatus, 14, 16, 17, 221
lysomes, 14, 16, 17
ribosome, 14, 16, 17, 223
See also Mitochondria.
Organ system, 48–49, 146–149, 150–153, 156–157, 162–165, 222
Organism, 34, 47, 52–53, 222
ancestor, 59, 80–81
and populations, 178–181, 182–185, 192–195, 196–197
survival of, 20, 72–75, 110–113, 126, 128–131, 146–147, 150–153, 180, 194, 196–197, 198–201, 214–217
and symbiosis, 124–127, 202–205
unicellular, 10
Organizing information, 49, 75, 85, 109, 118, 151, 154, 183, 189, 196, 197, 199, 203, 206
See also Making scientific illustrations.
Osmosis, 12, 222
Ovary, 54, 55, 222

P

Pancreas, 146–149, 223
Personal health, 64–67, 94–97, 99–101, 102–104, 150–153, 158–161, 166–169, 170–171, 172–175
Photosynthesis, 24–25, 27, 28, 188, 223
See also Chemical equation.
Phylum. *See* Classification.
Physiology and behavior. *See* Behavior.
Phytoplankton, 24
Pigment, 24–25
Plant, parts of, 55
Pollen/pollination, 124, 126, 223
Pope, Theodore W., 95
Populations and ecosystems, 80–81, 114–117, 118–121, 122–123
aquatic, 212–213
cane toads, 178–181, 182–185, 186–187
competition in, 180, 192–193, 219
desert, 188–191, 192–195, 229
protection of, 196–197, 206–207, 208–211, 212–213, 214–217
rain forest, 198–202, 202–205, 206–207
Populations, resources, and environments, 68–71, 76–77, 98–101, 108, 170–171, 178–181, 182–185, 186–187, 192–195, 196–197, 198–201, 202–205, 206–207, 220, 223
Predicting, 49, 58, 63, 72, 75, 77, 79, 98, 124, 127, 153, 165, 169, 188, 191, 192, 194, 195, 197, 202, 204, 212, 223
Producer, 188, 189, 223
Proteins, 14, 16, 17, 31, 223
Protons, 42
Protists, 20, 170, 223

R

Rapid eye movement (REM) sleep, 160–161
Reading skills
creating a K-W-L chart, 143
dictionary use, 42, 73
main idea/supporting details, 69
summarize, 69
Recognizing cause and effect, 10, 18, 19, 44, 45, 48, 49, 58, 63, 64, 67, 69, 76, 78–79, 94–95, 98–99, 102, 103, 131, 132–133, 140, 141, 154–155, 156, 158, 161, 178, 180, 181, 182, 186, 187, 196, 197, 201, 207, 208, 211, 212, 214
Recognizing limitations in the natural world, 58, 60–61
Red blood cell, 170–171, 223
Reflex, 43, 223
Regulation and behavior, 10–13, 20–23, 28–29, 34–37, 38–39, 40–43, 48–49, 104–107, 108–109, 110–113, 114–117, 118–121, 122–123, 156–157, 172–175
Reproduction
plant, 124–127, 132–133
Reproduction and heredity, 18–19, 30–33, 52–53, 54–57, 58–61, 62–63, 64–67, 68–71, 72–75, 76–79, 178–181, 182–185, 198–199, 223
Research activities, 29, 33, 35, 39, 43, 45, 49, 53, 61, 65, 67, 70, 81, 83, 85, 99, 111, 119, 121, 139, 151, 164, 167, 185, 191, 200, 201, 204, 207, 215
Resistance, 179
Respiration
and oxygen, 24, 25, 28, 29
plant, 28–29, 223
See also Cellular respiration.
Risks and benefits, 166–169, 206–207
Rolls, Dr. Edmund T., 139

S

Sabin, Dr. Albert, 166
Salk, Dr. Jonas, 167–168
Satellite, 206, 223
Science and technology
understanding, 18–19
in society, 76–79, 166–169, 172–175, 212–213
Science as a human endeavor, 18–19, 44–47, 82–85, 122–123, 158–161, 166–169
Science Scope Activities
A New Way of Looking at the World, 188B, 193
Bacteria Samples, 94B, 95
Classification of Animals, 82B

Classifying Microorganisms, 94B
Keeping Science Current, 40B, 41
Make a Grasshead, 20B, 25
Model of a Biome, 198B
Walk-in Cell, 10B
Scientific careers
biologist, 85, 114, 121, 122, 123
conservationist, 77, 207, 219
ecologist, 181, 192
entomologist, 82–83
forensics, 70
genetic engineer, 25
horticulturist, 58
research physician, 95
zoologist, 86
Scientific instruments and tools
bioreactor, 44–46
culture dish, 95
electroencephalography, 160
field techniques, 122–123, 167
hand lens, 27
hydrophones, 114
magnifying glass, 27, 96
microscope, 27, 96
periodic table, 29
photographic identification, 122
robots, 106, 123
Seed, 58, 59, 124–126, 202–203, 223
Sense organs. *See* Human body systems.
Sequencing, 30, 32, 41, 94, 95, 119, 158, 160, 167, 173, 183
Sleep, 158–161
Small intestine, 146–149, 224
Smooth muscle, 154–155, 224
Solving problems, 37, 71, 77, 152–153, 184–185, 186–187
Sonar, 119
Sound, 114–117, 224
Species, 30, 50, 54, 58, 60, 76–77, 80–81, 224
environment, 178–181, 182–185
identification, 122–123
predator, 72–75, 108, 110, 112, 118–121, 124, 128–131, 179, 182, 187, 188–189, 192, 198, 200, 223
prey, 118–121, 128–131, 188–189, 223
See also Classification.
Specimen, 83
Sperm, 18, 30, 224
Spinal cord, 40, 224
Stomach, 146–149, 224
Stomata, 26–27, 224
Structure and function in living systems, 10–13, 14–17, 18–19, 20–23, 24–27, 28–29, 30–33, 34–37, 38–39, 40–43, 44–47, 48–49, 52–53, 54–57, 58–61, 72–75, 81–81, 102–103, 104–107, 108–109, 110–113, 124–127, 128–131, 132–133, 136–139, 142–145, 146–149, 150–153, 154–155, 156–157, 158–162, 162–165, 198–201, 202–205
Sugars, 20, 22, 102
Symbiosis, 224
commensalisms, 124, , 219
parasitic, 124, 125, 128–131, 223
mutualism, 124–127, 132–133
Systems, order, and organization, 10–13, 14–17, 48–49, 82–85, 86–89, 90–91, 124–128, 170–171, 172–175, 178–181, 182–185, 192–195

T

Taste, 136–139
Tendon, 154–155, 224
Theory, 224
Thyroid gland, 48–49, 224
Tissue, 48, 128, 224
connective, 40, 44, 154
engineering, 45–47
epithelial, 44, 45
muscle, 40, 44, 47, 154–155
nerve, 40, 44
Touch systems, 142–145
Toxic, 183
Trait, 52–53, 54, 224
animal, 61, 76–77
desirable and undesirable, 61
dominant and recessive, 57, 59, 62–63, 64–67, 77–79, 219, 223
and environment, 68–71
plant, 58–60
selective breeding, 59, 61
single-gene human, 62–63
Tumor, 38–39, 224

U

Understanding about scientific inquiry, 82–85, 86–89, 94–97, 136–139, 158–161, 166–169, 214–217
Understanding that scientific findings undergo peer review, 166–169
Understanding that scientists change their ideas, 86–89
Understanding that scientists may disagree, 136–139, 159
Understanding that scientists share their results, 24, 26–27, 122–123, 166–169
Using numbers, 34–37, 42, 46, 77, 78, 100, 127, 138, 150–152, 162, 170, 204, 215
Using space/time relationships, 34–37, 114–117, 175

V

Vaccine/vaccination, 102, 166–169
Variable, 95, 132–133, 138, 158, 188, 224
Variation, 40, 53, 55, 60, 61, 69, 73
Venom, 182–185, 224
Vertical axis, 152, 158, 160, 204, 224
Virus, 94
and disease, 166–169, 172–175

W

Wada, Masamitsu, 24–25
Watt (w), 40, 224
Whiting, Michael, 85
Wildlife preserve, 202–205, 224
Writing activities
book, 145
description, 29, 57, 107, 117
dialogue, 17, 23, 67, 125
educational pamphlet, 65
explanation, 27, 29, 117
figures of speech, 57
letter, 181
monologue, 57
opinion article, 26
poem, 19, 47
research report, 137, 170, 215
science journal, 41, 160, 210
story, 21, 113, 125
summary paragraph, 41

Z

Zompro, Oliver, 82–84
Zoology, 86, 88–89, 224

Credits

10, 34 Hoagland, Mahlon, and Bert Dodson. *The Way Life Works: Everything You Need to Know About the Way All Life Grows, Develops, Reproduces, and Gets Along.* Reprinted by permission of Times Books, a division of Random House, Inc.

14 Shroyer, Jo Ann. *Quarks, Critters, and Chaos: What Science Terms Really Mean.* Prentice Hall General Reference. Reprinted by permission of the author.

18 "Clones: Double Trouble?" *TIME* for Kids. TIME Inc. (www.timeforkids.com/TFK/magazines/story/0,6277,93229,00.html). Used with permission of *TIME for Kids* magazine, 2002.

20 Excerpt from A WIND IN THE DOOR by Madeline L'Engle. Copyright ©1973 by Crosswicks, Ltd. Reprinted by permission of Farrar, Straus, & Giroux, LLC.

24 Netting, Jessica. "Gene Found For Chloroplast Movement." *Science News.* Reprinted with permission from SCIENCE NEWS, the weekly newsmagazine of science, copyright 2001 by Science Service Inc.

28, 38, 142 Reprinted by permission of *MadSci Network.* Washington University Medical School. (www.madsci.org)

30 Baeurele, Patrick and Norbert Landa. *The Cell Works: An Expedition Into the Fantastic World of Cells.* Reprinted by permission of Barron's Education Series, Inc.

40 "The BIG Questions." *Ask Dr. Universe,* sponsored by Washington State University. (www.wsu.edu/DrUniverse/body.html) Reprinted by permission of the author.

44 "Scientists Grow Heart Tissue In Bioreactor." Reprinted by permission of *Science@NASA.* NASA. (science.nasa.gov/newhome/headlines/msad05oct99_1.htm)

48 "Thyroid Disorders." *KidsHealth.* Reprinted by permission of The Nemours Foundation. (kidshealth.org/kid/health_problems/gland/thyroid.html)

52 Ridley, Matt. Genome: The Autobiography of a Species in 23 Chapters. Reprinted by permission of HarperCollins Publishers, Inc.

54 Henig, Robin Marantz. *The Monk in the Garden.* Reprinted by permission of Houghton Mifflin.

58 from THEY CAME FROM DNA by Bill Aronson, 1993 by Billy Aronson. Reprinted by permission of Henry Holt and Company, LLC.

64 Trost, Cathy. "The Blue People of Troublesome Creek." *Science 82.* Reprinted by permission of the author.

68 "Our Genetic Identity." American Museum of Natural History from the exhibit "The Genomic Revolution." (www.amnh.org/exhibitions/genomics/1_identity/nature.html)

72 Wollard, Kathy. "The Long and Short of Giraffes." *Newsday, August 11, 1998.*

76 "Poaching Creates Tuskless Elephants." Reprinted by permission of United Press International, June 19, 2001.

82 Trevedi, Bijal P. "New Insect Order Found in Southern Africa." *National Geographic Today.* National Geographic Channel – US, all rights reserved.

86 "Giant Panda." (www.nature.ca/notebooks/english/gpanda.htm) Illustration by Charles Douglas. Reprinted by permission of the Canadian Museum of Nature.

94 Netting, Jessica. "Dirty Money Harbors Bacterial Dangers." Science News. Reprinted with permission from SCIENCE NEWS, the weekly newsmagazine of science, copyright 2001 by Science Service Inc.

98 Moore, Pete. *Killer Germs: Rogue Diseases of the Twenty–First Century.* Reprinted by permission of Carlton Books Limited 2001.

102 "Bacteria" essay excerpt by Rachel Mock, Young Naturalist Awards 1998 winner. The Young Naturalist Awards is a program of the American Museum of Natural History. http://www.amnh.org/nationalcenter/youngnaturalistawards/1998/bacteria.html

104, 108 Text by Matthew Robertson from *Pathfinders: Insects and Spiders* ©Weldon Own Pty Ltd.

110 Pringle, Laurence. *A Dragon in the Sky: The Story of a Green Darner Dragonfly.* Reprinted by permission of Orchard Books, a Division of Scholastic, Inc.

114 Ford, John K.B., Graeme M. Ellis, and Kenneth C. Balcomb. *Killer Whales.* Reprinted by permission of University of British Columbia Press. Second Edition. 2000.

118, 122 Ford, John K.B., Graeme M. Ellis. *Transients: Mammal–Hunting Killer Whales.* Reprinted by permission of University of British Columbia Press 1999.

124, 128 Kneidel, Sally. *Skunk Cabbage, Sundew Plants & Strangler Figs: And 18 More Of The Strangest Plants On Earth.* 2001 John Wiley & Sons, Inc. This material is used by permission of John Wiley & Sons, Inc. ©2001

136 Raloff, Janet. "Surprise! Fat Proves A Taste Sensation." *Science News.* Reprinted with permission from SCIENCE NEWS, the weekly newsmagazine of science, copyright 2001 by Science Service Inc.

140 Reprinted with the permission of Simon & Schuster Books for Young Readers, an imprint of Simon & Schuster Children's Publishing Division from YIKES! YOUR BODY, UP CLOSE by Mike Janulewicz. Copyright ©1997 The Templar Company Plc.

146 "Your Digestive System and How it Works." *National Digestive Diseases Information Clearinghouse.* Reprinted by permission of the National Institutes of Health. (www.niddk.nih.gov/health/digest/pubs/digesyst/newdiges.htm)

150 "Amazing Heart Facts." From "NOVA" at www.pbs.org/wgbh/nova/heart/heartfacts.html
Copyright ©2002 WGBH/Boston.

154 "Muscles and Bones; Einstein; Stars Chat; Raptor Center." *Newton's Apple.* Reprinted by permission of KTCA. (www.pbs.org/ktca/newtons/newtonsclassics/classic11.html)

156 Barnes, Kate, and Steve Weston. *How It Works: The Human Body. Barnes & Noble Books.* Reprinted by permission of Award Publications.

158 "The Teenage Brain: Why Do We Sleep?" PBS: The Secret Life of the Brain. Public Broadcasting System. (http://www.pbs.org/wnet/brain/episode3/sleep/2.html)

162 Text: Whitfield, Philip, ed. *The Human Body Explained: A Guide to Understanding the Incredible Living Machine.* Henry Holt and Company, 1995. Reprinted by permission of Marshall Editions.
Illustration: *Visual Magic,* p. 39. Reprinted by permission from Breslich & Foss Limited.

166 Reprinted with the permission of Atheneum Books for Young Readers, an imprint of Simon & Schuster Children's Publishing Division from GREAT LIVES: MEDICINE by Robert H. Curtis, M.D. Copyright 1993 Robert H. Curtis.

170 Copyright 1999 *Epidemic!: The World of Infectious Disease* edited by Rob Desalle. Reprinted by permission of The New Press. (800) 233 4830.

172 "Facts About Infectious Diseases." Reprinted by permission of the Centers for Disease Control and Prevention. United States Department of Health and Human Services. (www.cdc.gov/ncidod/op/materials/opbrochure.PDF)

178 "The Unwanted Amphibian." *Frog Decline Reversal Project.* Reprinted by permission of the Frog Decline Reversal Project, Inc. (www.fdrproject.org/pages/TDprogress.htm)

182 "Cane Toads—Bufo Marinus." *Australian Museum Fact Sheets.* Reprinted by permission of Australian Museum. (www.amonline.net.au/factsheets/canetoad.htm)

186 Schulz, Dennis. "The Cane Toad Dialogues: Disaster or Disruption?" from *Savanna Links,* Issue 16, October–December 2000. Reprinted by permission of the Tropical Savannas Cooperative Research Centre. Northern Territory University. (savanna.ntu.edu.au/publications/savanna_links16/toad.html)

188, 192, 196 Bock, Carl E., and Jane H. Bock. *The View from Bald Hill: Thirty Years in an Arizona Grassland.* Reprinted by permission of University of California Press.

198, 202 Medici, Patricia, and J. Pablo Juliá. "Scientists Trap, Tag, And Track Tapirs To Design A Survival Strategy." *Eco–Exchange.* October–November 2001. Reprinted by permission of the Rainforest Alliance. (ra.org/programs/cmc/newsletter/nov01–2.html)

208 Diamond, Jared. "Easter's End." *Discover.* Reprinted by permission of the publisher and author.

212 The text was excerpted from the JASON Academy Course Human Impacts 101, Aquatic Ecology. For more information on online courses, go to www.jason.org/Academy(http://www.jason.org/Academy). Reynolds, Karen. "Human Impacts 101." (www.nsta.org/361/)

214 Pringle, Laurence. *Living Treasure: Saving Earth's Threatened Biodiversity.* HarperCollins Children's Books. Reprinted by permission of the author.